THE ARCHITECTURE OF EDUCATIONAL FRAMEWORKS

PAMELA SAWYER | ROSEMARY KARR | ELAINE ANN ZWEIG

Kendall Hunt
publishing company

www.kendallhunt.com
Send all inquiries to:
4050 Westmark Drive
Dubuque, IA 52004-1840

ISBN: 978-1-5249-1346-5

Printed in the United States of America

Table of Contents

CHAPTER 8: Reading 259

CHAPTER 9: Studying 301

CHAPTER 1
Transitioning to College

T.I.P.S.—(Tactical Information that Promotes Success)

Developing curiosity in life makes transitioning to college expectations and life easier.

© UniqueLight/Shutterstock.com

Curiosity motivates people to learn how nature works. The stars were one of the first points of curiosity.

© neftali/Shutterstock.com

cu•ri•os•i•ty: noun a strong desire to know or learn something.

Curiosity is experienced when we have a question that leads to inquiry. Being curious about how or why something happens leads people to increased interest in learning. Most of the time, learning that occurs as a result of curiosity does not feel like the traditional classroom experience.

Children are such curious creatures. They explore, question, and wonder, and, by doing so, learn. From the moment of birth, likely even before, humans are drawn to new things. When we are curious about something new, we want to explore it. While exploring, we discover (Perry, 2001).

Being curious in learning increases our motivation, focus, and connections among ideas in subjects.

While curiosity is fundamental to all learning, it is certainly the foundation of mathematics and science! Legend has it that Archimedes tried to discover if the king's crown was indeed made of gold. Curiosity led Archimedes to use the volume of water displaced to indicate the crown's metallic purity. He became so excited when he discovered this, he shouted, "Eureka! I have found it."

Curiosity led Pythagoras to contemplate what would later be named the "irrational numbers" when trying to calculate the hypotenuse of a right triangle with legs of equal length.

Curiosity is the foundation of reading! Out of curiosity we continue reading a good book to see how it ends. College students read research that explains outcomes initially inspired by curiosity.

Curiosity is the foundation of writing! Writing inspires curiosity in the forms of short stories, novels, song lyrics, and poetry. Writers often write about a topic they are curious about, attempting to gain understanding. The great American author William Faulkner stated, "I never know what I think about something until I read what I've written on it."

CHAPTER 1: OBJECTIVES

1.1 Acclimating to College

Objective 1 Understand College Culture
Objective 2 Recognize College Expectations
Objective 3 Understand Academic Integrity
Objective 4 Understand Emotional Intelligence
Objective 5 Understand Opportunities for Collegiate Involvement

1.2 Accessing College Resources

Objective 6 Understand the Nature of Peer Relationships
Objective 7 Understand the Benefits of Positive Relationships with Instructors
Objective 8 Recognize Academic Support Services
Objective 9 Recognize Relevant Student Support Services

CHAPTER CONCEPTS:

Some or all of the following terms may be new to you. Place a check mark in the column reflecting your knowledge of each term.

	Know	Don't know	Not sure	Page # where first found		Know	Don't know	Not sure	Page # where first found
college culture					collaboration				
acclimate					Grade Point Average (GPA)				
perseverance					syllabus				
academic etiquette					collegiate activities				
academic integrity					depth of learning				
plagiarism					emotional intelligence				
collusion					cognitive psychology				

1.1 ACCLIMATING TO COLLEGE

©Yuri Shevtsov/Shutterstock.com

Take a minute to cross your arms in front of you. Did you place the left or the right arm on top? Now, place the other (left or right) arm on top. Does the change to having the "other" arm on top feel awkward? Change constantly challenges our "comfort zone" by asking us to do something that may create discomfort at the outset. At first, adjusting to college may be as awkward as reversing the positioning of your arms
(You may unfold your arms, now!)

Welcome to college! By working through this textbook, you will increase your understanding of new things awaiting you as a college student. The concepts introduced will be similar to a map helping you navigate the many paths of college and successfully transition to this new chapter of your life.

Have you ever purchased a piece of furniture, like a bookshelf, that came in a box with the words "some assembly required?" Did you try to assemble the bookshelf without reading the directions to understand where and how the bolts or screws should be placed to stabilize and support the bookshelf? Often, we get so excited about a new item that we do not want to take the time to understand what we need to do and how we need to do it.

Many students arriving at college excited about the new environment jump in without any knowledge of what is necessary to succeed. Because your previous learning experiences may have taken place in high school, the work place, or the military, it is important to understand how the college learning environment can be different. High school, the work place, and especially the military have written policies and practices, written or unwritten expectations of behavior and conduct, and even long-standing traditions that describe the culture of the environment. Colleges are no different.

OBJECTIVE 1: Understand College Culture

College culture refers to a set of practices, philosophy, values, or codes of conduct associated with an organization and is typically different from high school culture. Within the college culture there are a set of behaviors, usually unspoken, that will increase your understanding of the events, classroom learning expectations, and many other imbedded nuances. For example, academic freedom is highly valued in college. This means your classroom experience may include a broader range of professors from different ethnicities with varied teaching styles and obvious political and religious affiliations which may not match your own. By understanding the unique culture in your college or university, you will be able to more easily adapt to the new environment.

Unlike high school, where your classification referred to the grade you were in, students at universities (freshman, sophomore, junior, and senior) and community colleges (freshman and sophomore) are classified by the number of course hours they have completed. Thus, a student just starting college, much like a student beginning high school, has traditionally been called a "freshman." In an attempt to make this term more inclusive to all genders, the term *first-year college student* is becoming more widely used for new students.

Are you aware of specific practices of your chosen college? For example, do you know if there is an established dress code or code-of-conduct? The information in the left column of the chart below explains the features of various categories directly related to some colleges' culture and serves as a point of initial understanding of the features. After you have read and understood each feature, personalize the information for your institution by completing the questions in the right-hand column.

EXERCISE 1.1: Categories of College Culture

Fill in the blanks as they relate to you.

Some College Cultural Categories	Personalization of Cultural Categories (search on your college website)
Traditions: dress code, code-of-conduct, climbing a mountain or pole, and many others can be identified on different campuses. Resources for this information include the student handbook, college website, or other college students.	List any of your school traditions: ______ ______ *Describe your feelings about one of these:* ______ ______
First-Year Experience Programs: include courses where incoming students are given support and guidance; the courses last from one week up to the entire first year of college. Upon application, you may have received information regarding required student orientations.	Determine if a seminar or course where first-year college students can learn about college is on your campus. If there is one, when and where does it meet? ______ ______
Residence Hall, Dormitory (dorms), or On- Campus Apartments/Housing: areas located on campus providing a room or suite for students to live. If your college has on-campus living, you would have received information about applying for a room in your acceptance packet.	Does your college/university have residence halls? ______ Explain which residence halls are recommended for first-year students, or policies concerning first-year students living on campus: ______ Explain why you chose to live where you are for this first year of college: ______
Greek Life: fraternities (derived from the Greek word meaning brothers) and sororities (derived from the Greek word meaning sisters) are social clubs whose focus is generally philanthropic work, academic achievement, leadership development, collegiate involvement, and community service. Greek life provides a ready- made social and support group.	Explain where can you go to learn about your college's Greek Life, if there are any on your campus: ______ ______ List a few advantages and disadvantages of joining a fraternity or sorority: ______
Social, Academic, and Professional Organizations: subject-specific interests such as math, science, photography, and art clubs whose focus is on academic achievement, or regional, state, and national affiliates of professional associations.	Explain where can you locate information on these types of clubs and their specific focuses: ______ ______
Athletics, Intramural Sports, and Campus Recreation: organized sports and recreational events established to promote physical development and socialization for students. Depending on your school, there may be varying levels of sports, activities, and competition. Be certain to visit your college website to find pertinent information.	Describe where can you locate the campus listing of recreational activities and sports: ______ ______ Describe the sports or recreational events of interest to you: ______ Clarify how you sign up for these events: ______

EXERCISE 1.2: Expectations

Walk around your campus and take notice of things such as dress codes, student/student interactions, student/professor interactions, "handouts," etc. Write a three to five sentence email to an imaginary high school student describing the culture you have experienced thus far at your college or university.

1. Getting the most out of my money
2. All around having a good experience

REFLECTION 1.A:

What were your expectations of your college or university life before you arrived on campus?

That is was exciting

Did you conduct a campus visit prior to enrolling in this college or university?
If not, why not? didn't have time
If yes, what did you see in the visit that attracted you to the school?

Now that you are here, how does college differ from your earlier expectations?
Explain. 1. You have to balance a lot more.
2. Time management is a necessity.

So far, you have focused on several features that reflect your current college's culture, but there may be a benefit in reflecting on the culture where you have previously learned. Looking back at previous learning environments may help you more quickly understand how they compare and contrast with the new school's culture.

EXERCISE 1.3: Learning Environments

For each of the following statements, evaluate if you have experienced the learning environment, which may have included a job or reserve or active duty in the military. Place a ✓ next to each one you identify through your evaluation.

I attended the same class or job daily.	✓	I took very few, if any, online courses.	✓
I was given time in class to do homework.	✗	I was required to have basic computer skills.	✓
I worked or went to class the same hours every day.	✓	I had to wear a uniform or specific clothing.	✗
I had to have a letter from a doctor or my caregiver to miss class or work.	✓	I was allowed to submit work late.	✓

continued

I was responsible for the quality of other people's work.	✓	I met with my teachers in their classroom where class was held.	✓
I was allowed to make up a missed assignment.	✓	My course grades were mailed or an online login was provided to my parents.	✓
My textbooks were provided at no cost.	X	I socialize with people "like" me.	X
I went to lunch at a scheduled time every day.	X	I was trained to do a specific job.	X
The number of tests given in one day was limited to no more than two (2).	✓	I was paid for the hours or work completed on the job.	X
I was given "progress" notices from my teacher to take home to parents.	✓	I was responsible for the quality of my work.	✓
I was evaluated yearly.	✓	My work was overseen by a single supervisor.	✓

Consider briefly how the previous learning culture compares and contrasts to those in college.

TABLE 1.1: College Learning Environment

In the College Learning Environment:
You may have different class schedules for different days of the week.
You are assumed to be an adult.
You may not have time to do homework in class.
Your permission is needed before anyone may see or discuss your grades.
Your absences may have no distinction between "excused" and "unexcused."
Your professor may not allow you to make up a missed test or assignment.
You pay for all your textbooks with personal income, financial aid, or scholarships.
* You may be required to work and be graded in groups in your classes.
You may have a test or major assignment due in each of your classes on the same day.
You may meet with your professor in his/her on-campus office or online "virtual office."
You will communicate with your professor and classmates through email.
You will meet the expectations of multiple instructors.

EXERCISE 1.4: Analyze the Differences

Identify the two or three most significant differences between your previous learning environment and those listed above.

1. Being graded by other class mates
2. Having different class schedules

REFLECTION 1.B:

Consider the differences between other learning environments and college. Review the items you recorded and identify the difference you believe will be the most challenging adjustment for you this semester.

___

Consider what you can do to minimize this challenge between the two learning environments.

organize and schedule everything

> **Student Tip:** As you work through this chapter, continue to identify ways to successfully adjust to or overcome the differences you have identified. When you see a possible strategy, place a check mark (✓) in the margin of the book (Yes, you may write in your textbook!) or record the difference on a sheet of paper you will use for the entire semester.

Depth of Learning

One of the biggest cultural differences incoming college students experience is how college courses may require a different level of subject understanding than previous learning environments. The concept of "deeper learning" and "strategies for learning" will be discussed in greater detail in Chapter 3 of this book, but it is advantageous for you to understand, early in the semester, what deeper learning is and how to begin applying this way of learning. Dr. Stephen Chew is a renowned **cognitive psychologist**. A cognitive psychologist studies how we think, remember, decide, and perceive information, as well as how we learn to acquire, process, and store it. ***Cognitive Psychology*** is the science of how we think. According to Dr. Chew, making *connections between the concepts* you are learning is the most important aspect of learning the materials more deeply. Perhaps in previous learning environments, you were successful by memorizing facts in isolation and recalling them long enough to pass a test. This type of learning is considered *shallow* learning. Refer to the continuum in Table 1.2 contrasting ***deeper learning*** with shallow learning. Basically, learning occurs through a range of strategies positioned between the two extremes of deeper and shallow.

TABLE 1.2: Continuum of Information Processing Levels

Shallow Learning--MEMORY--Deeper Learning		
Focus on minor aspects of information.		Focus on personalization of learning.
Example: Memorize dates or definitions just for the next test or assignment.		Example: Relating these dates or definitions to prior knowledge or making meaningful connections.
Memorizing the steps to solving a linear equation with two steps.		Understanding the steps to solving a linear equation with two steps.

Deeper learning typically requires more time to analyze what you are learning. You will be given the opportunity to learn with thoughtful connections in and among your course work. Here is the bottom line: if you are highly motivated to learn but use shallow learning strategies, you will not retain the concepts you are trying to learn. By employing the techniques discussed throughout this book, you will learn strategies to help you remember information for a longer period of time to help you thrive in this new environment.

Just as reading the directions prior to assembling a bookshelf is going to help you build a better bookshelf, understanding your college's culture will help you build a better first-year experience for yourself. Simply realizing college may take a little adjustment can be enlightening.

Recognizing the expectations of college will be the next stop on our journey to adjusting to college.

EXERCISE 1.5: Deeper Learning

Prepare your personal understanding of deeper learning by completing the following sentences:

1. In previous learning environments, I did not employ deeper processing when I read something. I know this was not helpful to my learning or deep processing because i wouldn't comprehend.
2. In previous learning environments, I exercised deeper processing when I personalized ______ ______. I know this was helpful to my learning and deeper processing because ______.

OBJECTIVE 2: Recognize College Expectations

Now that you have seen the bigger picture of your college's culture and how it may be different from high school, the work place, or even the military, how do you think your expectations of learning in college measure up to the reality of your college's culture? By understanding basic, yet often unstated, expectations, you are more likely to experience academic success. Most seasoned college students would agree that to do well in college requires commitment, ***perseverance*** (continued effort to succeed at something despite set-backs), self-sacrifice, and a great deal of time and hard work.

As an adult learner, you will be expected to think and act in a more mature manner. Classic movies like *Animal House* (1978), *Legally Blonde* (2001), and *21* (2008) glamorize the fun, antics, and myths of college students; these are not realistic expectations of college life. However, movies such as *Good Will Hunting* (1997), *Mona Lisa Smiles* (2003) and *Drumline* (2002) focus on the academic and emotional challenges which are more realistic depictions of what you might expect. This is not to suggest that attending college will not include opportunities for fun, but for the most part, students who attend college are expected to study. In a *National Survey of Student Engagement* study, research findings indicate students with the highest personal satisfaction and growth in college are those who "work hard and are asked to think at higher levels" (Belcheir, 9). "Higher level thinking" will be discussed in a later chapter in detail when Bloom's taxonomy for levels of thinking is introduced. It is mentioned here to help you understand college is going to stretch your mind, so deeper learning is going to take place. College includes hard work and the expansion of your mind!

EXERCISE 1.6: Collaboration on College Expectations

© Konstantin Chagin/Shutterstock.com

- Form groups of 3 or 4 students.
- Take a few minutes to introduce yourselves.
- Discuss your impressions of college expectations and what you anticipate learning in this course based on the textbook information. Share the primary challenge you identified and see who has the same challenges. Look through the table of contents to see which chapter addresses your challenge(s) and skim it to see what solutions you can use.
- Share your finding with the class when called upon.
- Depending on the group, you may want to obtain contact information for a few of your class mates.

NOTE: Students who make at least one connection with another student or instructor on the first day of classes are more likely to stay enrolled in college courses.

In order to familiarize yourself with the formal guidelines your college follows, locate a copy of your school's student handbook. You may have received this or a similar resource when you registered. If not, search your college's website for a digital copy. All of the expectations, as well as your rights, are included in the handbook. You will find behavioral guidelines such as a code of conduct and perhaps **email** and ***academic etiquette***. Included are practical guidelines such as:

- Withdrawal policy
- Final payment dates
- If/when a professor can withdraw you due to excessive absences
- Deadlines for scholarship applications
- Final exam calendars

Ultimately, it is *your responsibility* to become familiar with your college's guidelines and expectations.

EXERCISE 1.7: Using Your Student Handbook

Several expectations and guidelines found in your student handbook are listed above.

Identify three more expectations/guidelines and write them here, noting the page number on which you found it in your handbook.

1. ______________________________

2. ______________________________

3. ______________________________

REFLECTION 1.C:

Identify any expectations/guidelines that you are surprised to see in your handbook and explain why you might not have expected to see them.

Although these will be discussed in more detail later in this chapter, it is important to stress email etiquette and academic etiquette before you face the consequences of violating either one. ***Email and academic etiquette*** suggests you address your professors as Dr., (if appropriate), Professor, or Mr., Mrs., or Ms. depending on your college culture. First names are traditionally not used in an email, even if a professor allows the use of his/her first name in class. The following greetings are unacceptable: "Hey," "Yo," "Prof," as well as texting abbreviations, "bc," "B4," "C U," or any other slang language you might use in an email to your friends. A sentence written in ALL CAPS is generally interpreted as SHOUTING! More importantly, you need to consider the "tone" of your email—how your words might come across to someone else reading it. Never write anything in an email you would not say to the professor's face with another instructor present. If you are angry or upset, wait until you calm down and can think rationally before writing. Then, before sending your email, read it over three or four times to make sure you are saying only what you really want to say. Lastly, but certainly not least, proof your email. You are in college and your emails should reflect proper English and correct grammar and sentence structure.

Academic etiquette reflects how you interact with your instructors, college staff, and other students. There is an expectation of ***courtesy***, respect, and acceptance or tolerance of those who may not look or think like you or hold the same values or beliefs. The use of a professor's first name is never to be used to address him or her in class unless you have been given specific permission to do so. It is polite to say "thank you" and "you're welcome" when appropriate. Interaction with your classmates in the classroom or through email should follow the same suggestions mentioned in these last two paragraphs.

Instructor Expectations

Professor expectations will vary slightly from instructor to instructor, but you should

- have a working knowledge of the course ***syllabus***,
- attend every class,
- arrive on time and remain the entire class session,
- be prepared to learn upon arrival,
- communicate through verbal and non-verbal cues (meaning you are actively engaged in learning),
- and produce the best finished product for each assignment submitted.

Attending class is by far one of your professor's greatest expectations. Remember, professors are present for you in each class with vital information to share. By attending class, you are going to have a specialist teach you for a semester. While class attendance may sound like an obvious expectation, there are always a few students who believe attendance is optional, especially if it is not included in the final grade.

Unfortunately, not all students who attend class are prepared to learn. Arriving to class late, without the textbook or a notebook on which to take notes or a pen/pencil to write with, leaving class to answer or make a phone call, or leaving early is an indication you are not serious about this course. Failure to complete your written, reading, mathematics, or science lab assignment prior to class sends a message to your instructor that this course is not important enough to you to make the effort.

EXERCISE 1.8: Preparation for Learning

List three things you can do prior to or during the start of class to prepare for learning.

1. ______________________________

2. ______________________________

3. ______________________________

REFLECTION 1.D:

Analyze the three strategies you recorded above. Evaluate which of these you might need to improve in order to be successful in this course and in college.

Describe the actions and steps you will take to improve. List the strategies that will help you accomplish the actions and steps you described.

Appropriate Classroom Behavior

The use of technology in college is expected, but there are productive and non-productive ways to use it in the classroom. Your cell phone can be used productively in the classroom when instructors have you respond to a question by texting the answer to a multiple choice question and then reveals the correct answer. This gives you immediate feedback whether your answer is correct or not. In addition, the improvements in the graphing calculator apps for smart phones makes the calculator a useful tool to use within the first couple of weeks until you have had a chance to purchase one for your mathematics or science class. Your instructor will let you know whether these phone apps can be used in class but be prepared to have your calculator prior to test day!

The misuse of cell phones has become so prevalent that some restaurants are banning their use during dining because the service staff and other diners are distracted by patrons talking or texting. Imagine this distraction and disruption for students sitting in a classroom built to hold only 40 people. Most professors, and even many colleges, have some form of policy on the use of cell phones in class.

Other technology potentially interfering with classroom learning is the use of a laptop or tablet on which to take notes. The drawback to using these is that you must sit near an electrical outlet if you use your laptop or tablet in back-to-back classes or have a single three- or four-hour course. Generally, these outlets will be in the back of the room, removing you from the central "action" in the class. Although these devices are commonly accepted by most professors, there is the temptation to use them to search for other information, check your social media site, or simply browse the Internet instead of taking notes. This is inappropriate classroom behavior. In addition, the tapping of keys can be a serious distraction to those sitting near you. If you choose to use your laptop, turn off the sound to the keys, if this is possible on your laptop.

EXERCISE 1.9: Technology Use in Classrooms

Explain why you think note-taking with your computer may not be allowed by some professors. ____

____

Describe the messages you send to your professor when you check social networking websites or browse the Internet, text, or answer a phone call or even allow it to ring in class:

REFLECTION 1.E:

You are giving a graded presentation in class when a fellow student's phone rings. The student abruptly leaves the room to answer it. You begin your presentation again only to have the student return, pick up his books, and leave.

What kind of effect do you think the fellow student's actions will have on your presentation?

Describe the feelings you would experience as a result of the interruption.

____

Now, apply this scenario and your reaction(s) to your professor in the classroom while he or she is teaching. Explain how he/she would be affected if the same scenario occurred during his/her class.

____

____

Behaviors you have used to communicate positive interactions and active participation in previous learning environments will communicate similarly to your college professor. Some positive actions include:

- arriving on time,
- having supplies needed to learn,
- being attentive,
- being ready to discuss the homework,
- actively participating in any group activities,
- demonstrating your awareness of assignments and deadlines,
- and committing to being successful in the course.

By following your professor's expectations and role-modeling, you are learning what it takes to achieve greater personal and academic success.

EXERCISE 1.10: Learning Behaviors

Describe three behaviors you have demonstrated or observed in a previous learning environment that communicated a commitment to learning.

1. ______________________________

2. ______________________________

3. ______________________________

REFLECTION 1.F:

Create a procedure for you to use in improving one of the identified behaviors above in your college learning environment.

____

____

Understanding and Using Your Syllabus

A ***syllabus*** is a document written by your instructor to help you understand the course expectations. The syllabus is a contract among you, the professor, and the college you attend. It may be handed out on the first day of class or it may be ready for you to print from an online learning portal. Critical information in the syllabus includes your instructor's contact information, assignments, grading policies, due dates, and classroom procedures. While many professors will review the syllabus on the first day of class, it is intended to be your guide throughout the semester. Because you may not receive reminders of assignments and due dates, it is important to locate this information quickly. If you use the syllabus as your guide on how to do well in the class, it will provide critical information for navigating the course with greater ease. As such, review the syllabus each week.

Remember the person who assembled the bookshelf without reading the instructions? It can be a frustrating method of assembly yet many people attempt it. Reading and understanding your syllabus can minimize frustrations stemming from confusion or lack of understanding about the expectations of your instructor.

One of the many advantages of reading and understanding the course syllabus is its use as a study tool. The major concepts you will learn in the course are generally included on the syllabus and you can expect to see these on your assessments in the class. For example, the syllabus may include a statement regarding Student Learning Outcomes in this class: "A student will be able to demonstrate mastery in the following areas:

- Goal-setting
- Time management
- Textbook marking
- Note-taking
- Test-taking

This means that, by the end of the course, you will understand and be able to apply all of the information related to the bulleted concepts. By using this information in your test preparation, you will be more connected to the instructor's goals as they are stated in the syllabus.

Additionally, understanding your course syllabus includes knowledge of how the weighting of each coursework component is explained. For example, the weighting of categories for this class may look like:

Class work/Homework	20%
Tests (5 tests equally weighted)	30%
Group Project	15%
Essay	15%
Final Exam	20%

Knowing the weighting of assignments helps you understand the grades you are earning. You will want to complete every assignment so you will be setting yourself up for an "A" in every course. Apps are available for smart phones and tablets to keep track of your average as you enter each newly earned grade.

EXERCISE 1.11: Course Syllabus

Record how you would explain the purpose of this course syllabus to a student in high school.

REFLECTION 1.G:

Compare the syllabus for this course with the syllabus of a mathematics or science course.

Describe three (3) differences. ______________________

____

____

Describe three (3) similarities. ______________________

____

____

Explain your evaluation of why you think they have these similarities and differences.

____

____

Understanding Grade Point Average (GPA)

Each class taken in college changes your grade point average (GPA) by increasing or decreasing it. Some colleges have exceptions. For example, at some institutions developmental courses may not count toward GPA. Check with an advisor if you need additional information.

To better understand, your GPA might be compared to your credit score, which is a score assigned by credit agencies to reflect your payment history. A higher score indicates debts have been promptly paid with dependable accountability. Just as a credit score communicates how well you have promptly submitted payment for purchases, the GPA communicates how well you have completed the course-work. Your credit score communicates if you are a good risk for future credit. Similarly, your GPA is an indicator of your overall college performance.

So, how do you calculate your GPA? Many colleges use a four point grading system. To understand how this system works with a more traditional A, B, C, D, F grading system, see Table 1.4.

TABLE 1.4: Quality-Point Value of Earned Grade

Grade	Quality Points	Meaning
A	4.0	achievement of distinction
B	3.0	above-average achievement
C	2.0	average achievement
D	1.0	below-average achievement
F	0.0	unsatisfactory achievement (no credit is earned)

For example, if you take a three credit-hour class in which you earn an "A," you have earned 12 quality points.

4 Quality Points for the A
x 3 Credit Hours
12 Quality Points

The *average* of your total quality points equals your cumulative Grade Point Average (GPA).

EXERCISE 1.12: Grade Point Average

The following grades, based on a 4-point system, were earned for each course in one semester. Complete the chart. (You may need a calculator.)

		Grade	Value	Grade Points
History	3 hours	C		
English	3 hours	A		
Mathematics	3 hours	B		
Geology	4 hours	C		
Total Semester Hours		Total Grade Points		
Semester GPA: Total Grade Points divided by Total Semester Hours =				

In college, you may hear someone say, "Adrian has a 4.0!" This means Adrian has earned an "A" in all the courses he has taken, resulting in a high GPA. This does not mean Adrian has made 100% on every assignment or test in every class. It means for each class, his overall average is at an A level, usually a 90% or above. In contrast, a student who has a 1.9 or lower GPA has earned below average achievement in the courses taken. This is of concern because the student's continued college attendance could be in jeopardy. A low GPA could place the student on academic probation. The goal in college is to earn the highest grade possible in each of your classes, so your overall, or cumulative, GPA will be high.

The rewards of a high GPA may include membership in an academic honor society if eligibility is based on grade averages. Typically, these organizations have regularly scheduled campus meetings, perform service to the community, and may travel to state and national conferences. There are benefits to memberships in these academic honor societies beyond college as well. The directors of most College Career Services report employers who recruit on their campuses look for students with the leadership skills learned from student involvement in the honors societies. Understanding that every point counts toward your future, both in and out of college, may be a source of motivation for you. Just as earning a high credit score for lending purposes is critical to your financial success, earning a high GPA is critical to your academic success and may impact your career.

OBJECTIVE 3: Understand Academic Integrity

Academic integrity is defined as honesty and responsibility in scholarship or, more simply, intellectual honesty. This means you, as a student, will strive for honesty and take responsibility for the content of your work. A violation of academic integrity is called academic misconduct. Most institutions of higher education agree on three basic categories of academic misconduct.

Plagiarism is the use of someone's work, even a sentence or two, without proper citation. This will be discussed in a later chapter.

Collusion is the result of two or more people attempting to deceive an instructor.

Cheating is the unauthorized use of notes on a test, the sharing of information about an exam, copying on an exam, or acquisition of a test or questions prior to an exam.

EXERCISE 1.13: Excuses

There are many excuses students give for violations of academic integrity.

List two (2) that come to mind: ____

____

____

Another situation you may encounter is a student asking to copy your work. If you allow this, you are guilty of collusion. If you have not personally experienced this, you may have witnessed collusion when a student from another class section shares the answers on the test with a friend. In college, you are expected to report cheating or collusion. Some colleges have enacted an honor system, which requires you to report violations or risk personal disciplinary action.

EXERCISE 1.14: Academic Integrity

Record your college's formal statement concerning academic integrity.

___

___

___

___

REFLECTION 1.H:

Explain, with examples, what your college statement on academic integrity means to you.

___

___

___

Personal monitoring of academic integrity is expected in a wide variety of ways when students submit work to a professor. When submitting a group project with your name on it, you are indicating you contributed your portion of the project. Placing your name on an essay, paper, project, or exam is confirming the work you submit is your personal effort and understanding. Submitting a paper you previously submitted for another class may be a violation of the academic code as well. With technological advancements in which databases are created when you submit your work, resubmission of work is readily identified. Academic integrity is monitored today more actively, so it is crucial that you adhere to the college's policies.

The consequences of violating academic integrity guidelines range from a lower grade on the assignment, a failing grade for the course, or expulsion from the institution.

EXERCISE 1.15: Avoiding Academic Violations

Complete the chart.

Term	Definition	Example	Strategy to avoid it.
Plagiarism			
Collusion			
Cheating			

Research the group of people (or the single person), a council of students, instructors, or Dean of Students, who review any cases of academic integrity violations at your college. Explain who they are and what they do:

___

___

___

List the resulting procedures for students who commit academic misconduct at your school (this should be found in your student handbook): ______________________________

____

____

PERSON to PERSON

© Szasz-Fabian Ilka Erika/Shutterstock.com

In this exercise, you will be introduced to academic integrity issues. Let's discuss the possible actions and reactions.

Carlos and Gerry are both good students making A's and B's in their classes. They attended the same high school and served on Student Council together. Carlos and Gerry became reacquainted when they were in the same college Biology class.

Although they are not good friends, they have studied together a few times. During an exam, Carlos saw Gerry cheat. He does not know what to do. Gerry does not know Carlos saw her with written notes.

Based on this description, rank the following as Carlos' best possible course of action.

Do nothing ___ Talk with Gerry ___ Inform the instructor ___ Talk with the Dean of Students ___

Here is some additional information . . .

- Gerry made a 98% and Carlos made a 72% on the test.
- Grades are "curved," meaning that tests are given higher scores, with the highest original grade determining the curve.

Based on all the information you now know, rank them again as to what you believe is Carlos' best course of action. Has your ranking changed?

Do nothing ___ Talk with Gerry ___ Inform the instructor ___ Talk with the Dean of Students ___

1. What pieces of new information do you think should influence his decision?

2. What pieces of new information do you think should not influence his decision?

Here are your last pieces of information:

The instructor announces someone cheated on the exam.

The college has an Honor System in which students are required to report violations of academic integrity or risk disciplinary action themselves.

Carlos is on academic scholarship.

After class, Gerry tells Carlos she is the one who cheated, but begs him not to report her.

Based on all the information you have about this situation, rank these actions as to what you believe is the most appropriate.

Do nothing ___ Talk with Gerry ___ Inform the instructor ___ Talk with the Dean of Students ___

1. What pieces of new information would you still like to know about the situation?

2. Are there any pieces of information that could be viewed as more important as to why Gerry or Carlos chose to participate in cheating and, potentially, collusion?

OBJECTIVE 4: Understand Emotional Intelligence

Emotional intelligence, sometimes referred to as emotional quotient (EQ), is defined as "an array of non-cognitive capabilities, competencies, and skills that influence one's ability to succeed in coping with environmental demands an pressures" (Bar-On 2004, 14). When it comes to succeeding in college, and in personal relationships, emotional intelligence (EQ) is as important as your intelligence quotient (IQ).

Traditionally, the IQ score has been considered the measure of a person's cognitive knowledge potential in life. IQ scores have been used to place pre-collegiate students in various educational programs such as special education or gifted and talented. Yet, today EQ is considered important in determining if a student will do well in college. In general, EQ is a person's ability to identify, use, understand, and manage emotions in positive ways. This can be translated into the following categories:

- Self-awareness of personal feelings
- Self-management of personal feelings in a positive way

- Self-motivation to set, manage, maintain, and achieve goals; to delay gratification of immediate urges; to maintain a positive outlook
- Empathy toward other's emotions
- Social skills that create positive and productive interactions
- Apply emotions to tasks like thinking and problem solving

What does this mean for you? If you can manage your emotions, you are more likely to be successful in meeting the demands of several professors' assignments and the time needed to complete them. While you may have the IQ to succeed in college, a low EQ may hinder your success. However, if you have a slightly lower IQ but higher EQ, you may complete your academic goals with greater ease.

EXERCISE 1.16: EQ Assessment

Search the Internet for EQ assessments and complete one. (In order to receive a complete score and assessment details, you will have to pay for it. However, you will be given an overview of the areas contained in the EQ assessment.)

Explain why you do or do not agree with your overall assessment evaluation.

___

___

___

Sometimes, the EQ assessment results can "sting" when we know the results are describing us. What were your feelings when you read your evaluation?

List two (2) areas (if necessary) identified in the evaluation you will want to work on improving:

1. ___
2. ___

REFLECTION 1.J:

It is natural to try to justify why any negative result might not be true. Think about any negative result and give a candid response as to why it is true.

EXERCISE 1.17: EQ Areas of Improvement

Take a moment to review the areas indicated on your assessment that could use some work. Think of ways you can increase the two areas identified, and record them here.

EQ Area for Improvement	Current Tendencies	Ways to Improve this Skill
Example: Self- motivation	I have a hard time getting started or finishing an assignment. There are just too many other things I would rather do.	1. I can reward myself for completing an assignment by doing one thing I like to do.

Here are some suggestions for improving your EQ you may want to consider:

- Identify when you are stressed and think of techniques to manage that stress in a healthy way. What strategies do you have in place for when you are stressed or how do avoid getting stressed? Becoming more self-aware of your strengths and weaknesses can increase your EQ.
- Build a greater awareness of your emotions and learn constructive ways of handling them. Are you aware of your emotional triggers? These would include events or actions causing you to feel sad, angry, happy, or reluctant. If you feel a negative emotion, what steps do you take to rid it from yourself?
- Learn how to read non-verbal cues and how to comfort someone who is emotionally upset. Do you feel angry or frustrated when a person cries? Why do you feel this way? Do you think this is a constructive reaction? Can you feel the pain of another person when they are sad? If so, you are on the way to building a strong EQ.
- Develop humor in your communications. Laughter really is the best medicine! Are you able to find humor in most situations in which you arrive? According to research reported by NOVA/ WGBAH Science Unit, the physiological benefits resulting from laughing are increases in endorphins, dopamine, and relation responses and reduction in pain and stress. The cognitive benefits of laughter are increased creativity, improved problem-solving ability, enhanced memory, and better coping ability when stress occurs.
- Resolve conflict effectively and quickly. By allowing conflict to remain in your life, you give away energy and creativity that could be spent elsewhere. Ask, "How much of the conflict is due to your actions?" and "What will it take for me to resolve the conflict?" Put yourself in the other person's position and ask how they view you. Think of five characteristics you admire in the other person and five ways you can work toward resolving the conflict.

Increasing your EQ is something you can do with ongoing attention and by increasing your awareness of effective strategies for improvement. Take a moment to consider the following tips to continue improving your EQ to help in your success in college:

- Observe how you respond to other people. Do you make snap decisions about people based on stereotype? Are you able to put yourself in the place of another person and understand how they feel?
- Consider your environment. Do you always need to be the center of attention? Can you allow others to look and feel good?
- Perform ongoing self-evaluations. In an attempt to constantly improve yourself, conduct ongoing self-assessments to gain a better understanding of your areas of weakness. Do you always feel the need to be perfect or right? How can you maintain this unrealistic expectation?
- Recognize how you respond in stressful situations. When things take longer to accomplish or do not go your way, do you become irritated or angry? Can you control your emotions even under pressure?
- Take responsibility for your actions. Are you strong enough to be weak? In other words, are you able to admit fault, ask forgiveness, and attempt to right a wrong you may have committed?
- Examine how your actions will affect others—before you take those actions. Ask yourself how will my actions affect other people? Would you want someone you care about to act in a similar way? If not, consider alternatives to your actions.

Acclimating to College

In the months leading up to acceptance to your college, you may have spent time thinking about what it would be like to attend college. Perhaps you moved to campus housing or an apartment for the first time or you may have contemplated adjusting your work schedule, so you could be a part of the college scene. Either way, it is natural to consider the various options included in familiarizing yourself with the college culture. Both social and academic acclimation to college means adjusting to new environmental conditions, interpersonal relationships, social settings, and academic rigor. It also means engaging in activities with immediate and long-term benefits.

To ***acclimate*** means to adjust to a new temperature, climate, altitude, environment, or situation. Consider what happens when you go swimming when the water is cold. Do you just jump in or do you ease yourself into the cold water? After you have been in the pool for a while, your body temperature becomes adjusted, or acclimated, to the temperature. Similarly, when acclimating to altitude, it must be done slowly. If you try to do too much too quickly at a high altitude in which you are unaccustomed, you may spend your first few days of a snowboarding vacation in bed with altitude sickness. As a college learner, you are acclimating to the college culture, guidelines, and expectations which take time for you to become more comfortable. Although you will not become ill from trying to acclimate too quickly, the sheer numbers of things you must acclimate to will keep you from moving too quickly. A distinction should be made between the informality of the "college culture" and the formality of meeting the "college expectations" indicating an acclimation to the culture.

According to Jack Tupper Daniels, an American Olympic winner who has coached many of the premiere college track athletes over the last 35+ years, "within a month or two of training in a higher elevation, the body makes some physiological adjustments resulting in better altitude performance." Similarly, serious college students should expect the adjustment to college to take time to achieve maximum success in academic performance. Of course, this situation implies a high level of motivation, focus, and commitment.

Here are tips for easier acclimation, which are loosely based on Daniels' running theories.

- Believe in your ability to learn and grow.
- Maintain your motivation.
- Focus on opportunities to grow and to demonstrate your knowledge.
- Follow the directions (i.e., *Student Handbook*) for success.

When you are adjusting to the newness of your college, believe in your ability to learn and grow. As you are adjusting, reflect on prior successes resulting from conquering new challenges. Because you have succeeded before, you can succeed again. If your motivation begins to waiver, look for people, places, or inspirational books to give you a boost. One source of motivation may be to calculate your GPA. If it is high, there is your motivation—to keep it high. If it is low, there is a different, but equally powerful motivation—fear of failure. Study: to improve GPA, to avoid academic probation, or even to avoid dismissal. Additionally, seek out opportunities to increase your understanding of the new college to which you are acclimating. For example, contact your fellow learners or a professor for their insight on how to succeed in college. Finally, be sure to understand and follow the guidelines and policies of your college's expectations.

EXERCISE 1.18: Jack Tupper Daniels' Guidelines

Describe one of Daniels' four guidelines listed above. Explain how you will apply it in your life within the next seven days:

____

____

____

____

OBJECTIVE 5: Understand Opportunities for Collegiate Involvement

Student Life Office

There are many ways to connect with people in the college that extend beyond the classroom. The most obvious way to meet people is by getting involved in campus organizations, social clubs (such as are found in Greek life), athletic events, social networking, and professional organizations. Your college has numerous student organizations providing opportunities to socialize, work toward a common cause or goal, and/or represent your college at regional and state functions. One way to find the student organizations on your campus is to locate the office that coordinates these groups, which may be called "Student Life" or "Student Activities."

EXERCISE 1.19: Student Involvement

What is the name of the office who organizes the student activities on your campus? ______________

Where is it located? ____

Where did you access this information? ______________________________

Create a list of five student organizations available on your campus.

1. ______________________________
2. ______________________________
3. ______________________________
4. ______________________________
5. ______________________________

One or more of these may be of greater interest to you than others. Evaluate the top one or two student organizations that will connect you with other students on your campus.

Indicate these top two organizations with a check mark on the left side of the above list. Explain why these two organizations interest you enough to want to join:

Record when these two organizations meet:

REFLECTION 1.K:

Create a list of things you expect to gain from membership in these organization(s):

Describe the contributions you can make toward helping the organization(s) improve or thrive.

____

____

____

Most first-year students do not know many people on the campus, so attending a meeting opens the door to connect with the students who are members of an organization. If you tend to be shy or reluctant to meet new people, college is a great chance to learn how to overcome this. You have the opportunity to reinvent yourself if you wish, so prepare to step outside of your comfort zone. Just as crossing your arms with a preference to the left or right arm being on top and reversing them can be initially uncomfortable, moving outside your comfort zone by meeting new people may also be uncomfortable initially. The first leg of the journey of engaging with new people is to go where they meet, so when are you going to attend a meeting?

Is there someone you have met in one of your classes who you believe might share your interest in this group? Write down their name(s): ______________________________ Invite him or her to attend with you, and, then, you will know at least one person in the room. Most of the people who attend the group's meetings entered the room just like you . . . new, eager to meet others, and looking for socialization. For these reasons, and more, the people there will be excited to meet you.

Social Media and College

Social media websites also provide an avenue for communicating and connecting among college students. Facebook®, Myspace®, and Twitter® have become a fundamental aspect of most college's culture. In fact, research indicates, students who are involved in social networking are MORE likely to become involved in campus activities in general. It is common for colleges and universities to promote the positive events and people from their school through these social media outlets.

In 2007, a study from the *Higher Education Research Institute* found 94% of all college students have social networking accounts with the majority being members of Facebook®. This rate may seem high for 2007 and is expected to stay this high in the future. Interestingly, the research also shows a positive relationship exists between social media use and college engagement. Through social media you, as a college student, may:

- meet new friends on your campus,
- stay in touch with friends from other educational environments you have attended,
- communicate with and learn more about student organizations and campus events,
- and connect with current and past professors.

It is important to use social media responsibly. Unfortunately, all of us can think of examples illustrating how students demonstrate irresponsible use of social media, such as posting inappropriate, and sometimes illegal, social behavior. The outcome of this type of use can be life altering—once a posting is "out there," it can be accessed years later. Many employers are now reviewing Facebook® pages of applicants, so think before you post anything! It is important to read and understand your school's policy regarding social networking sites.

EXERCISE 1.20: Social Media

Write your college's social media use policy here:

Describe the usefulness of social media websites in college:

Explain the value of social media sites to your personal engagement in college activities:

REFLECTION 1.L:

Suppose "Student A" posts this comment on his/her Facebook® page: "I can't believe Dr. Z gave me a D on my accounting final. Now, I have to take the ****** course over and she's the only one who teaches it!"

Student A has applied for a summer accounting internship at Company C. As part of the vetting process, Company C routinely reviews Facebook® pages.

Describe what you would think as the Internship Coordinator about Student A. Consider academic potential, communication skills, attitude, etc.

____

____

____

Athletic Events

Another fun way to meet people and become a part of the college culture is through athletic events. Many universities and colleges have strong athletic programs that attract students to their school. If you are at a large school with such a program, but you are not a student athlete, there may be a booster club for you to join in support of your college's team. There may be a Twitterfeed (a digital feed from your college athletics program) with real time updates on events you can use to follow the team for greater engagement. You may also be able to participate in intermural contests, such as "flag football" in which teams comprised of members of specific dorms, "houses," or organizations compete against one another for championships.

Volunteerism

Volunteering can be a great way to extend your college learning beyond the classroom. Some college courses are actually designed to encourage volunteerism, but are termed "service learning" because the service is connected to learning and the application of the course concepts. Professors may include the opportunity for you to volunteer for causes and organizations in the community while you learn and include it as part of the course grade. In addition to courses with volunteerism as a focus, you will find numerous ongoing opportunities to engage in volunteering.

EXERCISE 1.21: Volunteer Opportunities

Research three opportunities to volunteer on your campus and list them here:

Giving freely of your time will increase your personal growth and extend your learning beyond the classroom. A secondary benefit you may realize from volunteering is the positive reflection it communicates to future employers. In a competitive work place, this may be the significant factor that sets you apart from all other candidates! Finally, volunteering for causes or organizations in your major provides a chance to network with people who are already working in your chosen profession.

Student Membership in Professional Organizations

Professional organizations offer another opportunity for connecting with like-minded individuals on your campus. Each profession (or career) has a professional association serving to maintain the professional standards and oversight of the practices within the profession. For example, Kappa Delta Pi (KDP) is an International Honor Society in Education for teachers. Go to their website http://www.kdp.org for information.

EXERCISE 1.22: Professional Organizations

Take a minute to survey the information on the website.

What does this link offer to the members of this professional organization?

Is there anything specific to careers in science on the website?

Describe how you think this information would be helpful for a graduating college student looking for a job in a science profession.

____

Now, take a minute to go to your college's website and locate three professional organizations that are available for students. You may want to look for recommended organizations for a field of interest, or your major or chosen profession, if you have already selected one.

1. ____
2. ____
3. ____

Are there any student activities or events listed for any of the three you identified? ______________

If so, describe one of the scheduled events. ______________________________

This event may be something you will want to attend, even if it is just to obtain more information on the group's purpose and upcoming activities.

Department-Specific Involvement

Each of the college courses you take is associated with a discipline. A discipline is a field of study you may call your ***major***, a group of courses (generally totaling between 24 and 39 credit hours) within a specific field of study, some required and some chosen from a set selection, necessary to fulfill the graduation requirements for a degree in a field. For example, a major could be Education. Universities and colleges organize their disciplines by associating them through schools (universities and colleges) and divisions (community colleges).

EXERCISE 1.23: Departmental Involvement

Review the schools/divisions in your college or university. List three here:

1. ______________________________

2. ______________________________

3. ______________________________

Identify the school/division THIS course is associated with in your school and write it here.

Understanding this organizational structure in college is another aspect of your college's culture. By understanding the way schools and divisions are organized, you will be better able to determine in which field of study your major is located.

Find the department for your major, or a field of interest, and write it here.

Every semester most college departments host events for students to attend to help participants gain better understandings of the discipline.

Locate a major event in any department of interest to you, and write down the information here. _____

____

Review the event information to determine who may attend, and if there is anything you may need to do prior to attending. Record this information here. ______________________________

____

____

____

Describe what you think the primary benefit of being involved on the departmental level of your discipline.

____

____

EXERCISE 1.24: College Involvement

Take a moment to consider some of the information readily available on your campus concerning involvement in college-sponsored activities. Locate general information on these campus opportunities.

Opportunities	Organizational Purpose	Why I Would Get Involved
Honors Organizations		
Social Networking (online)		
Fraternities and Sororities		
Professional Organizations		
Volunteer Opportunities		
Personal Interest Groups		

Which of your listed groups are you surprised to find on your campus?

____

Why are you surprised? ____

EXERCISE 1.25: Acclimation

You now have a clearer understanding of the wide variety of organizations and activities that will assist your acclimation to college, so it is time to determine how to best use this information. First and foremost, explain which ***collegiate activities*** can assist your college acclimation in the following ways:

Meet new friends: ______________________________
(college activity or organization)

Build understanding of the college culture: ______________________________
(college activity or organization)

Build school spirit/pride: ______________________________
(college activity or organization)

Engage with professors: ______________________________
(college activity or organization)

What collegiate activities have you determined to engage in this semester? ______________________________

Why did you select these activities/organizations? ______________________________

It can be exciting to consider the many ways you can learn beyond the classroom by dedicating time to social networking, student organizations, athletic events, professional, voluntary organizations, and departmental activities. College is a time to realize your potential; joining one or more organizations can encourage this personal and professional growth. These activities will require a time commitment and it sometimes may be necessary to forego the activities in order to concentrate on your required course work. At the same time, your investment in extra-curricular activities can offer you long-term benefits, such as establishing friendships, developing or improving leadership skills, improving community efforts by volunteering, and discovering new information about who you are. All this information can be included on your resume. Selecting your extra-curricular activity involvement wisely can help you realize long-term rewards because most employers are looking to hire well-rounded people.

COURSE CONNECTIONS:

Strengthening Your CORE in 39–48 Credit Hours

© Aleksandr Markin/Shutterstock.com

No, we are not talking about your physical core.
We are talking about your academic core or "required courses" for graduation.

Whether you are considering a career in medicine or modern dance, you will be required to take a number of "core" courses. These normally make up **39–48** credit hours required for graduation and traditionally include:

- English
- Lab Sciences (e.g., Biology, Geology)
- Mathematics
- Sociology or Psychology
- History and/or Political Science
- Speech
- Physical Education
- Foreign Language

© Billion Photos/Shutterstock.com

What do I gain by taking them?	Why do I have to take them?
These courses provide you with opportunities to: ■ Think critically, logically, and creatively. ■ Use the scientific process. ■ Write articulately. ■ Perform academic research. ■ Increase appreciation of classical literature or music. ■ Understand behaviors of individuals or groups. ■ Gain confidence in working with groups and public speaking. ■ Understand and participate globally.	1. To graduate! 2. To become a well-educated person. Knowledge is power! 3. To be exposed to disciplines in which you may discover an interest for a potential major.

With which of these core areas do you believe you will encounter the most difficulty?

Why?

If you were scheduling your courses right now, in which semesters would you want to take these courses?

____

Why did you choose these semesters? ____

____

State a positive and negative reason for taking your difficult courses.

i) in your first (or early) years

ii) in your last year

Has this information changed your plans of when you will take your difficult courses? ____________

Why or why not ?____

When selecting a course load or even a major, you should consider the different time commitments, activities, and your level of commitment. You may like the idea of being pre-med, but you must realize you will be taking time intensive courses which require many labs. Think through your time commitments to see if they can accommodate this level of work. Are you willing to make changes to your other commitments (i.e., work fewer hours)? This will be discussed in greater detail in the next Chapter.

Something to Think About

You will find at least one *Something to Think About* feature in each chapter throughout the text. This feature will be used to promote discussion on a topic covered in the chapter and how the topic is related to one or more of the following list of higher education concerns:

- **social responsibility** (a personal investment in the well-being of others)
- **personal responsibility** (taking responsibility and accepting the consequences for personal actions, and understanding the impact of those actions on others)
- **critical thinking** (ability to analyze, evaluate, and synthesize given circumstances)
- **empirical & quantitative skills** (ability to analyze data and draw valid conclusions)
- **communication skills** (command of oral, written, and visual skills)
- **teamwork** (a group working together for a common goal)

SOMETHING TO THINK ABOUT:

Complete the three steps in this section as written.

1. Take a minute to review the two pictures below. Do you think these are college students? How would you describe their behaviors as viewed in this picture?
   Which students would you want to associate with? Why?

   Write a paragraph (3-5 complete sentences) about the photographs as they relate to *college culture* and college life.

© Masterchef_Productions/Shutterstock.com

© wavebreakmedia/Shutterstock.com

2. Would your discussion be influenced if you knew the person in the left photo is a professor? . . . or if you knew, instead, he is a 35-year-old student?

3. Discuss the photographs again from the perspective of **social responsibility**, **personal responsibility**, **communication skills**, and **teamwork**.

1.2 ACCESSING COLLEGE RESOURCES

The best athletes surround themselves with support networks assisting in minimizing the challenges of stress, physical and social demands, and maximizing their training effectiveness. Similarly, you will experience many of these situations in the college environment. At times you may need to seek help in dealing with the stress, which is a natural byproduct of the new college environment. Where would you seek assistance? When conflicts arise from working with a small group of students on a project or with a roommate, who can you ask for help? Where do you go for instructional support? Knowing there is support for all of these challenges, as well as others, is like having your own private coaching staff to improve your college performance. By being willing to seek their assistance, if needed, you will have a competitive edge over your peers who do not ask for help.

Learning more about the nature of peer relationships and the benefits of positive relationships with professors will enhance your college experience. ***Collaboration*** is a key to long-term success in college and life. Have you ever hear the phrase "collaborate to graduate"? This expression is commonly stated by students who are working together, similar to a team, to earn a college degree. In many law schools, (refer to the movie *The Paper Chase*) creating the "right" study group may mean the difference in success and failure. It may be difficult to imagine graduating from college today if you are just starting your first year, but by understanding the college culture as it relates to connecting with fellow learners, you will achieve greater academic success and, perhaps, develop lifelong friendships.

OBJECTIVE 6: Understand the Nature of Peer Relationships

Have you ever taken a mathematics class and felt confident you understood the concepts presented while sitting in the classroom only to discover after arriving home to work on the assignment you really did not understand the process at all? Do you recognize the saying "the whole is greater than the sum of its parts?" By working with peers from the class, a group will have a breadth of knowledge no one person possesses alone. Working with a peer provides an opportunity to learn alongside another person who is also processing the information. You will each teach, and learn from, one another. Probably one of the greatest benefits of working with peers is the increased social interactions in and outside of class. Upon entering most college classrooms, you may not know a single person. By building relationships with fellow learners in your classes, you have the opportunity to connect with like-minded students.

Frequently, in college, you will be *required* to work with your peers in a small group on a semester-long project. As you know, the more people you try to gather for a meeting, the potential for increased conflict may arise. These may include schedule conflicts or differing perceptions of learning or perhaps just not seeing "eye-to-eye" on some aspect of the project. In spite of these challenges, you will be required to work with these learners and manage these conflicts. On the other hand, you may frequently meet people with whom you will become instant friends.

EXERCISE 1.26: Peer Relationships

Take a few minutes to write a list of ways you can work toward building lasting relationships with those you will meet in college:

____

____

____

____

Working with a partner or working with a group are two avenues for meeting and working with students who share your interest in attending college. Each type of connection has similarities and differences.

EXERCISE 1.27: Collaboration Compare and Contrast

- Form groups of two or three.
- Brainstorm with your group by discussing the benefits of working with a group and a partner and describe how both similar and different.
- Complete the following Venn diagram with information your group created.

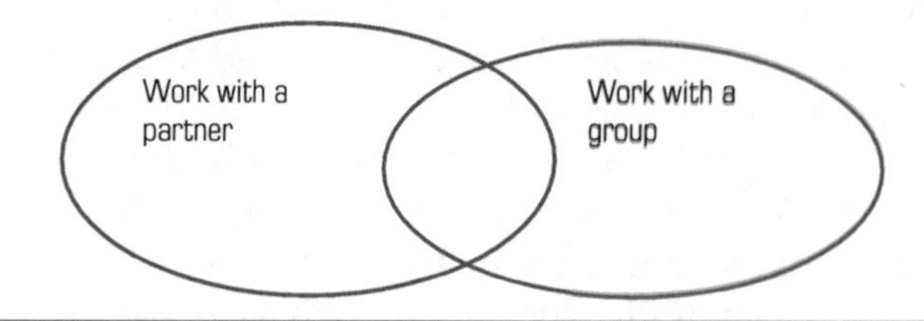

Summarize how these group and partner interactions are alike:

____

____

____

Summarize how group and partner interactions are different:

____

____

____

REFLECTION 1.M:

You have discovered the similarities and differences of working with a partner and within a group. In your past learning environment(s), you most assuredly experienced both types of peer interaction.

Which of the two (group or partner collaboration) did you encounter the most difficulty?

Why do you think this is so?

Consider any of your actions, attitudes, motivation, etc., that might have contributed to the difficulty.

Write them here. ____

What steps can you take, personally, to ensure more positive collaboration experiences during your college career?

____

OBJECTIVE 7: Understand the Benefits of Positive Relationships with Instructors

Establishing a relationship with fellow learners will take time to initiate and commitment to maintain. This is a different dynamic than you will have with your professor, but by combining the two opportunities you will learn the concepts in class more quickly. Establishing and maintaining positive relationships with your instructors will also require commitment. Taking time to meet with your professors regularly will provide benefits in improved communication, classroom learning, and quicker acclimation to the college culture. But how do you begin this process? One suggestion is to go to each of your professor's offices the first week of class and introduce yourself. By locating the professor's office when you are calm and focused on establishing a positive interaction with him or her, you minimize your stress when you need to ask for help. While your first meeting with your professors may seem a bit intimidating, most will support you and your goals.

Most professors welcome the opportunity to help advise you and provide additional academic support when you ask for it. Obviously, seeking a professor's advice will be easier if you have laid a strong foundation of numerous positive moments prior to asking for their assistance.

Beginning your semester with strong positive relationships with your professors, through office visits, classroom behavior demonstrating an interest in learning, or other positive interactions paves the way for the best probability for your personal enrichment and success.

EXERCISE 1.28: Instructor Interactions

List and explain two benefits of establishing a positive relationship with your professors.

1. ____

2. ____

Generate two useful questions to ask your professor that demonstrates your commitment to learning:

1. ____

2. ____

Most colleges provide a full support system with resources to help you meet most any challenge you might encounter. To assist with academic material, there may be a writing and/or mathematics tutoring center. When selecting a major, or choosing a transfer college, your academic advisor is a vital resource. The Financial Aid and Veteran's Affairs Officers are available to assist in these related areas. For stress issues and temporary psychological challenges, there are counselors available on campus for short-term intervention. Just as an athlete needs to employ a group to support his or her success, you will learn to access your support group for improving your academic performance. Success in college not only depends on your knowledge and determination but on your ability to recognize when you need help and reach out to the appropriate resource. Some of the resources offered by most colleges will be discussed here.

OBJECTIVE 8: Recognize Academic Support Services

Your most valuable resources are your instructors. They teach the material as well as write and grade the tests, so who else would know more about the requirements of the course? Think of this person as your coach who wants to see you succeed not only in their class but also in your educational goals.

If you have difficulty mastering course materials, contact your instructor immediately. As your "coach," he or she can explain the material again in a different way or provide additional resource information. It is likely your instructor will be able to identify how to address your learning concern as well as provide strategies to help you understand the material and study to maximize your learning. Giving you the opportunity to excel, as a coach would for an athlete, is what your professor wants.

Writing and/or Mathematics Tutoring Center

Sometimes an athlete has tried all of the suggestions given from their coach but is still not seeing the desired results on the field or court. When this occurs, he or she often seeks the advice of an individual whose expertise is in one specific aspect of the sport. For example, a baseball player may need to work with the team's batting coach and catcher to improve his ability to hit the ball. Most colleges have a writing center and/or a mathematics center (and possibly a science tutoring lab) for your support if you feel more attention on a specific skill is warranted. These centers may provide services such as tutoring, editing, resume writing, or general classroom concept explanations. This tutoring is usually provided at no extra cost to the student.

Academic Advisor

Do you think a college athlete will seek advice from a professional as to the best way to complete their training in hopes of entering the professional scene? Imagine you are seeking advice on how to move from the college classroom coursework to a chosen profession. Would you like to ask someone who knows how to complete the steps necessary for graduation and entering a specific profession?

You actually have this person on your support team now. Academic advisors have the experience of working with college students who are seeking directions on how to best select the courses needed to enter a desired profession. To find your academic advisor, contact the admissions office. Some advisors are assigned specific departments or disciplines. Students majoring in Education, for example, can speak directly to the education advisor. By meeting regularly with an advisor you will learn how to stay on a graduation plan and take the required courses in the minimum amount of time necessary. Since academic advisors do this on a daily basis, their expertise can offer you confidence you will meet your academic goals. Some college students are assigned an academic advisor while at other colleges an academic advisor is available only on a "walk-in" basis. Both provide

- information about transfer requirements,
- graduation requirements,

- help to develop a schedule which includes job hours and other responsibilities,
- advice concerning the sequence of courses,
- and guidance for scholastic probation.

If, after contacting your academic advisor, you find a need for additional information than provided, where could you go?

Consider visiting with an instructor, a dean of students, or even a classmate for alternative support.

OBJECTIVE 9: Recognize Relevant Student Support Services

Financial Aid Officer

Since most college students are not given full athletic or academic scholarships, the reality of paying for college can be stressful because they are working on paying for college. Think of the financial aid officer in your college as a valuable resource on the college student support team. He or she can provide information on acquiring money for college through scholarships, grants, student loans, or work-study programs. The priority to connect with your financial aid officer may be great, depending on your need.

Career Advisor

Just as a college athlete might seek a position to play for a professional team's "farm team," you may be seeking an entry level position in your profession. Working with someone who "knows the ropes" will be of great value, so seek out a career advisor in your first semester of college. The opportunity to take Career Aptitude tests will help you understand your abilities, interests, and values and is available in the Career Services office. Additionally, assistance with your résumé, job interviewing skills, and the ability to interview with companies recruiting on your campus may await you through the career services area. Many students wait until the end of their college career to seek out this resource, but the advantage of connecting with a career services advisor early is obtaining information to understand yourself and whether the career you are considering is a "good fit."

Professional Counselor

What types of stress do college students experience daily?

At times, do you wish you had someone to talk with confidentially about the stress in your life? The Counseling Office can provide you this safe environment. The information you share with a counselor is completely confidential and cannot be shared with anyone, not even your family or professors. College life and life in general can be overwhelming. These licensed counselors are for immediate and short-term therapy and can provide referrals for off-campus services for those in need.

Veterans Affairs Officer

Other support services are available for special student populations. For example, returning to college after serving in the military is riddled with a unique set of challenges. Just as the military men and women with whom you served are connected, the Veterans Affairs (VA) Office can become your support in college. Working alongside a VA Officer, you can learn about all your educational benefits and complete the necessary paperwork to access your benefits. Additionally, the VA officer may be able to provide information on veterans-only classes (if available), counseling services, and advisor services specifically for the returning veteran.

Colleges Adjusting to Returning Veterans	
 © Brandon Bourdages/Shutterstock.com	 © Straight 8 Photography/Shutterstock.com
The G.I. Bill Serviceman's Readjustment Act of 1944 provided money for college and living expenses for almost half of the 16 million veterans who served in World War II. The veterans changed the landscape of colleges because many were married and most colleges, up to this time, provided housing only for single students. Portable housing was brought in to meet the needs of these students.	Today's veterans face some of the same challenges as those returning from World War II. Many of these students have difficulty adjusting to college life. Most were enlisted and accustomed to a strict regimented existence. Colleges understand these challenges and embrace the veterans by offering veterans-only classes, special mentors, and counselors specializing in PTSD (Post Traumatic Stress Disorder).

EXERCISE 1.29: College Resources

List some other services or resources available for supporting your learning this semester:

____

____

Describe the psychological or emotional effect resulting from studying without using any of the resources the college provides.

____

____

EXERCISE 1.30: Student Support Services

Fill in the chart below.

Tip: You may want to enter this information in your phone now for use later in the semester.	**Location/Phone Number**	**Operating Hours**
Writing Center		
Mathematics Center		
Academic Advising		
Financial Aid		
Career Services		
Counseling Office		
Veteran's Affairs		
Technical Center		
Tutoring Services		
Testing Center		

Career Connection:

© suhendri/Shutterstock.com

Transitioning to college is similar to transitioning to a new job. The new environment, procedures, expectations, and evaluations may be very different from what you have experienced in the past. In this chapter, you have learned techniques to help you adjust to college—all adaptable skills to the adjustment to a workplace. Understanding the work environment, expectations, and peer and supervisor relationships, will contribute to healthier and happier job performance.

CHAPTER SUMMARY

In this chapter you have been introduced to ways in which college students acclimate to college and how to access support services. You have reflected on why you selected this school and you have explored the unique college culture on your campus. The experiences in and out of the classroom provide opportunities to understand what your professor expects and how college studying may be different from your prior learning environments. By following a code of conduct, you will increase your knowledge in the field by making connections between your courses.

Another critical component to successful transition to college is your comprehension of the course syllabus. Due to the unique features in the college culture, acclimating to college takes time, dedication, and persistence, realizing support services on campus can be critical to your success. Additionally, by connecting with peers, professors, and academic and student support services, you will engage in the complete college experience.

CHAPTER 1: Self-Check

Vocabulary: Define the following:

1. college culture
2. acclimate
3. academic integrity
4. academic etiquette
5. collegiate activities
6. collusion
7. deep learning
8. GPA
9. plagiarism
10. collaboration
11. perseverance
12. syllabus
13. emotional intelligence
14. academic advisor

Concepts:

15. Describe two ways college life is different from your former learning environment.
16. Describe the meaning of culture as it relates to college.
17. Describe the culture of the college you are attending.
18. Compare and contrast the culture of your college to the culture of your high school, the workplace, or military environments.
19. Discuss the depth of learning required for college.
20. Explain the difference between plagiarism and collusion.
21. Identify two services on your campus offering confidential support.
22. Discuss appropriate classroom behavior and instructor expectations.
23. Provide examples of academic integrity, its application, and its failure. Include strategies to overcome its failure.
24. State two reasons why it is important to know your professors' office locations and office hours.
25. Describe the purpose and content of an instructor's course syllabus.
26. Explain how to optimize the use of an instructor's course syllabus for determining grades, scheduling, and predicting test-taking items.
27. Explain a college GPA.
28. Write a paragraph explaining what you have learned about yourself concerning EQ.
29. Describe traits of emotional intelligence.
30. Explain how personal responsibility relates to emotional intelligence.
31. Describe a strategy to compensate for low emotional intelligence in one area, if appropriate.
32. Discuss how understanding emotional intelligence contributes to transitioning to college.

33. Describe the range of collegiate activities.
34. Identify social media and explain the benefits and drawbacks of using it in college.
35. Describe the value of athletic options.
36. Describe the value of involvement in student organizations.
37. Describe the value of social options and college-sponsored events.
38. Describe the value of volunteer opportunities and college credit options.
39. Describe the value of student membership in professional organizations.
40. Describe the value of department-specific events (e.g., art, culinary, theater).
41. Explain the differences between class-specific and project oriented relationships and the strategies one uses to establish and nurture each.
42. Identify strategies that enhance relationships with instructors.
43. Choose one of the strategies helpful in creating positive relationships with your instructors and explain how you will employ them over the academic term.
44. Explain the importance of meetings with professors.
45. Identify and describe the types of academic support services available at your college.
46. Describe the types of student support (non-academic) services available.

CHAPTER 2

Setting Goals and Managing Time

T.I.P.S.—(Tactical Information that Promotes Success)

Choices are critical components to college success. Making wise choices makes college more rewarding.

© Busara/Shutterstock.com

Versus

Africa Studio/Shutterstock.com

Just as you choose the type of food you eat, you may choose ways to invest your time. Will your choices concerning goals and time management be healthy?

Choosing to eat a donut or an apple means you have to weigh the long-term result of both. Everyone likes to indulge occasionally and eat a saturated fat and sugary donut. If a person only eats doughnuts, the long-term effects create an unhealthy body lacking energy.

Consider this as you make choices concerning class preparation and participation. . . . Every day, your professor comes to class prepared to serve you a five-star, fine- dining experience with balanced nutrition. You have the choice to partake in this exquisite menu through active learning. In contrast, many students opt out of the professor's healthy spread, leaving with a kid's meal because they are not as actively engaged in the learning or do not bother to attend a particular class session. Thus, you choose increased knowledge or a toy. It IS your choice.

In **mathematics**, the instructor provides you with multiple examples to increase conceptual understanding. Mimicking those examples is not enough. You must learn how to apply instructor-led techniques to other new and varied situations for in-depth learning. If you choose to learn at a deeper level, it will take time. However, the menu is prepared by your instructor to build on these abstract concepts allowing you to complete different problems involving similar processes.

In **reading**, you experience deeper learning and increased comprehension by annotating a textbook prior to class. Upon entering class, the learning is easier as a result of choosing to pre-read actively.

In **writing**, choosing to begin an essay early means the final draft will be more easily read and understood. College writing requires time for ideas to incubate. Allowing time for this process to fully occur means your final product is well developed!

In **education**, arranging observations in a public school to connect theory taught in the college classroom allows for easier, more practical applications of theory and learning.

CHAPTER 2: OBJECTIVES

2.1 Setting Goals

Objective 1 Understand Maslow's Hierarchy of Needs

Objective 2 Learn Strategies for Setting Long-term Goals

Objective 3 Understand How to Set Goals for Individual Classes

Objective 4 Apply Backward Planning to Goal Setting

2.2 Managing Time

Objective 5 Understand the Relationship between Personal and Academic Priorities

Objective 6 Establish Priorities for Course Requirements

Objective 7 Learn Strategies for Establishing Schedules

2.3 Identifying Strengths, Challenges, Opportunities, and Choices

Objective 8 Learn How to Identify and Enhance Strengths

Objective 9 Recognize and Advance Challenges

Objective 10 Understand Opportunities and Choices

CHAPTER CONCEPTS:

Some or all of the following terms may be new to you. Place a check mark in the column reflecting your knowledge of each term.

	Know	Don't know	Not sure	Page # where first found		Know	Don't know	Not sure	Page # where first found
tenacious	X				time management	X			
priorities	X				short-term goals	X			
grit	X				long-term goals	X			
persistence	X				procrastinate	X			
strength	X				intermediary goals				
opportunity	X				"rule of thumb"	X			
challenge	X				"SMARTER" goal	X			
threat	X				backward planning				

© Pushkin/Shutterstock.com

"Alice came to a fork in the road. 'Which road do I take?' she asked." "'Would you tell me, please, which way I ought to go from here?'"

"'That depends a good deal on where you want to get to.'"

"'I don't much care where—'"

"'Then it doesn't matter which way you go.'"

— Lewis Carroll, *Alice in Wonderland*

2.1 SETTING GOALS

Just as Alice is perplexed as to which direction or road to take because she is not sure where she is going, attending college classes without an end-goal may be perplexing and frustrating. Goals are aims or the predicted outcome of a process. If Alice had taken time to determine the place she wanted to go, then she would have been equipped with the necessary information to help her to decide on how to get there. As the White Rabbit suggests, because Alice did not know where she wanted to go, then there was no choice to be made, either road would have taken her somewhere.

Perhaps of more importance, what motivates Alice to run or rest? Before you can determine the direction you are going, it is helpful to know the reasons you are inspired to begin and complete a task. Maslow's work on *A Theory of Human Motivation* offers a foundation for understanding how and why you are motivated.

OBJECTIVE 1: Understand Maslow's "Hierarchy of Needs"

Imagine your world came under some unknown attack rendering all electronic impulses useless. As a result of this catastrophic event, all technology from water purification, electricity, and electronic devices would no longer work. Humans would survive but would need to learn to rebuild civilization as they know it. If you know about Abraham Maslow's "Hierarchy of Needs," you could help rebuild society by understanding the order of events, needing to occur to maximize the efforts of everyone and everything.

In 1943, psychologist, philosopher, and leader of the Human Potential movement, Abraham Maslow, wrote a paper entitled *A Theory of Human Motivation.* His writings produced one of the most useful diagrams (see Figure 2.1) for understanding the human development which is called the "Hierarchy of Needs." This hierarchy demonstrates the order in which human needs must be met. In order to progress from a lower to higher level, success must first be met in the lower levels.

FIGURE 2.1

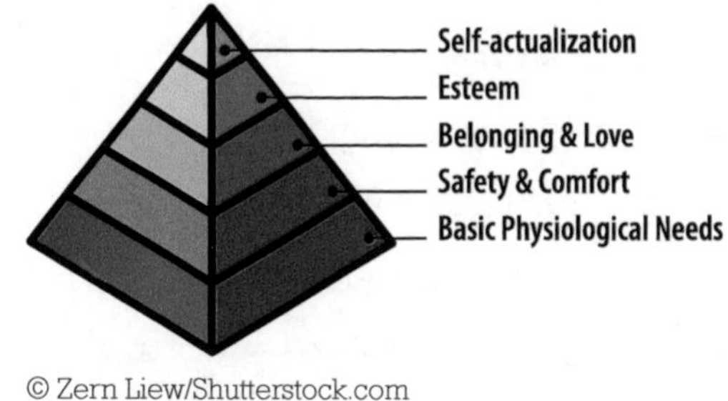

© Zern Liew/Shutterstock.com

The initial level, entitled "***physiological***," includes the basic needs to stay alive. This seems like a logical point of beginning. Unless you can keep your body healthy and meet the basic needs you cannot move to any of the higher levels. These needs are the first to be met in order to the start the journey leading to self-actualization, the highest level.

Once you have your physiological needs met, you progress to the "***safety***" level of Maslow's hierarchy. At this stage, you begin to protect the basic needs you have established and seek safety for your body. Along the way, you may have acquired property, a family, some resources, and employment. Being physically safe and keeping your property, resources, and family safe requires you to now consider what is morally right or wrong. Imagine you are in the group of survivors after the Earth was attacked, as discussed in the opening of this section, and that you found resources for your basic needs for survival. It only seems natural that you would want to protect and keep them safe. You would want everyone to follow the rules to keep their families and possessions safe and some type of punishment for those who violated those rules. If a person lives in a neighborhood where drive-by shootings occur, he or she may not be able to reach the final step of Self-Actualization in Maslow's Hierarchy, but may be able to move to the next level of "love and belonging" by interacting with friends and loved ones.

Love and belonging is the next stage of progression in the hierarchy. In this stage you seek friendship, family, and intimacy. Having secured your basic needs, you are better equipped to realize the need for companionship, familial connections, and intimacy. A homeless mother who is literally sleeping on the streets may build and provide intimacy for her child even when food cannot be temporarily found. This is an extreme case of being at the level of love and belonging without meeting the very basic needs, but there are always exceptions to these models presented. Although it would be unusual, do you know someone who has achieved a higher level without meeting a lower level?

Esteem is the fourth level of Maslow's hierarchy and, just as the name implies, your self-esteem, confidence, personal achievement, as well as respect from and for others, is achieved. After connecting with humans in relationships that create love, belonging, and intimacy, this level seems to be a natural progression. According to Maslow, all human beings want to be respected and highly regarded by others. When a positive self-esteem is achieved, you are more confident and more likely to achieve more because you are willing to take risks. Sometimes this level has been negatively affected due to experiences in education.

The fifth level of Maslow's Hierarchy is the ultimate level of needs having been met, ***"self-actualization."*** At this stage, having met all of the previous four stages, you realize your full potential with the ability to be creative, spontaneous, and problem solve. Along with these critical thinking abilities, you have moved to a higher level of morality which is demonstrated by an acceptance of diversity (lack of prejudice) and the realities of the world you live in (acceptance of facts). Maslow believes until you master the first four levels of need, you will not be able to actualize.

EXERCISE 2.1: Maslow's Hierarchy of Needs

Rank the five levels in order of needs.

__2__ safety

__5__ self-actualization

__3__ love and belonging

__1__ physiological needs

__4__ esteem

EXERCISE 2.2: Hierarchy Needs

Match the categories with their needs (not all contents will be used).

B safety	A. achievement and confidence
C self-actualization	B. morality, family, property
E love and belonging	C. morality, spontaneity
D physiological needs	D. food, water, breathing
A esteem	E. friendship and family intimacy

EXERCISE 2.3: Summary of the Hierarchy

Write a brief summary of Maslow's "Hierarchy of Needs:" A diagram set up to easily explain the needs of humans in order to live a successful life with Basic needs, safety, love, esteem, and self-actualization

REFLECTION 2.A:

Evaluate and explain on which of the five levels you perceive yourself living today.

I believe the levels that i have in common are safety, love, needs, and actualization

OBJECTIVE 2: Learn Strategies for Setting Long-Term Goals

Goals are the destinations you establish for yourself that help you move to higher levels of Maslow's Hierarchy. To attain these goals, you build road maps of activities guiding you toward achieving your purpose. Have you ever used your GPS to go to a new location? How did you start your journey? Most people type in the address of their destination and the GPS generates a map to follow. This is the same process you need to follow when establishing your goals. You specify your goals (*type in your destination*), and then determine the actions (*generate a map to follow*) necessary to reach them.

Making choices and having a wide variety of choices is what goal-setting allows you to do. It is a way to prioritize the use of your time and it allows for periodic check-points of progress. Goals are the motivation for most of the things you do. For example, owning a home is a goal for a large number of people. This goal motivates them to obtain the best jobs they can find, to start saving money for a down payment, and to work to establish a good credit rating.

Specifying a goal involves more than merely thinking about it or even writing it down. A well-specified goal should be a ***"SMARTER" goal***. The acronym "SMARTER" refers to the series of seven attributes of a well-written goal.

- **"S" is for Specific.** Being specific holds you accountable to the goals you are establishing. Specific goals include the actions you will take. For example, if you set a goal to pass a mathematics course, you might decide you will devote a minimum of 12 hours each week to study for it and seek assistance from a tutor if you need help.
- **"M" is for Measurable.** The measure may be quantitative or qualitative, but it must be set against some standard of performance and a standard of expectation. Simply passing a course is not a measurable goal; a "D" is passing at most colleges but is not sufficient for moving to the next course. Passing a course with at least a "C" is a measure of the goal.
- **"A" is for Attainable.** Setting goals is a balance between making them too easy or too hard. When you think of attaining your goal, you must consider availability of resources (i.e., time, money, and people). If you set a goal of completing 15 hours of courses in one academic term, you may be taking on more work than you can successfully accomplish, particularly if you are also working or caring for a child. The extra load may require too much of your time and your grades may suffer. You must ask yourself if the lower grades are worth completing the extra course. However, if you are attempting to enter a program that begins only once a year and the extra course will allow you to apply next term rather than waiting another year, then the chance may be worth it. If you are taking lab-based courses, they usually require additional expenses as well as the additional class time, so you may not have the financial resources to take on more than one in a given term. Think through your goals and ask yourself if each one is attainable.
- **"R" is for Relevant.** A goal must be relevant to you and your life. Will the achievement of your goal advance you toward your vision of a career? Relevant goals help you to keep focused on what is important. In college, you will have opportunities to take courses in subjects not specifically necessary for your degree or certificate; these are usually called "free electives" and you have the chance to study areas outside or only slightly related to your primary coursework. It will be necessary for you to consider how much any course will be adding to your desired college or personal goal by asking how relevant is it? For example, if you want to get in better shape, a fitness class will meet both a college requirement and personal goal. If you have always been interested in meteorology but your major is in political science, taking a course in meteorology may fulfill a personal interest.
- **"T" is for Time-bound.** A timeline or date should be part of your goal. Being time- bound helps you to measure your success toward reaching your goal. It also can assist you in developing an action plan of objectives and strategies for obtaining your goal. Because any college degree or certificate will require a huge investment of your time, typically several years, your goal becomes easier to manage if you establish a series of shorter-term goals (semesters or quarters) and set times when you can reasonably expect to accomplish each step.
- **"E" is for Evaluate.** Setting a goal with the first five attributes is not enough to ensure its attainment. Frequent evaluation of your goals is essential to reaching them. Conditions such as a change in your major, a change in job responsibilities, or a change in available resources may affect your stated goals. At the end of each term, you should consider how well you have met your established goals, or how much you have advanced toward their achievement.
- **"R" is for Revise.** Your goals are not cast in stone and they, along with the conditions for their achievement, will change from time to time. For example, courses in the "hard" sciences (mathematics and lab sciences) generally must be taken linearly, meaning one course is a

prerequisite for another. Because of this, it is difficult to take multiple courses in the field in one term. If you are attending a small college or in a field with a lower enrollment of students, it is possible not every course you need will be offered every term; some may only be offered every other year. You may find yourself in a situation where you may need to re-evaluate whether you can remain in this major without adding additional years to the attainment of your goal. After evaluation, you should revise the goals needing changes and continue the SMARTER goal-setting process.

EXERCISE 2.4: Parts of SMARTER Goals

Write the word represented in each letter for SMARTER goals.

Specific

Measure

Attainable

Relevant

Time-bound

Evaluate

Revise

EXERCISE 2.5: Identifying Parts of a SMARTER Goal

Identify each of the components of a S.M.A.R.T.E.R. goal in the following:

"To enter a competitive nursing program, a successful applicant typically earns a 3.8 GPA. Therefore, I will earn A's and B's in all of my college courses. I typically achieve A's in my college mathematics courses, so this seems attainable. This means, I study a minimum of three hours a week in the mathematics tutoring center working on my homework. If I do not understand a concept, I will make an appointment with my instructor as soon as possible to improve my learning of the course materials. By the mid-course, I will reflect on course average to make sure I am on track to earning an "A," and seek more tutoring or instructor assistance if needed."

S ____________________

M ____________________

A ____________________

R ____________________

T ____________________

E ____________________

R ____________________

Can you see how stating your goals in SMARTER terms will help to clarify your intent and focus the subsequent actions necessary to achieving them?

Goals may be long-term, short-term, or intermediary. A long-term goal takes two or more years to achieve but a short-term goal can take from one week to two years to realize. ***Intermediary*** (or intermediate) goals are the smaller steps you need to take in order to achieve either short-term or ***long-term goals***. An example of how this would work is setting a long-term goal to buy a new car. This long-term goal, when written as a SMARTER goal, reads something like: "I will purchase a new Ford truck within the next twelve months." Establishing the ***intermediary goals*** includes answers to questions such as:

- "How much money will I need to save for the down payment?"
- "How much money will I be able to finance?"
- "How much money can I realistically afford for a car payment?"
- "What is my credit score?"

By brainstorming questions such as these and all of the necessary steps needed to purchase the truck, you can determine if the time set for achieving the long-term goal is realistic. If not, you may need to adjust your time frame or how much money to save in order to purchase the truck. Writing goals requires time to think about what you want to do and how you can do it. After you establish long-term and ***short-term goals***, record them on your calendar. Additionally, record your intermediary goals to chart your progress.

EXERCISE 2.6: Goals in SMARTER Form

Identify a long-term (at least one year) educational goal you wish to achieve. Answer the following questions in order to help you write your goal in SMARTER form.

What do I want to accomplish? getting into UT Austin

How will I measure my success? Education and achievements

What resources do I need to achieve this success? Patience, money, perserverance

How does this goal relate to my degree or certificate? ______

When can I realistically reach my goal? ______

How will I evaluate my progress? ______

I will need to revise my goal if this happens: ______

My goal written in SMARTER form is: ______

______

______

The intermediate goals I need to accomplish include: ______

______

______

I will adjust my time line (if necessary) based on my intermediate goals in the following way(s): ______

______

______

REFLECTION 2.B:

Select a recent goal you did NOT complete. Now, you know the framework for writing a goal in SMARTER form. What components of this framework could you have applied that would have allowed you to complete your goal?

______

Finishing building my tesla coil

______

______

______

______

______

______

______

______

OBJECTIVE 3: Understand How to Set Goals for Individual Classes

Start setting your goals in this class. You may not have considered what you want to learn, but you probably have thought about the grade you want to make. Many students want to earn an "A" in every class and at the beginning of the academic term their intentions are good. However, most students do not understand the perseverance, dedication, commitment, and amount of work involved to earn your "A." For whatever grade you want to achieve in this course, you will need to candidly consider what you are willing to do to earn it.

EXERCISE 2.7: Supporting Goals

Answer the following questions for THIS course.

What grade are you willing to work for in this course? 

What steps will you take to earn this grade? (Possibilities might include: form a study group, attend class regularly, visit the Writing Center, submit all assignments on time; set aside a specific time to study every other day, or meet with my instructor.)

How many hours per week do you *realistically* believe you can devote to this one course? __________

(Time management will be discussed later in this chapter.)

EXERCISE 2.8: Setting Goals

Repeat Exercise 2.7 for the other classes you are taking. Remember, your success in college is most likely a goal you set; you owe it to yourself to do whatever is necessary to ensure your success.

____

____

____

OBJECTIVE 4: Apply Backward Planning to Goal Setting

Backward planning is one way to set a goal for an academic term, or long term, and to set realistic intermediate goals for its completion. Just as the name implies, this strategy requires you to begin with the end in mind and work backward on the time required to accomplish all of the steps successfully. This is a process used in bidding for a construction contract or marketing account. In order to complete the project on time, the team plans backwards to realize the projected date of completion and its cost. Of course, some may realize there is not enough time to complete the project.

For example, if you have to write a term paper which is due in one month, look at a calendar for the next month. Write the due date on the calendar if you have not already done so. Then, set small attainable goals to achieve the written product by the submission deadline. For the term paper, you might plan something such as:

4th week: Term paper ready to submit to professor.

3rd week: Final revision of term paper.

2nd week: Submit the rough draft to the campus Writing Center for revision and editing.

1st week: Write the thesis statement and a working outline, and research the topic in the library or ask a librarian for research assistance.

As you can see, this means you will need to set a goal and break down the steps necessary for achieving it. You might not need a full week before going to the writing center and your final revision.

However, allotting extra time between steps will allow you to attend to more urgent assignments with an earlier deadline. In some subjects, such as mathematics, backward planning is not as important as simply keeping up with the homework assignments!

EXERCISE 2.9: Backward Planning

Review your assignments in this class or another class in which you are currently enrolled. Select one of the longer assignments and describe the tasks you need to complete to meet the goal.

Assignment Title: ______________________________

Class: ______________________________

Submission deadline: ______________________________

List the steps or tasks you need to accomplish.

Step 1: ______________________________

Step 2: ______________________________

Step 3: ______________________________

Step 4 (the submission deadline): ______________________________

(Insert additional steps should you need them.)

Now, reverse the list to determine the end-date when each step needs to be completed.

Step 4: ____ Date to complete: ______________________________

Step 3: ____ Date to complete: ______________________________

Step 2: ____ Date to complete: ______________________________

Step 1: ____ Date to complete: ______________________________

(Insert additional steps should you need them.)

Take a moment to consider the resources you need to accomplish the tasks you are using in your backward planning. For example, the resources for a term paper may include meeting with a research librarian, spending time in the library, and spending time in the campus writing center. All of these require some degree of scheduling ahead of time.

What types of resources will you need to complete the assignment?

Resource 1: ______________________________

Resource 2: ______________________________

Resource 3: ______________________________

(Insert additional resources should you need them.)

Now that you have applied the strategy of backward planning, you can use the deadlines you have set (date-to-complete) as markers or milestones to track your successes. Write the information you have generated in your calendar to more easily track your intermediary goals. By recording the dates, you will have constant reminders of the next step to complete in the predetermined deadline. Finally, the recording of the dates for all assignments in the term will help you to always be prepared!

The use of backward planning will help you to manage your time so you are less stressed and more focused, allowing you to submit your best work for each class. You may even realize you have more time to celebrate your work by doing the things you enjoy most. Be sure to reward yourself along the way so you can increase your motivation to complete your established goals.

PERSON to PERSON

© Rawpixel.com/Shutterstock.com

In this exercise, you will be introduced to three students, all first-term college students. Each student has a unique background and personal circumstances.

Let's meet them!

Terence is married with two children, ages three and seven. He recently returned from serving four years in the military. Terence works two part-time jobs for a total of 35 hours a week and is enrolled in 12 credit hours. He hopes to become a police detective.	Becka lives at home with her mother and received a scholarship to attend college. She does not work outside the home and is enrolled in 12 credit hours. Her goal is to earn a certificate in the Dental Hygiene field.	Tamisha is a first-generation college student, meaning she is the first in her family to ever attend college. She has a part-time job, 25 hours a week, and is enrolled in 12 credit hours. Although she is not certain of what she wants to do, she enjoys science and mathematics classes.

Based on these descriptions, rank the students as to whom you believe will be most successful this term with "1" being the most successful, "3" the least successful.

Terence ____ Becka ____ Tamisha ____

Here is some additional information to consider:

Terence's only access to a computer with internet connection is at his 2nd job.

Becka's mother suffers from Alzheimer's but has professional help from 8am–5pm Monday–Friday for her mother.

Tamisha's part-time job is at the college and her employer allows her to attend class three hours of her work week, which she must make up some time that week.

Based on all the information you now know about these three students, rank them again as to who you believe will be most successful this term with "1" being the most successful, "3" the least successful. Has your ranking changed?

Terence ____ Becka ____ Tamisha ____

1. What pieces of new information do you consider to be a positive influence on success?

____

____

____

2. What pieces of new information do you consider to be a negative influence on success?

____

____

____

Here are your last pieces of information:

Terence's 2nd job is night clerk at a local motel three nights a week from 11 pm to 7 am.

Becka's siblings watch their mother two weekends a month.

Tamisha lives in a college dormitory.

Based on all the information you have about these three students, rank them one last time as to who you believe will be most successful this term with "1" being the most successful, "3" the least successful.

Terence ____ Becka ____ Tamisha ____

1. Why did you rank them this way?

____

____

2. What pieces of new information would you still like to know about each student?

____

____

3. What are the pieces of information that could be seen as both positive and negative influences on success?

____

____

2.2 MANAGING TIME

© xtock/Shutterstock.com

According to *Psychology Today*, *time management* "is the ability to plan and control how you spend the hours in your day to effectively accomplish your goals." This means you can actually control and manage the resource of time. Most research indicates that acquiring this skill will create a more productive, less stressful, and more fulfilling life. Understanding the relationship between achieving academic success and achieving personal success is a vital first step toward this accomplishment.

Before discussing anything about how to manage your time, take a few minutes to see how you are *currently* spending your time. One way to put into perspective how you use your time is to create a pie chart. **There are no right or wrong answers in this exercise; it is based on your opinion.** For the most effective outcome of this exercise, be honest as to how you spend your time.

EXERCISE 2.10: 24-hour Pie Chart

Complete the pie chart for one of YOUR 24-hour days.

You might find it helpful to use different colored pencils for each of the areas. Each segment of the chart represents one hour in the day. Shade in the number hours per day spent. —working at outside employment (including commute time) —sleeping —preparing/eating meals and dressing for work and/or class —attending class (including lab hours, plus commute) —exercising —with family and friends —on other entertainment —any other activity you want to track	**24-hour Pie Chart** 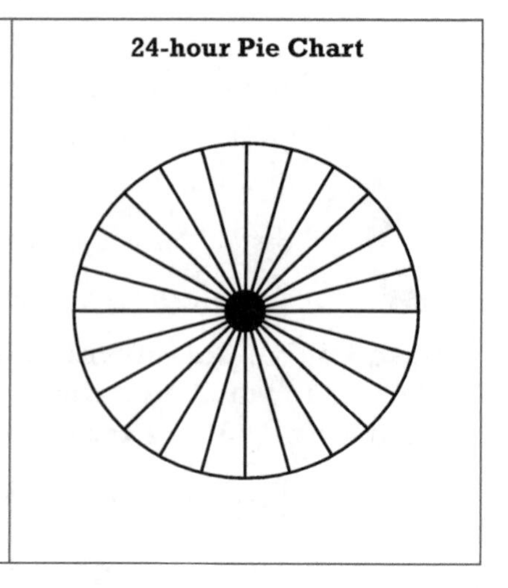

Do the results of your "pie" surprise you? ______ Why or why not? ______________________________

____

Obviously, you have to sleep, prepare and eat meals, and dress for the day. These are "musts." You have to spend time on them. If you go to class, then this becomes a "must." Perhaps you have a job. If so, this is added to the "must" list. The rest of your time is yours to spend any way you want.

Did you notice studying was not on the list? ______ Did you even consider it? ______________________

How much time of your day is left for studying? ______

The number of hours in your day shaded for each of the listed areas is a reflection of how much you currently value this activity or need. The larger blocks of shaded area are your current priorities.

OBJECTIVE 5: Understand the Relationship between Personal and Academic Priorities

Priorities refer to the arranging of tasks you want to complete in an order of urgency, or ranking them in a way to systematically complete each one. Of course, what is considered "urgent" or important will vary by individual. Your enrollment in this class implies the priority you place on attending college. Whether you are seeking a degree or certificate, taking courses to meet new job requirements, or taking courses for personal fulfillment, you have prioritized attending college. Depending on why you are attending college, it may be considered an academic priority, personal priority, or both.

Academic Priorities

Academic priorities are the level of importance you place on activities or accomplishments relative to your academic career. Some examples of goals needing to be "ranked" or prioritized may include achieving a certain grade-point average, graduating, increasing your understanding of a specific subject, gaining entrance into a particular honor society, transferring from a community college to a university, or passing all your courses with a "C" or better.

EXERCISE 2.11: Identifying Academic Priorities

List three academic priorities you have for this academic term:

1. Classes
2. AP tests
3. Sanity

Personal Priorities

Learning in the college culture takes place both inside and outside the classroom. For this reason, personal priorities are equally important. A personal priority is the importance you attach to an individual accomplishment. Some examples of these may include: exercising regularly, seeking employment, developing a romantic relationship, starting a family, improving your skills on a musical instrument, joining a student organization, volunteering for a local cause; the list is endless. As a college student, you need to consider how your personal goals will impact your college success. For example, if you are seeking employment, obtaining a job will definitely impact the number of hours you have available for study. However, if not having a job is placing undue hardship on meeting your financial responsibilities, obtaining a job will motivate you to find time to study.

Both academic and personal priorities are important. Sometimes these priorities are the same. For example, graduating from college can be both an academic and a personal priority. Other times, personal and academic priorities support one another. For example, volunteering for a local cause may be a personal priority. However, if service learning or volunteering in the community is part of a course requirement, then it can also be an academic priority. If achieving a high grade-point average is an academic goal, it could fulfill a personal goal of transferring to a highly competitive university or entrance into a graduate program.

EXERCISE 2.12: Personal Priorities and College Success

List three personal priorities for the academic term and state what impact they may have on your college success. Write NONE, if applicable.

Personal Priority	Impact on College Success
1.	
2.	
3.	

After you have considered your three personal and academic priorities, how would you rank them overall? For example, your first choice might be personal or academic.

Rank	Previously Listed Academic and Personal Priorities
1.	
2.	
3.	
4.	
5.	
6.	

OBJECTIVE 6: Establish Priorities for Course Requirements

Setting priorities is a necessary strategy for college success. Merely understanding this concept is only the beginning; through prioritization, successful time management will be realized. Since you are currently enrolled in college courses, consider the variety of these courses and the demands on your time.

EXERCISE 2.13: Course Preparation Time

Write the names of the courses in which you are currently enrolled, the hours you spend in class each week, and the hours you *currently* spend preparing for each course outside of class. Be sure to include any lab or recitation classes in the hours in class. Note, in mathematics courses, homework and outside labs are part of the preparation time.

Course	Hours in Class	Hours Preparing

There are many factors influencing the amount of preparation time you will need for each college class you take. One primary factor determining the time you need to study is the amount of prior knowledge you have in the subject. If you have taken courses in the subject being studied, you probably have a firm grasp on the vocabulary used to describe the concepts. For example, if you have taken prerequisite courses to prepare you for chemistry and microbiology, you have heard the language of the discipline, so learning in the next class may be less encumbering. In contrast, if you take a microbiology class without having the foundation of the vocabulary, it may take you a significant amount of time to learn the material. This is because you are learning the basic language of the course and learning the newly introduced materials at the same time. Therefore, the stronger your foundation and preparation prior to entering a course, the less time you may be need to study for the course.

Rule of Thumb for Out-of-class Study

© Noppanun/Shutterstock.com

Learning can be compared to the effect a small trickle, or drip, of water over time has on a large bolder. Over time, a small drip can bore a hole through a solid rock or cliff. Imagine every time you study the effect is like the slow drip of water on the rock. Eventually, you will realize the concept has become a permanent memory which has left a lifelong impression on your brain. Slowly dripping water producing a hole in the solid stone takes repeated drips. By learning with the slow drip process, the concepts will be more manageable, less stressful, and last longer! This process will be discussed in detail in Chapter 3.

In college, there is a recommended study-time formula necessary for a student to be academically successful. The ***rule of thumb*** for the average number of hours expected for a student to spend on outside of class study are 1:2 "one to two" for face-to-face classes and 1:3 "one to three" hours for online classes. This means for every hour you attend class, you need to plan for two or three hours of studying outside of class to yield greater success. Remember, this is just a generalization! If you are lost in the complexities of a class, then more time will be needed to comprehend and retain the required course information.

EXERCISE 2.14: Predict how You Use Your Time

Evaluate the time you anticipate investing in the courses you are taking this academic term.

How many course-hours have you enrolled in for this academic term? ______

If you invested *three* additional study-hours per week for EACH of these course-hours, how many additional hours would be required each week? ______

Does this number surprise you? ______

Do you think you have this many additional hours to spend on college work? ______

The questions above were predictions. Now, by looking at a week, you will be able to see how well you predicted your study time.

EXERCISE 2.15: Week at a Glance

Earlier, you filled out a 24-hour chart to view how you spent your time in one day. To obtain a clearer perspective of your time management, complete the following chart for a typical week.

Account for EVERY hour with one of the following codes:			
S (Sleep)	W (Work plus commute)	C (In class/lab)	F (family/friends)
P (Preparing for work/class; meals; eating; exercising)	ST (Studying)	E (Entertainment)	

Typical Week for This Academic Term							
	Sunday	**Monday**	**Tuesday**	**Wednesday**	**Thursday**	**Friday**	**Saturday**
6:00–7:00am							
7:00–8:00 am							
8:00–9:00 am							
9:00–10:00 am							
10:00–11:00 am							
11:00—Noon							
Noon—1:00 pm							
1:00–2:00 pm							
2:00–3:00 pm							
3:00–4:00 pm							
4:00–5:00 pm							
5:00–6:00 pm							
6:00–7:00 pm							
7:00–8:00 pm							
8:00–9:00 pm							
9:00–10:00 pm							
10:00–11:00 pm							
11:00–12:00 pm							
12:00–1:00 am							
1:00–2:00 am							
2:00–3:00 am							
3:00–4:00 am							
4:00–5:00 am							
5:00–6:00 am							

After reviewing your weekly schedule and knowing the number of hours of outside study recommended, is there enough time to meet the "rule of thumb?" 1:2 or 1:3.

If yes, congratulations!

If not, explain how you can better manage your time to include more study time.

OBJECTIVE 7: Learn Strategies for Establishing Schedules

In business, the term *Return on Investment* (ROI) is used to express if businesses are getting a positive return on their investments. By borrowing this term for your college success, determine if you are investing adequate time and energies to earn a positive ROI. Just as businesses have to evaluate their ROI frequently, you will want to review your time and energy weekly to make certain you are receiving a positive return. If you were a business, would others be confident in investing in you?

Often, the challenge in completing schedules is to strike a healthy balance between personal and academic priorities. To arrive at the perfect balance, manage your time, so you are not "over-extended" or "over-committed." It is easy to agree to meet a friend for coffee or a workout, as both are healthy ways to spend your time, but remember your priorities before saying "yes!" Most people fail to take time to evaluate how these commitments, although small, may impact their academic success.

Two Weeks at a Glance

A single day as represented by the pie chart at the beginning of this section reveals only a "snapshot" of your time. A 24-7 chart helps you visualize how you are spending every hour of every day for a single week. However, to get the "big picture" it is more useful to view at least two weeks, and preferably an entire month, or even an academic term, to see if there are any conflicts between assignments and/or personal commitments.

Have you ever missed a deadline to submit course work?

A schedule helps to create a reminder of important deadlines, reducing the possibility of an oversight.

EXERCISE 2.16: Schedules and Work Conflicts

In this case study, you are to assume the perspective of this student. You are given the following information:

- Susie and Kenley are your elementary aged children.
- Kelly is your only niece.
- Fred is your loved one's father.
- You work 4 hours (2–6) on days you are scheduled.
- You attend classes in the mornings (Monday–Friday) from 8:00 until noon.
- English is the class creating the biggest challenge for you.
- One Saturday a month you volunteer at the local food bank for three hours (9:00 am–noon).
- Review the two weeks on the calendar on the next page.

Sun **7**	**Mon** **8**	**Tue** **9**	**Wed** **10**	**Thu** **11**	**Fri** **12**	**Sat** **13**
	English paper outline due	Dentist 1 PM. Work	Work	Mathematics test	Susie's School Play—need 24 cupcakes	Volunteer work Kelly's swim meet (8-11 AM)
Sun **14**	**Mon** **15**	**Tue** **16**	**Wed** **17**	**Thu** **18**	**Fri** **19**	**Sat** **20**
Sociology Group project meeting 2:00 pm	Work Kenley's Dr. Appt. 2:30	Turn in History paper Math lab due	Read History Chapters 13-15	Sociology Group project due Work	English paper due Fred's BD dinner 7:00	

Do you see any potential scheduling conflicts based on *your* list of priorities?

If you have to work on Tuesday and Wednesday, the 9th and 10th, when do you study for the mathematics test on the 11th?

Your plan: ____________________

Will you try to bake the cupcakes for Susie's school play or purchase them? ____________________

Why? ____________________

What will you do about the conflict on Saturday the 13th

Your plan: ____________________

As you may notice, the 2nd week is busy with many assignments. What strategy (or strategies) can you use to complete them all on time?

Your plan: ____________________

Because English is your most challenging subject, more time will need to be devoted to writing the paper due on the 19th. How can you adjust your schedule to include four additional hours over the two week period?

____

REFLECTION 2.C:

Form a group of three or four members and compare your answers to the previous questions on priorities and time management. Discuss the ways in which each group member approaches time conflicts. After the small group discussion, write a paragraph on how your approach to conflicts may have been different from others in the group. Try to include support for approaches *different* from yours.

____

____

____

____

____

EXERCISE 2.17: Two-Week Calendar

Now, you have reviewed and evaluated the two-week schedule in the case study. Use the blank two-week calendar below to enter all your due dates for assignments for the courses you are taking, any work, volunteer and family commitments, for these next two weeks. You might want to include your scheduled study times.

Sun	Mon	Tue	Wed	Thu	Fri	Sat
Sun	**Mon**	**Tue**	**Wed**	**Thu**	**Fri**	**Sat**

REFLECTION 2.D:

I (will/will not) be able to do everything I have on this calendar and still maintain my personal and academic priorities because:

____

In order to complete my course work for these two weeks I will need to:

____

Considering your class load, your personal, family, and work commitments, review your 24/7 schedule and your two-week schedule. Do you have the additional hours needed to study outside of class in order to be successful in all your courses? ______

If not, is it possible for you to find the additional hours to help you be successful? ______

Are you able and/or willing to adjust your schedule to find this time? ______

Explain your answer. ____

If your schedule limits the additional hours needed to ensure your success, consider cutting back on your work hours or involving your family in taking ownership of some of the obligations you normally handle.

If this is not an option, you may have to consider withdrawing from your most difficult course because it requires more time preparing outside of class. However, please discuss this with your instructor prior to making this decision. There could be financial ramifications for withdrawing from a course, especially if it is past the time for receiving any refund or if you are on financial aid or a scholarship.

The benefits of taking time to organize your weekly and monthly schedule include:

- managing your time
- minimizing your stress
- enabling prompt submission of your course work
- providing more time for socializing

As you have seen from the production of your own weekly and two-week schedules, planning ahead will make your life less stressful and create more productive use of your time. Knowing what is coming up before the moment it arrives allows for more predictability in your day as well as your week. Additionally, by effectively managing your time, there may be more time to include a few social activities. Knowing the most important items on your schedule have been completed allows for relaxation when attending those social activities.

Ideally, you should use all your syllabi from the courses you are taking and write down the due dates for every assignment for this term. Most colleges provide students with some sort of academic year calendar and this would work well. Having all due dates on the same calendar will help you to avoid overlapping deadlines for assignments and papers, especially around midterm and the end of the term.

With the increased popularity of electronic calendars, you may find it more convenient and effective to keep all your activities on your phone calendar. Because most smart phones have accessibility to online storage, the contents of your calendar can be downloaded to your computer and iPad© or tablet for accessibility at any time. Any update made to one automatically updates the others, so you always have a complete view of your weeks.

To-Do Lists

Knowing how creating a schedule can make you more productive and relaxed, you should be ready to create one for every week. Of course, just writing items on a calendar is not enough reinforcement for most people. To increase the benefits of using the schedule you have created, developing a "to-do" list focuses and prioritizes your tasks. A "to-do" list consists of the tasks and appointments you have to complete in a week or a day.

After you have recorded the deadlines, events, work hours, and other important dates on your schedule, *write a list of the smaller steps* you may need to complete in order to meet the pending deadlines. For example, you may not typically include "run to the grocery store" or "go to the bank" in your schedule. These are essential tasks in managing your life, but may not be deemed worthy of writing on your schedule. A typical to-do list might look like this:

Run to the bank to make a deposit

Pay rent

Grab a loaf of bread and some milk

Pick up dry cleaning

Call Uncle Joe regarding Mom's gift

In order to manage your day and the many tasks necessary as an adult, a to-do list can be essential for planning. Now, the list has been created, so it is time to prioritize the items. Go back to the list and place an "A" by the most important, a "B" by the somewhat important, and a "C" by the least important. The ranking may look similar to:

A Run to the bank to make a deposit

A Pay rent

B Call Uncle Joe regarding mom's gift

B Grab a loaf of bread and some milk at the grocery store

C Pick up dry cleaning

By using the "A, B, C system" to prioritize your tasks, you will be more focused on completing the A list first, then the B list, and if time allows complete the C list. By doing this daily, you will have two rewards. The first is:

- maintaining the focus on every task which needs to be completed, with the highest priority being given to the more urgent tasks,
- setting a visual reminder of all the tasks you accomplished in the day.

The second reward has psychological benefits because you will realize you have been productive, even on the days you may feel like very little has been accomplished.

At this point you may be thinking something like, "this is going to take too much time." How much time do you spend on tasks every day, but cannot recall what you completed? Investing a little time in organizing and prioritizing your time at the beginning of the day will actually increase the amount of productivity in the day! Making certain every day is invested on the areas needing your focus will have its own rewards. You will have control of your time. Remember, the ROI at the beginning of this section? Are you investing your time in the things with the potential to generate the greatest return on your investment (time)?

Distractions

Feeling frustrated by the little things that arise in your day may mean you are trying to do too much or you have too many distractions. Are you aware it takes up to 20 minutes to regain your focus for every interruption occurring in your day? For example, you are reading a chapter in your geology textbook when a text message from your friend pings on your phone. You stop, read it, and reply. The time you took to respond to the text message might have taken less than two minutes. However, those two minutes may have cost you an additional 15 to return to your reading at a level where you comprehend what you are reading. You may even need to re-read the section you were on when the text message came in. Research studies on employees in the business world have shown for every "minor" distraction from work-focused activities, 20 minutes of productivity was lost.

When studying, it is important to work in an environment containing a minimum number of distractions. College libraries generally provide study rooms—some sound-proofed rooms when the door is closed are an option to consider. If you are living with a roommate, set aside study time when he or she will not be present or agree upon a certain "study time" when you are both studying. Of course, if your phone is left enabled to ring or notify you of a text, you have not eliminated the distractions. To minimize distractions, turn off the ringer and texting notification. Plan your week by dedicating two to three hours of undistracted time to maximize your learning.

SOMETHING TO THINK ABOUT

Take a minute to review this picture.

© Phovoir/Shutterstock.com

Do you think this student looks stressed?

1. Write a paragraph, three to five complete sentences, about the photograph as it relates to goal setting and time management.

2. How would your discussion be influenced if you knew:
   - the time when he began studying (30 minutes ago, versus three days ago)?
   - the subject he is studying (mathematics or history)?

3. Discuss the photograph again from the perspective of: social responsibility, personal responsibility, communication skills, and teamwork.

COURSE CONNECTIONS:
Hard and Soft Sciences

Hard Sciences

Generally, more technical;

may require more study time

on a daily basis

Soft Sciences

Generally, more conceptual;

may require large blocks of

time to write papers

	Sample Courses	*Mis*perceptions	Realities	Study Time Commitment
Hard Sciences	*Algebra* *Statistics* *Biology* *Chemistry* *Physics* *Geology* *Ecology*	Courses are more difficult and require a lot of study time	Classified as "hard" sciences due to specific research methods Usually take more time to work through problems or experiments in order to understand a concept	Requires skill mastery, technical vocabularies, and lab procedures
Soft Sciences	*English* *History* *Sociology* *Psychology* *Government* *Speech* *Education*	Courses are easier and do not require much study time	Classified as "soft" sciences because of different research methods than "hard sciences" Usually takes time because of extensive reading	Requires writing papers and preparing and presenting projects

How are the "hard" sciences and "soft" sciences the same?

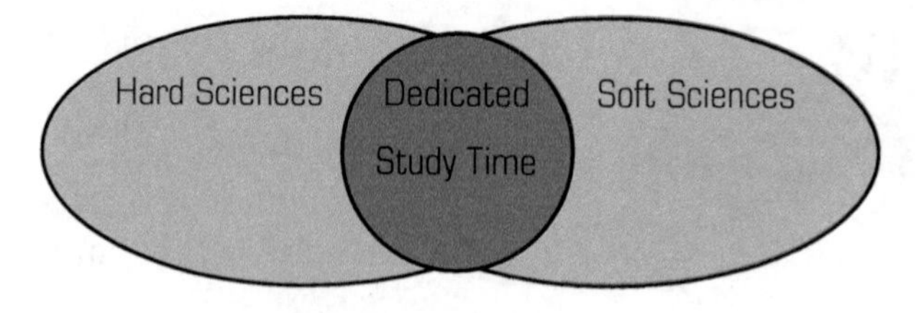

They both require study!

REFLECTION 2.E:

List each "hard science" course you are enrolled in for this semester.

____

____

____

Why did you choose this/these?

____

____

____

Describe a positive experience you have had in each one thus far.

____

____

____

List each "soft science" course you are enrolled in for this semester.

____

____

____

Describe a positive experience you have had in each one thus far.

____

____

____

Even though you may be experiencing some difficulty with the content, how have these positive experiences affected your attitude toward both the "hard" and "soft" sciences?

____

____

____

____

2.3 IDENTIFYING STRENGTHS, CHALLENGES, AND CHOICES

© hurricanehank/Shutterstock.com

Have you ever seen a bull dog grab a hold of a pet toy? Bulldogs are known to have such a strong bite that it is almost impossible to pry the toy out of their jaws. This is where the term "bull dogged tenacity" originated. It refers to a person who has the determination of a bulldog.

Imagine you have "bull dogged tenacity" regarding your course work. This means you complete the assignments with the determination of a bulldog refusing to release the goal or object, even if obstacles occur. This type of determination creates the focus necessary to complete the goals you have established and prioritized.

OBJECTIVE 8: Learn How to Identify and Enhance Strengths

The skills involved in prioritizing, planning, and focusing take time to develop and manage. There are a myriad of ***strengths*** contributing to a successful college experience such as intelligence, emotional intelligence, patience, tolerance, and determination. The traits of tenacity, ***grit***, and persistence are premier strengths. One of the biggest differences between students who succeed in college and those who are less successful is tenacity. A ***tenacious*** person is one who is committed to completing the task no matter what obstacles may occur.

A recent report from the Department of Education suggests **"*grit*"** is a critical component of the successful student equation. Per the report (Duckworthetal 2007, 1087–8): Grit entails working strenuously toward challenges, maintaining effort and interest over years despite failure, adversity, and plateaus in progress. The gritty individual approaches achievement as a marathon; his or her advantage is stamina. The last eight miles of a marathon may be the most challenging, so the key to completing it is focusing on the short-term—on the road in front of you, one stride at a time. Completing the smaller steps eventually add up to the end goal. In contrast, not completing the individual steps toward your goals can lead to disappointment or boredom, which, to some, signals it is time to change trajectory and cut losses. The gritty individual stays the course.

Persistence is another critical characteristic you will want to develop as a college student. When a student continually strives to achieve a goal or overcome an obstacle, he or she is demonstrating persistence. Thomas Edison is a great example of an American who persisted in everything he attempted. Between 1881 and 1933, Edison filed for 1,093 patents; this is still the highest number of patented inventions from a single American citizen. His persistence is commonly noted in his quote, "Our greatest challenge lies in giving up. The most certain way to succeed is to always try just one more time." Edison offers you, as a college student, the inspiration to try again and again. This may become frustrating, but the return on your investment is definitely worth it.

EXERCISE 2.18: Academic Strengths

Identify several personal strengths that have helped you succeed at something in the past. List these in the chart below and describe how they can help you succeed in college. An example is given to help you get started.

Strengths	How This Can Help Me Succeed in College
focus	I have the ability to stay focused on a task until it is completed.
grit	
tenacity	
persistence	

EXERCISE 2.19: Persistence

Go to the website http://www.values.com/inspirational-sayings-billboards/37-Persistence to read about Abraham Lincoln's persistence. List three of Abraham Lincoln's failures.

1. ______________________________

2. ______________________________

3. ______________________________

List one success, other than being elected President of the United States.

REFLECTION 2.F:

Consider a time in your life when you did not achieve a wanted goal (to win a swim meet or track event, being selected first chair, or passed over for a promotion, etc, but "persisted.")

How did this event make you feel at the time?

____

____

Did you consider giving up swimming or track or leaving your job? Why or why not?

____

____

Since you did not give up on your "goal," what strength kept you moving forward?

____

____

Now, consider an event in your past in which you did not achieve a particular goal and DID give up. What was different about the two events resulting in such divergent decisions?

____

____

How did you feel about giving up on your goal?

____

____

____

Knowing what you know now about setting goals using the SMARTER format and the identification of some of your strengths, what could you have done to keep from giving up on this goal?

____

____

____

OBJECTIVE 9: Recognize and Advance Challenges

Some people appear to be naturally tenacious or persistent, and some are, but most people who demonstrate these characteristics have had to learn them over time. The first way to work toward this type of discipline is to discover your own strengths and ***challenges*** as they relate to achieving your goals. A persistent person will evaluate if there is more than one way to achieve the goal, adjust their strategy and try again. The determining factor for most success is the ability to look at the relevance and approach of the goal with honesty. This requires self-evaluation to determine your strengths and challenges.

Procrastination

The Merriam-Webster dictionary defines ***procrastinate*** as "to put off intentionally and habitually." Remember Maslow's "Hierarchy of Needs?" According to his theory, human needs are met by progressing from one level of satisfying a need to another in order to self-actualize. Self-actualization is the point at which humans realize their full potential with the ability to be creative, moral, spontaneous, problem solvers, and to accept diversity and reality. A person's self-actualization takes time to achieve. Thus, set-backs may need to be considered along the way. One such set-back may be seen in the form of procrastination.

Procrastination can be more readily understood by considering how motivation is a catalyst for greater success. Success breeds success, which is the means for greater successes. Consider how Maslow's "Hierarchy of Needs" acts as a powerful means of motivation. As a person achieves the journey leading to self-actualization, it seems logical that procrastination becomes less of an influence.

EXERCISE 2.20: Procrastination

Predict how procrastination fits into your current level of Maslow's "Hierarchy of Needs:"

____

____

On a practical level, forgetting about an assignment can generally be overcome by keeping an academic calendar, whereas procrastinating is knowing an assignment is due and intentionally avoiding completing it. It is so easy to say to yourself "I'll work on my essay tomorrow." Unfortunately, the tomorrows keep coming and you are still planning on "getting to the essay later." Overcoming procrastination requires focus and time.

It is tempting to eat dessert before consuming healthy foods. As much as most people might prefer to eat dessert first, most people have learned to eat their vegetables first in order to stay strong and healthy. In general, humans prefer to complete enjoyable things first. For some, completing a mathematics assignment is much more enjoyable than writing a demonstration speech. Overcoming procrastination is similar to learning to eat the most nutritious food first. Setting aside a little time each day to work on certain assignments you may find less interesting or more challenging may help with procrastination. Rewarding yourself with a phone call to a friend or watching a favorite TV show after working for an hour or two will motivate you to complete a less interesting assignment.

Identifying Challenges

It is important to identify your educational challenges and understand how to advance them. As you begin your college coursework, perhaps you have identified an academic challenge. An example of how you discovered this challenge may be a time you performed poorly on a test. You have an opportunity to assess your challenges when a test is administered, graded, and returned in a class. Upon reading through the test, you may notice consistently missed information. This may demonstrate a fragile retrieval of information (this will be discussed in detail in the next chapter). For now, consider another way to interpret this outcome. In light of your challenges, is it possible you may not have studied well enough, which resulted in the inability to retrieve or apply the needed information?

In general, recognizing your challenge as it relates to accomplishing your goals is the first step in overcoming it. Take a minute to think of one or two areas where you might not perform as well or where you feel you could improve your skills. Next, think of ways in which you could overcome or advance those challenges. You will want to consider your strengths and think of ways to use them to overcome your challenges. Briefly note ways in which you plan to challenge your challenges. See the example given for you in the exercise below.

EXERCISE 2.21: Strengths and Challenges

Complete the chart with your understanding of your challenges and strengths.

Challenges	Strengths	Ways to Advance Challenges
easily distracted	organization	Set my phone for a specific amount of time and work on homework until time is up. Change the amount of time I work from assignment to assignment so I do not get distracted knowing time is almost up.

OBJECTIVE 10: Understand Opportunities and Choices

In the same way strengths and challenges appear to be polar opposites, so are the concepts of maximizing your ***opportunity*** to make wise choices. Taking time to weigh the outcomes of your choices will allow you the opportunity to make better choices.

Opportunities come in many forms. Many professionals are brought onto college campuses as guest speakers who will readily share their experiences in their field. Often, they are invited to lecture to specific classes, but sometimes they will give a college-wide speech. Events such as these provide you with a chance to advance your learning outside of the standard course content. There are many ***opportunities*** presented to you, and it is your decision whether to avail yourself of those prospects. Although your attendance to these events is usually not mandatory, some professors will insist you attend for their class. Occasions to volunteer for special events or to work in service organizations provide opportunities for you to enhance your college experience.

EXERCISE 2.22: Opportunities for Success

Describe two or more opportunities you envision for success.

Success in college depends upon your ability to recognize when opportunities are presented, so you can benefit from them. In the same way, recognizing the potential choices to your success will enable you to give some thought to the ways in which you can minimize their impact.

It is helpful to identify and manage the ***choices*** that improve your success. One of the most common choices college students often fail to consider is if there are sufficient resources for accomplishing a goal. Resources come in the form of time, money, and personal energy. Allowing too little time to research or write a term paper could threaten a good grade in a course. Not understanding and accounting for all of the financial costs involved in setting up a dorm room or apartment may mean you are spending more time earning money and less time on your studies.

Taking on too many tasks at one time or trying to help other people too much results in a reduced energy level, which is a very real threat, but often less recognized. It is generally easy to say "yes" to someone's request for assistance, particularly if they are a friend. If you are trying to work a job, raise a child, care for an elderly parent, and take a full load of college courses, it can be taxing to the point you suffer from a depletion of your own energy. This makes the accomplishment of the necessary tasks even more difficult because it is harder to work at something when you are tired. This might look similar to your phone when you are running too many "apps" at the same time. Each "app" drains the phone's battery, so it has less power to run. When you really need to use your phone, you will not have the ability to text or answer a call.

A great example of how prioritizing your energy to better insure you are able to lend help to others is seen on a commercial plane. The flight attendant always describes what to do in case of a drop in cabin pressure. When traveling with a child, you are told to put your oxygen mask on first then place a mask on your child. In other words, you cannot help anyone else unless you take care of yourself.

One assistive strategy in understanding choices is to always look at the tasks you must accomplish and realistically estimate the costs in time, money, and energy associated with getting them completed. By having these valuable estimates, you can accurately schedule your activities as well as a plan for paying for them.

EXERCISE 2.23: Choices to Success

Describe one or more choices you envision to your success.

Discuss two strategies you can employ to manage or eliminate the choices to your academic success:

____

____

____

Career Connection:

© Viorel Sima/Shutterstock.com

In the workplace, you may report to different people requiring reports and projects with close or overlapping deadlines. In addition, the rest of the duties of your job need to be completed on time. Also, you will be maintaining a balance with your personal life. By making wiser choices you will be able to set goals and establish their priorities, develop schedules and manage your time, and identify things helping or hindering your progress. The same college success strategies will contribute to workplace advancement.

CHAPTER SUMMARY

In this chapter you learned about motivation as it relates to "Maslow's Hierarchy of Needs," how to manage your time, set goals, and self-identify choices to your envisioned college successes. You contrasted personal and academic goals you identified, as well as the comparisons between them. Realizing the connections between the two types of goals may act as a motivator, because accomplishing the academic goals so closely aligns with achieving your personal goals. Additionally, learning to manage your time with weekly scheduling and backward planning will create a less stressful and more productive life.

"Maslow's Hierarchy of Needs" is a theory of motivation built on five stages. Each stage defines a level of human achievement with the ultimate goal being to achieve self-actualization. The lowest level is physiological in which basic needs such as food, clothing, and shelter must be met. Safety, the ability to protect your body and belongings, is the second level. The third level, love and belonging, anticipates you will find healthy intimacy in your life. Esteem is the fourth level of need to be met and implies your self-esteem, confidence, personal achievement, and respect from others will be achieved.

The final stage is self-actualization. In this ultimate level of meeting your needs, you will realize your full potential with the ability to be creative, moral, spontaneous, problem solvers, and the acceptance of diversity and reality. This theory explains how humans are motivated to develop through stages to achieve their full potential in life.

Goal setting is the foundational component enabling your weekly calendar to work toward achieving balance in your life. Your weekly schedule should reflect your goals. If you have a goal to be on the dean's list this academic term, then your weekly schedule will include all of the necessary elements for a well-designed goal.

Also discussed is the need to self-assess your strengths and challenges. In addition to those already mentioned in this summarization, tenacity, grit, and perseverance were included. By combining tenacity and persistence, you are more likely to succeed in college.

Finally, the ability to recognize opportunities and to predict the potential choices to your envisioned successes will play a critical role in your college success. Beginning with realistic visions of your success and employing effective ongoing management strategies will aid in the focus necessary to attain your goals.

CHAPTER 2: Self-Check

Vocabulary: Define the following:

1. perseverance
2. tenacity
3. grit
4. procrastination
5. priorities
6. short-term goal
7. long-term goal
8. intermediary goal
9. strengths
10. challenges
11. choices

Concepts:

12. List and describe the five levels in "Maslow's Hierarchy of Needs."
13. Explain how understanding "Maslow's Hierarchy of Needs" can increase a person's motivation.
14. Describe Maslow's self-actualization theory.
15. What is a goal?
16. What does each letter of SMARTER represent in relation to setting goals?
17. How long does it take to achieve a:

    long-term goal a year or longer

    short-term goal less than a year
18. Describe how methods of achievement relate to long-term goals.
19. Analyze the similarities and differences between academic and personal goals.
20. Determine the criteria for establishing individual class goals.
21. What is "backward planning"? How can backward planning be useful to you as a college student? Describe the milestones that must be met to stay on track.

22. Explain the relationship between personal and academic priorities.
23. Rank order your top five personal priorities for succeeding in college and support your reasoning.
24. Define priorities as it relates to time spent studying.
25. Describe the course requirements in need of prioritization.
26. Describe what criteria should be used to prioritize course requirements.
27. Discuss the conflicts that may arise between personal priorities and academic course requirements and describe methods for dealing with the conflicts.
28. Describe the differences between a weekly and monthly calendar.
29. What is a to-do list and how can it be used to make sure the most important items are completed first?
30. Describe "rule of thumb" for study time and explain how it can reinforce learning.
31. Describe the content (and range) of a schedule.
32. Discuss review and revision of schedules.
33. Describe the "slow drip" learning process and explain the advantages of employing it.
34. What is the difference between "hard" and "soft" sciences? Give one example for each type.
35. Discuss strategies for managing procrastination.
36. Explain how tenacity and persistence assist in achieving academic goals.
37. Explain what is meant by the phrase "time is not a replenish-able" resource as it is use in this chapter.
38. Discuss two strategies you can employ to manage or eliminate the choices to your academic success.
39. Explain distractions and how one manages them, identifying strengths, challenges, opportunities, and choices.
40. Create three note cards for this chapter, the first with a True-False test question, the second with a multiple choice test question, and the third with an essay question.

CHAPTER 3

Processing and Learning Information

T.I.P.S.—(Tactical Information that Promotes Success)

Achieving an "Aha!" moment leads to prioritizing various aspects of your life and balancing time which can increase the likelihood of future "Aha!" moments.

Scientists and physicians frequently experience "aha" moments.

© Hulton Archive/Stringer/Getty Images

© Sergey Peterman/Shutterstock.com

Time is the foundation that allows for more "Aha"' moments.

Merriam-Webster defines an **"aha moment"** as a moment of sudden realization, inspiration, insight, recognition, or comprehension.

Doing well in college reflects your personal priorities to learn over working too many hours or having too many social commitments. Your ability to maintain focus is increased as your commitment to learning increases. This leads to more connections between subjects such as languages, mathematics, and science.

In **mathematics**, have you ever experienced the satisfaction of getting a problem correct? Or rather, have you experienced sudden understanding of a concept that might be described as a "light bulb" moment, especially during class? How do you increase the frequency of that feeling? Practice! While all tasks require practice, mathematics may take even *more practice* than other subjects.

In **education**, have you ever answered a question from a student who is confused about an explanation in class? During your answer to the student, his eyes light up and he states, "Oh, I get it!" As children receive more information about a topic, they relate their own experiences to the concepts and understanding takes place. Jean Piaget calls this constructivism.

As you apply what you have studied in **science** class to actual laboratory experimentation, you will likely experience more "Aha!" moments in your lab courses. Of course, in science, those moments may be when anomalies occur, a recognition that something "different" is happening and the need to explain that difference.

In **reading**, "Aha" moments are increased when ample time is dedicated to annotation and active learning strategies that increase your comprehension. That's when you "get it" and create endless "Aha" moments!

In **writing**, "Aha" moments are realized as you allocate enough time in your writing to learn ways to communicate more effectively. This means writers start early to create ideas that will create "Aha" moments for the reader. Of course, this type of writing happens best when others review your writing prior to submission.

CHAPTER 3: OBJECTIVES

3.1 Processing Memory and Learning

Objective 1 Recognize How Memory Systems Process Information

Objective 2 Understand the Relationship between Schemata and Long-Term Memory

Objective 3 Understand the Relationship between Selective Attention and Cognitive Processing

Objective 4 Understand the Relationship between Metacognition and Learning Strategy

Objective 5 Recognize Strategies for Developing Long-Term Memory

Objective 6 Recognize the Importance of Whole-Brain Learning

3.2 Determining Learning-Style Preferences and Adjusting to Multiple Teaching Styles

Objective 7 Apply Strategies to Strengthen Learning Modalities

Objective 8 Understand How to Adjust Personal Learning Preferences to Different Teaching Styles

Objective 9 Learn Methods for Studying Independently

CHAPTER CONCEPTS:

Some or all of the following terms may be new to you. Place a check mark in the column reflecting your knowledge of each term.

	Know	Don't know	Not sure	Page # where first found		Know	Don't know	Not sure	Page # where first found
sensory input	X				memory systems	X			
sensory memory	X				selective attention	X			
working memory	X				deep processing	X			
long-term memory	X				metacognition	X			
schema	X				"forgetting curve"	X			
recursive learning	X				whole-brain learning	X			
constructivism	X				distinction	X			
magical Number 7+/- 2	X				elaboration	X			
	X				retrieval	X			

3.1 PROCESSING MEMORY AND LEARNING

Pulling it down from the cloud . . . Just as we store songs, movies, books, apps, and even calendars in the "Cloud," we store personal memories and a LOT of other information in our personalized cloud . . . our brain.

Have you studied for a test and felt confident about your preparation only to go "blank" when you begin the test? This lack of ability to recall stored information is not just frustrating but can have serious consequences.

The memory process is a complicated system, but the information provided in this section will help you understand its processes and provide techniques you can use to improve your ability to retain learned information. Before you can be concerned about retrieving information, you must first understand how memories are stored.

OBJECTIVE 1: Recognize How Memory Systems Process Information

Perhaps you have gone out to socialize with your friends on a Friday night and met someone you want to call later. Would you remember the phone number if the person repeated it to you, or would you ask to have it written on a napkin or even entered in your cell phone? Most of us would need to have the number written down or entered into our cell phone because committing a 10-digit number to memory is inefficient. (Technically, our short-term memory can hold only three to seven pieces of information at a time, but this will be discussed later.) You may have to repeat the phone number over and over numerous times and then there is still no guarantee you would remember it when you got home.

What would happen if, at just the moment the person begins telling you the phone number, your favorite song begins to play? Would you be able to remember the number now? Would you even hear the whole thing? You probably would not hear it, because the momentary distraction of the song caused you to stop paying attention to listening to the digits in the phone number. Therefore, if you want to be able to call this person, you must first pay close attention to the information you are receiving.

How Memory Processes Work

The brain has a unique way of processing information which includes gathering, storing, and retrieving information or memories when needed. The terms *information* and *memory* will be used interchangeably. There are four levels of processing information into memory as seen in Figure 3.1. Understanding these stages can provide important insight into the learning process.

FIGURE 3.1 Stages of memory processing

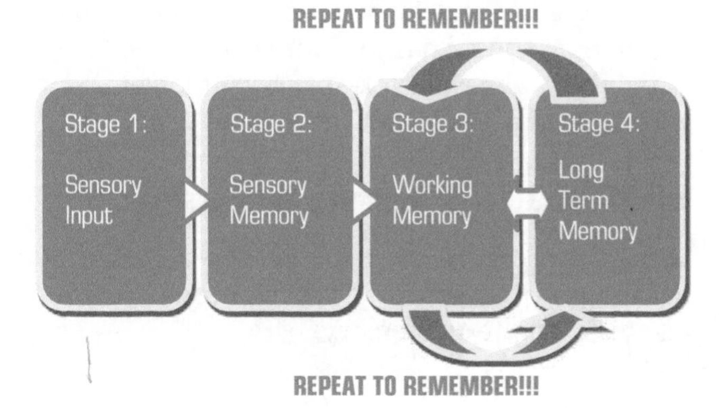

The first step in the memory process, ***sensory input***, is a heightened awareness of stimuli (new information) to the brain from the physical world. You will first become aware of this new information when one or more of your five senses are alerted to something new or different *(i.e., hearing the phone number of the person in the previous example)*.

Sensory input creates your ***sensory memory***, the second stage in the memory process. Once information enters the sensory memory, the brain attempts to determine the size, color, shape, smell, and location of the stimuli. The sensory memory can only process three to five bits of information and hold it for merely a second. This is your short-term memory and, as you have seen from the phone number scenario, the brain is inefficient at remembering information short-term. At this point, you can either ignore the new memory or move it to your working memory *(you determine whether you want the person's phone number)*.

Have you ever watched a glow stick or a sparkler and noticed the trail it leaves behind in the dark sky? The stream left behind the light is not really there; this is the sensory recognition existing in your brain. Another example of this sensory recognition is if you are listening to a lecture but begin thinking about how hungry you are. In the brief moment you were distracted, you did not hear the words of your professor. When your attention returns to the lecture, you can recall the last two or three words spoken. This is an example of how your sensory memory's ability to hold information, although briefly, allows you to return to the information *(the song playing momentarily distracted you from hearing the phone number)*. Because sensory memory lasts for just a second, it is critical to consciously process the information received to the next stage of the memory process.

In order to turn a short-term memory into a long term memory, the memory must first be moved into the ***working memory***, where information is stored between 15-30 seconds. The working memory can hold five to nine bits of information. In this stage, information is prioritized by the ***central executive*** (Baddeley 1986), a name given to the process, and either discarded or continued to be processed *(i.e., recalling the new phone number)*. In other words, in this section of memory impulses are controlled, new information is being evaluated, correction of information is created, and the recognition occurs that some information may require deeper thinking.

For example: you are studying for an exam when the smell of smoke enters your consciousness (*sensory input*). Immediately, you stop studying to identify the source of the smoke (*sensory memory*) and determine if you are in personal danger (*working memory*). Your brain helps you determine the greater priority in less than a minute, whether to continue studying or leave your house. Of course, when you inspect the cause of the smoke, you remember you left a bag of popcorn in the microwave too long (*discard the memory*).

The last stage of memory processing is ***long-term memory*** where a limitless capacity for storing different types of information that has been processed and stored exists. The storage can begin without any conscious activity on your part; for example, recognizing the smell of your father's after shave or remembering what you were doing years ago when you hear a particular song played today. In other cases, it may take years for your long term memory to form, for example, being able to think in a foreign language without translation.

EXERCISE 3.1: Memory Processing

Label the following flow chart with the stages of memory processing. Try not to look at the example in an attempt to test your working memory. This is the beginning of your review for working these stages into your long-term memory!

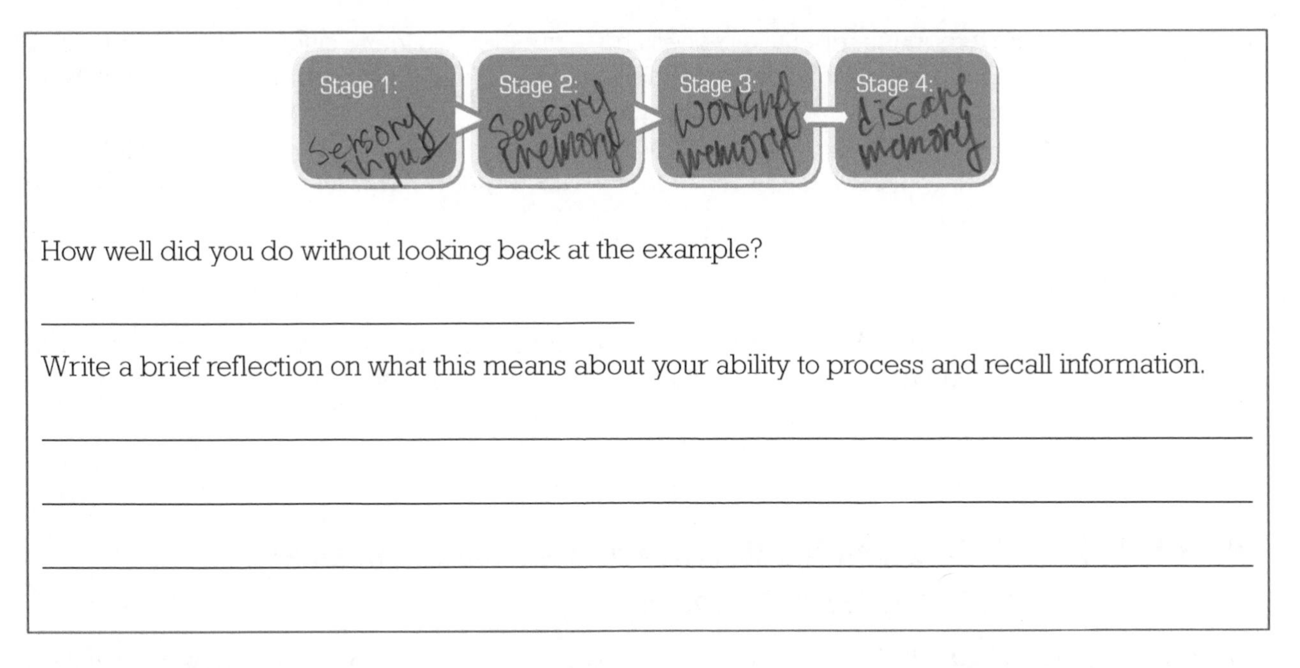

How well did you do without looking back at the example?

____

Write a brief reflection on what this means about your ability to process and recall information.

____

____

____

For the information needed for most college courses, storing information in the long-term memory will not be a quick process. A naturally occurring phenomena that demonstrates this long-term storage formation is the formation of hail as illustrated in Figure 3.2. Hail forms in a storm cloud when raindrops are sucked into a strong updraft moving them to a higher altitude, above a "freeze" line. The air is much colder, the raindrops freeze, and the heavier raindrops fall below the freeze line. Here, they pick up more moisture, only to be caught in the updraft again and tossed back into the colder air where they freeze and become larger. This process is repeated until the weight of the hail becomes heavy enough to break through the force of the updraft and gravity pulls it to the ground. The size of hail depends on the force of the updraft, the height of the storm cloud, and the number of repetitions hail has made before developing large enough to fall to earth. Just as hail is created by the repetition of a cycle, memories are created by the repetition of information moving back and forth between the working memory and long-term memory until it becomes "heavy" enough to stay in your long-term memory.

FIGURE 3.2 Example of Stages 3 and 4

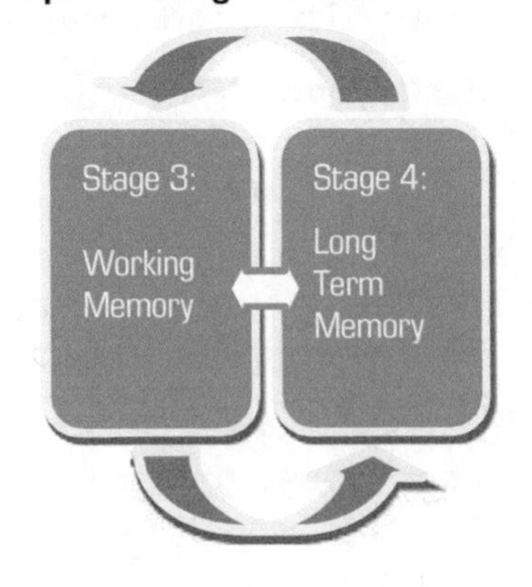

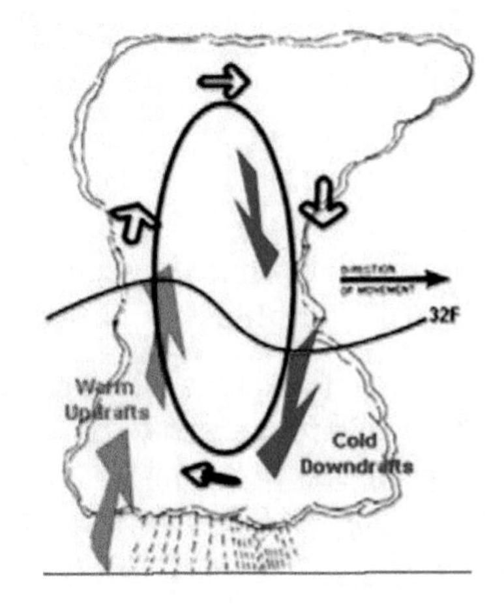

To learn something new requires repetitive processing—whether it is information in statistics or a skill in a sport. You will need to keep bouncing the information back and forth between your long-term memory and your working memory (or practicing the skill over and over) for the information to become so fully engrained in your long-term memory or "muscle memory" for a physical skill) that it can be retrieved at any time. Creating long-term memories requires constant and repeated efforts in the right conditions.

REFLECTION 3.A:

Consider the steps it took you to learn to learn to ride a bicycle. List the steps you went through, from using training wheels to riding alone and identify the memory processes you went through at each stage.

OBJECTIVE 2: Understand the Relationship between Schemata and Long-Term Memory

Schema (schemata, plural) is an organizing method individuals use to process new information based on prior knowledge, experiences, and perceptions. Jean Piaget (1952) called the schema the basic building block of intelligent behavior—a way of organizing knowledge. Indeed, it is useful to think of schemas as "units" of knowledge, each relating to one aspect of the world, including objects, actions and abstract (i.e., theoretical) concepts. People develop this personal schema, it affects how new information, correct and complete, or incorrect and incomplete, is stored in the brain and retrieved. For example, if a student is taking an astronomy course and can already identify a number of constellations in the sky (*prior knowledge*), she can learn to locate new constellations more quickly based on their proximity to the ones she already knows.

Another example, a person might have a schema about buying a meal in a restaurant. The schema is a stored form of the pattern of behavior which includes looking at a menu, ordering food, eating it, and paying the bill. This is an example of a type of schema called a "script." Whenever you are in a restaurant, you retrieve this schema from memory and apply it to the situation.

> ***Mathematics and Schema***
>
> Stored *incomplete* or *incorrect* information can influence your ability to process new information. For example, to add the following two fractions with the same denominator $\frac{5}{9} + \frac{8}{9}$, you write a new fraction with that denominator and add the numerators $\frac{13}{9}$.
>
> If you try to apply this same rule to the addition of two fractions with different denominators, you may miss a large number of exercises because this rule does not hold true for fractions with different denominators. The fractions must be converted to the same denominator to be added.
>
> In order to learn how to add fractions with different denominators, you must first identify what is incomplete or inaccurate in your understanding of adding fractions (when denominators are different, you must first find a common denominator and write each fraction with that denominator before adding and you must "unlearn" your misconception before replacing it with the correct information). Of course, repetition of this information will be critical in storing it accurately into your long-term memory.

The process of learning the information needed for college courses requires a deliberate effort on your part to work through information with the primary focus on the interaction between working-memory and long-term memory. This type of deliberative learning requires you to employ ongoing review, recitation, rehearsal, rereading, rewriting, and recursive thinking. It is said "perfect practice makes permanent," and if you are to have immediate recall of information when you need it, you must take the time necessary to process it deeply.

EXERCISE 3.2: Personal Schema and Memory Process

Describe schema and explain how it enhances the memory process.

it organizes how we think
and put together things like math

REFLECTION 3.B:

Describe an incident in your life for which you used *prior experience* to develop new knowledge.

For example, your friend convinces you to try a habanera pepper with your dinner. Not being aware of the "Scoville Scale" for hotness of peppers (habanera peppers 150,000–300,000 Scoville units), you take a bite and spend the next ten minutes trying to breathe. The following semester in your culinary arts course, you take a test and you are asked to rank the following peppers based on the Scofield Scale: serrano, cayenne, jalapeno, habanera, and bell peppers. Because of your experience with the habanera, you are able to correctly rank the peppers.

Now it is your turn.

?

Describe an incident in your life for which you used prior *perceptions* to develop new (or correct incorrect) knowledge.

For example, you attended a private high school where any type of profanity resulted in some form of punishment. During your political science class, your instructor uses several of these words during a lecture. You are shocked to hear this, but no one else in the class even seems to notice. You discuss this with your roommate and she explained that professors have "academic freedom" to teach their classes in any manner they choose and that in this particular instance, the professor was quoting an opponent's viewpoint.

Now, your turn:

COURSE CONNECTIONS:
Math Myths

There is a math gene.
Men are better at math.
Good math students work problems
quickly and find it easy.

Myth 1: ***There is a math gene.*** This is sometimes referred to as a math "brain," suggesting you need dominance of the left brain to be good at mathematics. This myth continues with the misperception you are either good at it or not. Some go so far as to think mathematics ability is "higher" than other abilities.

Myth 2: ***Men are better at mathematics.*** Research has shown no difference in mathematics ability based on gender. What may partially explain this misperception is the cultural importance of the subject. It is possible some women are simply less interested in mathematics and also are more willing to admit difficulty.

Myth 3: ***Good math students work problems quickly and find it easy.*** Speed does not indicate ability, it usually indicates practice! With experience, the time needed to work a problem is generally reduced.

Learning takes practice . . . and time! In mathematics, do you memorize the processes or do you work to abstractly understand the concepts? Do you simply apply a series of memorized steps or do you try to understand the process behind the steps? When you experience an "Aha" moment in mathematics, it can be rewarding and motivating.

Which, if any, of these "math myths" have you believed in the past?

none

Does it surprise you that they really are not true?

no

OBJECTIVE 3: Understand the Relationship between Selective Attention and Cognitive Processing

A critical component of maximizing your brain's potential to retain information in the long-term memory is ***selective attention***. This level of attention requires intentional focus on the information being learned. Cognitive researchers report setting goals is the best way to achieve selective attention. For example, many students like to study while listening to music. During this time, the focus is on the studying (the selected attention) and the music is merely in the background. However, if a warning sign goes off indicating bad weather, the brain switches its attention to the more important issue. Protecting yourself is a higher priority than studying. When the "all clear" sound is given, your brain will be able to return to studying. When sitting in a psychology class taking notes, do you suddenly sit up straight and become more focused only when the instructor mentions "be sure to write this own because it will be your test?" When you recognize your personal learning motivations, you have surprisingly remarkable recall!

EXERCISE 3.3: Selective Attention

Write your definition of selective attention.

choosing or prioritizing what you should pay attention to

Describe the situation you experience when are you most aware of it in your learning.

Describe how you have successfully focused on your learning in the past.

____

____

Explain why that experience produces effective learning.

____

____

REFLECTION 3.C:

Describe a time in your past learning when your selective attention was so strong on studying that you missed dinner, a favorite TV show, or a phone call. What were you studying and what made the subject so interesting that you could "tune out" everything else around you?

Chunking

Due to the limited capacity of storage for short term memory, which is approximately five to nine bits of information, it is important to learn how to manage information efficiently. George Miller's foundational research coined the term ***Magical Number 7+/- 2*** to suggest information can be "chunked" to maximize working memory. Trying to put more than five to nine items in your short term memory will actually cause your brain to be overloaded and function poorly. Chunking information creates predictable patterns for the brain to temporarily store information for later processing as well as creating the ability for long-term learning to occur. In Miller's research, he asked participants to recall a string of digits, such as seen in this nine-digit number:

6 3 1 9 8 0 2 5 7

The participants were most successful at recalling five to nine digits, but became less accurate with longer numbers. This means the working memory was overworked, so Miller suggested a person can chunk the longer digits to create fewer pieces of information with which to work. Chunking looks like:

6-3-1 9-8-0 2-5-7

When the information is reorganized into three three-digit numbers, the working memory will store them longer so it can be processed for long-term purposes.

Students often think cramming at the last minute or writing an essay the night before it is due is an effective study strategy. Obviously, the brain, if given the opportunity to speak, would whole-heartedly beg for a steady stream of shorter practice periods to learn the information that has been chunked. This stage of memory is only temporary and requires deliberate effort to retain the information initially processed.

When studying, it is important to understand the limitation of working memory (7+/- 2 chunks) as previously stated. In less than one minute short-term memory has to process the stimuli from sensory memory to determine if it is important. This means that, in order for the learning process to occur, you will need to locate similarities or differences in the concepts you are learning and organize the information in five to nine chunks. When information is chunked, you will have greater success in your learning for later recall. You may have done this to memorize a locker combination or a phone number. For example, chunk

- dates in a history class.
- vocabulary words by meaning or similar features.
- foreign language words by categories such as household or occupation.
- fewer words or ideas in which relationships cannot be determined.

EXERCISE 3.4: Chunking Information

Review the information concerning hard and soft sciences in Chapter 2. Then, explain chunking and how you can apply it in the following types of courses.

a) soft science courses ______________________________

____

____

____

b) hard science courses ______________________________

____

____

____

REFLECTION 3.D:

Create a list of ten vocabulary words used in your sociology (or government) course.

List the words and then "chunk" them so their definitions will be easier for *you* to remember. Not everyone will "chunk" in the same way!

Ebbinghaus' Forgetting Curve

A concept serving as another motivational foundation for repetition while learning is the "***forgetting curve***." In 1885, Hermann Ebbinghaus published the results of his research concerning a theory of forgetting (see Figure 3.3) which was entitled *Memory: A Contribution to Experimental Psychology*. Even though his research was published almost 130 years ago, his findings continue to inform students in the twenty-first century how to remember information. Basically, people in Ebbinghaus' test groups were taught information and then asked to recall it, so psychologists could measure their recall abilities. As Figure 3.3 indicates, the best opportunity to recall information is when it is fresh. The following chart includes the information reported by Ebbinghaus' study on the amount of time passed and the ability for the students to remember the information taught.

FIGURE 3.3 The Forgetting Curve

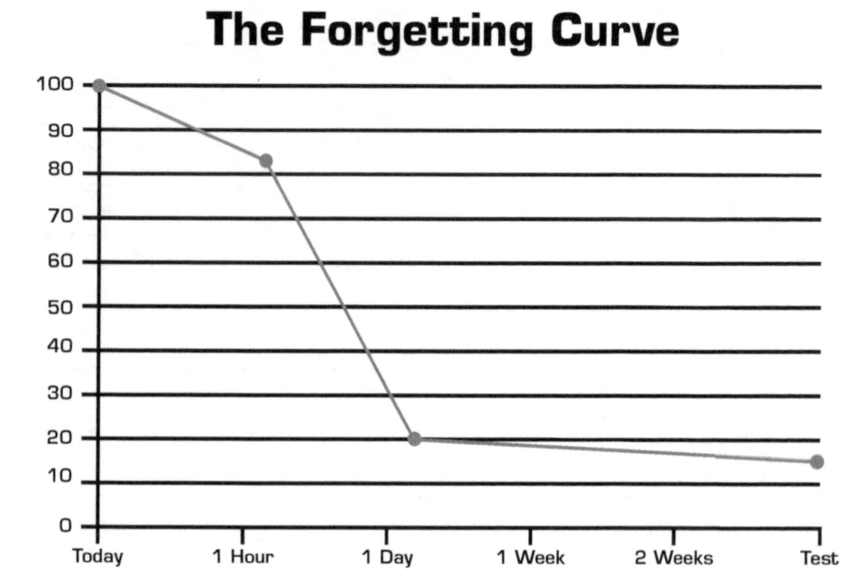

Time Passed Since Learning Occurred	% of Information Forgotten
19 minutes	41.8%
63 minutes	55.8%
8 hours 45 minutes	64.2%
1 day	66.3%
2 days	72.2%
6 days	74.6%
31 days	78.9%

http://mylearningnetwork.com/?tag=memory

The research findings translate into many practical implications for learning new material. First, ongoing review takes time for learning. Most college classes last from 50 minutes to one hour and twenty minutes (longer for laboratory or recitation components). According to the forgetting curve, you will only be able to recall 44.2% of the lecture after a little more than an hour, meaning you have forgotten 55.8% of the information. Often students sit and listen without taking notes while the professor is lecturing, so taking clearly-written notes is crucial.

Depending on the course, you will most likely cover a chapter per week (mathematics and lab science courses may cover less.) If you read the chapter prior to attending class, this will increase your learning recall because you have thought about the material prior to the lecture. Because almost 75% of new learning is lost in six days, you will need to include repeated exposure to the course materials for long-term recall.

Finally, consider the fact that most of your courses will have about four tests per semester, which may or may not include a midterm and final exam. This means you will be tested over three to four chapters or weeks of material per test. If your course includes a cumulative (covering all material to date) midterm, you are now responsible for half of the course material. If you have a cumulative final exam, the full term's material will be covered on a single test! The forgetting curve indicates in 31days only 21.1% of the learned information is readily available for recall if you have done nothing to review during that period. Imagine how much you would not be able to recall two or four months after learning something new without any review. Thus, you will need to review all of the course materials for an extended time period to remember it for your test.

Overcoming the Curve of Forgetting

After reading how much effort is required to remember and learn, you might be thinking, "There goes any social life for this term!" However, learning new material with long-term retention will not take as much time as you may think. Remember the hailstone analogy? As long as the hailstone was being bounced back into the colder atmosphere, it continued to become larger as it picked up more moisture along the way. Learning means you will incorporate periodic reviews of the material, which will take less time than waiting until the night prior to the test!

Look at Figure 3.4. If you review new material right after class (moving the information into long-term memory), rather than retaining 50% of what you learned, you could retain between 75% and 100%. If you review the same material 24 hours later (bring it back into your working memory), you would only need about ten minutes to maintain the same retention (send it back to your long-term memory) rather than just 33% with no review at all. Reviewing the material one week later (bringing it back to your working memory) should only take about five minutes a day and then one month later (or when the test is given) two to four minutes a day. This shows studying just a few minutes a day is far more efficient, and definitely less stressful, than trying to cram the night before a test. Of course, this time will vary depending on the subject area. For example, mathematics tends to build conceptually throughout the academic term and you will use previous concepts to connect new ideas. Thus, mathematics usually requires more daily preparation and less cramming the day prior to the exam.

FIGURE 3.4 Overcoming the Curve

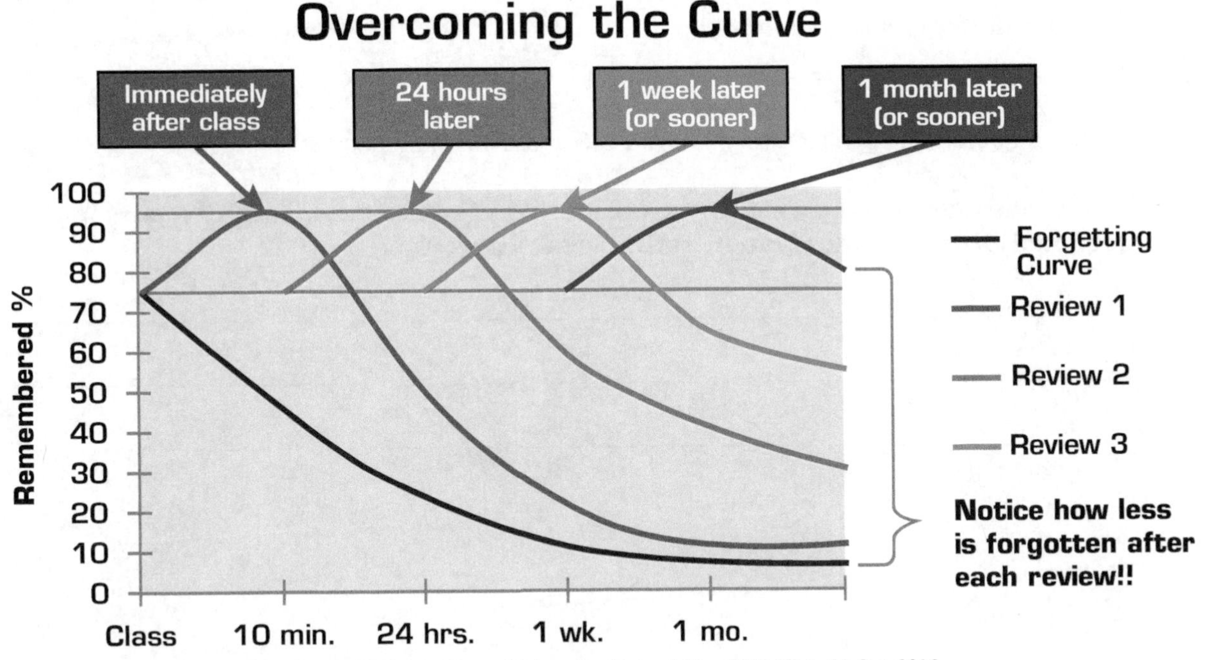

Source: Teichert D.J. "Lest They Forget." Brigham Young University: Idaho. 9 Nov. 2010. Web. 29 Oct. 2013

SOMETHING TO THINK ABOUT:

Take a minute to review picture. Do you think these students look like they are learning?

© Rawpixel.com/Shutterstock.com

1. Write a paragraph, three to five complete sentences, about the photograph as it relates to *memory*, *learning*, and *strengths* and *weaknesses*.

   ____

   ____

   ____

2. Would your discussion be influenced if you knew:
   - The group had just created a humorous mnemonic device to remember pertinent examination facts?
   - The man on the right is the recorder for the brainstorming session?

3. Discuss the photograph again from the perspective of **social responsibility**, **personal responsibility**, **communication skills**, and **teamwork**.

   ____

   ____

   ____

OBJECTIVE 4: Understand the Relationship between *Metacognition* and Learning Strategy

Consider the reality shows *The Voice* or *So You Think You Can Dance*. During the initial screening process, the judges go to various cities and listen or watch numerous people vie for one of the coveted spots and progress to the next level. Generally, the first episode of these shows reveals many people who cannot sing or dance. (Apparently, this is considered entertainment!) Why would these people wait in line for hours just to be cut off when it is obvious they cannot sing or dance well? Perhaps they know they are poor performers, but are seeking their "15 minutes of fame." Maybe believe they are good, perhaps based on the praise of family and friends. This lack of understanding may stem from weak metacognitive thinking—the ability to know what you know. If a person knows they are above average in singing, they have thought about it and can understand the feedback from listeners. In contrast, a person who thinks their talent is above average, but fails to understand the negative feedback they have gotten in previous experiences lacks the ability to candidly judge their singing or dancing.

Metacognition "refers to people's abilities to predict their performance on various tasks (e.g., how well they will be able to remember various stimuli) and to monitor their current levels of mastery and understanding" (*How People Learn*, 12). Study and learning strategies focusing on analyzing how well you performed on a test, understanding how well you remembered the procedure or task, or understanding what areas need improvement, are ways you can apply the concept of metacognition to learning. By including reflective pauses (stopping to review what you just learned) in your learning, you will be able to understand what you know and what needs more attention. In so doing, unlike our contestants described previously, you will be able to take the necessary measures to learn material and know what you know. You will use metacognition to determine which strategy is the most effective for learning.

In order to apply metacognitive strategies you will need to employ ***recursive*** learning strategies. Experiencing, reflecting, thinking, and acting are ways in which recursive learning occurs. In other words, learning is not a linear process but one requiring you to go back and forth to make sure you understand what you are learning. Some professors and subjects (mathematics) tend to incorporate this type of learning naturally, but many do not. For this reason, you will need to become familiar with ways to manipulate information in a variety of ways to better guarantee it is stored adequately in your long-term memory and it can easily be retrieved.

Some strategies encourage and support metacognition and recursive thinking and include:

- Recognizing the importance of your *internal dialogue* where you ask questions such as:
  - "So what does this have to do with the topic?"
  - "What do I already know about this topic?"
  - "What questions do I still have concerning this topic?"
  - "What can I do to learn more about the topic?"
  - "Is there a person or support system available to help me learn more?"
- Monitoring your inquiry processes through written reflections and summaries.
- Solving problems with a team to enhance problem solving solutions.
- Asking what learning strategy is best for the type of material covered in your course.
- Different strategies will be discussed in Chapter 7.

Two easy ways to incorporate metacognition and recursive practices in your study time are:

KWWL: Asking questions to determine prior knowledge, lingering questions, where or what resources are available to locate answers to lingering questions, and recording what you have learned.

What do I Know?	What do I Wonder about?	Where can I find the answer to my lingering questions?	What did I Learn?

SQ4R: Reading strategy activating prior knowledge through **Survey**, requires you to write **Questions** and **Read** for answers, **Record** your answers, **Recite** the information (aloud), and **Review** the material read. See Chapter 7 for more information on this strategy.

EXERCISE 3.5: Exit Slip for Today

Exit Slip: At the end of class, write (3) three things you learned in class, (2) two ideas you found surprising, disagreeable, or you agree with, and (1) one question you have about the content that day.

For today's class session, identify:

Things I've learned today:

1. ______________________________
2. ______________________________
3. ______________________________

Things I found surprising, disagreeable, or very much agree with.

1. ______________________________
2. ______________________________

One question I still have about the materials covered in class today.

1. ______________________________

EXERCISE 3.6: Case Study Yolanda

© bikeriderlondon/Shutterstock.com

At the age of 30, Yolanda reentered a formal college mathematics class. She was nervous because she had not taken a test or seriously thought about mathematics for so long. Yolanda is a seamstress for the local dry cleaner and enjoys creating quilts for her family. Both activities require her to determine order, patterns, relationships, and the various parts to construct something new. Mistakes in her seamstress job result in ill-fitting clothing and unhappy customers, unlike many of the mathematics exercises with less practical consequences.

Hopefully, Yolanda realizes her prior knowledge and experiences lend support in her new learning environment. Additionally, Yolanda could realize she is able to employ metacognition as well as recursive learning to expand her mathematics skills. She could develop the ability to visualize a new learning identity. In the end, Yolanda's learning identity will be altered as the result of her new social surroundings in a college classroom and the mathematics curriculum she learned.

A *learning identity* is the development of a new personal identity shaped by the social and educational setting a person is in. The environment of a college classroom and the learning in which you are participating will shape your learning identity. The correlation between your social identity and academic learning compose a "learning identity" affected by your successes and challenges within the college environment. The primary benefit of developing an awareness of your learning identity is the sense of belonging and contributing to the learning environment. Additionally, those with a better understanding of their learning identity are more willing to learn through new or different ways. The bottom line is students with a strong comprehension of their learning identity are "more successful in school" (Kolb and Kolb).

In 2007, G.K. Hutt reported in his study how students in a college mathematics class who focused on building a stronger self-awareness of their learning identity overcame their math anxiety. Basically, the instructors of the lower level mathematics class improving the learning identities of the students emphasized the building-up of confidence. This was completed through metacognitive reflections, positive self-talk, and supportive learning environments.

According to research, changing your learning identity will take time and deliberate efforts. First, position your experiences in learning at the center of your learning identity because you can control your choices. By doing this, you are taking control over your ability to learn. Secondly, value how learning is a process and allow yourself sufficient time to learn. Typically, no one single test or grade will demonstrate your learning of a subject. For this reason, you will want to chart your successes as you achieve them. Remember, failure is a good teacher! As Edison said, "Each time I fail, I am one step closer to the solution." Learning to control your emotional reactions to failure is another vital step in creating your learning identity. Learning to lose or fail is learning to win and succeed. Think about what you do well in a learning environment for a moment. Do you speak about this in the same way as you do something you have experienced failure in? Try to employ positive self-talk to improve your weaknesses. For example, rather than saying "I am not good at math," say "I am not good at math, YET!" Just this one word changes the message sent to your brain from a negative to a positive one. Finally, keep an account of your success and failures over time and see how success breeds success.

Another practical way you can begin to improve your learning identity is by taking time to visualize or "see" yourself succeed in the social and academic settings reinforcing the likelihood of your success. To do this, close your eyes and picture yourself successfully using knowledge and experiences in your most challenging classes. Then, visualize taking a test and earning an "A." Continue to do this; over time, you will realize your new learning identity.

In the classic movie *"The Music Man,"* (2003 TV version) a con man sells instruments and uniforms to the parents of children in a small turn-of-the-twentieth century town and tells the children to "not worry about the notes—just use the 'think system.'" Of course, when it comes time to actually play the instruments, the children could not. Just visualizing your learning identity is not going to be sufficient if this is all you do.

The ability to visualize yourself succeeding in college is similar to a literary technique originated by Samuel Taylor Coleridge which is termed "willing suspension of disbelief." Simply stated, "willing suspension of disbelief" is the mind's ability to visualize or fill in the blanks when you read or see a movie that seems unbelievable as actually real or believable. When a magician saws a person in a box in half, we know the events are not occurring as they appear. This is the mind's ability to fill in the missing information through visualization. You may have experienced this while playing video games such as *Grand Theft Auto®*, *Spiderman®*, or *Metal Gear Solid 2®*. These require your mind to fill in the missing details yet still see the events as "real."

Applying "willing suspension of disbelief" to visualizing yourself as a student who will graduate with a 4.0 GPA is similar. Your mind will need to fill in the missing information as you visualize yourself walking across the stage upon college graduation while showing off your many honor ropes and awards. This concept, when applied in your daily learning routine, allows you to visualize yourself studying diligently and productively. Of course, this can only become a reality IF and WHEN visualization is personalized. Learning takes time, effort, and thinking. Visualizing your new self in addition to good study habits will allow you to become a successful student.

REFLECTION 3.E:

Describe an academic goal you are working to achieve this semester.

A's on everything

Close your eyes and visualize what the sensory details will be like when you achieve this goal. Write the additional details you see while visualizing the completion of the goal.

Predict what will happen if you take time to visualize this goal every day for the next month.

OBJECTIVE 5: Recognize Strategies for Developing Long-Term Memory

The desire of many students is to be able to perform well on course assignments and earn an "A" in each class. Few students realize the effort necessary for learning and achieving high grades or even how life-long learning is necessary for most careers. Knowing the best way to process information for long-term storage is of tremendous value in achieving academic goals.

To effectively conduct all the stages in memory processing in a timely manner, prior knowledge is retrieved to determine your current level of understanding in your long-term memory. This requires the brain to think of a set of behaviors that have worked in the past to determine their use in this specific situation. For example, you may read about the hydrological cycle in a textbook with the visual aid in Figure 3.5.

FIGURE 3.5 Dynamic Interaction among Humans, Agriculture, and the Environment

Photo: Engle, Stephanie. "FEW Diagram 1." USDA Food and Agriculture

Per USDA/NIFA: The Food-Energy-Water system is the combined complexity of food production, energy requirements, and water availability. The system integrates physical (such as built infrastructure and new technologies), natural (such as biogeochemical and hydrological cycles), biological (such as agroecosystem structure and productivity), and social and behavioral entities (such as decision making and governance). Innovative approaches that study the intersection of these components will promote sustainability within the food–energy–water system.

This may be a topic you have very little prior knowledge about, but take a minute to see what you know. When you look at the visual aid from above you may review the words written on the picture, as well as the caption. If you lack the vocabulary to understand it, you will study the pictures to make more meaning. You may recognize the clouds in the symbols provided for water, electricity, and food and fiber. After reading the text more closely in the image, more information will be revealed. Probably, the information included your prior knowledge makes the most sense. Now, you can review the arrows and text to understand the connections between them and any prior knowledge currently stored in your long-term memory. Eventually, you will use the picture, caption, and your prior knowledge to understand the connections between sustainability and human consumption. By reviewing the new information and vocabulary and comparing it to previously learned materials stored in your long-term memory, you realize learning more about the study of sustainability and human consumption can be added to your memory. Of course, you may have learned that more background information is going to be needed before you can grasp this concept completely. (For more on this topic, complete a Google search using the key phrase, "NIFA Research Addresses the Food–Energy–Water System."

This type of learning allows for the discovery of how concepts connect to one another, and this requires us to think on the deeper level in an ongoing way suggested by Dr. Stephen Chew. For additional information on ***Deep Processing***, see Chapter 1.

FIGURE 3.6 Dr. Chew's Method

Deep Processing **Level**	**Point of Inquiry**
Elaboration	How does this concept relate to other concepts?
Distinction	How does this concept differ from other concepts?
Personal	How can I relate this information to my personal experience?
Appropriate ***retrieval*** and application	How am I expected to use or apply this concept?
Result	
Automaticity	Practiced to the point knowledge recall is not a conscious effort.
Overlearning	Extending learning to the point where the information is recalled quickly and easily.

EXERCISE 3.7: Applying Deep Processing Learning

© amid999/Shutterstock.com

Take a minute to visit Encyclopedia Britannica (http://www.britannica.com/science/human-skeletal-system) and learn the four major bones in the leg (femur, fibula, patella, and tibia).

For the topic "Identify the four major bones in the leg of a human," answer the questions for each phase of the learning process.

Deep Processing Level	**Question**	**Response**
Elaboration	How does this concept relate to other concepts?	
Distinction	How does this concept differ from other concepts?	
Personal	How can I relate this information to my personal experience?	
Appropriate retrieval and application	How will my professor want me to apply and retrieve this information? Objective tests? Essay or application questions?	

By applying Dr. Chew's practical suggestions for learning on a deeper level, you are actually using the Constructivist Theory to learn.

Constructivism

One of the best ways to learn is through ***constructivism*** (a.k.a. Constructivist Theory) in which "learning is an active process where learners construct new ideas or concepts based upon their current past knowledge." Jerome Brunner developed this theory in 1966 in response to the cognitive research on how the brain processes information for long-term storage and retrieval. He suggests we need to build knowledge and skills. His theories were generated from research on how students learned mathematics and science. Brunner's theory of learning suggests you need to pull forward prior knowledge when learning new information. Then, you can build the newly learned information into new constructs. By actively seeking ways to attach new information to prior knowledge, long-term memory is enhanced.

Constructivism is a learning theory suggesting experiences shape and create knowledge for humans. Problem solving and experiments are the foundation of this theory, so learning is constructed through these two processes. For example, if you were enrolled in a business communications class the professor might give you a company case study in which you would review the company records. Then, you would be asked to determine the problem and recommend a solution. The solutions would include inquiry and the application of your course materials. Constructing new knowledge is the ultimate result of applying this learning theory. Ways in which students can apply constructivism are:

- Arguing for or against a point or position
- Inquiring about information while studying or in class
- Building on prior knowledge of a subject
- Discussing during class or in a study group
- Understanding the process of knowledge in subjects such as mathematics, science, or computer programming

EXERCISE 3.8: Applying Constructivism

Apply the principles of constructivism to "addition of two fractions with different denominators" by answering the following questions.

Questions	Answers
What do I already know?	For example, you might say "I know how to add two fractions with the same denominator."
What do I need to know?	For example, you might say "I need to know how to convert a fraction to a new fraction with a different denominator."
How will I use this new information?	
How will this help with the problem?	
How will knowing how to work this help me with future problems?	

Learning with these strategies takes time and encourages connections in the way Dr. Chew suggested with the use of elaboration, distinction, personal application, and retrieval cues matching the type of knowledge you will be asked to use for assessment. All in all, this encourages automaticity and over learning, practiced to the point that knowledge recall is not a conscious effort creating long-term memories. Driving is a good example of automaticity and overlearning because most people have been driving for a significant amount of time and limited energy is expended on this task.

By applying constructivism to your classes you will begin to learn through inquiry as well as with deeper processing. Both of these enhance your long-term memory. The results should be better grades in your courses!

EXERCISE 3.9: Deep Processing and Constructivism in a College Course

Complete the information in the chart for one of your other courses. The first row has been completed to serve as an example for you.

Course	Topic	Deep Processing	Constructivism
English	Problem-Solution essay	**Elaboration:** describe the problem and other's solutions. **Distinctions:** Explain how this situation is different from the group's overall purpose. **Personalization:** How has this problem affected me? **Retrieval:** What are the parameters of the assignment and how can I apply my ideas to the professor's expectations?	In what organization am I a member that I see a problem? How would I describe the problem? What would others say about this problem? How have other groups attempted to solve a similar problem? How can I create a solution to this problem?
		Elaboration: **Distinctions:** **Personalization:** **Retrieval:**	

Now you understand how to apply constructivism and deep processing to your courses, take time to apply them to some of the skills we learned in the previous chapter.

EXERCISE 3.10: Combining Skills

Study Skill	Deep Processing	Constructivism
SMARTER Goal Setting	**Elaboration:** **Distinctions:** **Personalization:** **Retrieval:**	

Study Skill	Deep Processing	Constructivism
Learning Environment	**Elaboration:** **Distinctions:** **Personalization:** **Retrieval:**	

By learning to apply the theories of constructivism and deep processing to your life, you will become a life-long learner, seeking to learn in most situations and at every stage of life. Sometimes learning will occur as the result of a job or different career track (promotion to manager), new technologies requiring learning for efficient use (wireless home DVR systems), or the desire to know more about a topic of interest (classic cars) or need (how to fix a broken water pipe). The capacity for storage in the long-term memory is endless. Curious people look for new things to learn, so learning to learn in college is actually the beginning of actualizing your life-long learning skills.

COURSE CONNECTIONS:

Left Brain and Right Brain

What do Sean Combs, A.K.A. Puff Daddy or P. Diddy (rapper), members of Coldplay (musical group), John Urschel (NFL athlete), Teri Hatcher (actress), Bram Stoker (author), and J. P. Morgan (financier and banker) have in common?

They all studied mathematics in college.

Left Brain

analytical
logical
quantitative

What do Oprah Winfrey (media mogul), John Audubon (artist), Desmond Tutu (South African theologian and leader of apartheid movement), Natalie Portman (actress), and Leonardo da Vinci (artist) have in common?

They all began careers in "right brain" areas.

Right Brain

artistic
creative
imaginative

Do you consider yourself a "left-brain" or "right-brain" person?

What in your past has led you to believe you are one or the other?

Are there situations or activities in your life that would qualify as the "opposite" of what you believe your brain dominance is?

How will this information on "brain dominance" influence your choice of major or career path?

OBJECTIVE 6: Recognize the Importance of *Whole-Brain Learning*

Pop culture and the media have generated some myths concerning learning and the brain. One of these myths is people with left hemisphere dominance and right hemisphere dominance should be taught differently. Current research, which incorporates current technologies from neuroscience, cognitive psychology, and educational psychology does not support this notion of brain learning. What research does suggest about the brain and learning is everyone has to "fire and wire" to learn.

Some basic information on how the brain works is essential for understanding how you fire and wire it. Very simply stated, firing occurs when a neuron, or nerve cell, receives information from other sensory organs and communicates with your body (e.g., muscles) that interacts with your surroundings. See Figure 3.7. Dendrites, the tree- like structures, receive the electrical charge and send the incoming information to the axon. Typically, numerous neurons are fired simultaneously which "integrates the information it received from the synapses and determines its output" (*How People Learn,* 85). The latter constitutes the wiring of your brain. The challenge is that there is actually a small gap between your neurons and the synapses, so repeated firing is necessary to build the connection to form a memory.

FIGURE 3.7 Brain cell

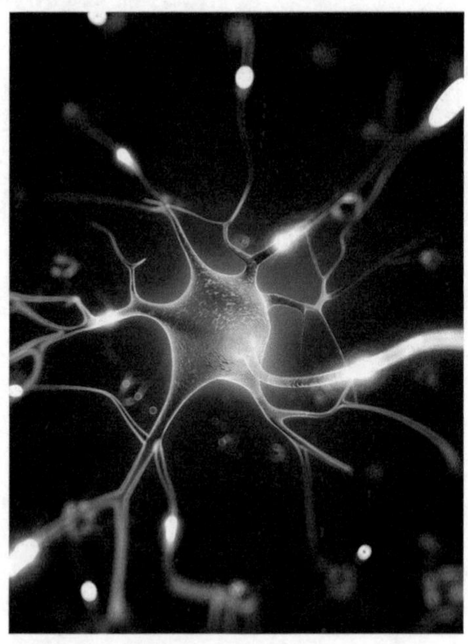

To make this more understandable, relate the wiring of your synapses to climbing a mountain. The first time you climb the mountain is always the hardest, but the more you climb the same path, typically the easier it becomes. Very rarely do mountain climbers take the most direct route to the precipice of the mountain. Instead, they traverse left and right and up and down until they safely arrive at their desired destination. Wiring your brain with a concept the first time is the most challenging, but it becomes easier the more frequently you traverse the same path.

Another important point concerning the brain and learning is there are two types of memory processes, **declarative** and **procedural**. Declarative knowledge is information based on facts or events. An example of declarative knowledge is identifying all the parts of the brain for an anatomy and physiology course or listing and describing the three branches of government. Procedural knowledge consists of multiple pieces of information that must be used collectively. An example of procedural knowledge is performing an experiment in a chemistry lab. There is the specific knowledge needed for the experiment, but also the handling of equipment and the safety procedures to be followed. Another example is solving a quadratic equation in an algebra course; there are several methods for accomplishing this, each with their own set of steps to follow.

The brain is a remarkable organ requiring the "firing and wiring" of synapses for learning to occur. Becoming actively engaged in learning, through experiences heightening your senses, will increase your opportunity for "firing and wiring" to occur. This means you need to seek ways of learning that engage both processes of firing and wiring. Often students think reading a chapter or sitting through a lecture is sufficient for learning, but our brain is not created to remember passively. Active learning means you engage the nervous system in learning through physical activity, listening, speaking, or any number of ways that the senses are activated. You may recall the memory model presented at the beginning of this chapter reinforces the need for your senses to be activated because this is the beginning point for information to be put into the brain. In order to "fire and wire" your brain, you will need to use your senses and make connections.

REFLECTION 3.F:

Create an analogy by completing this sentence, "Learning with firing and wiring my brain is like . . . "

____

____

Explain what is being compared to "firing and wiring."

____

____

Howard Gardner's Multiple Intelligence

Many educators have had the experience of not being able to reach some students until presenting the information in a completely different way or providing new options for student expression. Perhaps it was a student who struggled with writing until the teacher provided the option to create a graphic story, which blossomed into a beautiful and complex narrative. Or maybe it was a student who just couldn't seem to grasp fractions until he created them by separating oranges into slices.

Because of these kinds of experiences, the theory of multiple intelligences resonates with many educators. It supports what we all know to be true: a one-size-fits-all approach to education will invariably leave some students behind. The theory of multiple intelligences challenges the idea of a single IQ, where human beings have one central "computer" where intelligence is housed. Howard Gardner, the Harvard professor who originally proposed the theory, says that there are multiple types of human intelligence, each representing different ways of processing information:

Verbal-linguistic intelligence refers to an individual's ability to analyze information and produce work that involves oral and written language, such as speeches, books, and emails.

Logical-mathematical intelligence describes the ability to develop equations and proofs, make calculations, and solve abstract problems.

Visual-spatial intelligence allows people to comprehend maps and other types of graphical information.

Musical intelligence enables individuals to produce and make meaning of different types of sound.

Naturalistic intelligence refers to the ability to identify and distinguish among different types of plants, animals, and weather formations found in the natural world.

Bodily-kinesthetic intelligence entails using one's own body to create products or solve problems.

Interpersonal intelligence reflects an ability to recognize and understand other people's moods, desires, motivations, and intentions.

Intrapersonal intelligence refers to people's ability to recognize and assess those same characteristics within themselves.

However, the theory is also often misunderstood, which can lead to it being used interchangeably with learning styles or applying it in ways that can limit student potential. While the theory of multiple intelligences is a powerful way to think about learning, it's also important to understand the research that supports it.

3.2 DETERMINING LEARNING-STYLE PREFERENCES AND ADJUSTING TO MULTIPLE TEACHING STYLES

Now that you understand that learning is the result of firing and wiring your brain, take a moment to determine through which of the senses you prefer to learn. Since firing the brain is the result of sensory input, there are three primary means of processing information: visual, auditory, and tactile (touch) or kinesthetic (movement) pathways. If you are a culinary arts student, you will probably need the olfactory (sense of smell) and gustatory (sense of taste) pathways to learn, as well.

OBJECTIVE 7: Apply Strategies to Strengthen Learning Modalities

Take a minute to review the characteristics of the three most recognized learning preferences in the chart below.

Learning Preferences	Characteristics of learning preference
Visual	Prefer written information, pictures, charts, diagrams, videos, flow charts, and time lines. Can easily organize information into categories.
Auditory	Prefer listening to a lecture, talking to peers, and learning in study groups. This may include eloquent speakers who tend to enter professions requiring strong verbal skills.
Kinesthetic	Prefer learning through touch, movement, and space. Learn best when someone demonstrates or shows them how to do something. Often times, people who are kinesthetic learners are athletes, dancers, engineers, or other professions requiring more movement.

Based on the brief overview, which one do you guess is your learning preference?

all of them
___

Now, take a few minutes to complete a self-assessment on your learning preferences.
http://vark-learn.com/the-vark-questionnaire/

Did you guess accurately? ___

EXERCISE 3.11: Learning-style Preference.

Summarize your findings with the Learning Preference Assessment:

Learning-style preferences

Visual learners are most comfortable with learning environments including written information, pictures, charts, diagrams, videos, flow charts, and time lines. In most college classes, there are limited opportunities to learn with visuals. Of course, some disciplines are more conducive to visual learning than others. For example, mathematics and science classes will have more visual learning than an English course. Even if you are a visual learner, you will want to learn how to turn the less visual courses into visual learning and study tools. First, take notes during the lecture. This will allow you to convert the auditory information into a visual form. Next, convert your traditional linear notes into visual note-taking such as mapping (See Chapter 7). Finally, be aware you may prefer to read and write rather than meet and talk with your peers.

Auditory learners are students who listen and talk to learn. If you are an auditory learner, you may prefer to sit in a lecture-based class, tell people about the concepts you are learning, and join study groups to verbally exchange information. This is the format of most college classes, so you may find college learning is "easier" than other learning environments you have experienced previously. As an auditory learner you will want to make sure you are seated in the classroom so you can hear the professor. When reading your books, notes or mathematical procedures, read aloud to yourself to gain the richest learning opportunity. If you do join a study group, be sure everyone comes prepared to talk about the course materials.

Tactile or ***Kinesthetic*** learning is completed through bodily movements. Typically this is completed through deliberate movement of your body in activities such as walking, running, pacing, bouncing a ball, or even writing on a large white board or on the side walk with chalk. Obviously, most traditional college classrooms are not going to have as much kinesthetic learning as you will need. This means you will need to seek deliberate opportunities to review your course materials in ways encouraging bodily movement.

Figure 3.8 provides an overview of learning style preferences with practical study tips for each style.

FIGURE 3.8 Learning Preferences and Practical Study Tools

Learning Preference	Note-taking/Reading	Lecture	Studying
Visual	Mapping, highlighting, annotation.	Write notes while watching for visual cues on the most important information to include.	Map the chapter and your notes. Draw pictures as often as possible.
Auditory	Outline, mapping, Read concepts aloud and listen to audio books as needed.	Listen and take clear notes that will act as a prompt for your recall later.	Group study sessions; explain or describe what you are learning to someone else. Read your notes aloud.
Tactile (or kinesthetic)	Mapping, note cards, computer. Read with a pen or pencil in your hand ALWAYS! Annotate your textbook.	Take notes that will allow you to focus on the information being presented.	Read or repeat your learning while engaging your large motor muscles (arms, legs, big movement muscles) in ways such as: walking, pacing, writing on a large dry erase board, or use sidewalk chalk.

EXERCISE 3.12: Effective Learning Strategies

Identify three learning strategies in this chapter you think will be most effective for your learning.

1. ______________________________

2. ______________________________

3. ______________________________

Decide which of the three you chose will be the first one you use and describe how you are going to apply it.

____

____

EXERCISE 3.13: Using Learning Preferences for Lectures, Reading, and Studying

Explain how you use your learning preference when studying in the following activities:

Classroom lecture:

____

____

____

____

Reading:

____

____

____

____

Studying:

____

____

____

____

Understand your dominant learning preference and how to use it for learning can help you earn "A's" in all of your classes. Additionally, understanding in how to strengthen all of the learning modalities boosts your whole brain learning opportunities. This means you can have triple and quadruple strength learning. Imagine you have to tow a car by tying a rope around the rear and front bumpers of two cars. You need to make sure they are firmly connected, but then you realize your rope is too flimsy and weak to use. After a few minutes of thinking you realize if you double the rope it may work better, but if you triple the strength by using three strands of rope, you will have an even stronger rope. The triple-strand rope is strong enough to tow the car to the repair shop. Notice how increasing the number of ropes in the following scenario creates a more successful opportunity to tow a car. The car is representative of a new concept and the towing is similar to learning new information.

The single strand of rope too flimsy and weak to do the job of towing is comparable to only using one learning preference to learn. For example, the auditory learner who only uses his or her listening skills to learn may realize it is inadequate. If the auditory learner adds both the visual and kinesthetic modalities, learning may be easier. Simply understanding which one of the learning preferences is your best learning modality is actually the beginning point of applying learning styles for maximizing your learning retention and recall.

Finally, because of the challenge to fire and wire your brain, it is logical to try and use as many of your senses to learn new material. It is through the senses the "firing" of the brain is initiated. "Wiring," on the other hand, requires repeated energy. Rather than trying to tow the information from your chemistry textbook with one flimsy strand as a single learning pathway, try employing triple strength learning with all three learning modes. Learning by seeing, listening, speaking, body movement, as well as reading and writing may help you earn an "A" in the class. Of course, the real benefit is you will store the information in your long-term memory for retrieval throughout your life.

REFLECTION 3.G:

What is your primary learning preference? ______________________________

Which learning style have you NEVER used? ______________________________

Evaluate how you can add this modality to your learning style. ______________________________

OBJECTIVE 8: Understand How to Adjust Personal Learning Preferences to Different Teaching Styles

You have probably already figured out that not all of your instructors teach in the same style you learn.

EXERCISE 3.14: Identifying Instructor Teaching Styles

Describe the teaching/learning style preference of your professors.

Course	Observed Teaching Style	Characteristics

Did you notice any similarities differences in teaching styles for instructors of "hard science" and "soft science" courses? ______

Write your observations here:

____

____

You are not going to be able to change your instructors' teaching styles. Therefore, you will need to adjust how you take notes in class for those courses whose instructors do not teach in your preferred learning style. Most instructors use auditory and visual methods to teach their classes. They lecture, lead discussions, use PowerPoint presentations, bring in guest lecturers, write on the board and ask questions in class.

If you are a visual learner, it may be hard for you to take notes if your instructor is lecturing. Still take notes, but as soon as you leave class, transfer those notes into lists, mappings, figures, and any other means necessary to translate them into a form you can study effectively. You might ask your instructor if you could record the class sessions. This will allow you to focus on the writing portion and fill in the auditory later.

If you are an auditory learner, it may be hard for you to take notes if your instructor is also writing on the board or going through a written presentation. Your brain will be trying to catch all the words your instructor is saying which will conflict with your trying to write down the notes on the board. You might ask your instructor if there are handouts of the material presented in written form which would allow you to focus on what he/she is saying in class. Many instructors have notes available online. In many classes, there are videos explaining many of the concepts. These incorporate visual and auditory components.

If you are a tactile/kinesthetic learner, you may have a more difficult time because not many instructors teach in this manner. Those instructors who employ a lot of group work will appeal to you because you will be able to move around during the class. Physical education courses and the lab portion of science classes will be well-suited for you. In the lab classes, you will be using your hands and possibly walking around the room to gather materials or to confer with other groups. Some mathematics professors ask their students to volunteer to work problems on the board. However, in the classroom, you will still need to learn to take notes. When you leave class, transfer those notes via computer, large white board, or any other means in which you can use your hands and/or body for movement.

REFLECTION 3.H:

Which of your instructors (the course, NOT his/her name) teaches the least like you prefer to learn?

____

What is his/her predominant teaching style? ________________________________

What is your predominant learning style? ________________________________

Students very often do not recognize ALL the different types of teaching styles that instructors use. For the next three class sessions, try to pay attention to everything your instructor does during his/her teaching.

What types of teaching styles did your instructor use? ___

Were any of them YOUR style, even if for a short period of time?

If not, create a list of three things YOU can do to adjust your learning style *slightly* (we are not asking you to completely change how you learn) to help yourself succeed in this course.

1. ___
2. ___
3. ___

Try this for 3 weeks and then come back to this question and report on how your choices worked.

Write the date you will report back here: ___

How did your adjustments help? ___

During this time, did you consider any other changes you might consider to help yourself succeed?

___

OBJECTIVE 9: Learn Methods for Studying Independently

Once you try to use all of the modes to learn, you will be a more independent learner. Learning independently is going to empower you in college and in your career. Most employers of any profession seeking to hire college graduates will expect you to be able to learn independently. They will want you to take tests, just as you did in your college classroom, for a variety of reasons. Typically, you will be given a test to measure your knowledge of the information or skills necessary to perform your job well. Occasionally, you will be required to take a certification exam prior to your employment. The tests you take for your career have a higher stake than those you take in college because passing the career tests will make the difference between getting, keeping, or advancing in, a job. If you fail one of these tests, you may be looking for another place to work, which could be circumvented if you are an independent learner.

There are numerous men and women in history who have demonstrated independent learning, but Malcolm X (1925-1965), a militant black activist, is probably one of the most remarkable examples. He had been a good student in junior high school and was, at one time, encouraged to become a lawyer, but he felt there was no hope for a black man in America to become a lawyer. This realization discouraged him to the point of dropping out of school after the eighth grade. When he was twenty-one years old, he was incarcerated for armed robbery and served six years in the Charleston, MA state prison. While he was there, Malcolm X was motivated to read for personal improvement. He began by writing the numerous unfamiliar vocabulary words from the dictionary in a notebook and repeatedly reading them out loud to learn them. Eventually, he was able to read everything he could get his hands on for the duration of his imprisonment. As he states in his autobiography, *Literacy Behind*

Bars, "reading had forever changed the course of my life." His self-motivation to learn independently did alter the course of his life as well as the lives of many African Americans.

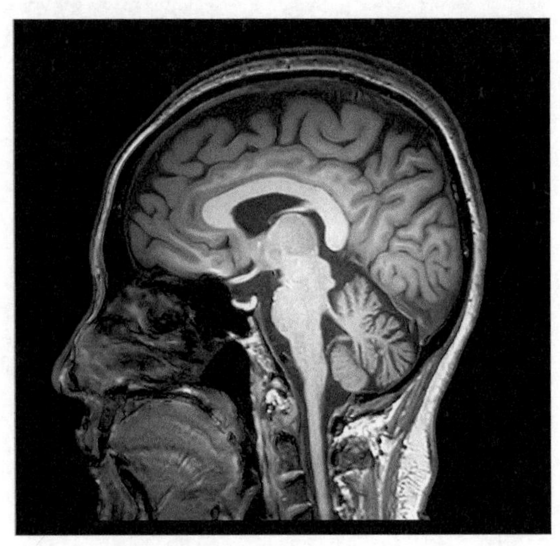
© AkeSak/Shutterstock.com

Becoming an independent learner means there are many factors influencing your desire to learn. Your inquisitiveness or curiosity to learn can create the motivation to seek out more information on a topic. Additionally, you will ask questions that can act as a catalyst for acquiring more information on a specific topic. Motivation to learn is the foundation of independent learning. When you are motivated to learn more than the minimum, you will seek out ways to increase your knowledge. Of course, metacognition plays a critical role in independent learning. Thinking about what you know, or do not know, will aid in your learning. Critical thinking, thinking of ways to analyze, synthesize, or evaluate material, is a powerful tool for learning independently. If you can do this without a professor or boss telling you what to do next, you are going to learn faster and more comprehensively. Finally, an independent learner exhibits persistence, tenacity, and grit. When learning becomes challenging, the students who can learn independently will continue trying, hang on tightly to their goal, and recover more rapidly from setbacks.

EXERCISE 3.15: Whole Brain and Independent Learning

Complete the chart below by describing learning strategies promoting whole brain learning with independent learning strategies.

Independent Learning Factor	Learning Strategy
Inquisitiveness	
Self-motivation	
Metacognition	
Critical Thinking	
Persistence	
Tenacity	
Grit	

Return to the self-assessment of your strengths and weaknesses in Chapter 2. Describe how you would employ independent learning strategies to develop your learning weaknesses.

____

____

____

PERSON to PERSON

In this exercise, you will be introduced to a classroom environment with unique interactions. Let's meet the individuals!

© Shutterstock.com

Elena is taking a philosophy class as an elective. She checked an online website to see if anyone made comments regarding the various instructors of that course. Although most of the comments were negative for the instructor of the section she wanted, she decided to enroll in the section anyway. She reasoned because she is a hard worker, making A's and B's in all of her classes for two years, she would be fine. After two weeks, Elena grew increasingly anxious. During class, she felt little instruction occurred. The classroom was chaotic as students chatted in groups, texted, and generally disregarded the instructor's PowerPoint™ presentations.

Based on this description, rank the individuals as to whom you believe is most responsible for learning.

Elena ____ Instructor ____ Classmates ____ Dean ____ Online rating site ____

Here is some additional information.

- The instructor is not a native speaker of English.
- The division dean has received multiple complaints against the instructor each semester for three years regarding classroom discipline.
- The instructor said the students showed little interest in the subject or respect for the learning process.

Based on all the information you now know, rank them again as to who you believe is most responsible for learning. Has your ranking changed?

Elena ____ Instructor ____ Classmates ____ Dean ____ Online rating site ____

1. What pieces of new information do you consider to be a positive influence on learning?

____

____

2. What pieces of new information do you consider to be a negative influence on learning?

____

____

Here are your last pieces of information.

- After investigation, the division dean finds the complaints were based more on high academic standards and rigorous tests rather than ineffective instruction or lack of classroom management.
- Elena wanted to meet with her instructor to express her concerns but the instructor's office hours conflicted with Elena's availability.

Based on all the information you have about this situation, rank them one last time as to who you believe was most responsible for learning the class material.

Elena ____ Instructor ____ Classmates ____ Dean ____ Online rating site ____

1. What pieces of new information would you still like to know about the classroom?

____

____

2. Are there any pieces of information which could be seen as both positive and negative influences on learning?

____

____

Career Connection:

© kryzhov/Shutterstock.com

In college, you will process, retrieve, and learn a great deal of seemingly unrelated information. What you learn in history will most likely have little to do with what you learn in chemistry. However, when you have selected a major (an area of study), you will find what you learn in your first courses in that area is necessary to succeed in the future ones. It is critical you be able to retrieve critical information without thinking about it or referring to your textbook or notes. Once you move into the workplace, this ability to retrieve multitudes of dissimilar information will be crucial to your success.

CHAPTER SUMMARY

This chapter has offered scientific information concerning the cognitive process necessary for learning. This means when your senses have a heightened awareness of stimuli it processed, the information is sent to your sensory memory, where it can sit briefly (up to three seconds). If the information is processed from the sensory memory, the information will arrive in the working memory stage. While in working memory you will have 30 seconds or less to determine the importance and relevance of the information. This is a short-term memory storage area of the brain, so the final stage of the memory process is long-term memory which has unlimited capacity for information. In this final stage of memory, schema are created. When learning a new idea, it is automatic for the brain to file through your schema to see what you have seen, heard, or learning about the concept previously. Of course, all of this is assuming you are dedicating your attention to learning through selective attention. Because we learn through the engagement of our senses, there are wide varieties of ways to take in information.

Constructivism, "learning is an active process where learners construct new ideas or concepts based upon their current past knowledge," encourages you to think about what you have learned, about the concept being taught, and link your old knowledge with the new knowledge. In so doing, you are constructing strong pathways in your brain for greater recall later.

Another strategy for learning is through metacognition. This strategy requires you to think about what you are learning and make connections with prior knowledge. For example, you have identified the style of learning you prefer in this chapter. There are three basic modalities for learning with your senses: visual, auditory, and tactile or kinesthetic. If you process information through your primary channel of learning, you will think about which strategies are best for you. It is always a good idea to use as many of the learning styles (multiple modalities) as is possible in every learning situation.

Repeat to remember is another learning strategy discussed in this chapter. Ebbinghaus' forgetting curve demonstrates our mind is fragile when it comes to retaining information. Since you progressively lose information from the minute you learn it, ongoing review is essential. Elaboration, distinctions, personalization, and retrieval are four strategies provided by Chew to increase your learning to deeper processing levels. These allow for multiple reviews of your course materials in innovative ways.

Being an independent learner means you have identified your strengths and weaknesses for the purposes of improving your weaker learning strategies. This will require you to understand why you are motivated to learn in the first place. Inquisitiveness is a critical component for learning because asking questions engages your mind to think about the topic at hand.

CHAPTER 3: Self-Check

Vocabulary: Define the following:

1. Sensory input
2. Sensory memory
3. Working memory
4. Long-term memory
5. Constructivism
6. Schema
7. Selective Attention
8. Brain and cognition language
9. Metacognition
10. Recursive learning
11. Chunking
12. Grit
13. Tenacity
14. Perseverance

Concepts:

15. Define the stages of memory process.
16. Explain working memory components and limitations.
17. Explain the capacity for information in working memory and describe strategies that will increase your working memory.
18. Explain the constructivist theory of learning.
19. Apply the constructivist theory to personal learning strategies that will enhance long-term memory by engaging schema.
20. Describe Ebbinghaus' forgetting curve and list three strategies you can use to retain information you are learning.
21. Describe your learning identity.
22. Explain what a strength and weakness in learning is and include strategies one can use to overcome weaknesses.
23. Explain the four strategies from Chew to increase our learning to deeper processing levels: elaboration, distinctions, personalization, and retrieval.
24. Explain how a learner can "fire and wire" for long-term learning.
25. Explain the memory stages as the stages apply to learning in college.
26. Recognize how all of the parts of the memory process create the whole of memory.
27. Explain Brunner's learning theory as it relates to schema supporting long-term memory and learning.
28. Explain the measures needed to attend to stimuli.
29. Apply study strategies encouraging focus for selective attention to compliment working memory.
30. Explain the following learning strategies: learning goals (SMARTER), physical and mental needs in place to learn; constructing meaning in learning through conversations with peers; learning through applications; deeper learning/processing; practicing; and committing to learning for a life-time.
31. Discuss time required to learn.
32. Discuss left and right brain functions.
33. Describe the benefits of whole brain learning.
34. Describe independent learning strategies promoting whole brain learning.
35. Recognize the importance of "fire to wire" for learning.
36. Describe the characteristics of a visual learning style.
37. Describe the characteristics of an auditory learning style.
38. Describe the characteristics of a read/write learning style.
39. Describe the characteristics of a kinesthetic learning style.
40. Explain your learning preference as it relates to classroom lecture, studying, and test taking.
41. Describe how each of the four modes could support learning.
42. Describe the characteristics of a multi-modality style.
43. Describe the learning/teaching style preferences of two of your professors.

44. Explain strategies to adjust to a learning/teaching style different from your learning preference.
45. Describe how independent work is fundamental to a career.
46. Describe independent learning strategies promoting metacognition.
47. Describe independent learning strategies requiring a student's strengths to increase proficiency of learning weaknesses.
48. Create three note cards for this chapter: the first with a true-false test question, the second with a multiple choice test question, and the third with an essay question.

CHAPTER 4

Thinking Critically

T.I.P.S.—(Tactical Information to Promote Success)

Recognize how familiarity with the patterns existing in subjects will improve learning.

Examples of patterns:

Patterns in the **Tartan plaid fabric** used originally in Scotland helped clans identify who was the opposing group in battle.

Fibonacci Sequence:
1, 2, 3, 5, 8, 13 . . .

© michal4r/Shutterstock.com

© clarissa harwell/Shutterstock.com

Did you know that patterns surround you, in life and in all college coursework? A good step in transitioning to college, and the level of learning that is needed, is to understand the patterns in your course materials.

Mathematics is about the discovery of patterns. It is the result of observing the world and developing a *language* to describe shapes and movement.

Mathematics is a way of communicating, a way of thinking, and a way to analyze patterns. Mathematics is NOT simply about solving equations; it is about developing the ability to think logically and abstractly, skills needed for daily decision making.

Similarly, **reading** is about discovering the pattern of organization. Accomplished readers read and predict the pattern of organization. A few of these patterns include: cause and effect, compare, contrast, and definition. Effective readers predict the pattern of organization which increases their reading comprehension.

Teaching is about observing the patterns of student behavior in a classroom. Students react to specific situations with similar behavior patterns. This allows teachers to understand the student and attend to the student's needs.

Finally, **writing** requires authors to use logical patterns when organizing the information they write. Most scholarly writers know the thesis statement is written in the first paragraph as the last sentence. Additionally, scholarly writers formulate a topic sentence for each paragraph that connects to their thesis statement.

A pattern of writing is deductive logic which originated in the 5th Century B.C.E. with syllogisms like:

Cicero is a man.
+ All men are mortal.
Cicero is a mortal.

© Cris Foto/Shutterstock.com

CHAPTER 4: OBJECTIVES

4.1 Investigating Bloom's Taxonomy

Objective 1 Understand the Meaning of Bloom's Taxonomy Levels

Objective 2 Understand the Relationships Among the Taxonomy Levels

4.2 Making Connections between Bloom's Taxonomy and Learning

Objective 3 Understand How to Use Bloom's Taxonomy to Increase Learning

Objective 4 Explain Connections in the Course Materials That Are Created Through the Use of Bloom's Taxonomy

4.3 Thinking Creatively

Objective 5 Understand the Components of Csikszentmihalyi's *Creative Thinking Flow*

Objective 6 Determine Connections between Creative Flow and Maslow's Self-Actualization

Objective 7 Understand How Creative Flow Components Can Affect Goals

4.4 Thinking Critically in Everyday Life

Objective 8 Understand How Critical Thinking Influences the Decision-Making Process

Objective 9 Understand Strategies for Improving Critical Thinking Skills

Objective 10 Understand Real-Life Applications for Creative Problem Solving

CHAPTER CONCEPTS:

Some or all of the following terms may be new to you. Place a check mark in the column reflecting your knowledge of each term.

	Know	Don't know	Not sure	Page # where first found		Know	Don't know	Not sure	Page # where first found
Analysis					Bloom's Taxonomy				
Synthesis					higher order thinking skills				
evaluation					creative thinking "flow"				
self-actualization					critical thinking				
thinking clearly					creative problem solving				
focus on the point					Four Stages of Critical Thinking				
question your questions					core curriculum				

Career Connection:

© bokehart/Shutterstock.com

In college you will have the opportunity to develop analytical and *critical thinking* skills. These will not be limited to mathematics and science courses. You will be required to think critically in sociology, psychology, government, English, speech, foreign languages, and humanities. These are skills that will transfer to the workplace. The Occupational Outlook Handbook produced by the Bureau of Labor Statistics (http://bls.gov/ooh/) lists analytical skills and critical thinking skills as additional skills needed for almost all occupations.

Do you ever wonder what it means when someone tells you to "think like your professor" to increase your success in a class? This term is used by many to encourage students to learn how to study, but what are the "secrets" stored in the cognitive vaults of higher education? What would you pay or do to learn these secrets? Well, lucky for you, you have already paid to learn this vital information by taking this class. In this chapter you are going to learn how to think like your professor by learning about ***Bloom's Taxonomy***, creative thinking, problem solving, ***self-actualization*** according to Maslow's "Hierarchy of Needs," and how to use these "secrets" to enhance your critical thinking.

4.1 INVESTIGATING BLOOM'S TAXONOMY

Corner Stone

© Radovan1/Shutterstock.com

One of the most well-known sections of a building is the "corner stone." It must be laid with the utmost precision and an understanding of the entire structure and how to align all of the components of the structure. If the corner stone is ill-positioned, then the entire structure will not stand strong or straight over an extended period of time.

Learning is similar to the construction of a building because both require a step-by-step process with the end result in mind from the beginning. One of the ways educators have been successfully accomplishing this task is with the use of Bloom's Taxonomy.

OBJECTIVE 1: Understand the Meaning of Bloom's Taxonomy Levels

Think back to when you were in elementary school learning the multiplication tables. At the time, you were required to memorize the facts with, perhaps, little association or understanding of how you would eventually use them. Some students may have been taught that this was another way of understanding repeated addition, but most students were asked to memorize and restate the tables with automaticity. The foundation of mathematics requires the use of multiplication and division. As a matter of fact, all of the concepts you learned from kindergarten through eighth grade were preparing you to learn how to master the higher-order thinking skills that are required in high school mathematic courses—algebra, geometry, trigonometry, calculus, and statistics. In order for you to have done this successfully, the teachers and schools you attended were deliberately building the foundation for your success by incorporating tasks that built upon and strengthened one another. Each task became progressively more challenging with the rote learning serving as the corner stone that aligns the rest of the mathematical building.

FIGURE 4.1 Bloom's Taxonomy

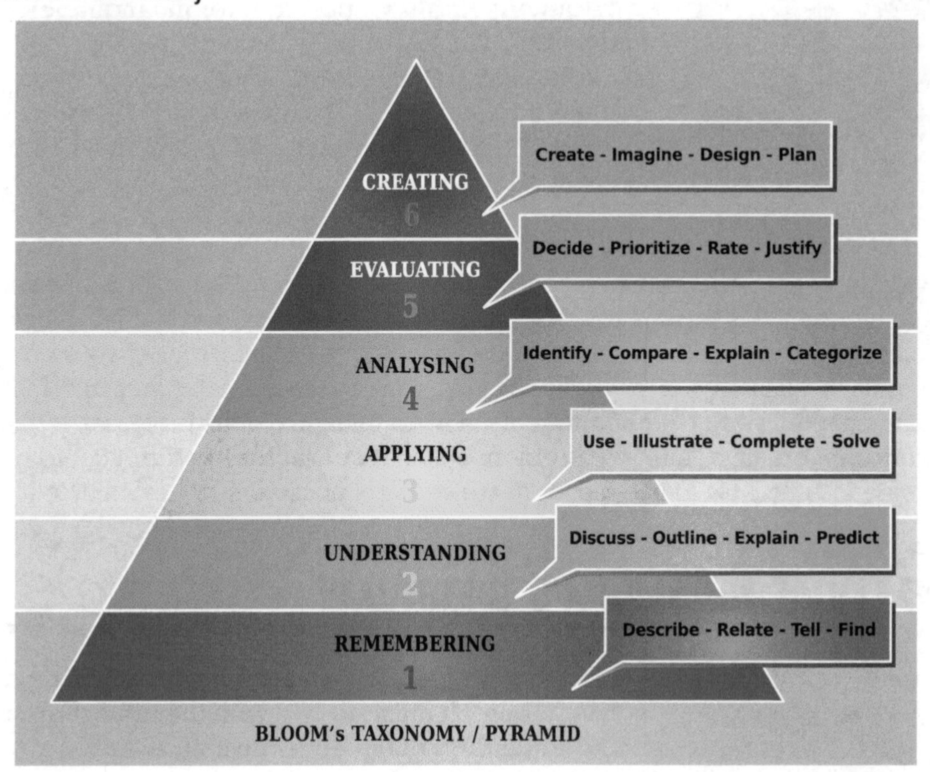

Bloom's Taxonomy is a cognitive learning continuum consisting of six levels that move from simple to complex as seen in Figure 4.1. Typically, the first three levels of Bloom's Taxonomy are considered the lower levels of learning because the depth of learning is focused on a basic understanding of the facts. The levels of Bloom's Taxonomy are:

1. ***Knowledge*** is the basis for Bloom's Taxonomy and requires you to remember new factual information such as multiplication or periodic tables or sight words.

   Comprehension follows knowledge by expecting you to understand a concept to the point that you can use it correctly as in simplifying an expression or solving an equation or perhaps using a sight word in a sentence.

   Application is the next level of learning and requires you to use information to solve a word problem in science or mathematics and understanding a passage that contains many of the new sight words.

The remaining three stages of Bloom's Taxonomy are considered the ***higher order thinking skills*** because students are challenged to think on a conceptual level.

2. ***Analysis*** is the first level of higher learning and requires learners to recognize main points or explain the connections between complex ideas. This usually means you are asked to compare and contrast or interpret information from a graph.
3. ***Evaluation*** is the next level of Bloom's Taxonomy. Most students in college have been asked to research a topic and evaluate the sources for validity, credibility, and relevance.
4. ***Creation/Synthesis***, the highest level of learning in Bloom's Taxonomy anticipates that you will be able to take two or more ideas and combine them to create something new. You may have been asked to do this if a professor or teacher required you to research a topic you are unfamiliar with and use the sources to create your own conclusion about it. ***Each of these*** six levels comprise the corner stone for learning.

OBJECTIVE 2: Understand the Relationships Among the Taxonomy Levels

Understanding the relationship among the levels in Bloom's Taxonomy is necessary for you to use them as a practical learning tool. When they were originally formulated in 1956, it was determined by Benjamin Bloom and his research group that they were a hierarchy of cognitive learning because it was agreed that a person needed to master one level of learning in order to learn at the next level. Over the last few years, researchers have questioned the hierarchical aspect originally implied—the need to become accomplished in one level in order to move to the next. In addition, *Evaluation* and *Creation* have been switched from the original with Creation forming the apex. All of this is to say that the best use of Bloom's Taxonomy in learning is to recognize ways to achieve the higher-order learning skills. In college, you will be expected to operate on the upper levels that are often referred to as ***higher-order thinking*** or ***critical thinking***.

By comparing and contrasting the six cognitive levels, you will be able to understand the distinctions between each more clearly. *Knowledge* dictates that learning is demonstrated through

- *Defining* a concept.
- *Describing* a concept.
- *Naming* a concept.

In contrast, *creation (or synthesis)* is requiring you to be able to:

- *Create a new process from others you have learned.*
- *Combine multiple skills to solve a new type of problem.*
- *Consider everything you know about a topic to apply the information in a different way.*

Suffice it to say, you will struggle with *creation (or synthesis)* if you have not learned the basic knowledge necessary for combining the components of a concept. An illustration of this is found in the ***core curriculum*** (required classes) that is in most colleges for the purpose of establishing a foundation for learning in the upper division courses. Classes that are established by each state for state schools and that are generally included in the core curriculum include courses in:

- *English*
- *Science*
- *History*
- *Social sciences*
- *Speech communications*
- *Government*
- *Mathematics*

The aim of the core curriculum is to assist college students to advance from the basic information of facts, toward critical thinking of concepts through creation of ideas. Columbia College explains the core curriculum well when they state, "The habits of mind developed in the core cultivate a critical and creative intellectual capacity that students employ long after college, in the pursuit and the fulfillment of meaningful lives" (Columbia College, 2013).

EXERCISE 4.1: Reflecting on Bloom's Taxonomy

Review the information you have read so far in this chapter and explain how it will help you think like a professor.

____

____

____

____

____

4.2 MAKING CONNECTIONS BETWEEN BLOOM'S TAXONOMY AND LEARNING

OBJECTIVE 3: Understand How to Use Bloom's Taxonomy to Increase Learning

With the progression of cognitive learning being perceived as similar to building a structure, it is essential that you learn the facts of a course as well as the various ways of analyzing, synthesizing, and evaluating them. Most educators write learning Objectives by using verbs that describe the desired level of learning for the student. See Table 4.1 for the list of key words and how they connect to Bloom's six levels of cognitive learning. This chart includes the characteristics for each of the cognitive levels, an example using one of the key words, and stems (possible beginnings) for formulating your own questions.

TABLE 4.1 Bloom's Taxonomy for Practical Applications

Level	Characteristics	Key Words	Example	Question Stems
Knowledge	Remember, recall factual information	Define, describe, list, itemize, name, state	Define plate tectonics using the language of	■ Define the word . . . ■ Describe the properties of . . . ■ Name the characteristics of . . .
Comprehension	Understand concepts	Explain, predict, translate, infer, exemplify, interpret, extrapolate, hypothesize	Explain the causes of plate formation, continental drift, and seafloor spreading.	■ Explain the plot, process, or concept. ■ What is the inference about in the . . . ■ Write a hypothesis for . . . ■ What inference or conclusion can you make?
Application	Use information and generalizations to solve original or real-life problems	Compute, apply, solve, prove, calculate, illustrate, show, manipulate, manage, decide	Identify and name the plates on a map. (knowledge and application needed)	■ Describe the ______ changes that occur in ______________________.
Analysis	Recognize main points; reduce multifaceted information to explain how the parts relate to the whole; understand connections.	Compare, contrast, identify, analyze, trace, relate, organize, outline, distinguish, separate	Compare and contrast three types of plate boundary.	■ Outline the parts or features of ■ Identify how is ______ related to . . . ■ List the parts . . . ■ How would you categorize . . . ? ■ Can you identify the difference parts . . . ? ■ What evidence can you find . . . ? ■ What is the relationship between . . . ?
Evaluation	Understand values, judge something against given or stated standards	Assess, evaluate, rate, judge, determine, accept, reject, argue a point of view, qualify,	Using the concepts in plate tectonics, evaluate the theory of Intelligent Design.	■ Prove (or disprove) the theory of . . . ■ Defend the actions, ideas, or perceptions of . . . ■ Assess the need for . . .
Creation/ Synthesis	Innovate, create something that did not exist before, alternative solutions	write an essay, design an experiment, draw, create, express, discuss, propose, visual representation, invent	Discuss the implications of plate tectonics for life on Earth.	■ Formulate a theory for . . . ■ Propose a solution for . . . ■ Predict the outcome of . . . ■ Construct a model that would change . . .

EXERCISE 4.2: Identifying Taxonomy Levels

Identify the level where the following learning Objectives belong in Bloom's taxonomy.

Question	Level
Explain how the word "work" is used in each of the following sentences: "It will take a lot of work to learn Chinese." "'Work!' Shelby hasn't even looked for a job since graduating.'" "'Men at Work' is the name of a band from the '80s.'" "The Mona Lisa is a work of art."	(evaluation)
Identify the parts of speech used in the sentence: "Sandy drove her new car to the mountains."	(application)
Name the eight parts of speech.	(knowledge)
Define conjunction. Define verb.	(comprehension)
Write a sentence that contains all eight parts of speech.	(creation/synthesis)
What is the difference in an adjective and an adverb? A noun and a pronoun?	(analysis)
(Based on information included in Lepionka, Mary Ellen. *Writing and Developing Your College Textbook: A Comprehensive Guide to Textbook Authorship and Higher Education Publishing,* 2nd ed. Gloucester, MA: Atlantic Path Publishing, 2008.).	

REFLECTION 4.A: Taxonomy Levels in Course Work

Use the information from the chart on page 124 to write a question for each of the six levels of Bloom's Taxonomy for **American History Since the Civil War**. If your instructor agrees, work in groups to help write the questions.

Level	Question
Knowledge	
Comprehension	
Application	
Analysis	
Evaluation	
Creation/Synthesis	

Through the application of Bloom's Taxonomy to your studying in college, you can learn to generate goals for your own learning; these are similar to SMARTER goals from Chapter 2. Prior to beginning your study session, write your goals for the session in the form of Objectives, clearly state the behavior, skills, or attitudes that you will demonstrate when learning has occurred. These should be written in the following way:

After reading Chapter 4, I will be able to identify and explain the six levels in Bloom's Taxonomy.

Describes when/what, and the action or behavior that is based on the description words in Bloom's Taxonomy.

Examples of Education Objectives

Learning Objectives can be of a general/global nature or they can be more specific in nature. Whatever perspective you take, a learning Objective must be quantifiable, clearly stated, and action-oriented. When related to a Service Learning project, the Objective(s) must be related to coursework and or the course professor's instructions. Global General Learning Objectives are written using action verbs such as: LIST, DEFINE, RECOGNIZE, IDENTIFY, DEMONSTRATE, or DRAW. Specific Learning Objectives are written using verbs such as ANALYZE, WRITE, CONSTRUCT, SYNTHESIZE, COMPARE, CONTRAST, OBTAIN, DEVELOP, or SOLVE.

Examples of Learning Objectives:

1. IDENTIFY five methods teachers use to manage behavior in the classroom.
2. "COMPARE and CONTRAST the treatment and behavior of boys and girls in the classroom as it relates to gender equity." (English or Psychology student tutoring at Meadows Elementary School).
3. Develop three strategies for encouraging reading in the classroom.

Making connections between Bloom's Taxonomy and learning means you can increase your ability to learn through a systematic approach to guide you. As you have probably already noted, moving beyond the lower level learning in Bloom's Taxonomy becomes progressively more challenging for your mind. Being asked to identify a word or concept is easier than using the information to solve a problem. For example, being asked to identify the Pythagorean Theorem is much easier than using the Pythagorean Theorem to determine the length of the hypotenuse. An even more challenging task would be if you were asked to analyze the Pythagorean Theorem's qualities as they apply to architecture.

The point of learning Bloom's Taxonomy is for you to use the increasingly complex cognitive levels to prepare for the assignments and tests you will take in college. Quite frankly, your professors are going to expect you to generate ideas within the higher order thinking skill level, not the lower levels. Of course, this does not mean you will be able to omit the lower levels of learning. In contrast, you will be expected to have mastered the lower levels prior to entering in a class discussion that will be on the higher levels of learning.

EXERCISE 4.3: Test Questions for Each Taxonomy Level

Select a topic from **this course** that you have studied in depth and develop a test question for each taxonomy level.

Level	Question
Knowledge	
Comprehension	
Application	
Analysis	
Synthesis	
Evaluation	

REFLECTION 4.B:

Although we have not discussed study strategies in detail, how helpful do you believe the last two exercises would be in preparing for a test?

OBJECTIVE 4: Explain Connections in the Course Materials That Are Created Through the Use of Bloom's Taxonomy

The connections in this course's materials were created through the use of Bloom's Taxonomy. The authors determined what information and on what level you needed to learn. Once the learning level was determined, the contents of the book were created by using the questions from Bloom's Taxonomy. Primarily, the purpose for this organizational structure was to guarantee that you would learn the concepts progressing from simple to complex. Professors who use this textbook are using Bloom's Taxonomy when they assigned your readings, projects, and essays. Because you have read the assigned pages or chapter prior to class arrival, your professor will expect more of the higher level thinking skills to be demonstrated in class discussions and activities.

When you use Bloom's Taxonomy to generate questions, deeper learning connections will occur in a course. Think about it. By generating questions with the verbs from Table 4.1, you are processing the information from simple information to the construction of complex ideas. When you do this, you are thinking like your professor, so you will perform better in the class. As previously mentioned, you are learning the *secrets* of how to think like your professor. Consider, who designs the test questions? The professor creates the exams using the verbs in Bloom's Taxonomy. Thus, you have learned one of the techniques of how professors create a test!

As you have seen, Bloom's Taxonomy is a valuable study tool for creating questions. You also can apply this same technique for reading, active listening, and note taking.

Reading while using Bloom's Taxonomy will require you to generate questions from the text. Then, as you read with a more defined purpose, you will look for the answers to the questions you generated. A good way to do this is to turn the headings and subheadings within the textbook into questions by using the stems given to you above in "Bloom's Taxonomy for Practical Applications." For example, to learn on the analysis level, write a question with the stem that begins "List the parts . . . " As you read with this heightened sense of purpose, you will identify the list and record your answers. You may use the Cornell Note taking system (described in Chapter 7) or write the information in the margin of your text book. You can use the stems that pertain to each level, so you will increase your thinking as you build toward using higher order thinking skills.

Active listening means you make a deliberate effort to listen to a speaker's meaning, not just the words that are uttered. This may sound unusual, but do you know how easy it is to become distracted? Traditionally, people hear and learn between 25-50% of information that is delivered verbally. By using your active listening skills you will increase your retention and recall. Exactly how do you listen actively? To begin, pay attention to all of the verbal and non-verbal cues. For the next step, demonstrate encouragement where you will nod, smile, gesture, or utter a statement to the speaker. Ponder the points being made by the speaker by asking higher order thinking level questions to yourself to determine your level of understanding. For example, you may want to summarize or restate the points made by the speaker. In so doing, you will be seeking clarification of your understanding. Try to think of a few questions that can extend your understanding of the speaker's material. Notice how much active listening requires you to generate questions. Now imagine that the speaker is your professor giving a class lecture. By employing listening skills during a lecture, you will be learning the material with an active learning mindset.

Note taking with the use of Bloom's Taxonomy means you will predict what the professor is going to say in a lecture while taking notes. Of course, this means you have invested adequate time in preparation prior to attending class. As you know, this means you will have already read the course materials, so you will have connections in your mind based on the readings. While your professor is lecturing, you can predict the next point in the lecture based on your understanding of the course content. Predicting during a lecture means that you are employing the various levels within Bloom's Taxonomy through your thinking process. An illustration of this is a student who has completed the pre-reading, using Bloom's Taxonomy in the procedure previously listed, and is able to listen to the course lecture with the ability to predict the next point to be made by the professor. Additionally, the student is able to generate questions to extend his or her learning through the active listening strategy previously mentioned. Basically, by generating questions in all of these activities you will be an active learner who employs critical thinking throughout all of your learning and studying sessions.

COURSE CONNECTIONS:
Deductive and Inductive Reasoning

Deductive Reasoning

considered "top down" reasoning; generally moves from general to specific

Inductive Reasoning

considered "bottom up" reasoning; generally moves from specific to general

	Deductive Reasoning	**Inductive Reasoning**
Characteristics	Original premise MUST be true. Secondary premise MUST be true. CONCLUSION: The result MUST be true.	Original premise may or may not be known to be true. Secondary premise may or may not be known to be true. CONCLUSION: The result may or may not be true.
Example	Premise: $5x - 3 = 7$ TRUE $5x = 10$ TRUE because adding 3 to both sides does not change the meaning of the equation. Conclusion $x = 2$ TRUE because dividing both sides by 5 does not change the meaning of the equation.	Premise: $x^2 = 16$ TRUE $x = 4$ TRUE because $4^2 = 16$. BUT x could also be $^-4$ because $(^-4)^2 = 16$.

For each group of statements below, determine whether they would be considered *deductive* or *inductive* reasoning. Explain to another student how you arrived at the answer.	
Tom is five years older than his sister Samantha and his sister Samantha is three years younger than her sister Kayley. Therefore, Kayley is younger than Tom.	(deductive)
Susie is older than Mike and Mike is older than Kason. Therefore, Susie is older than Kason.	(deductive)
Humans inhale oxygen and exhale carbon dioxide. Trees absorb carbon dioxide and produce oxygen. Therefore, deforestation reduces the amount of oxygen available.	(deductive)
"Fracking" is a process use to bring natural as to the surface by injecting high-powered water into the earth near a known gas field. Earthquakes have been registered near known fracking sites. Therefore, fracking causes earthquakes.	(inductive)

SOMETHING TO THINK ABOUT:

Complete the three steps in this section as written. Take a minute to review the picture below. Do you think this student looks like she is learning?

1. Write a paragraph, three to five complete sentences, about the photograph as it relates to *thinking critically*.

____

____

____

continued

2. Would your discussion be influenced if you knew the student has either a GPA of 1.9 or of 3.8?

___

___

___

3. Discuss the photograph again from the perspective of, personal responsibility and communication skills.

___

___

___

4.3 THINKING CREATIVELY

OBJECTIVE 5: Understand the Components of Csikszentmihalyi's *Creative Thinking Flow*

Have you ever experienced a time in your life when you were working on a project that brought you such satisfaction that you lost track of time? This may have been when you were working on a class project, thinking about how to improve the performance of your car's engine, or when you were producing a piece of artwork. If you have experienced something similar to this, you may have realized what it was like to have "**creative flow**." According to **Mihaly Csikszentmihalyi**, a world renowned psychologist who has spent years trying to understand creativity and flow, flow is a "feeling when things [are] doing so well as an almost automatic, effortless, yet highly focused state of consciousness" (*Creativity,* 110). Through his research, he has found seven conditions that describe flow. These are:

1. Completely involved in what you are doing—focused, concentrating
2. A sense of ecstasy—of being outside of everyday reality
3. Great inner clarity—knowing what needs to be done, and how well you are doing
4. Knowing that the activity is doable—that your skills are adequate to the task
5. A sense of serenity—no worries about yourself, and a feeling of growing beyond the boundaries of the ego
6. Timelessness—thoroughly focused on the present, hours seem to pass by in minutes
7. Intrinsic motivation—whatever is produced becomes its own reward

To help you understand the various components of "creative flow," consider an artist who enjoys painting. Before the artist can begin his project, he must have some idea of what he will paint. Most likely, he will paint something that he feels is within his "comfort zone" of skills (#4). As he begins to paint, the portrait becomes clear in his mind and he begins to develop it on the canvas (#3). He realizes as he paints that the softness of the child's skin reflects exactly what he wanted. This is a new experience for him and his focus becomes much more directed (#1). As he focuses on his painting, time has no meaning. He continues until the light fades and he must stop. He realizes that he has been at his easel for hours (#6). When he returns the next day to continue working on his project, and the portrait develops as he perfectly mixes the colors to reflect his original vision, whatever is going on around him becomes irrelevant. He is "in the zone," as some would say (#2). He has pushed himself and a feeling of comfort envelops him. He is not arrogant about his portrait, he is simply proud of his accomplishment (#5). This painting was not produced for a grade or a project; it was something he wanted to do for his grandchild. He is happy with his work and no one can take that away from him (#7).

As you can see, the steps for the creative flow do not necessarily happen in the order they are listed here. Your creative flow could be an experience of a day of playing baseball, an evening of dancing, writing a paper on a topic that greatly interests you, trying a new recipe, or preparing for a violin concert.

EXERCISE 4.4: Creative Flow

Forgetting the order, describe a time in your life when you experienced a sensation that could be identified as "creative flow."

____

____

____

____

____

____

____

REFLECTION 4.C:

Identify all 7 of Csikszentmihalyi's conditions as they relate to your creative flow experience.

____

____

____

____

____

____

____

This offers a visual way of understanding flow and the balance between the challenged and skill level. Flow occurs when the person's skills are high and the challenge is great. For example, a scientist who has researched for 20 or more years to find the cure for cancer will feel the creative flow when his or her skills in research and knowledge are high and the challenge is great. Suppose an undergraduate has learned to use a microscope to interpret microorganisms that were grown slides, to the point that his or her knowledge concerning staphylococci, streptococci, and e coli is high. The challenge of learning to identify more microorganisms increases his or her motivation to learn. This means that the student becomes so focused on reading the slides with a microscope that he or she is intrinsically motivated to go beyond the professor's assignments to learn more. In turn, this means he or she is so focused on the learning that he or she loses track of time, has a sense of calm, and clarity.

If you lack either the skill or the challenge, flow cannot occur. In Figure 4.2, notice that the left side lists progressive states of emotions from apathy, worry, and anxiety. These are the end result of a low skill level combined with a task that is either too challenging or not challenging enough. For example, a student who studied physics in high school may be bored with the "rudimentary" homework assigned at the beginning of a college physics class. This lack of challenge may create a situation where the student is frustrated with the class and loses motivation. Similarly, when a student feels that he or she is not doing well in a class (low skill) and have a significant challenge in learning for a variety of reasons, he or she will feel apathetic or anxious. Either scenario has a disappointing outcome and limits the opportunity for creative flow to occur.

FIGURE 4.2 Mihaly Csikszentmihalyi: "Flow"

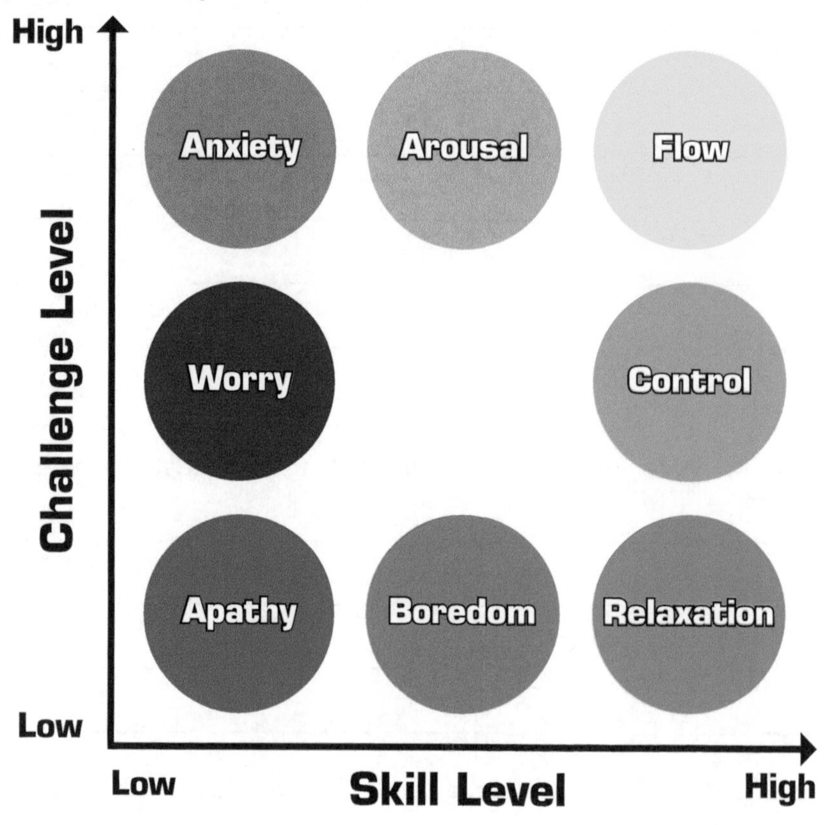

(Source: Csikszentmihalyi, Mihaly. *Flow: The Psychology of Optimal Experience*. 1997.)

Csikszentmihalyi suggests that arousal is the point where learning can occur because this is the "area that you are pushed beyond your comfort zone." You sense a heightened awareness of new information or a greater challenge that grabs your attention. An example of this is when you are studying a language, say Spanish, and feel as if you have a firm grip on it. Then, you travel to Spain for a semester and your emersion into the new culture presents a new set of challenges. As a result you are eager to sit and sip coffee while visiting with the local people and lose track of time. You are aware that this is not a normal event for you and experience serenity. This set of naturally occurring events that result from entering the culture of a language you have studied in a classroom offers you a new, more challenging level of learning. Thus, your arousal of the novel parameters of this situation push you easily into creative flow.

Control is another good position for entry into flow because you feel confident in your skills. This comfort in your skills means that an increase in the challenge will create the opportunity for entering flow. To illustrate this point, think about people who have been working at the same company for 20 or more years. It seems likely that they would become very competent in their skills, but over time lack any serious challenges. In order to seek out flow, these people would need to find opportunities to challenge their skills by increasing the difficulty of the task. This might be accomplished by requesting a transfer to a different department where their skills would be used in a different way or possibly leave the company for a new challenge.

Students who have a firm grasp on the course contents and are challenged to learn more, are more likely to experience flow. The optimum condition for flow to occur is when the skill level is high and the challenge is also high. In everyday life, this means that in order to experience flow once you have mastered the skill in an area that you find happiness, you will need to increase the challenges.

EXERCISE 4.5: Flow Figure

Considering your performance in this course through TODAY, describe where you are in Csikszentmihalyi's flow Figure 4.2. **Use the vocabulary** in the chart in your description.

REFLECTION 4.D:

Describe the information in Figure 4.2 to a student not in your class. Use your **own words** in your description (NOT the vocabulary in the figure).

Again, you are being given another *secret* to the inner workings of higher education. Have you ever observed a professor who is passionate about his or her subject? These professors have a hard time ending class on time, may be very interesting to listen to their lectures, and inspire you to learn all you can about this topic due to their enthusiasm. More than likely a professor who acts this way is experiencing flow during your class because they are in a profession that challenges them intellectually as well as the fact that they are masters of the skills necessary to perform well in the profession. Because your professor is experiencing flow, they anticipate that you will eventually share their passion. In college, it is understood that when you take a class, you are as dedicated to the learning as your professor is to his or her profession.

For more information on happiness and "flow," with Dr. Csikszentmihalyi, visit http://www.ted.com/talks/mihaly_csikszentmihalyi_on_flow.html. (The video is approximately 18 minutes long.)

OBJECTIVE 6: Determine Connections between Creative Flow and Maslow's Self-Actualization

Understanding flow is one way of increasing your motivation to learn or to self-actualize. Another, perhaps, more widely known strategy is by grasping Maslow's "Hierarchy of Needs" and self-actualization. Both of the theories offer a way of understanding how you learn to "pursue your passion"—find the profession, major, sport, or hobby that engages all of your talents and interests. Before you can do this, you will need to find out how to meet all your basic needs.

Take a moment to review the five stages in Maslow's Hierarchy of Needs that were presented in Chapter 2. Recall that each stage leads to self-actualization, the highest level. *Self-actualization* includes creativity, morality, problem solving, acceptance of reality, and a lack of prejudice. This is the ultimate level of needs that humans have to realize their full potential. Do you think that it is interesting that Maslow feels that creativity is a need?

EXERCISE 4.6: Review of Maslow's Hierarchy

Using the triangle below, list Maslow's hierarchy of needs with a short description of each out to the side.

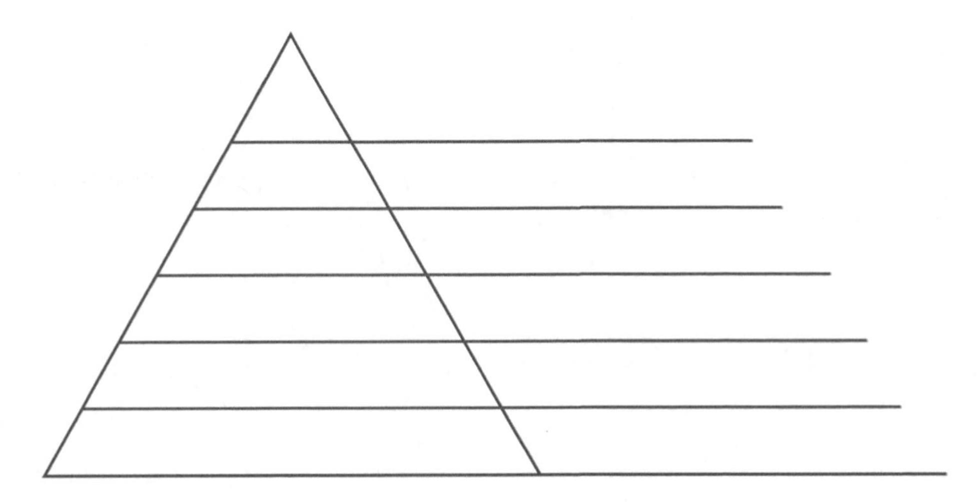

Applying creative flow to pursuing your passion will affect your personal goals. What do you most enjoy doing in life? This may or may not be in a college class. It may be something you are involved in as a volunteer in your community, at your place of worship, at work—anything that makes you passionate about life. Perhaps it is working with children, attending a sporting event, participating in a theatrical or chorale presentation, restoring a classic car, building things, or working with animals.

EXERCISE 4.7: Self-Assessment of Talents

Check the appropriate column that represents your **talent** and/or **interest** in the categories below.

Categories	**Talent** Innate or natural ability to do well	**Interest** Read, watch, or do with focus; natural curiosity.
Athlete: tennis, basketball, swim, etc.		
Cook: ability to combine ingredients with positive outcome		
Decision Maker: use math to solve problems and communicate		
Influencer: can easily persuade people to action		
Interpersonal: cooperate with others		
Life-long Learner: seeks knowledge in all areas		
Listener: listen actively		
Musical: sing, instrumental, etc.		
Observer: observe critically		
Organizer: sees the order of things and is able to put things together in a practical way		
Socializer: plan events or social gatherings		
Visualizer: good eye for color, arrangement, detail		
Writer: convey ideas in writing		

OBJECTIVE 7: Understand How Creative Flow Components Can Affect Goals

With your newly realized, or perhaps recent, reminder of your talents and interests, consider how these will guide your long-term goals. If you disregard these natural abilities in determining your lifetime goals, you will be challenged to discover creative flow in your chosen occupation. You have unique characteristics to offer the world, but if you disregard them, the world will not benefit from your aptitudes. Joseph Campbell, mythology scholar, coined the phrase, "Follow your bliss." He further clarifies this sentence by stating,

> "If you follow your bliss, you put yourself on a kind of track that has been there all the while, waiting for you, and the life that you ought to be living is the one you are living. Wherever you are—if you are following your bliss, you are enjoying that refreshment, that life within you, all the time" (*The Power of the Myth* 1988).

Working diligently at something you enjoy, sparks curiosity, and energizes you; you are on the path to realizing creative flow. Considering your bliss, natural talents and interests, determine how you can best apply them in your goals.

REFLECTION 4.F:

Making the information from the previous self-assessment practical means that you will need to review the steps included in a SMARTER goal in Chapter 2. Write a personal goal based on the desire to pursue your passion through creative flow.

Next, apply the seven conditions recommended for creative flow to one academic goal. Be sure to review the steps included in a SMARTER goal in Chapter 2.

Finally, identify ways to apply creative flow to long-term goals. This may be an intermediate or short term goal that is related to the goal you wrote concerning pursuing your passion. Reviewing the steps included in a SMARTER goal from Chapter 2 will make this easier.

____

____

____

____

____

____

PERSON to PERSON

In this exercise, you will be introduced to three students who are adjusting to college life.

© Monkey Business Images/Shutterstock.com

Let's discuss the possible outcomes based on the information provided.

Sheila, Patrick, and Michael met in their American history class the first semester of their college career. They ended up sitting next to each other because they did not know anyone in the class. Michael took the initiative to meet the other two. He stated, "I'm the guy you want to call when Friday night hits! I'm kinda' of party phenomenon." Sheila, being kind of shy, said "I'll try to remember that fact, but I don't party very often." Patrick, being eager to meet new friends, since none of his friends attended his college, encouraged Michael by giving him his phone number.

Quickly, it became clear that Michael and Patrick were spending time together over the weekends. They come to class reveling in the fun they had over the weekend. Sheila decided that she would continue to sit near them, as they were friendly, but spent her weekends studying and reviewing her notes from the course. She did find a group of friends in the Student Government Association with whom she spent any extra time.

Three weeks into the semester the first round of tests arrived. Sheila felt nervous about what to expect, but Patrick and Michael agreed that the first test in any class was usually a wash, so they said "why study too hard?" As soon as the tests were passed out, the tension in the room thickened.

Based on this description, predict the order of successful completion of the history test.

Sheila ____ Pat ____ Michael ____

Here is some additional information.

- Michael was able to find time to study in between classes that was more than 6 hours a week for history.
- Patrick was too distracted when the time to study arrived, and chose to take a nap in an attempt to catch up on some much needed sleep.

continued

Based on all the information you now know, rank them again as to what student will do best on the test. Has your ranking changed?

Sheila ____ Pat ____ Michael ____

1. What pieces of new information influenced your ranking decisions?

____

____

____

2. Explain why this new information helped shape your opinion.

____

____

____

Here are your last pieces of information.

- The instructor announces that the majority of the students (2/3) failed the test.
- Sheila typically spends the class period shopping and checking Facebook®.
- Patrick is the first person from his family to attend college.

Who do you think is most likely to have performed well on the history test?

Sheila ____ Pat ____ Michael ____

1. What pieces of new information would you still like to know about the situation?

____

____

____

2. What advice would you offer each student in light of the information in this chapter?

Sheila: ____

Michael: ____

Patrick: ____

4.4 THINKING CRITICALLY IN EVERYDAY LIFE

If you think about how difficult college is, or how easy it is, your images may become a reality. In other words, if you think it is hard, it usually will be hard. However, if it REALLY is hard, you must give it 100% effort! If you think it is easy, it will be easier. Attitude influences your ability to think critically.

EXERCISE 4.8: Thinking and Outcome

Henry Ford, creator of Ford Motor Company, is credited with the saying "Whether you think you can or think you can't, you're right." In your own words, what do you think this statement means?

___

___

___

REFLECTION 4.G:

"You become the person you are, based on what you are thinking."

Do you agree or disagree with this statement? Explain why.

Comparing the two statements above, do you believe they are saying the same thing? Why or why not?

OBJECTIVE 8: Understand How Critical Thinking Influences the Decision-Making Process

By learning Blooms' Taxonomy, Maslow's "Hierarchy of Needs," and how to achieve creative flow, you are beginning to think like a professor and become a student who will more easily succeed in college. It is essential that you understand how these theories promote the critical thinking that influences your decision making process. According to CriticalThinking.org, "Critical thinking is the disciplined art of ensuring that you use the best thinking you are capable of in any set of circumstances." Basically, this means that you will need to take time to analyze your current thinking patterns, determine those that are productive, and apply these to your decisions.

Over the last three to six months, you have made many decisions about college. "Should I listen to people who influence me by telling me what they think I should do? What have I read about colleges' programs that I am considering? Do I want to study in a discipline where I know very little based on a scholarship offer? How did I perform so poorly on the college entrance exams? What are my options now? If I move out of my parent's home, where is the best place to live?" Do you get the point? Decisions are parts of everyone's life, so it is important that you learn a process for arriving at your decisions.

Just as you typically consult your family, friends, school counselors, or teachers concerning your major decisions, the government structure is designed for the president to consult with experts when making major decisions. The vice president and fifteen members who serve on the Presidential Cabinet aid the United States President in making the best decisions for the majority of citizens in each situation. There are numerous examples of how people are required to make critical thinking a part of the decision making process throughout history as well as in current times. As you have seen, the presidential cabinet is organized to aid the president in decision making.

Consider how critical thinking skills may be needed in situations in your life. Discuss with a classmate. You may want to consider critical thinking skills in fields such as law enforcement, fire science, or medical science.

OBJECTIVE 9: Understand Strategies for Improving Critical Thinking Skills

FIGURE 4.3 Four Stages of Critical Thinking

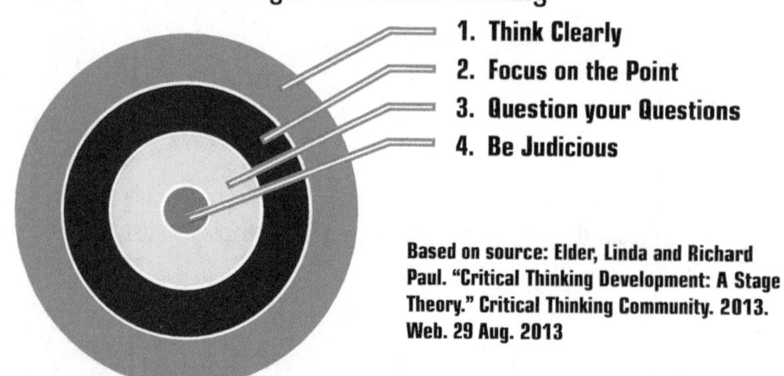

You have the opportunity to learn how to use critical thinking in making decisions for yourself. Learning to think critically when making decisions means that you will need to learn to discipline your mind in a new way.

By learning a more logical approach to decision making, you are more likely to make constructive decisions that will increase your ability to self-actualize and experience flow.

© Gumpanat/Shutterstock.com

Thinking clearly **means that you will want to examine carefully any ideas that you read or hear that are strange, or just do not make sense to you. As the old adage states, "If it looks like a duck, swims like a duck, and quacks like a duck, then it probably is a duck." In other words, review all of the information available to determine the full and complete meaning.**

Two ways to clarify your thinking is to try restating what you understand through a summary, and then conducting research by asking follow up questions. Pointers for improving this are:

Direct: direct your retelling to one point at a time

Understand: relate as many details as you understand them

Connect: connect your ideas to your life experiences

Kick-it-around: explain your ideas using synonyms or words that create a metaphor.

For example, your psychology professor has assigned you to read an article entitled "Identical twins reunite after 35 years." Alex Spillius' article, which was published in The Telegraph (2007), reports on a newly-discovered research project conducted in the late 60s in America. Basically, these sisters, as well as many other sets of twins, were knowingly and deliberately separated at birth but the adoptive parents were not told about the sibling twin. Psychologist Peter Neubauerg designed this study to learn how much effect an environment has on the development of twins. It is reported that this type of study ended in 1980. Some readers of this article might automatically wonder, "Was it legal to separate twins at birth in the 60s?" or "Is this a moral or ethical dilemma created by science?" Obviously, there are more questions you might ask, but for the sake of understanding in how to "think clearly" by using DUCK, applications will be limited to these questions.

Direct: *I will only focus on addressing "Was it legal to separate twins at birth in the 60s?"*

Understand: *My understanding of the information in this article is that Peter Neubauerg was given consent to separate twins at birth, but I am not sure if this originated from state or federal laws.*

Connect: *Based on my experience from reading about twin studies, I understand that twins have been separated for various reasons and then studied by psychologists.* Usually, they learn that twins have many of the same mannerisms and interests. The primary question studied by psychologists by studying twins is "does nature or nurture have greater influence on human development?"

Kick-it-around: *Separating twins at birth without telling the adoptive parents is like adopting a child and never telling him he was adopted.*

Here is a more personal use of the DUCK method. For example, you are having trouble arriving on time for your class because of unpredictable traffic during peak times. Review the steps for critical thinking:

1. **Think Clearly**: use DUCK to determine the specific reason you are late.
2. **Focus on the Point:** How can I arrive at class early or on time every day?
3. **Question your Questions:** Is the fact that I am late due to unpredictable traffic or not starting early enough to allow for the unexpected? Is the fact that I am late, due to getting up too late to arrive on time? Is the fact that I am late due to disrespect for authority?
4. **Be Judicious:** What is the root of this random thought, "I am an adult, so why do I have to follow the rules made up by the college?" Perhaps, this is the reason I do not abide by the starting time for this class, and I really need to work on understanding that the purpose of the rules is to protect me as well as offer me an opportunity for self- improvement.

Now that you have seen an example of clear thinking, you are ready to learn ways to **"focus on the point."** Sometimes when people are trying to think about a decision, too many variables arise and cloud their clear thinking. For example, Sally and Fran are looking for decent housing that is not too expensive to live in next year. Unrelated thoughts or irrelevant ideas such as Sally thinking, "I am going to paint the kitchen blue." Or Fran thinking "Who is going to do the grocery shopping?" may force you to lose focus on the decision concerning affordable housing. To avoid irrelevant thinking frequently ask: "What is the crucial question? Is this or that relevant to it? How does it relate?"

While maintaining your focus, you will need to **"begin questioning your questions."** This means that you will examine your original questions to determine what other questions need to be addressed before making a decision. For example, consider the situation where Sally and Fran find an apartment but it has a large bedroom and a much smaller bedroom. How will they decide who gets the larger bedroom? And how can they be fair about it? The result of this type of questioning is being a critical thinker who can make more informed decisions.

Finally, you have arrived at the fourth criteria to guide your decision making—"**being judicious."** To become a judicious person you will need to learn to employ all of your senses (vision, hearing, smell, taste, and touch) to observe the behaviors of other people and your own. Sally is insisting on taking the larger bedroom but is unwilling to pay a larger part of the rent. She says that since she found the apartment, she is entitled to the larger bedroom without paying any more. Fran may think "I have never seen her act so selfish!" Watch for signs of illogical or unprovoked behavioral reactions in a variety of situations. Ask yourself: "Why did they act like that? What else is going on that may have influenced that reaction? What has happened in the past to provoke such an extreme response?" Is Fran sure she wants to share a place with someone like that?

Be aware of the times when you are behaving illogically or have an extreme emotional reaction to an event or statement. Ask yourself: "Why did I say or do that? Do I really believe this? Am I wrong?" Few people are willing to probe this deeply to determine how to make the best decision. Those who do will learn to be more open to new or novel ideas. When this occurs, better and more creative decisions will be the outcome.

EXERCISE 4.9: Decision Making Through Critical Thinking

Think of a recent decision that you have made and analyze how critical thinking affected your decision.

If you realized that little if any critical thinking was used in making your decision, how could you have used it in this situation to arrive at an alternative decision that may have been more productive or creative? Determine what step you omitted that would have helped you make the best decision.

Review the critical strategies that have been presented and discuss two ways that you can personalize them in your decisions concerning your course work this semester.

Critical Thinking and Creativity

Critical thinking and creativity are both skills that enhance your learning and life. While we have discussed creative flow, we have not directly discussed creativity. What exactly is ***creativity***? According to Csikszentmihalyi, creativity "is [the ability] to bring into existence something genuinely new that is valued enough to be added to the culture" (*Creativity*, 25). Simply stated, this means that a creative act will be novel and appreciated by others in a community. Knowing this definition, who do you consider to be a creative person? A couple of examples of creative people are:

© lev radin/Shutterstock.com

Nobel Prize Winners: (All of them!) In 2006 a Nobel Prize was awarded to Muhammad Yunus. This economics professor is noteworthy for many reasons, primarily being that he created the concept of micro-loans and the Grameen Bank in a poverty stricken Bangladesh, India. He is heralded as the "banker to the poor" through loans granted from the Grameen to impoverished people.

© Eugene Ivanov/Shutterstock.com

Artists: Pablo Picasso (25 October 1881–8 April 1973) and Georges Braque are credited for inventing "cubism" the most influential art form of the twentieth century. This art form is recognized by the process where cubists deconstruct a subject and then construct a new abstract representation of the subject. It reflects the events in history that were taking place during World War I and II that constantly challenged the traditional political and personal beliefs of the population. Look at the picture above to understand how the two-dimensional objects create many interpretations. Influences of cubism are evident in: Orphism, Futurism, Vorticism, Suprematism, Constructivism and Expressionism art forms.

While these examples of creative people and your ability to become their equal may seem a bit intimidating, it is possible. Keep in mind that many creative people come from humble origins. How can you be creative as a student? If you invest the time and energy to learn how to connect the concepts in your courses you will then be able to construct or synthesize them into a new idea or form. This in and of itself is a sign of a critical thinker, but is it really fulfilling Csikszentmihalyi's criteria for creativity? He would agree that is a creative act if you were to get a positive response in the form of a grade or addition to the body of research because it would be and into the "culture." If this sounds like it is a discipline that is learned over time, it is.

EXERCISE 4.10: Creativity and Critical Thinking

Having learned the definition and seeing an example of creativity and critical thinking, compare and contrast them in the graph below.

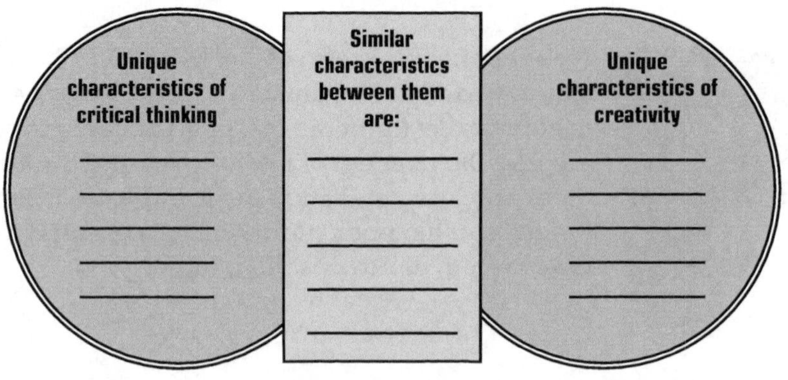

Write a brief summary of how critical thinking and creativity are similar and different.

____

____

____

Do you think that creative thinking enhances critical thinking? Explain the relationship between critical thinking and creativity.

____

____

____

Multiple Perspectives

Because it is often challenging to understand how to view a problem from multiple perspectives, as mentioned briefly in the four steps for critical thinking, you will be given instruction on how to apply this information. Multiple perspectives are simply that, more than one point of view or ways of looking at a situation or an event. A classic example of this is seen in the Indian folkloric story of how blind men who are feeling different sections of the elephant explain it from their perspective. For example, one man touches the trunk of the elephant and describes it very differently from the man who is touching the elephant's tail. Depending on what version you read, there are between three to six men trying to explain what an elephant is to the other men from their experience and perspective. The story is told that these men eventually begin to argue as to who is right or wrong. In the end, they realize that they are all describing the elephant from different perspectives, and that accounts for the disagreement. This story is similar to real life as it demonstrates that a personal perspective is based on experience.

EXERCISE 4.11: Interpreting a Graph

Could the sport of fishing produce a graph like this?

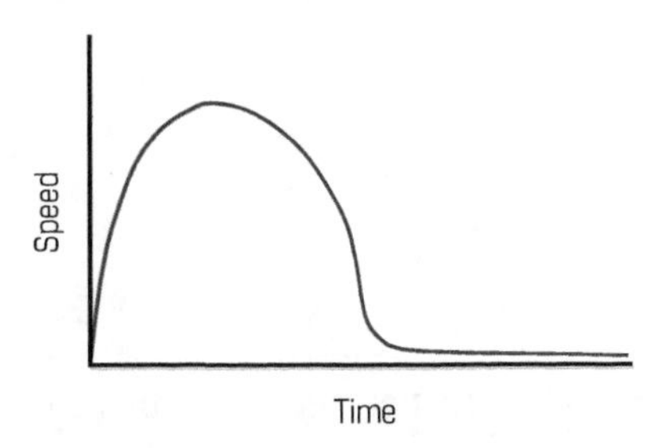

Give a reason explaining why you think it does fit or does not fit the graph. Describe what other information you might need to know to answer this question. How does your personal perspective affect your comments?

OBJECTIVE 10: Understand Real-Life Applications for Creative Problem-Solving

In today's society there are multiple perspectives that are based on each person's unique viewpoint. If each person clings too tightly to their one true perspective, there can be limited agreement or ***creative problem solving***. As a college student, you are going to be given numerous opportunities to see the world from new and different perspectives. Often students want to argue, much like the blind men and the elephant, but the students who are willing and eager to seek another person's perspective will be the beneficiaries of greater insight, knowledge, and creative problem solving. The increased knowledge and insight actually support the creative problem solving process.

Have you heard the expression to "think outside the box?" This is what can happen by being willing to see multiple perspectives on a particular situation. The opportunity to see more than one perspective means that you will acknowledge the validity of race, gender, religion, experiences, and attitudes that will enhance your ability to think outside the box.

Consider car keys. For years, you needed three keys for your car: one for the ignition, one for the doors, and one for the trunk. Years went by and someone thought of a way to only require two keys: one for the ignition and doors and one for the trunk. More time went by and someone created a way to use a single key for the ignition, doors, and trunk. Now, some cars have no keys. That's thinking "outside the box!"

EXERCISE 4.12: Different Perspectives

Consider the following scenario:

© BlueSkyImage/Shutterstock.com

The young woman at the counter is the only customer service representative available at the moment.

Customer Service Representative (we'll call her "Rep"): Your refund will be reflected on your credit card within one bill cycle. Please let us know if it does not appear.

Man: Thank you for the assistance.

Rep: Have a good day, Sir. Next?

Woman: I've been waiting for over five minutes to get some service.

Rep: I apologize for the delay, but currently I am the only one here. I am working as quickly as I can. How can I help you?

Woman: I purchased this vase as a present and I need to return it.

Rep: Do you have your receipt?

Woman: <with attitude> No, I don't have the receipt. As I said, it was for a gift.

Rep: OK, that's all right. Do you have the gift receipt that would have come with it?

Woman: <attitude and eye rolling> Of course not! The receipt was given with the gift.

Rep: The person who received the gift should then be the one to return it.

Woman: < exasperated> The gift was returned to me when it could not be delivered.

Rep: Then I'm not sure what you're asking for, if you say you don't have the gift receipt, but the gift was returned to you.

Woman: <angry, now.> Look, you can see that I purchased it here because your store logo is on the price tag. I removed the price but you can scan it in your computer to see the cost and just give me my money back.

Rep: I'm sorry, but the store policy is not to refund items without a sales or gift receipt. Ma'am, there are other people waiting in line that I need to help and I cannot help you with your situation.

Woman: Is there a manager that I can speak with?

Rep: Absolutely. I will call her and she will be here as soon as possible. In the meantime, would you please step aside and let me assist our other customers?

Woman: <huffy> Okay.

Manager: Good afternoon. How may I be of service?

Woman explains situation to the manager. She has calmed down just a bit.

Manager: I understand your situation, but our store does have policies about returns. Let me look at something. <Manager takes the vase and scans the bar code on the bottom of the box.> The scan indicates that the final cost of the vase was $19.97.

Woman: <incredulous, voice getting louder> But I paid $27.95 for that vase!

Manager: I understand that may be true, but the vase was put on sale after the holidays at $19.97.

Woman: But I want the full price I paid for this vase refunded!

Manager: The absolute best we can do is give you a store credit for $19.97 because you do not have the original receipt or the gift receipt.

Woman: But I want my money back, not some store credit. I don't shop here all that often!

Manager: Unfortunately, that is all we can do. It is your choice. You can accept the store credit for the $19.97 or take nothing.

Woman: Is there someone else that I can talk to about this? This is ridiculous!

Manager: I am the manager of this department, so there is no one else you can talk with here.

Woman: What about the store manager? Surely he or she is interested in a regular patron. You don't want to lose a valuable customer like me.

Manager: In order to speak to the store manager, you will need to call his office and make an appointment. I will write down the number for you.

Woman: <huffy and sarcastically> Thanks a lot for the "service." I will tell all my friends and neighbors just how your treat your customers!

How would you describe the **perspective** of the customer service representative in this scenario?

____

____

____

____

How would you describe the **perspective** of the woman in this scenario?

____

____

____

____

How would you describe the **perspective** of the customer service manager in this scenario?

____

____

____

____

How would you describe the **perspective** of the man standing behind the woman in this scenario?

____

____

____

____

Describe any discrepancies you found in the scenario.

____

____

____

____

Is there anything you can think of that the customer service representative could have done differently which might have diffused the situation?

____

____

____

____

Finding creative solutions to life's challenges can be accomplished by reviewing critical thinking stages listed in this chapter and combining it with creativity. The ***four stages of critical*** decision making are 1. Think Clearly; 2. Focus on the Point; 3. ***Question your Questions***; and 4. Be Judicious. While you are brainstorming solutions using this method, you begin to think outside the box by considering all the possible perspectives involved in the situation. Brainstorm as many possible scenarios as you can. After you have exhausted your brainstorming of different perspectives, determine if there is one that stands out as the optimum solution or if there is a combination of two that will be the best choice. Write out your thinking through each stage, so you can follow your logic to completion.

Now try to apply the creative problem solving process to a real-life situation.

EXERCISE 4.13: Conflict Resolution

Describe a recent conflict you witnessed or were engaged in and its outcome.

____

____

____

____

Elaborate on the various perspectives that should have been considered in determining a solution.

Write an alternative solution based on the creative problem solving you just learned.

COURSE CONNECTIONS:

Job Prospects in the STEM Fields

Science
Technology
Engineering
Mathematics

Have you ever considered a job in a STEM field? One thing to know is that jobs are available and predicted to grow! Consider this: employment in Science, Technology, Engineering, and Mathematics areas is expected to grow almost twice as fast as non-STEM areas through 2018.

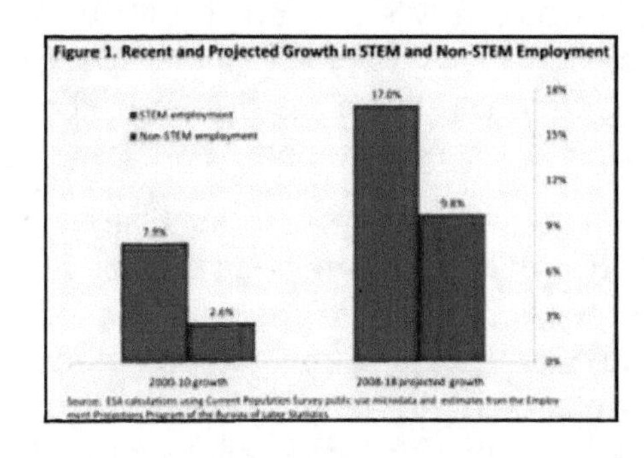

Source: http://www.esa.doc.gov/sites/default/files/stemfinalyjuly14_1.pdf

Possible Careers:

	Biostatistician	Apps Software Developer
Park Naturalist	Astronomer	Product Safety Engineer Auditor
Cost Estimator	Engineer	Automotive Engineering Technician
Architectural Drafter	Auditor	

Using your college catalog, identify one introductory course in each STEM field that you might be interested in taking.

Field	Course
Science	
Technology	
Engineering	
Mathematics	

CHAPTER SUMMARY

In this chapter you have acquired the knowledge of how to think like a professor through learning the "secrets" stored in the vaults of higher education.

The first "secret" is to use Bloom's Taxonomy to create questions of inquiry and set learning goals. The ultimate goal of using Bloom's Taxonomy is to employ your higher order thinking skills that include analysis, synthesis, and evaluation. And, of course, this will help you anticipate potential test questions.

The second "secret" is to strive for creative flow because most of your professors have experienced flow during their research and are probably experiencing it during a lecture. Your professors are modeling how to become interested in a topic to the point that you are learning to master a discipline or skill and they are challenging you to use this discipline or skill in novel ways. Eventually, you will experience most of the seven characteristics of creative flow.

The third "secret" that will help you think like a professor is to strive for self-actualization. In order for your professor to master the philosophical and intellectual challenges he or she has achieved self-actualization. Because your professor is on this level, he or she is expecting you to learn through dialogue and questioning of facts that offer the opportunity to be creative, moral, and spontaneous problem solvers, and achieve the acceptance of diversity and reality. In so doing, you will be motivated to fulfill your potential. By understanding in that Maslow's "Hierarchy of Needs" is a framework for you to use as a scaffold to construct your basic needs, safety, and intimacy, you are better equipped to increase your self-esteem and arrive at self- actualization.

The fourth "secret" in learning to think like your professor is to employ critical thinking when learning and making decisions. Professors are typically eager to think about various ways to solve a problem to discover the best solution because their minds are trained to think this way. When you are a student in a class and realize there is a challenge, using critical thinking skills will open up more possibilities for the best solution.

The fifth "secret" to thinking like a professor is to see multiple perspectives in any given situation. This will allow you to be more creative in resolving problems because you can see the bigger picture. Remember that the elephant being described by the men in the folktale was really the same animal that was described from different perspectives. In order to seek multiple perspectives you will need to think outside the box.

Throughout this chapter we reviewed a variety of ways to understand critical thinking as it is related to creative problem solving. This information concerns your current standing as a college student but has far reaching effects throughout your life. Decision making becomes progressively more challenging as you go through life. Now, you are deciding on important matters such as what to choose for a college major, what you want to do for the rest of your life, and whether you will get married and start a family. Decision making is an endless task that will be a learning process throughout your life.

CHAPTER 4: Self-Check

Vocabulary: Define the following:

1. Bloom's Taxonomy
2. Objectives
3. Creative Flow
4. Critical Thinking
5. Creative Problem Solving Process
6. Decision making Process
7. Creativity
8. Multiple perspectives
9. Question your Questions
10. Focus on the Point
11. Thinking clearly
12. Judicious
13. Core Curriculum

Concepts:

14. Explain the states of Bloom's Taxonomy and describe how they can be used to increase your learning.
15. Describe the connections in the course materials that are created through the use of Bloom's Taxonomy.
16. Explain how questions can create deeper learning connections in a course.
17. List and discuss the components of Csikszentmihalyi's creative thinking flow.
18. Describe the seven characteristics that indicate a person is experiencing creative flow.
19. Compare and contrast creative flow and Maslow's self-actualization.
20. Describe how creative flow components can affect goals.
21. Explain how critical thinking influences the decision making process.
22. Explain the five steps suggested for improving a person's critical thinking skills.
23. Explain how a critical thinker can view a problem from multiple perspectives.
24. List the taxonomy levels and describe the skills at each level.
25. Give an example of each taxonomy level using a single topic.
26. Discuss the hierarchical nature of the levels.
27. Compare and contrast the contiguous levels.
28. Classify stated objectives by taxonomy level.

29. Discuss the academic rigor of each taxonomy level.
30. Select a topic from this course and develop a test question for each taxonomy level.
31. Describe the process used to write questions through the use of Bloom's Taxonomy.
32. Explain how the questions create deeper learning connections in a course.
33. Predict how the use of Bloom's taxonomy for question generation will affect your future learning in college courses.
34. Discuss two strategies for engaging taxonomy during note-taking.
35. Discuss two strategies for engaging taxonomy during reading.
36. Discuss two strategies for engaging taxonomy during active listening.
37. Describe creative flow and self-actualization as it relates to one personal experience.
38. Apply the creative flow components to one personal goal.
39. Apply the creative flow components to one academic goal.
40. Identify ways to apply creative flow to long-term goals.
41. Analyze how critical thinking affected a recent decision.
42. Discuss how critical thinking can improve the decision making process.
43. Discuss two strategies for improving critical thinking.
44. Contrast critical thinking and creativity.
45. Explain the application of critical thinking and creativity.
46. List the options for different perspectives.
47. Describe multiple perspectives for a given scenario.
48. List two strategies to improve critical thinking.
49. Apply the creative problem solving process to a real-life situation.
50. Create three note cards for this chapter, the first with a true-false test question, the second with a multiple choice test question, and the third with an essay question.

CHAPTER 5

Maintaining a Positive Attitude

T.I.P.S. (Tactical Information that Promotes Success)

Maintaining (or developing) a positive attitude will contribute to a meaningful college experience.

Going up!

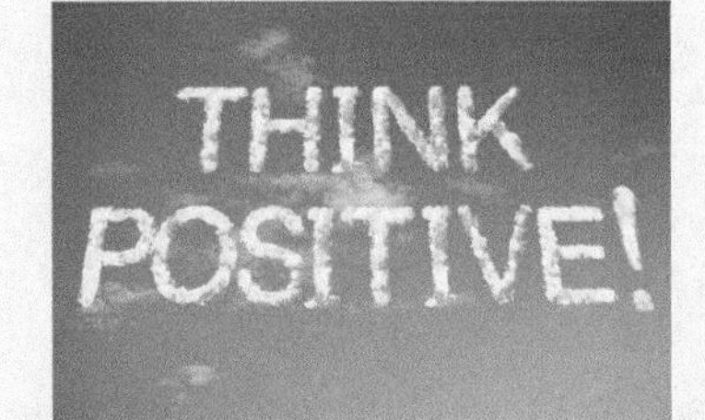

© phloxii/Shutterstock.com

Students with a positive attitude can turn learning into a positive experience!

© wow.subtropica/Shutterstock.com

© marekuliasz/Shutterstock.com

Zig Zigler, a motivational speaker, is credited with saying, "Your attitude, not your aptitude, will determine your altitude."

Approaching tasks of any type with a positive outlook will increase your altitude! It may be seen in simple ways such as feeding your mind, body, and soul with positive ideas. One practical way to accomplish this is positive self-talk. Before you get out of bed in the morning, say "This is going to be a great day!" You will be surprised how much better your day will become after saying this to yourself.

Mathematics: One little word makes a big difference . . . "I'm just not good at math" is often heard from frustrated students. Notice how the addition of one three-letter word can offer an elevated attitude when one says, "I'm not good at math, **YET**." You will be positively surprised how this little word changes your attitude toward mathematics.

Reading: Reading positive and insightful materials that increase an optimistic outlook feed the mind to become more positive.

Writing: Reading to write allows authors to experience more flow in the process. Striving to experience this positive energy when writing offers rewarding outcomes.

Education: A teacher's positive attitude causes a chain reaction of positive thoughts, events, and outcomes. It is a catalyst, sparking extraordinary results. Additionally, teacher's attitudes can determine a student's success. According to the "self-fulfilling prophecy," teacher attitudes towards a student will determine their success or failure. If a teacher was found to have a positive attitude of a student, the student was more likely to be successful. In contrast, teacher's negative attitudes toward a student seemed to lead to failure. Thus, teacher's attitudes matter significantly!

CHAPTER 5: OBJECTIVES

5.1 Developing a Positive Attitude

Objective 1 Understand Attitudes Associated with Classes and Assignments

Objective 2 Understand the Relationship between Grades and Self-Efficacy

Objective 3 Understand How to Redirect Challenges

5.2 Creating Intrinsic Motivational Strategies

Objective 4 Understand Locus of Control and How it Can be Adjusted

Objective 5 Understand the Relationship between Locus-of-Control and Self-Actualization

5.3 Managing Stress

Objective 6 Understand Strategies to Maintain Good Mental Health

Objective 7 Understand Strategies to Facilitate Good Physical Health

Objective 8 Understand Strategies to Manage Finances

CHAPTER CONCEPTS:

Some or all of the following terms may be new to you. Place a check mark in the column reflecting your knowledge of each term.

	Know	Don't know	Not sure	Page # where first found		Know	Don't know	Not sure	Page # where first found
psychological pollution					eustress				
Expectancy Theory					distress				
self-efficacy					endorphins				
intrinsic motivation					Federal loans				
extrinsic motivation					private loans				
locus of control					grants				
internal locus of control					Federal Work-Study Program				
external locus of control									

5.1 DEVELOPING A POSITIVE ATTITUDE

© TinaImages/Shutterstock.com

"People are just as happy as they make up their minds to be." Abraham Lincoln

"If you say you can or you can't you are right either way." Henry Ford

"Change your thoughts and you change your world." Norman Vincent Peale

"The worst disability in life is a bad attitude." SupaNova Slom

"Sometimes I succeed, sometimes I fail, but every day is a clean slate and a fresh opportunity." Gretchen Rubin

In 1956 Norman Vincent Peale wrote *The Power of Positive Thinking*, which continues to garner attention because of the practical suggestions he offered to his readers. Peale's words of encouragement inspired leaders to greatness and offered inspiration to all who met him. Many of the topics he wrote about are still in vogue today. For example, his book includes a chapter entitled "How to Create Your Own Happiness," which is still a much written about topic as evidenced by Gretchen Rubin's book, *The Happiness Project: Or, Why I Spent a Year Trying to Sing in the Morning, Clean My Closets, Fight Right, Read Aristotle, and Generally Have More Fun* (2009). Finding happiness by developing a positive attitude may sound as if one is stating the obvious, but for many the connection is a mystery. In this chapter you will learn how a positive attitude contributes to your long-term happiness and methods for maintaining a positive attitude.

EXERCISE 5.1: Positive Attitude

On a scale of 1 to 10 with 1 being "extremely negative" attitude and 10 being "extremely positive" attitude, how would you rate your attitude TODAY? Circle the number reflecting your attitude.

Extremely negative									**Extremely positive**
1	2	3	4	5	6	7	8	9	10

REFLECTION 5.A:

Seriously consider your answer to the exercise. Explain your reasons for your attitude TODAY.

____

____

____

Describe your attitude today. Would you say it is typical for you or are there extenuating circumstances affecting your current attitude? Explain how your overall attitude for this academic term compares with your current attitude.

___

___

___

OBJECTIVE 1: Understand Attitudes Associated with Classes and Assignments

In your course work there will be some classes and assignments with greater interest to you than others. It seems easier to complete the work when the assignment appears relevant or more interesting. The challenge of doing well in college, and life in general, is knowing how to motivate yourself to maintain a positive attitude when the work seems irrelevant and perhaps even boring. Face it: even the most optimistic people have days that seem darker when the motivation to perform well is lost.

According to the *National Mental Health Association*, there are some basic tips for enjoying life:

1. Balance work and play.
2. Engage in activities you enjoy and look forward to.
3. Discover the "elf" in yourself. Learn to have fun.
4. Improve your laugh life. He who laughs, lasts.
5. Participate in activities with people who share your interests.
6. Reward yourself with little things that make you feel good.
7. Live a healthy lifestyle (i.e., eat well, exercise, and get sufficient sleep).
8. Challenge yourself to do something new.
9. Surround yourself with cheery people. Avoid stress carriers.
10. Shun the "superman" or "superwoman" syndrome. No one is perfect.

Applying these tips to college means you need to seriously consider each of the ten suggestions as they apply to your current life. Initially, you will learn to balance work and play through the suggestions on scheduling offered in Chapter 2. In that chapter you were encouraged to proactively plan time for study, classes, work, and healthy life choices.

Perhaps you are thinking tips 2, 3, and 4 suggest the same thing, so take a moment to understand the unique features of each. The first of these suggests you identify activities you enjoy and in which you look forward to participating. For example, plan time in your weekly schedule to do what you enjoy. This may be participating in an intramural activity, reading a novel, painting, or having coffee with friends. It is necessary to devote most of your free time to studying, but the old saying "All work and no play makes Jack a dull boy" really is true! You will not be much fun to be around if all you can talk about is schoolwork. Another way to view this is to select a major and future career you find fun. Confucius said "Find a job you love and you will never work another day in your life." Recent findings suggest taking a vacation is a positive event, but it is the anticipation of the fun during the vacation that boosts happiness. Learning to laugh, according to tip 4, helps your endurance.

Laughter really is the best medicine; it lowers your blood pressure, increases oxygen flow, improves your immune responses, aids in pain management, and increases memory. It is interesting to realize a joke can actually help you remember test materials.

Tips 5–7 focus more on relationships with the potential to reinforce your pleasure in life. It is important to participate in activities with people who share the enjoyment of the event. In college, this may mean meeting with people from your classes who are enjoying learning! Enthusiasm is contagious. Be sure to reward yourself for a job well done, as was discussed in Chapter 2's discussion of SMARTER goal setting. Sometimes, just knowing you are going to do something pleasurable after completing a task makes the task easier. Living a healthy life style is often easier to imagine intellectually than actually doing it. Perhaps finding an exercise buddy will help you change your attitude towards living a healthy lifestyle. Tips for living a healthy life style will be discussed later in this chapter.

"Challenge yourself to do something new," is tip 8. Although you are probably thinking this means trying a new sport or learning to dance, the challenge presents a wide variety of possibilities related to college. For example, when studying, you might want to try new and different strategies. If you have not worked in groups or studied with a partner, consider that approach.

Tip 9, "surround yourself with positive people," is very wise advice. Have you ever spent time with a "Negative Nancy," or "Danny Downer?" If so, you know how much energy this type of person can drain from your reserve, so avoid them. Additionally, have you ever noticed how great you feel after spending time with a positive person? Hanging out with people who are optimistic increases the chances you will be more optimistic.

Finally, trying to be a "superman" or "superwoman" will not bring you long-term happiness. Even Superman® had to make choices as to which situation he could handle at one time. You may be able to accomplish everything for a while, but inevitably, you will fall short at something because you cannot continue to spread your time, energy, and emotions too thinly. It is important to know how much you can take on at any one time and say "no" to additional requests or activities with the potential to overburden you. It is important to realize when to ask others (family or team members) for help in completing some of these tasks.

EXERCISE 5.2: Attitude

You were given ten tips to help you enjoy life. List the three (3) tips that "speak to you" and explain why you believe they are important (Write out the tip—do not just list the number.)

1. ______________________________

____

____

2. ______________________________

____

____

3. ____

____

____

Some of the tips from the *National Mental Health Association* are those you may have learned from influential people in your life. If you have not had the opportunity to learn from such a person, begin looking for inspirational materials to read on a regular basis to increase your understanding of positive choices. Perhaps start with *The Power of Positive Students* by Dr. William Mitchell!

You might automatically think the previous ten tips to enjoy life would be the same as those suggested for a healthy attitude. However, there are six different pointers from the *National Mental Health Association* for developing a healthy attitude:

1. Set realistic goals for yourself.
2. Be flexible in dealing with people and events. Avoid "psychosclerosis," a hardening of the attitudes.
3. Accept the things you cannot change in yourself or others.
4. Forgive yourself for mistakes.
5. Take satisfaction in your accomplishments. Don't dwell on your shortcomings.
6. Clean up "psychological pollution." See the "positive" in events.

These six tips are specific ways to develop a healthy attitude. Notice the first, "set realistic goals for yourself," was addressed in Chapter 2. Realistic goals mean you understand how to exercise your personal strengths and weaknesses to increase your success. Realistically, it is improbable a person with a low GPA who applies to medical school is going to be admitted. It is unrealistic a first year college student can work a full-time job and perform well when enrolled in a full schedule of college credit work. Unrealistic goals can result in negative thinking, frustrations, and possible failure. In order to avoid these undesired outcomes, set realistic goals.

Flexibility with people and events is necessary for a positive attitude. This means you will need to be aware of how your actions affect the lives of others. For example, perhaps you are a person who likes to go to bed early to get up early and complete your morning routine. Your new roommate, however, loves staying up late as well as sleeping late. Living with another person requires flexibility. You could try to make your roommate follow your routine, but compliance to your schedule is not very likely. Since you really do not have the power to control your roommate's behavior, you can only control your own. Trying to work out a compromise would be the best option.

The next tip for developing a positive attitude is to accept things you cannot change about yourself or others. This one is probably the most challenging. Perhaps you are not athletic or not as attractive as you would like to be. These are things you most likely cannot change. Rather than dwell on these, focus on your strengths. Perhaps you are a good leader or very artistic. The second half of this tip, "to accept the things you cannot change in others," is more difficult. For example, you may have a professor you believe has characteristics that challenge your ability to remain positive in the learning environment. Do you think you will be able to change the distracting tendencies of your professor? This seems unlikely. By convincing yourself to accept this professor may never be able to please you, you take control to maintain a positive attitude by telling yourself you are going to focus on learning the course material.

Forgiving your mistakes will help you maintain a positive attitude even when the circumstances are not at an optimum. Perhaps you failed the first test for the semester. Rather than letting this grade result in a negative attitude, visit your instructor to determine why you may have earned such a grade and move on to the next opportunity to do well in this class. Henry Ford stated, "Failure is simply an opportunity to begin again, this time more intelligently."

Being able to take satisfaction in your accomplishments rather than focusing on your shortcomings is necessary for maintaining a positive attitude. Too often, it is human nature to focus on your failures rather than your successes. Learn to enjoy the moment of your accomplishments by pausing to recognize them. Perhaps you have successfully achieved an "A" on your Physics test, but earned a "C" on a term paper for English. Be sure to slow down and congratulate yourself for the "A" in physics. You might not be happy about the "C" on the term paper, but acknowledge the fact that it is a passing grade! Consider putting the "A" test along the edge of your mirror or on a bulletin board as a reminder of what you have done well. Without dwelling on the less than desired grade of "C" on the essay, meet with your instructor or attend the writing center to determine what you might need to work on before the next paper is due. Focusing on the positive achievements rather than obsessing on the less than perfect attempts will generate a healthier attitude.

Finally, the last tip listed for maintaining a positive attitude is to clean up "psychological pollution. See the 'positive' in events." In order for you to understand this tip, you will need to understand the meaning of **psychological pollution** as the elements in your environment creating anxiety, fatigue, or distress. Psychological pollution is similar to the contaminants in an ecological environment threatening its stability. In other words, you will need to identify the events (or even people) contributing to your anxiety, fatigue, or distress. Then, deliberately focus on the positive events constantly occurring around you. For example, perhaps you are not doing well in your sociology class. This knowledge may cause anxiety when you go to class. Rather than letting the anxiety increase, recognize a good friend or create a new friendship with a person who is taking the class. Talk with your friend prior to class starting about common interests to relieve some of your anxiety. After class, ask your friend about forming a study group. By explicitly determining what the pollutants are in your psychological environment, you can more easily focus on the positive events.

Once you understand the mechanics of developing a positive attitude, you will be able to determine how a more optimistic perspective can alter your course work.

EXERCISE 5.3: Healthy Attitude

You were given six tips to help create a healthy attitude. Considering your answer to Exercise 5.1, list the two (2) tips you believe will be the most effective to help improve your attitude and explain why you believe they will be helpful. (Write out the tip—do not just list the number.)

1. ____

____

____

2. ____

____

____

COURSE CONNECTIONS:
Positive Self-Talk

FIGURE 5.1

As stated earlier, Henry Ford is known for saying, "If you think you can or think you can't—you're right."

What is meant by this is if you believe you can accomplish something, you are willing to work for it. If you do not believe you can accomplish something, then you will not put in much, if any, effort.

If you are having difficulty in your mathematics course, try positive self-talk. No, you're not being asked to walk around mumbling to yourself! Instead, mentally, or aloud when you are alone, say to yourself: "I may not very strong in math, YET, but I am capable of learning the concepts necessary to pass my mathematics course. I will work to improve my skills."

FIGURE 5.2

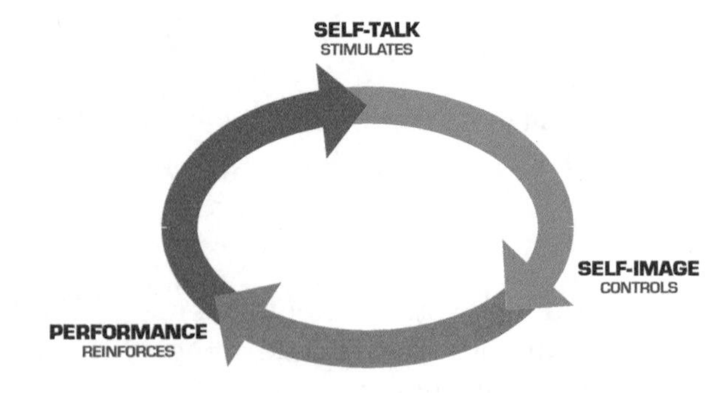

As illustrated in Figure 5.2 positive self-talk stimulates you to make changes in your thinking. These changes, in turn, will improve your self-image. When you believe you can work math problems correctly, your performance will improve. Once your performance improves, you have more reason to continue positive self-talk. However, all these changes are dependent on the fact that you are willing to work to improve your mathematics skills by whatever means are necessary.

In spite of occasional setbacks, use your positive self-talk and increase your efforts to be successful!

REFLECTION 5.B:

Try positive self-talk for ONE WEEK for a course in which you might not be performing as well as you would like. After one week, answer the following questions about your experience.

1. How often did you repeat your positive self-talk during the week? ____________________
2. Do you believe the positive self-talk made a difference in your PERFORMANCE in class over the week? Y/N Explain your answer.

____

____

____

3. Do you believe the positive self-talk made a difference in your ATTITUDE toward class?

____

4. In what ways was your attitude changed? Give specific examples.

____

____

____

EXERCISE 5.4: Attitudes toward Coursework

Describe your attitude concerning your courses and upcoming assignments by completing this chart.

Current Courses	**Upcoming assignment**	**My current attitude toward the assignment is ________. Briefly explain the origin of this attitude.**	**Which of the six tips can I use to overcome or improve my attitude? (Write out the tips)**
EXAMPLE: Microbiology	Test	Negative because I never do well on Dr. M's tests.	Forgive my mistakes and see the positive in events.

Summarize the discoveries you made from analyzing your attitudes.

____

____

____

____

OBJECTIVE 2: Understand the Relationship between Grades and Self-Efficacy

Try to remember what you have written while moving forward in understanding the **Expectancy Theory**. This motivational theory suggests people anticipate an outcome by the effort made toward the desired outcome as illustrated in Figure 5.3.

FIGURE 5.3

Expectation	*This paper in English is going to be difficult because I don't like to write.*
+Effort	*+ I will read the directions, go to the Writing Center, and try my best to do well.*
Desired Outcome	*I will earn an "A" or a "B" on this essay.*

When students study or work diligently to achieve a specific grade, they expect to make the grade for which they worked. Generally, a lesser effort is translated into lesser success but it is possible to work hard and receive a disappointing grade. However, this theory suggests your expectations and efforts produce desired outcome.

EXERCISE 5.5: Application of Expectancy Theory

Look back at the responses you gave in exercise 5.4. Compare your expected approach to class assignments to those within the Expectancy Theory.

Course	Assignment	Expectancy Theory

The Expectancy Theory intersects with **self-efficacy**, the belief in your ability to finish a project or meet a goal. Self-efficacy is often confused with self-esteem, which is your perception of your overall worthiness. It is possible to have a strong self-efficacy with a low self-esteem or even a high self-esteem and weak self-efficacy. Your self-efficacy can actually perpetuate a motivational cycle. This means you reflect on the successes in the past to determine how effectively you anticipate your performance in the current challenge.

FIGURE 5.4 Self-Efficacy and the Learning Cycle

Strong Self-Efficacy

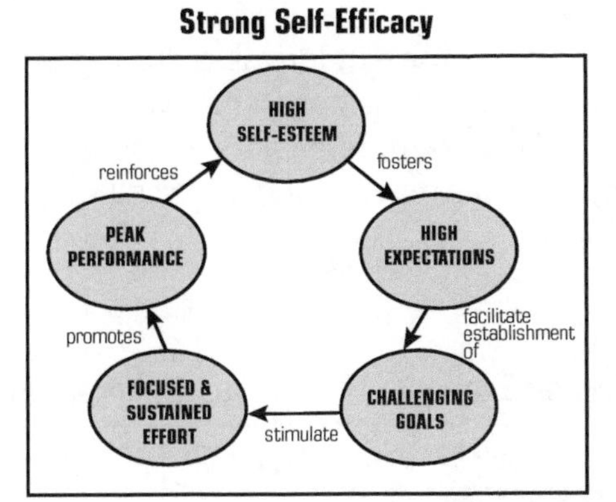

Weak Self-Efficacy

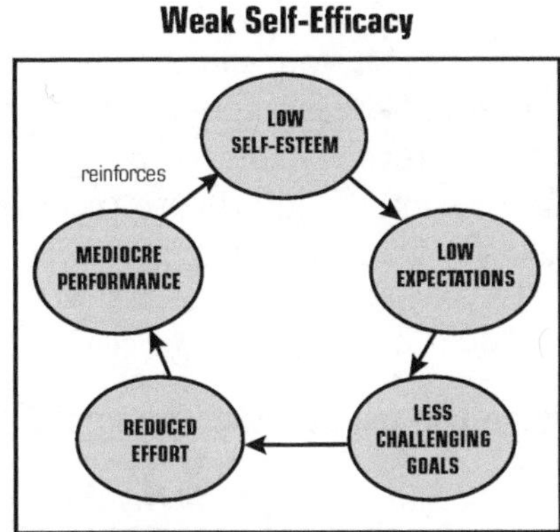

Basically, if you anticipate success, you will achieve it through your sustained efforts in studying. Success leads to success. In contrast, if you have not experienced success in learning, it is more likely you will suffer with a weak self-efficacy and be less motivated to try or employ new learning strategies. Whatever your level of self-efficacy regarding learning new course material, you will unconsciously defer your judgment concerning success or failure to your previous experiences. Thus, the motivation is either ignited or extinguished.

EXERCISE 5.6: Self-Efficacy and Self-Esteem

Discuss the difference between self-efficacy and self-esteem.

____

____

EXERCISE 5.7: Self-Efficacy and Course Grades

Discuss the connections between self-efficacy and course grades.

____

____

____

____

____

Students with a strong self-efficacy will be more persistent, tenacious, and able to recover more readily from failure. Significant research has been published to aid in the understanding of how self-efficacy alters a student's motivation to learn. For this reason, learning strategies increase a student's self-efficacy are beneficial for college success.

Learning strategies to increase self-efficacy may include reflection, double-checking, and comparative studies.

Reflection

Keep a learning journal for your class. Self-monitor what you are learning, how well you are feeling about your progress in the class, specific ways you have seen success, and even a learning log allows you to chart your progress visually as in Figure 5.5. For example, most textbooks include a quiz for each chapter. After taking it, record your progress. You may want to include multiple attempts in your chart to more fully see your progress.

FIGURE 5.5 Learning Log for Self-Monitoring of Success Example: Humanities Chapter Quizzes

	Chapter 1	Chapter 2	Chapter 3
100%			
75%			
50%			
25%			
10%			
0%			

You may wonder if the benefits in keeping a reflective journal are worth the time. Basically, the point in keeping this journal is to increase your self-efficacy by seeing your successes. The more you see and understand your personal successes, the more you will understand what is effective in your learning strategies.

A journal is also beneficial in determining how effectively you are using your time when you include questions concerning your schedules. For example, if you begin writing your English essay four weeks prior to the due date, you will be able to record you started on the research and writing with ample time to write well. When you go to the writing center for assistance, you will be able to record this positive step as well. By taking this journal through the entire writing process, you will see its effectiveness on the positive outcome.

Double-Checking

Since written homework in college, generally associated with hard sciences, is not traditionally taken up and given a grade, the need to check your work rests upon your shoulders. As you complete the exercises in your textbook, check the answers (usually in the back of your book or at a companion website). When you check your work, do not merely see what you got wrong or right. Ask yourself, WHY you missed it and HOW you can change your thinking for the next time you encounter this problem (one like it) or question.

Comparative Studies

Frequently, students believe learning is easier for "smart" people. In other words, a person with a perceived high IQ does not have to put forth as much effort as those with a lower IQ. While this may have some truth, it does not mean "smart" people do not have to work for their successes. In addition, there are some people who are naturally "smart" in mathematics or history. Naturally "smart" people may have to work harder in their more challenging subjects. All of this to say, working to learn is required by everyone!

Typically, students who earn higher grades understand the amount of effort necessary to do well. Seek out three students who are earning "A's" or high "B's" in a course in which you might be having trouble. Interview them using these questions:

1. How many hours per week do you study?
2. If you know you have a major test in a week, how do you pace your study time?
3. When you write an essay, how much time do you allow to complete it? Do you have someone read it over? Do you include multiple drafts?
4. What advice would you offer to a student concerning the time and effort you invest in studying and the outcome?

Once you have completed the interviews, analyze the information for what is most effective for you.

EXERCISE 5.8: Comparative Study

Since you have completed the comparative study, discuss why you agree or disagree with this line of thinking.

____

____

____

____

____

____

Reflect for a moment on your most recent successes in studying for a class. Success may have come in the form of an "A" on a test, report, paper, or project. Or it may have been reflected in an increase from a lower to higher grade or overall grade average in a class.

EXERCISE 5.9: Examining Successes

Write down three (3) of your most recent successes, describe them, and list the strategies you applied to attain this success.

Successful moment	Description	Strategies I applied to create this success.

Based on the information you have written in the above chart, discuss how your applications of successful strategies can be used to predict greater college success.

____

____

____

____

Reveling in the victories or successful accomplishments in your college career is rewarding. Perhaps they are rewarding because you understand the amount of focus and energy expended on achieving them. Have you ever heard understanding joy requires a person to experience pain? Without the understanding of pain, joy loses its significance. Similarly, understanding the fullness of success means there may need to be a few setbacks or challenges along the way. Without the setbacks and challenges, success is marginalized. It is through your ability to redirect challenges that success increases as well as the pleasure of overcoming the challenge.

OBJECTIVE 3: Understand How to Redirect Challenges

Have you ever considered the positive role of failure as it concerns motivation? This may be an unusual statement in a college success textbook, but failure can be beneficial—when you *learn* from failure! All Steven Spielberg, multi-Academy Award winning Director, ever wanted to do was make movies. However, he was denied entrance into his desired program, the University of Southern California School of Theatre, Film, and Television, *three times* because of low high school grades. He finally gave up and enrolled in a similar program at another college. He dropped out of school before graduating to pursue directing on his own. The rest is history. Failure does not mean the end of goals and dreams; it can be a catalyst for their achievement. Failure on an examination can help you identify areas of the subject matter requiring additional effort to learn . . . if you choose to use the failure as a learning experience.

Reduce the pressures to pass the test by focusing on learning. Have you ever achieved a love of learning? Do you feel joy when understanding a concept? Do you have a good feeling from achievement? Or, do you equate an "F" with failure of yourself? Separating self-worth from grades is critical if you want to learn from mistakes. Go to visit your professor to discuss strategies for improvement. Remember, activity does not result in progress all the time.

Setbacks can come in all walks of life. Perhaps you have had a setback in a personal relationship has come from a breakup, received a "D" on a test you felt you passed, or had to replace a tire on your car unexpectedly, causing a financial burden. Some other setbacks may have occurred in your previous learning environment, when you were not selected for a competitive team or organization, or promoted in rank as soon as expected. Setbacks are manifested in a wide variety of forms, but all require you to learn to successfully work through them. Take a moment to contemplate a recent setback.

EXERCISE 5.10: Setbacks and Causes

Describe a setback you have experienced.

____

____

____

____

Describe the factors contributing to the setback.

____

____

____

____

What happened at the end of this setback? Hopefully, you were able to successfully work through it and realize its positive benefits. A classic example of someone overcoming a setback is one of Julian Michaels' "Biggest Losers." Julian Michaels is the well-known weight loss motivator from the "Biggest Loser" show. She works with extremely obese people to overcome the setbacks they have experienced in attempting to lose weight. In her book, *Unlimited: How to Build an Exceptional Life,* she states:

> "Part of abandoning the all-or-nothing mentality is allowing yourself room for setbacks. We are bound to have lapses on the road to health and wellness, but it is critical that we learn how to handle small failures positively so that we can minimize their long-term destructive effects. One setback is one setback—it is not the end of the world, nor is it the end of your journey toward a better you."

While your challenges or setbacks may not come in a physical form, the inspiration offered by Michaels it is still applicable. Her philosophy, "One setback is one setback—it is not the end of the world, nor is it the end of your journey . . . " is applicable in your college course work. Learning how to overcome setbacks is a part of life. Once you see you can successfully overcome a setback, you are learning and growing stronger for the challenges of any future setbacks.

EXERCISE 5.11: Setbacks into Successes

Describe how your previously stated successes (Exercise 5.9) can contribute to reversing a setback into a success.

____

____

____

____

Happiness is a natural byproduct of successfully overcoming life's setbacks. Have you ever met someone who you think is a positive person who told you their life story of heartache? It always seems surprising when the people who seem to be bright and full of life explain the hardship they have endured. There seem to be a large number of professional entertainers who have had this type of life. Rapper and actor LL Cool J's autobiography, *I Make My Own Rules* (1997), tells his story of growing up in the home of a single-mother whose live-in boyfriend abused him. He found solace in rapping. He could have chosen to remain bitter, but he chose to change his life. As a result, he found a happier life with his longtime wife, Simonne, and their four children. Choices you make will determine your lifelong happiness as well.

The term "happiness" has been used in this book and is found routinely in today's media. What does this term mean? Sometimes it can be a vague concept with a wide variety of meanings or applications. Basically, it means learning to be content with who you are and what you have. In psychologist Ed Diener's book, *Happiness: Unlocking the Mysteries of Psychological Wealth* (2008), he explains "subjective well-being" [happiness] is the combination of life satisfaction and having more positive emotions than negative emotions." If you are happy today, it may or may not mean you will be happy in the long run. Happiness is measured in both the short term and the long-term.

The understanding of happiness begs the question, how can you strive for a happier life for your entire life? This can be explained by comprehending the connections between your choices made today and happiness for your life. One way to realize the effect of your immediate choices on your future is to write your obituary. While this may sound morbid, it really is a great way to determine your current choices. For example, if you want to be remembered for your generosity in giving money for the betterment of children, you will need to learn how to earn enough money with which you can be generous. Additionally, you will want to become familiar with worthy organizations caring for children. Take a minute to read a few obituaries online or in your local paper to help you understand how obituaries serve as a brief synopsis of a person's life.

EXERCISE 5.12: Write Your Obituary

A few suggestions to help get you started include:

- *Full name of the deceased (including maiden name, nickname, or any other name by which your loved one might be identified).*
- *Dates and locations of birth, marriage, and death.*
- *Cause of death.*
- *Predeceased and surviving loved ones' names.*

- *Schools attended.*
- *Military service.*
- *Place of employment and position held.*
- *Membership in organizations (for example, civic, fraternal, church).*
- *Hobbies or special interests.*
- *Charities to which you have donated money.*
- *Remarks or comments about you made by influential people in your life.*
- *Funny or interesting fact about your life.*
- *Passions in your life.*
- *Personal quotes or statements defining your life.*
- *Your source of happiness.*

____

____

____

____

____

Describe your feelings writing your obituary. Be specific and include any challenges you experienced during the process.

____

____

____

____

____

____

Hopefully, you found the writing of your personal obituary to be beneficial in predicting the current choices you will need to make. Based on your writing, predict where you will be in:

Five years: ______________________________

Ten years: ______________________________

Twenty years: ______________________________

Discuss your attainment of happiness: ______________________________

____

____

____

Now that you understand the meaning of happiness, how your choices determine your immediate and long-term happiness, and what you want people to say about you after you die, identify the elements of your long-term happiness. In other words, what will you need to do to insure your personal happiness?

EXERCISE 5.13: Components of Happiness

Write three of the most critical components of your happiness: what will you need to do to insure your personal happiness?

1. ______________________________

   ____

   ____

2. ______________________________

   ____

   ____

3. ______________________________

   ____

   ____

Describe and discuss two strategies supporting your long-term happiness.

1. ______________________________

   ____

   ____

2. ______________________________

   ____

   ____

5.2 CREATING INTRINSIC MOTIVATIONAL STRATEGIES

Educational psychologists and cognitive specialists define motivation as either intrinsic or extrinsic. **Intrinsic motivation** originates from within you and extrinsic resides externally. Intrinsic motivators are manifested within you in such ways as achieving your goal, learning something interesting, or working a problem alone and getting the correct answer. These bring satisfaction in and of themselves. In contrast, **extrinsic motivation** stems from external factors. Positive extrinsic motivation can come from monetary compensation, earning tangible things, or verbal praise from parents or instructors. An illustration of external motivation would be if you worked to earn straight A's in your first year in college in order to be rewarded with a new car by your parents. While this is an extreme example, it demonstrates the ultimate reward is outside of you.

Not all extrinsic motivation is positive, however. Fear of failure is a strong extrinsic motivator! For example, perhaps your parents are paying your expenses for college and all have agreed should your first semester grades be less than a "C" average, their support will end. You would then be responsible for all your expenses if you want to continue attending college. Failing a course would have serious personal consequences. Sometimes a negative extrinsic motivator is stronger than a positive one.

EXERCISE 5.14: Intrinsic and Extrinsic Motivation

Give an example of an intrinsic motivator and an extrinsic motivator in your life. Try to relate each to your college experience.

Intrinsic ____

____

Extrinsic ____

____

While the educational and cognitive psychologists have determined internal motivation is the better of the two, it seems both (intrinsic and extrinsic) are necessary depending on the situation. In the working world, most people enjoy their job. Being able to satisfy a personal dream is an intrinsic motivator. Outside of volunteers, how many people will be able to stay motivated to work if they do not earn a pay check? Payment for services rendered or duties fulfilled is another important part of positive motivation in the work place. The value of earning a paycheck is real. However, neither external nor internal motivation will satiate a person's ambition in isolation, but when combined, offer a balanced form of motivation.

Take a look at how this balance affects your motivation to earn a good grade in a class. Intrinsic motivation in this situation means you are trying to earn a grade to satisfy something within yourself. Perhaps you did not apply yourself in previous learning environments, but now you want to prove how capable you are to yourself. On the other hand, extrinsic motivation may be seen in earning a grade to avoid being placed on academic probation.

Try to find what motivates you to do your homework. Perhaps you will find it is extrinsic motivators such as money; being paid for good grades. In a way, you are paid through course credits toward a degree. Short term payoffs may include money for passing a course or making an "A." Identifying the type of courses that require some type of external motivation initially, and, then, eventually become realized through internal motivation might be the first step to becoming a successful student and employee in the work place. Maybe the payoff is admission to a four-year institution or graduate school, a better job, or being granted an interview.

EXERCISE 5.15: Motivators for Your Courses

Compare and contrast your internal and external motivations as they relate to your current courses.

Courses	Examples of my INTRINSIC motivators	Examples of my EXTRINSIC motivators
Example: Mathematics	I have studied the chapter, gone to speak with my professor, and have reviewed my notes, so I should be able to do well on this test.	My parents said if I don't well in this class, I can't go snow skiing during spring break.

Most long term satisfaction and the motivation to do well stem from intrinsic motivation. To begin the transition to this intrinsic motivational drive and independence, you must first believe in yourself and your ability to succeed! Be patient in learning. Some subjects take more time and effort than others. One example for learning a concept in mathematics or chemistry might not be enough. To develop intrinsic motivation, you might need to begin with small changes. One such change might be attending a college tutoring lab for mathematics to improve your skills. Developing intrinsic motivation will allow you to become more open to college requirements and see them as opportunities to grow as an independent thinker.

EXERCISE 5.16: Extrinsic to Intrinsic Motivation

What is one small change you might consider to begin the transition to intrinsic motivation in one or more of your classes?

____

____

____

OBJECTIVE 4: Understand Locus of Control and How it Can be Adjusted

In addition to understanding extrinsic and intrinsic motivators in your life, it is important to understand your **locus of control** or self-determination. The degree to which people perceive their environment controls the outcomes in their life suggests they have an **external locus of control**. For example, as a first year college student, you may have stayed out late and skipped several classes. Then, when you failed the midterm exam, you may have blamed the professor for not explaining things well enough for you to pass. This is an external factor you claim is out of your control. If you perceive your ability to control the circumstances of life is within your control, it is said to be you have an **internal locus of control.** Considering the previous example, had you had an internal locus of control, you would have responded to failing the midterm exam by accepting responsibility for not attending class. To discover if you have an internal or an external locus of control, consider the information in the following sections.

Experts agree an internal locus of control puts you in control of making decisions and modifications necessary to meet the demands of college. If you have an external locus of control, you may struggle with those decisions and modifications that could lead to your success in college. Take a look at the statements found in Figure 5.6 to understand the difference in the attitudes of individuals with an internal and those with an external locus of control.

FIGURE 5.6

External locus of control	Internal locus of control
"I do not know why the school required me to take this college success course."	"I hope to gain skills in this course that will apply to my other courses."

Explain which of the two statements sounds more like your attitude toward taking this class.

____

____

____

You may have heard student comments such as:

"The professor did not explain it well."

"This course is too hard for me to understand."

"The tests are not like the material taught in class."

Sometimes it is accurate to say the instructor does not give you what you need to learn well, but you are still responsible for doing everything in your power to be successful. When you feel short changed in a learning environment, seek help from fellow learners, your professor or teaching assistant, or from relevant student services. Learning to ask for help in college demonstrates an internal locus of control because you are still in control of your learning outcomes. This tenacity and internal locus of control will benefit you throughout life. You cannot always accurately predict or dictate what will happen in your life, but you can control your response.

Who do you blame when or if you fail? Who gets credit for your success? Do you say, "I am not good at . . . ?" Or do you say "I could have studied differently"?

EXERCISE 5.17: Locus of Control

Consider the following statements; identify them as *internal* or *external* control.

____________ I cannot believe I am required to visit our instructor during office hours.

____________ I cannot believe I have the opportunity to talk with my professor one-on-one.

____________ My spouse demands a large amount of my time.

____________ I have too much homework.

____________ My boss keeps changing the work schedule, but I need this job so I will rearrange some other things.

Explain if your locus of control is primarily external or internal.

____

____

____

If you have realized you have an external locus of control, list three (3) ways you can work toward making it more of an internal locus of control.

1. ____

2. ____

3. ____

REFLECTION 5.C:

List two (2) areas in which you are internally motivated and two (2) in which you are externally motivated.

Internally Motivated	Externally Motivated

List two (2) areas in which you have an internal locus of control and two (2) areas in which you have an external locus of control. These do not necessarily need to be college related.

Internal Locus of Control	External Locus of Control

As you have seen above, being internally (externally) motivated and having an internal (external) locus of control are NOT the same thing.

1. Compare YOUR *internal* motivation and *internal* locus of control for your examples above and explain how the circumstances of these two areas are different.

____

____

____

____

2. Compare YOUR *external* motivation and *external* locus of control for your examples above and explain how the circumstances of these two areas are different.

____

____

____

____

OBJECTIVE 5: Understand the Relationship between Locus-of-Control and Self-Actualization

Finding ways to shift your external locus of control to an internal locus of control can help you become an independent learner. If you believe you have the power to control your environment, then you will have more motivation to study for an "A." In contrast, if you have an external locus of control, you may believe a professor just arbitrarily assigns you a grade at the end of the semester. By understanding you have the ability to affect the grades you earn, studying will become an area in which you will want to invest your energies.

EXERCISE 5.18: Locus of Control and Self-Actualization

Take a minute to review Maslow's Hierarchy of Needs and self-actualization from Chapter 3.

Make a list of how locus of control and self-actualization are similar.
Make a list of how locus of control and self-actualization are different.
Explain how locus of control contributes to self-actualization and motivation.

Sometimes, attitudes toward certain subjects are developed as a result of previous experiences, but attitudes can also be developed by the people or circumstances around you. Can you break the barriers of societal views of mathematics? Why does it seem socially acceptable to say "I cannot do math" while saying "I cannot read" would not be socially acceptable?

EXERCISE 5.19: Attitudes toward Mathematics and English Composition

Explain your attitude regarding mathematics. ____________________

____

____

Describe some of the attitudes you hear around you regarding mathematics. Do these attitudes sound more like a person with an internal or external locus of control?

____

____

____

When a negative attitude is prevalent, it may result in poor academic performance. A recommendation to overcome this obstacle is to find your internal locus of control and begin working to change this attitude. Rather than giving the power of your success in mathematics to external forces, assuming the internal locus of control (*I can do this! I will need to allow more time.*) Some students in English composition exercise an external locus of control through avoidance (*My boss needs me to work, so the essay will need to wait.*) and a negative attitude (*I can't write well, so why bother!*). The key is taking back the power to succeed with an internal locus of control. This level of control sounds like: *I need to allow more time to write or do the mathematics homework, since I will need to seek assistance in the Writing Center or math lab.*

One of the challenges in learning mathematics, and most any college level class, is due to the fact that each topic builds on the previous topic. This means a strong foundation is necessary in order to continue learning. An analogy of this is the foundation of a house. If the house is not built on a strong foundation, it will not stand the test of time. Eventually, the walls will cave in. In learning, our ability to learn ideas that are built on top of one another is only as strong as our foundation. Did you enroll in higher level coursework than you have the solid foundation to support? The key to success is to learn concepts for long-term retention in order to increase your strongest background knowledge.

One way to increase the learning in two subjects at one time is to find ways in which they are similar and different. Consider how a student taking a speech and mathematics class finds connections between them to increase her learning in both classes. In her speech class, she was given a requirement to compare a personal characteristic to an inanimate object in a three minute speech. She finds an analogy that clearly communicates the relationships of her perception of mathematics and self in the following way:

"Why I Am Like An Integer"

> *Integers are both positive and negative numbers. Similarly, I have positive and negative sides. For example, I volunteer with children in an afterschool program by tutoring them in math, which is positive. In contrast, I am very selfish with my chocolate . . . No one gets to share MY chocolate, not even my best friend.*
>
> *As with integers, I believe people can count on me. My little brother, he's 15, counts on me to pick him up after school or basketball practice. He and I commiserate over our challenges with mom and dad, too. He counts on me to listen and be there for him.*
>
> *Integers can be prime, having no factors but one and themselves, or composite, having multiple factors. While I sometimes complain about my mom, it's obvious I have inherited many traits from her. There is no denying this makes me similar to an integer because traits from my mother are visible in my eyes, nose, mouth, and hair color. I have traits shared by my mother and father, like composite numbers. This is seen in my mocha colored complexion.*
>
> *In conclusion, what I like most about integers is they have no limit. I am like an integer in this way, too. The opportunities in life are endless and there is no telling how far I can go.*
>
>

This creative-thinking student demonstrates a positive attitude toward speech making and mathematics as she makes connections between these two classes. As you know, the more connections you can make, the greater your successes.

COURSE CONNECTIONS:

Mathematics Anxiety

© Creativa Images/Shutterstock.com

What is Mathematics Anxiety?

Mathematics anxiety is a fear of mathematics, especially when taking tests. Math anxiety generally stems from negative past experiences. It can vary from feeling butterflies in your stomach during a test to throwing up before each one. The physical effects of general anxiety are illustrated in Figure 5.7.

Many students with math anxiety have tried to memorize (rote) their way through courses. While this may have been successful at lower levels and for certain subjects, memorization will not always work. The long-term result is avoidance of math, increased anxiety, and ultimately failure, which begins the cycle.

FIGURE 5.7

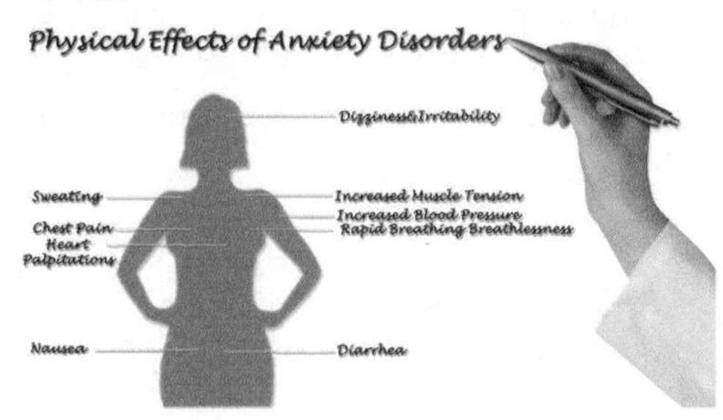

© arka38/Shutterstock.com

Do you have mathematics anxiety?

Probably the easiest way to determine if you have math anxiety is to stage the test-taking situation by reworking one of your tests (covering up the answers) at home. If you are able to work the problems with the correct answers, you most likely have some level of anxiety. If, however, you still miss problems, the difficulty is more likely a misunderstanding of concepts and/or lack of preparation.

What can you do to help yourself?

- avoid trying to memorize steps
- work to understand the connections between concepts
- visit your instructor for ways to refocus your learning
- visit your instructor or the college math center for additional or different explanations of concepts
- if you truly have math anxiety, visit your counseling center where you may be given some information on how to reduce, if not eliminate, your anxiety

You will gain confidence in your mathematical ability, which should result in success followed by the desire to learn more, repeating the cycle, as shown in the top of Figure 5.8.

REFLECTION 5.D:

List the courses you are taking this term. Extra lines have been provided if you are taking more than five courses and/or or science lab portions and/or recitation portions of a course.

Courses:	**Perceived Anxiety Level**
______________________	______
______________________	______
______________________	______
______________________	______
______________________	______
______________________	______
______________________	______

Out to the side of each course, evaluate your anxiety level about the course (not on taking a test) on a scale of 1 to 5 with 1 being "not anxious at all", 3 being "neutral," and 5 being "I get anxious just thinking about it."

Considering ONLY the courses with a score of 1, 2, or 3, describe why you believe you feel little or no anxiety in these.

____

____

____

____

____

____

Considering ONLY those courses with a score of 4 or 5, describe why you believe you feel so much anxiety in these.

____

____

____

____

____

____

Considering ALL courses, are there any circumstances in those lower anxiety courses you may be able to "tap into" to help you lower your anxiety level in those higher anxiety courses?

____

____

____

____

____

____

5.3 MANAGING STRESS

Life's choices are challenging even when they are the "right" choices. Even if you know where you are going and how you are going to get there, stress will be natural. Managing stress is essential to good mental health, overall physical health, and a happier life.

OBJECTIVE 6: Understand Strategies to Maintain Good Mental Health

By understanding a variety of strategies, you will be able to maintain positive mental health. According to the *National Mental Health Association* there are ten characteristics of positive mental health. People with a positive mental health:

1. . . . feel good about themselves.
2. . . . do not become overwhelmed by emotions, such as fear, anger, love, jealousy, guilt, or anxiety.
3. . . . have lasting and satisfying personal relationships.
4. . . . feel comfortable with other people.
5. . . . can laugh at themselves and with others.
6. . . . have respect for themselves and for others even if there are differences.
7. . . . are able to accept life's disappointments.
8. . . . can meet life's demands and handle their problems when they arise.
9. . . . make their own decisions.
10. . . . shape their environment whenever possible and adjust to it when necessary.

At times, stress will serve a positive function, termed **eustress**, as a motivator to complete a task or generate a euphoric feeling. This type of stress can actually be healthy and produce positive attitudes and mental health. The most common example of eustress is the participation in any type of competition. Although the competition is stressful, you are also filled with a rush of adrenalin can increase your oxygenation and interest and result in a better performance.

In contrast, **distress** can trigger the same physiological symptoms, but with less positive outcomes. For example, if entering a room to meet new people causes distress, the physical results may be aggression, anxiety, passivity, or withdrawal. Distress may be triggered from a single event and alter a person's mental health if left untreated.

FIGURE 5.8 The Relationship Between Stress and Learning/Performance

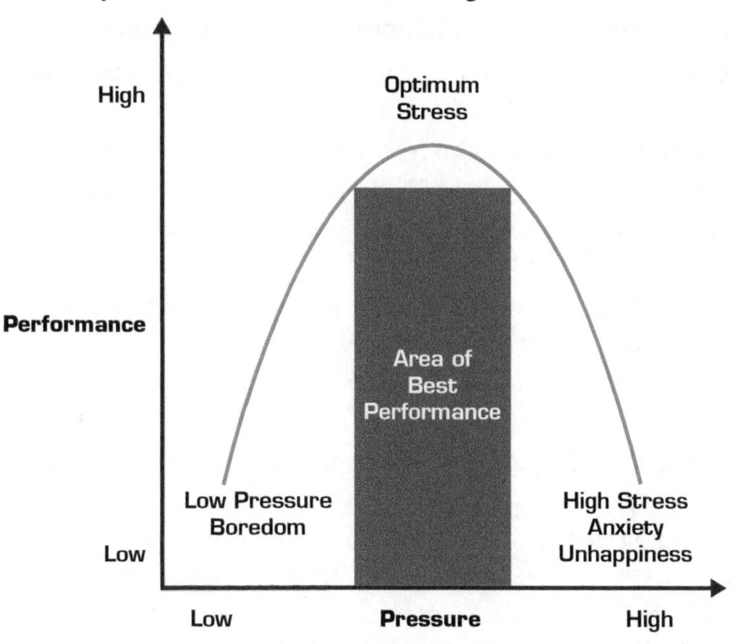

The Inverted-U relationship between pressure and performance

Our minds and bodies are created to deal with stress for short periods of time, but if left unattended, stress can result in a wide variety of negative physical and mental outcomes such as:

- Fatigue
- Headaches
- Loss of sleep
- Loss of concentration
- Difficulty making decisions
- Inability to control anger
- Loss or gain of weight
- Loss of interest in outside activities

Imagine a pan is full of water on the brink of boiling over as representing a person who walks around with high levels of negative stress. Like the pan of water on the stove, he is on the verge of boiling over at any moment. Then, for example, as he is commuting home from school a car cuts him off on the highway. Since he is already distressed, an ordinary event can cause him to "boil over" to the point of committing road rage. People who are walking around with high levels of stress may react with extremely erratic behavior when a minor offense is committed. At this point it might be wise to seek professional help. This is not healthy and can have very serious long-term consequences if left unmanaged.

Ten ways to cope with stress and manage your healthy life choices

1. **Connect with others.** Find a friend! Make new friends and cultivate the relationships you currently have with your friends.
2. **Stay positive.** Increase your optimism with positive people, inspirational readings, and music.
3. **Get physically active.** Take a brisk walk or run to increase your **endorphins** (chemicals released in your brain that trigger positive feelings)!
4. **Help others.** By serving others who are less fortunate, you can realize how good your life is.
5. **Get enough sleep.** This may be the most underrated and most abused step to coping with stress! By getting enough sleep (seven to eight hours) you are able to think more clearly and increase positive connections in your relationships.
6. **Create joy and satisfaction.** As was previously written, "Laughter is the best medicine," so liberal doses on a daily basis are highly recommended.
7. **Eat well.** Eating healthy foods fuels your ability to think clearly, improves your mood, and allows your body to remain healthier.
8. **Take care of your spirit.** Prayer and/or meditation allow you to connect with your deeper self which can richly enhance your life.
9. **Deal "better" with hard times.** Keeping a journal by writing your emotions or events in your life with the feelings you are experiencing, can increase your self-awareness and generate solutions to events troubling you.
10. **Get professional help if you need it.** As a college student, you have professional counselors available to assist you who are experienced in working with students and the challenges you are facing.

(Source: "Live Your Life Well: 10 Tools to Live Your Life Well." *Mental Health America*. 2013. Online. 19 Aug. 2013.)

Developing a heightened awareness of your stress levels will help you process the stress in your life. This means you will need to first understand how you feel and react to life's situations when you are not stressed, or at least minimally stressed. When less stress exists, do you tend to let things "roll off your back" or do you tend to defend your position? Have you ever watched the behaviors of people in reality television shows who are under distress? For example, there is a program about brides whose behaviors are over the top due to distress. Many brides feel the need for their wedding day to be perfect even if their behavior has to be imperfect to achieve it. It seems to capture a person at their worst and allows it to be entertainment. Most people who watch this type of show understand the bride is acting in an extreme way due to stress.

COLLABORATIVE ACTIVITY

Explain your perspective on ways entertainment (like the show mentioned above) normalizes "over-the-top" responses to stress, or creates a heightened sense of what distress looks like?

Defend your position on why this behavior is normal and acceptable or not.

Discuss this as a group and report your conclusions to the class.

REFLECTION 5.E:

Describe your top two (2) strategies out of the ten listed above you can integrate into your life to help control your stress level.

1. ______________________________

2. ______________________________

Consider the effect these two changes could make in your life and describe how they can help you reduce your overall stress level. Establish a time-line for which these strategies will be applied.

____

____

____

____

____

____

____

EXERCISE 5.20: Self-Inventory for Reaction to Stress

Complete the self-inventory by going to the URL below to determine your "normal" reaction to stress:

http://www.stress.org/self-assessment/

Locating the professional counselor on your college campus before you are in distress is a positive step. If you have not already done this, there is no time like today to do so. In addition to your campus counseling, there are many resources, as listed in Figure 5.9 below, to aid you in managing your stress and improving your overall mental health.

FIGURE 5.9

Organization	Contact information
Association for Behavioral and Cognitive Therapies	305 7th Avenue, 16th Fl., New York, NY 10001 Phone (212) 647-1890 http://www.abct.org/Members/?m=FindTherapist&fa=FT_Form&nolm=1
American Association for Marriage and Family Therapy	112 South Alfred Street, Alexandria, VA 22314-3061 Phone: (703) 838-9808 http://www.aamft.org/TherapistLocator/index.asp
Gay and Lesbian Medical Association	1326 18th Street, Suite 22, Washington, DC 20036 (202) 600-8037 info@glma.org http://www.glma.org/index.cfm?nodeid=1
Mental Health America	http://mentalhealthamerica.net/go/find_therapy

SOMETHING TO THINK ABOUT:

Complete the steps in this section as written.

1. Take a minute to review picture below.

© LuckyImages/Shutterstock.com

2. Do you think this group looks like they are managing stress? At the end of the meal, when the bill is presented, how do they handle the tab? (*something free, calculating tab of restaurant bill)

3. Write a paragraph, three to five complete sentences, about the photograph as it relates to *a positive attitude.*

   - Would your discussion be influenced if you knew: the person calculating the tab was an engineering student or if she was a theatre student? Male or female?

4. Discuss the photograph again from the perspective of **social responsibility**, **personal responsibility**, **empirical and quantitative skills,** and **teamwork**.

OBJECTIVE 7: Understand Strategies to Facilitate Good Physical Health

As was generally mentioned, maintaining and managing your physical health will be necessary for successes in college and your career. Specifically, physical health includes your personal hygiene, food choices, sleep, and exercise.

Personal hygiene includes the habits you have established to care for your cleanliness. By attending to details such as bathing, dental hygiene, and washing your hands, you will increase your self-esteem and contribute to your personal health.

- Bathing daily is essential for your health as it allows you to cleanse off dirt, sweat, and bacteria causing diseases. Of course, liberal use of antiperspirants, deodorants, and fragrances AFTER bathing are always good for your social life!
- Healthy dental hygiene means you are brushing with toothpaste and flossing your teeth at least two times per day (after each meal is best). By flossing daily, you are decreasing the odds you will have a heart attack. Research indicates the plaque building up on your teeth, if introduced in the blood stream via a bleeding gum, acts the same as that created in your arteries. Finally, attending to your dental hygiene increases the beauty of your smile . . . and results in fewer cavities.
- Washing your hands may sound like a nebulous task, but it is essential for your personal health as well as for the health of the community in which you work and live. Colds and flu are typically spread as a result of poor hygiene. Did you know washing hands is the number one way to prevent the spread of diseases? The best way to wash your hands is to soap up your hands and allow water to rinse them off for at least 15 seconds. Since you may be living in a communal setting, this is an easy but critical step toward maintaining your health.

Food choices in college are often relegated to the cheapest and fastest foods available. Cafeterias typically serve foods high in fat with low nutritional value. This is related to the term "freshmen ten," the ten pounds or more many first-year college students gain. Fortunately, this does not have to be your only choice. The recommendations on healthy eating in college include drinking water, eating fruits, drinking alcohol in moderation (if at all), controlling portions, and looking for healthy choices in dining halls. Many fast-food restaurants are responding to this need for better food by offering "healthy" options.

To begin healthy choices, be sure to drink plenty of water. This is probably not the first time you have heard this sage advice, so if you are not already drinking this naturally healthy and primarily free substance, begin drinking more water today. "The Institute of Medicine determined an adequate intake (AI) for men is roughly 3 liters (about 13 cups) of total beverages (this does NOT include alcohol) a day. The AI for women is 2.2 liters (about 9 cups) of total beverages a day" (*Nutrition and Healthy Eating*). In the past, you may have heard the "eight by eight" guide in which people are encouraged to drink eight eight-ounce glasses of water by 8:00 PM every day. This general guide, although lower than now recommended, may help to remind you to drink plenty of fluids. When you feel the dry sensation in your mouth indicating you need water, reach for good ole' H_2O.

Next, grab a piece of fruit rather than a high-fat over-processed choice. The health benefits of fruit are inclusion of full of fiber, calcium, and water. Typically, fruit is found in the dining halls of most colleges and it is easy to carry with you for a quick healthy snack. Compare the calories in fruit, as shown in Figure 5.10 on the next page, to a piece of chocolate cake with icing (235 calories) and it is clear fruit is healthier. Also, the fruit will satisfy your hunger longer than the sugar laden cake.

FIGURE 5.10 Chart: 100 Calories of Fruit

Fruit	Amount	Calories
Apples	2 extra small	105
Apricots	6 whole	101
Bananas	1 medium	105
Blackberries	100 berries (or 1 1/2 cups)	100 (93)
Blueberries	125 berries (or 1 1/4 cup)	97 (103)
Cantaloupe	2 cups, diced	106
Cherries	20	103
Clementines	3 whole	104
Cranberries, raw	2 1/4 cups	98
Dates, medjool	1 1/2 whole	100
(Source: "What 100 Calories Looks Like: Fresh Fruit Edition." *PopSugar Living.* 2 June 2010. Web. 20 Aug. 2013.)		

If you want to be successful as a college student, abstaining from alcohol is the best decision. However, if you choose to drink **and are of the legal age in your state**, alcohol consumption should be in moderation. Moderate drinking for women is one drink per day and for men it is two drinks per day (one four-ounce glass of wine, one 12-ounce beer, or one ounce of liquor all contain the same alcohol content). Of course, since most first year students are under the drinking age, students who engage in underage drinking are assuming a big risk. Those who choose to engage in drinking need to be aware of the long-term consequences attributable to the lack of inhibition resulting from drinking alcohol. Remember the high caloric content in beer, wine, and hard liquor. Habitually consuming these beverages will cause you to gain weight. The results of indulgence in alcohol can be manifested in the following ways:

- Lower GPAs
- Memory Loss
- Injuries, alcohol poisoning, and other fatalities
- Damages to others (i.e., vomit, litter, property damage, fights, and sexual violence)
- Car accidents, many leading to human fatalities
- Engaging in risky sexual behaviors which can result in the contraction of sexually transmitted diseases or unwanted pregnancies

This list is based on well-documented data and research. All of this is to say, if you choose to drink, do so in moderation.

Healthy eating also requires portion control. For meals, a rule of thumb is a healthy portion of meat or vegetables is roughly the size of your fist. However, controlling portions at meals is usually not a college student's problem; snacking is. This means it is important for you to read the labels of the food you are eating. Maybe you have grabbed a two-pound bag of M&Ms because it is cheaper. There are approximately 21 servings in this size. Bear in mind, one serving of M&Ms consists of 30 pieces, so a serving has 103 calories, 4.4g of fat, 15g of carbohydrates, 13.4g of sugar, and 0.9g of protein.

Controlling how much you eat requires education on serving sizes. One smart way to avoid large portions of snack foods is to purchase the smaller 100 calorie bags. These are easy to grab on the run and will not add unwanted food intake to your diet.

Sleep is often a struggle for college students, as well as most Americans. College students tend to stay up late and get up early which, obviously, limits the number of hours they will sleep. Sleep deprivation has many causes, but it is seen in college students as they study late, adjust to new sleeping patterns, experience interrupted sleep, or suffer from anxiety and stress. Very often sleep deprivation goes unnoticed. Its symptoms include the inability to focus, slower reaction time, taking longer to process new material, irritability, and possibly depression. The importance of getting eight hours of sleep for every 24-hour period is probably more important than you think. Since sleep experts have reported memory is enhanced through sleep, sleep needs to become a priority. Some studies have suggested the student who manages eight hours of sleep will earn a letter grade higher than their peers who are sleep deprived. Some suggestions for getting adequate sleep are:

- Establish a routine and schedule so your body and mind know when it is time to sleep.
- Avoid stimulants such as caffeine and alcohol four hours (or more) before going to bed.
- Find a dark, quiet, temperature-controlled place to sleep.
- Purchase and wear ear plugs to help block out noise, if necessary.
- Indulge in short "power naps" during the day, so your brain can reboot.
- Create and maintain a schedule that allows ample time for studying.

For many college students, proper sleep will be the most challenging healthy habit to form, but the rewards are worth the energy invested. A good night's sleep can do more for your GPA than most anything else.

Resting, or doing absolutely nothing, is another essential habit that can lead to greater personal health. Throughout your day, allow yourself some down time so you can pause to breathe and think. It is recommended you take 15 to 30 minute breaks between classes or during your work day. In so doing, you are restoring and resting your body and mind. This includes frequent breaks from working on the computer!

The final suggestion for taking care of your body in college is to plan time to exercise on a regular basis. Aerobic exercise is known to increase blood flow, release endorphins, and aid in the ability to fight infections and improve the quality of your sleep. Did you know vigorous exercise actually makes you smarter? Researchers from Saginaw Valley State University in Michigan conducted extensive research on this and reported students who exercise vigorously seven days a week had 0.4 higher GPAs than students who did not exercise. Of course, it is necessary to note increased exercise combined with studying contributed to the academic success of the students. Exercise without hitting the books will not increase your knowledge or GPA. Finally, adding exercise throughout the day has healthy benefits as well. For example, choosing to take the stairs instead of an elevator on your way to class burns extra calories and increases the oxygen flow to your brain. If you are a commuter student, consider parking farthest from the building for a brisk walk twice a day. Look for other ways to add more exercise into your daily routine.

Since stress in life is unavoidable, it is important you learn how to manage it through a healthy lifestyle including personal hygiene, food choices, sleep, and exercise. By managing your personal hygiene you will be able to meet people more easily and ward off unwanted bacterium naturally developing through daily activities and interactions. Eating foods that have a high nutritional value feed your body, soul, and mind. Would you ever consider putting sugar in your car's gas tank? No. It would ruin the engine. Similarly, putting low nutritional food in your tank will decrease your energy, motivation, and thought processing. Sleep, or lack of it, will alter your ability to think and respond to stress. If you are waking up during the night thinking of all the things you have to do, you are experiencing sleep deprivation due to stress. Rather than lying in bed and worrying about the tasks at hand, work with a well-organized schedule to accomplish the various demands but still provide the necessary sleep. Exercise can be a helpful sleep agent, too, as long as it is completed at least two to four hours prior to going to bed. Establish the time and day you will exercise and try to find an "exercise buddy" who will help you stay on track, then follow through with action. The health benefits of exercise are numerous but the use of exercise to manage stress is essential. According to the Anxiety and Depression Association of America, "Studies show that [exercise] is very effective at reducing fatigue, improving alertness and concentration, and enhancing overall cognitive function. This can be especially helpful when stress has depleted your energy or ability to concentrate." Combining these four traits of a healthy lifestyle can result in greater success throughout life.

EXERCISE 5.21: Healthy Changes

After reading and reviewing the four categories offered in this unit to increase your overall health, complete the following chart. This is intended to help you recap what you learned, evaluate how well you are doing in each of these areas, and to organize a game plan for improvement.

	Personal hygiene	Food Choices	Sleep	Exercise
What I am doing now:				
Recommendations:				
What I need to do:				
How will I incorporate this into my daily life?				

OBJECTIVE 8: Understand Strategies to Manage Finances

Another source of stress in college and in life is the management of personal finances. Attending and paying for college can be challenging. In reality, the struggle usually stems from a limited knowledge and experience in managing personal finances. This, coupled with additional expenses of tuition, books, and housing, can contribute to increased stress levels. According to the 2012 Kiplinger online article by Janet Bodnar entitled "Personal Finance Advice for College Students," "College students take a lot of heat for being poor money managers. But I'm convinced all it takes to sharpen their skills is a little knowledge.'' The article also recommends four points of focus for college students who want to better manage their finances. These include:

1. Stay on top of your student loans. Be sure the money you are getting in the form of college loans will be a realistic amount for you to repay. This means you need to project your future earning and determine how long it will take for you to repay them. Finally, be sure to check on the interest attached to the loans, so you can most accurately determine the affordability of the loan and its repayment.
2. Keep track of your money. This may seem too obvious to mention, but you need to keep up with where and when you are spending your money. You may have a pencil and paper, spreadsheet, or online tracking system to monitor your expenditures. All of these systems are only as accurate as the information you add to them, so keep a daily account of your spending habits.
3. ''Take a pass on credit cards.'' Studies consistently show college students struggle with credit card debt. One recent survey of undergraduate business students published in the International Journal of Business and Social Science found 90% of student cardholders carried a balance from month to month, and fewer than 10% knew their card's interest rate or what they would be charged if they made payments late or went over their limit. To avoid the debt trap, students should forgo cards at least until they are ready to graduate and have acquired several years of experience and confidence managing their cash.
4. Start saving today. The earlier you begin saving the more you will have to spend later in life. Save as much as you can even it is only 5% of your earnings because the key to building personal wealth is time. Allow your money to earn you more money in a 401K, stock market, or IRA. For example, if you invest $100 a month, which equals $1,200 (about 7% earnings) annually, in forty years you will have $142,720.

These four focus **points** are the beginning of taking charge of your personal finance, but they all assume you have a personal budget. Budgeting means you estimate your income and expenses for a predetermined time period, which can help you learn to live within your means. If this is a new idea for you, track how you are spending your money for three days. Then review the recorded spending to see how much you spent and on what items you purchased. This will help you realize if you are living within your means and on what types of items you may be able to live without.

EXERCISE 5.22: Analyze Elements of a Budget

Use a calculator to analyze how realistic the budget is for this student.

Devon is a server in a restaurant. He earns $2.71 per hour plus tips and works Wednesday through Saturday nights, averaging five hours per night. He averages sales of $700 per night and generally receives a 20% tip.

How much does Devon average per night? ______ per week? ______ per month (use four weeks)? ______

Because he is single, his employer deducts 15% from his paycheck each week for taxes and Social Security. How much does Devon pay in taxes each month? ______

How much does Devon take home each month? ______

Use the following expense chart, Figure 5.11 to answer the remainder of the questions.

FIGURE 5.11

Expense	Budgeted costs	Actual costs this Month
Share of Rent	$504	$504
Share of Electricity	$125	$130
Share of Water	$50	$48
Cell Phone	$70	$82
Car payment	$351	$351
Car insurance	$198	$198
Renter's insurance	$25	$25
Gasoline	$200	$163
Food	$272	$270
Clothing	$100	$96
Entertainment	$100	$175
Savings	$50	$50
Total Expenses		

What is the total amount budgeted for expenses? ______

What is the actual amount spent for expenses this month?______

Did Devon bring home enough money this month to cover his budgeted costs? ______ To cover his actual costs? ______

Explain. ____

____

____

Is Devon living within his budgeted amount? ______ Explain. ____________________

____

____

If Devon has $638 in his savings account, does he have enough to cover expenses if he is sick and cannot work one week this month? ______

As most of us have experienced, there are going to be unexpected expenses that strain even the best formulated budget. Unplanned expenses are things like car repairs, increased tuition, and higher utility bills. If you have been saving money and it is accessible, then you may be able to meet this type of obstacle with financial success. In contrast, if you have been living beyond your means, the unplanned expense will create financial instability as well as increase your stress level.

EXERCISE 5.23: Unexpected Expenses

Describe an unexpected expense you have had in the last year and how you handled the challenge.

____

____

____

____

Money and stress seem to go hand-in-hand. A 2013 study (conducted by EverFi and sponsored by Higher One) entitled, "Money Matters on Campus. How Early Attitudes and Behaviors Affect the Financial Decisions of First-Year College Students," reported that 80% of college freshmen (about 18 years old) are experiencing stress due to worries concerning money. Of the 40,000 students included in this study, 20% reported they purchased items they knew they could not afford and 24% would be "horrified" to let anyone know about their spending habits. The great irony here is most students have not had the opportunity to learn about handling money or the stress coming with it. The lack of information given to you, or learned by you, means you may not know where to turn for help when money problems stress you. Since the majority of college campuses are working to help students with this financial and learning deficit, there are counselors on most campuses to help you. However, developing and living on a budget is the best way to manage financial stress because you experience a sense of accomplishment and establish control of your money.

The previously mentioned Money Matters on Campus study also reported students having better attitudes toward money and paying their bills in a timely manner were more likely to graduate from college and repay their loans. Rather than worrying over where the money will come from, managing the funds you have is more likely to minimize your stress and increase your college success.

Federal and Private Loans

School loans create a conundrum for most college students. Affording college tuition and books is costly and the majority of students secure a college loan, so why would you not apply for one? First, know there are federal and private loans you may consider. **Federal loans**, if you qualify, have lower and fixed interest rates, so they are easier to repay. Additionally, federal lending practices may allow for the government to pay your interest while in college. The downsides to federal loans are you have a limited amount of money you may borrow and the government can take a portion of your earnings and taxes if you fail to make payments on the loan. A **private loan**, one from a bank, does not have a fixed rate and offers little flexibility on repayment deadlines. Of course, with a private loan you can shop around to find the lowest interest rate. The downside to personal loans is the interest rate and monthly payment can change, which means you have limited options on the payback. In general, it is best to procure federal loans for as much of your college funding as is possible and then obtain private loans as needed. If you determine the need to get a loan, ask the following three questions:

1. What is the cost (interest rate) for borrowing this money?
2. When do I have to start paying off the debt?
3. When will I have the funds to repay this debt?

Grants and Federal Work-Study Programs

Grants are another source of funding for your college expenses. These are by far the best way to pay for your college education because they are "free." **Grants** are awarded based on financial need and you will not have to repay the amount you are given. In order to qualify for grants and federally funded loans you need to complete the Free Application for Federal Student Aid (known as the FAFSA). This form may be completed annually to determine the funds you may be awarded as well as if you qualify for **Federal Work-Study Programs** (work for the college on-campus part-time). The money is distributed on a first come, first serve basis, which means a student who may need less money will win the funds over the student who needs more money who applies later. Apply by January 1 to be first in line.

Scholarships

Scholarships, money awarded by individuals or institutions based on specific criteria not requiring repayment, are another wonderful means of paying for college. You may begin locating scholarships awarded from the financial aid office on your college or university. There will be lists of institutional and private scholarships with the criteria for qualifying for them. Most have merit-based criteria, meaning you must have a specific grade point average to qualify. Some have career criteria, meaning you must be majoring in a specific field, such as theater. Others may require you belong to a specific ethnic group, religion, or be a child of a fallen soldier, firefighter, or police officer. The application process may take a significant amount of time, but the money is well worth the effort. Remember, you can go online to your college's website to research scholarships and apply every year!

Finally, the education portion of the Montgomery GI Bill is available for veterans who were discharged from one of the US military branches prior to September 10, 2001. These benefits include tuition and fees and a monthly allowance, depending on the number of hours enrolled, for up to 36 months.

For veterans who served at least 90 days of active duty after September 10, 2001, the Post-911 GI Bill, the benefits could include:

- payment of tuition and fees for up to 36 months issued to the school when certificate of enrollment is processed
- monthly housing allowance prorated monthly payment to student
- a stipend for books and supplies issued directly to the student when the school certifies and VA processes the enrollment
- college fund ("kicker") payments based on full or part time college enrollment
- rural benefit payment given to the veteran living in an unpopulated area
- "Yellow Ribbon" benefit based on tuition rates higher than the funds awarded to the veteran.

Some states provide additional tuition and fees when either of the GI Bills is exhausted. Check to see if your state is one of these. All of these benefits are, of course, contingent upon an honorable discharge from one of the US military branches.

EXERCISE 5.24: Paying for College

There are multitudes of ways to pay for college. Based on the information in this section, identify which method(s) fit the description. An answer may be used more than once.

____ **1.** may be limited to some religious or ethnic groups	**A.** Federal loans
____ **2.** interest rates may change before you graduate	**B.** Private loans
____ **3** only military serving prior to September 10, 2001 are eligible	**C.** Grants
____ **4.** interest rates do not accrue until six months after graduation	**D.** Scholarships
____ **5.** based on academic or subject interest	**E.** Work/study grants
____ **6.** do not have to be repaid	**F.** GI Bill
____ **7.** only post 9/11 military are eligible	**G.** Post 9/11 GI bill
____ **8.** money delivered on "first come, first served"	
____ **9.** based on financial need	
____**10.** have academic requirements (GPA)	

To minimize the stress in your life concerning personal finances, make choices that can build a more positive future for yourself. In so doing, you are managing the potential distress comes from overcommitting your money to purchase temporary happiness. By learning to live on a realistic budget, you will be able to manage your finances and focus on doing well in college.

PERSON to PERSON

In this exercise, you will be introduced to a first semester student with unique personal circumstances. Let's meet her!

© Nejron Photo/Shutterstock.com

continued

Carlita had a major test scheduled for 10 a.m. The instructor's syllabus states clearly there are no makeups regardless of the reason for missing an exam.

She lives in off-campus housing in a one-bedroom apartment with a roommate. Although Carlita remembers clearly she set the alarm, she suspects her roommate turned it off.

She woke up at 9:30 a.m. Although she would be late, she would still make it in time to take the exam. However, her vehicle did not start! She missed the exam.

Based on this description, rank the individuals as to who you believe is most responsible for the missed exam.

Carlita ____ Roommate ____ Instructor ____ Parents ____

Here is some additional information.

- Carlita did not get home until one in the morning the day of the exam.
- There was a power outage in her area last night.

Based on all the information you now know, rank them again as to who you believe is most responsible for the missed exam. Has your ranking changed?

Carlita ____ Roommate ____ Instructor ____ Parents ____ Power Company ____

1. What pieces of new information do you consider to be important in this ranking?

____

____

2. What pieces of new information do you consider to be unimportant in this ranking?

____

____

Here are your last pieces of information.

- She told her parents she thought her battery was weak since she had difficulty starting the vehicle last week.
- She worked last night.

Based on all the information you have about this situation, rank them one last time as to who you believe was most responsible for the zero she will receive for the exam.

Carlita ____ Roommate ____ Instructor ____ Parents ____ Power Company ____

1. What pieces of new information would you still like to know about the situation?

____

____

2. Are there any pieces of information pertinent to the situation?

____

____

Career Connection

© Alitsiya/Shutterstock.com

Maintaining a positive attitude is important to your college success. There will be challenges and setbacks, but with a positive attitude, you can persevere. One of your biggest challenges will be managing the unique stress college life creates. Your ability to manage this stress by good mental, physical, and financial health will be invaluable in your transition to the workplace as well as in your personal life.

CHAPTER SUMMARY

In this chapter you have learned how to develop a positive attitude, manage stress, and create intrinsic motivational for managing stress in college and beyond.

This type of positive outlook on life requires you to understand the Expectancy Theory of motivation. The basic premise of this theory is desired outcomes or goals can be achieved when the expectation is clearly defined and the right amount of effort is invested.

The Expectancy Theory intersects with self-efficacy, as a person's self-efficacy can actually perpetuate a motivational cycle. In other words, the stronger your self-efficacy the more likely you will experience success because you expect to succeed.

By maintaining a positive attitude, you are more likely to experience long-term happiness. Happiness is a critical component to realizing your success and a natural byproduct of successfully overcoming life's setbacks. Setbacks are inevitable, but learning to overcome them and then doing so increases your self-efficacy and long-term happiness.

Intrinsic and extrinsic motivations are pivotal concepts that can increase your success. Intrinsic motivation is deemed to be more advantageous for long-term happiness and success. Extrinsic motivation is considered best for short term solutions to motivation. A combination of the two will work to increase your overall motivation and success.

Understanding how to maintain an internal locus of control rather than an external locus of control was also considered in this chapter. A person with an internal locus of control has the perception of control in their life. This person is viewing life from the perspective of controlling the circumstances in their life rather than giving away power to others or external events. By working on increasing your internal locus of control you can increase your positive attitude.

There are two types of stress. Eustress is a motivator to complete a task and it generates a euphoric feeling. This type of stress can actually be healthy and produce positive attitudes for mental health. In contrast, distress can trigger the same physiological symptoms, but with less positive outcomes. Stress is a natural byproduct of long-term demands on your physical, mental, and emotional state. A college student attending college for the first time is going to experience eustress and distress. For this reason, it is important you learn how to identify and manage stress through ongoing healthy choices. Some of the areas in which managing physically healthy choices will be found in personal hygiene, food choices, sleep, and exercise.

Finally, in this chapter you were given some basic direction in managing your personal finances. As the lack of money is a significant stress for most college students, learn to locate grants, scholarships, student work on campus, or benefits from the Montgomery GI or Post 911 GI Bills as they relate to you. Then, if you still need money to pay for college, consider obtaining a federal or private loan.

There are a wide variety of elements contributing to your positive attitude and overall happiness. Making healthy well-reasoned choices about each element will provide you the opportunity to enjoy life and minimize your stress.

CHAPTER 5: Self-Check

Vocabulary: Define the following:

1. psychological pollution
2. Expectancy Theory
3. self-efficacy
4. intrinsic motivation
5. extrinsic motivation
6. locus of control
7. internal locus of control
8. external locus of control
9. long-term happiness
10. eustress
11. distress
12. positive stress
13. endorphins
14. federal loans
15. private loans
16. grants
17. Federal Work-Study Program

Concepts:

18. Explain the connections among expectation, effort, and perception of challenges.
19. Describe self-efficacy and discuss how self-efficacy might affect course grades.
20. Describe three learning strategies from this chapter aiding in the creation of greater success which stem from a positive attitude.

21. Explain how a setback can be used as a platform for success.
22. Describe the characteristics of good mental health.
23. Discuss the effects stress can have on mental health.
24. Describe the characteristics of good physical health.
25. Discuss the effects stress can have on physical health.
26. Describe the relationship between mental and physical health.
27. Describe how your financial plan budgets for unexpected expenses.
28. Discuss how financial difficulties contribute to stress.
29. Explain how locus of control can be either external or internal.
30. Compare and contrast intrinsic and extrinsic motivation.
31. Compare and contrast locus of control and self-actualization.
32. Explain how locus of control contributes to self-actualization and motivation.
33. Describe the types of choices you expect regarding classes and assignments.
34. Describe your approach to selecting classes.
35. Describe your approach to making decisions about assignments.
36. Explain Expectancy Theory and describe how it relates to motivation.
37. Compare approaches to class assignments, selections, and general decision making to those within the Expectancy Theory.
38. Discuss how self-efficacy might affect course grades.
39. Identify two strategies to improve self-efficacy.
40. Describe strategies employed to create success.
41. Discuss the application of the identified successful strategies to predict greater college success.
42. Identify a recent setback and describe the factors contributing to that setback.
43. Describe how previously stated successes contribute to changing setbacks into successes.
44. Understand influence of choices on long-term happiness and include two strategies supporting long-term happiness.
45. Identify the elements of long-term happiness as described in *The Happiness Project* by Gretchen Rubin.
46. Determine if you have a greater propensity for the internal or external locus of control.
47. Discuss two strategies for increasing an internal locus of control.
48. Explain how these two strategies increase intrinsic motivation.
49. Explain how a student can access support services specific to good mental health and explain the variables can hinder good health habits.
50. Describe the relationship between mental and physical health.
51. Develop a realistic budget to manage your personal and college finances.
52. Describe three sources of educational funding and how to access them. Explain the benefits or lack of benefits in taking out school loans.
53. Give an example of a situation where stress was beneficial.
54. Create three note cards for this chapter, the first with a true-false test question, the second with a multiple choice test question, and the third with an essay question.

CHAPTER 6

Communicating and Exchanging Ideas

T.I.P.S.—(Tactical Information that Promotes Success)

Communicating ideas effectively is a skill demanded in every profession.

Effective communication, the ability to express your ideas clearly, allows you to demonstrate your knowledge and understanding of the course material. Fortunately, effective communication **can be learned**. This may take a life-time of learning and refining, but college is a great place to start!

Learning how to communicate your thoughts, as well as science and mathematics skills, happens as you read and listen.

Read to understand the author's meaning and learn to put aside your personal opinion on the topic.

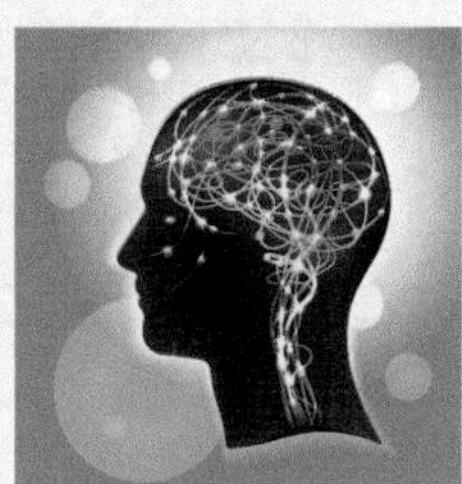

© Sergey Shenderovsky/Shutterstock.com

© Kalakruthi/Shutterstock.com

According to *Merriam-Webster*, communication is defined as "the act or process of using words, sounds, signs, or behaviors to express or exchange information or to express your ideas, thoughts, feelings, etc., to someone else."

Communication is a two-way process. There is an old saying that states, "we have two ears and one mouth so we may listen twice as much as we talk." Based on this quote, how much attention needs to be placed on listening when communicating?

The changes in technology have increased the methods of communication: email, texting, and social media. Each may be appropriate for different audiences.

In **mathematics and lab sciences**, symbols are used to communicate concepts and processes. Learning the associated vocabulary facilitates understanding through active classroom discussion, exploring ideas and making connections. Listening to the perspective of others may strengthen your appreciation for the beauty of the mathematical language.

Reading skills require a two-way process of communication while reading, which is critical. Reading the perspectives of others will require a distancing of your bias at times. If your opinions interfere with your ability to listen to the author's message, limited comprehension can occur. This means you need to listen to yourself and monitor your reactions as well as listening to the author's message.

In **writing**, predicting your audience determines the way you address the topic. Writing about the effects of underage drinking for your peers is very different than writing to your 13-year-old sister. Before writing, consider your audience and how you can best communicate your ideas.

In **Education**, the ability to write newsletters and notes to parents in a professional manner helps determine your credibility. The utilization of communication logs empowers parents to write questions and thoughts about their child's progress as well as establishes an open line for the teacher to engage in written conversation.

CHAPTER 6: OBJECTIVES

6.1 Communicating with Others

Objective 1 Understand Active Listening

Objective 2 Understand the Difference between Assertive and Aggressive Behavior

Objective 3 Understand How to Develop Healthy Relationships in College and Careers

6.2 Relating to the Professor

Objective 4 Understand the Need to Connect with Each Professor

Objective 5 Understand Writing Arrangement and Style of an Email Communication

6.3 Relating to Groups

Objective 6 Understand the Stages of Group Dynamics

Objective 7 Understand Conflict-Resolution Strategies

Objective 8 Understand Synergy as it Relates to Group Dynamics

6.4 Collaborating Outside of Class

Objective 9 Learn how to Identify a Study Partner

Objective 10 Understand the Role of Diversity

Objective 11 Understand Strategies to Connect with Others In and Out of Class

CHAPTER CONCEPTS:

Some or all of the following terms may be new to you. Place a check mark in the column reflecting your knowledge of each term.

	Know	Don't know	Not sure	Page # where first found		Know	Don't know	Not sure	Page # where first found
assertive					egocentric				
aggressive					active listening				
synergy					email communication				
diversity					ethical dilemmas				
collaboration					stages of group dynamics				
ethnocentric					conflict resolution				

© pathdoc/Shutterstock.com

Have you ever had someone you were talking to seem inattentive? Maybe he was looking over your shoulder as if watching for someone, shuffling papers on his desk, or even checking emails or texts on his phone? Sometimes a person might even act like he is listening, but when asked a question concerning the information in your conversation, he does not know how to respond. Either way, it is annoying when someone is not listening to you.

In this chapter you will learn skills to help you communicate effectively with your instructors, peers and groups.

6.1 COMMUNICATING WITH OTHERS

OBJECTIVE 1: Understand Active Listening

There are certain behaviors a person exhibits when **actively listening,** making a concerted effort to understand what the other person is saying. He will focus on the meaning of the words uttered by the speaker and watch for non-verbal cues. He will make eye contact and his body language will determine a steadfast attention. He will be considering a question to ask and will use nonverbal cues to communicate he is listening and understanding by perhaps giving a nod or a smile or even a verbal "yes" or an "uh oh."

Active listening is a fine art and sometimes requires the ability to remain calm and even silent. The possibility exists that your personal bias may lead to misunderstandings. If you are listening to a person and it appears like she is being critical of you or is expressing a different opinion than yours, you may ask follow up questions, tactfully and without confrontation, for clarification. By offering respect to the speaker it is more likely she will return your respect. Responding appropriately suggests you may be candid but must communicate respect appropriately. One way to accomplish this is to repeat or summarize what you understand she is saying and allow her to respond. At times it is difficult to remain unemotionally involved, especially if it seems as if she is attacking your personal opinions or beliefs. In this case, it is wise to allow the speaker to communicate her idea without interruption. Waiting offers the speaker time to communicate her ideas more fully; it is possible what you heard was not the whole story. When you apply these steps in active listening, the opportunity for engaging and productive communication can occur.

When people are not listening actively, they seem preoccupied or act as if they have "zoned out." At times people can even offer the verbal and nonverbal cues noted for active listening, but are not processing the information on a meaningful level. It becomes apparent when a misunderstanding or conflict arises that active listening may not be evident if the listener storms off or slams down their phone. Active listening in a classroom is critical to your college success because the price you may pay if you do not listen actively is a low or failing grade.

EXERCISE 6.1: Active Listening Skills

Take a minute to complete the following self-evaluation of how strong your active listening skills are. https://www.mindtools.com/pages/article/listening-quiz.htm.

EXERCISE 6.2: Improving Active Listening

Now that you have assessed your current ability to listen actively, what will you do to work on improving this skill? Write a plan of action by including the elements of a SMARTER.

Goal:

Area for improvement:

What I can do to increase this skill:

REFLECTION 6.A:

Consider a time when you believe you were utilizing active listening. Describe the situation and evaluate the degree to which you believe the other person was, or was not, actively listening to you.

____

____

____

____

____

Building an awareness of your ability to listen actively in class will help you think more clearly, generate constructive questions, and offer you another repetition in the learning cycle. Active listening can also assist in building strong interpersonal relationships. Try active listening with your significant other and see the difference it will make in your relationship. When someone sees you are listening actively, positive results in the learning and relationship will be the outcome.

SOMETHING TO THINK ABOUT:

Complete the three steps in this section as written.

Take a minute to review picture below. Do you think these individuals are not communicating with others?

© Vlad Teodor/Shutterstock.com

1. Write a paragraph, three to five complete sentences, about the photograph as it relates to *communication*.

2. Would your discussion be influenced if you knew:

    - The girl on the left is a mother of an infant who needs her immediate assistance in child care.
    - The man in the middle is texting the girl on the left.
    - The girl on the right is trying to focus on learning with notecards from a digital website.

3. Discuss the photograph again from the perspective of **social responsibility**, **personal responsibility**, and **teamwork**.

OBJECTIVE 2: Understand the Difference between Assertive and Aggressive Behavior

Active listening is one of the many communications skills increasing success in your college and career life, not to mention the positive effect it will have in your personal life! When things in a college class go differently than you expected, do you become frustrated, feel threatened, or even angry? How do you proceed?

Sal, a first year college student, was struggling in his biology class. He had attended every class and spent hours studying, but was always receiving low, near failing grades. The lab grade was his only hope of passing the class, but his lab partner, Weston, was not working with him as a team player. His partner would get to the lab early to try to have it all done before Sal arrived, because Weston had to go to work at the college library. Due to the recurrence of Weston's eagerness to finish and eliminate Sal, Sal would complete the lab and then try to track down Weston to confirm they had the same outcomes on their lab reports. This had happened twice and on the third time it occurred, Sal, having not uttered a word to Weston about this frustration previously, got in Weston's face and yelled, "You are destroying me, man! Why are you trying to finish the lab without me? This will make me fail the class!" Weston was insulted and shocked at Sal's accusation.

EXERCISE 6.3: Collaboration

© wavebreakmedia/Shutterstock.com

Collaborate with your fellow learners on this conflict.

Do you think Sal's behavior was justified? What do you think Weston's reply was to Sal? If you think Sal was out of line, how do you think he could have been more constructive in his interaction?

Sal would have benefited from understanding that a critical skill for working toward improving his ability to communicate effectively is by becoming **assertive** without being **aggressive**. Aggressive behavior is "an act directed towards a specific other person or object with the intent to hurt or frighten, for which there is a consensus about the aggressive intent of the act" (Maccoby). In other words, aggressive behavior is an action intentionally seeking to threaten or intimidate another person while defending your personal rights.

Additionally, the behavior demonstrated by the initiator is generally accepted as threatening by the general population; behaviors toward another person such as:

- inflicting punishment, guilt, or shame,
- anger,
- body language,
- and threatening or bullying.

In contrast, assertive behavior is demonstrated when a person expresses their opinion or need with confidence and respect toward others (Smith). Often people believe they must be aggressive to obtain things or persuade others, but exercising assertive communication skills will help gain the respect of others as well as obtain what you want. An illustration of assertive behavior is seen when Walt asked Caroline out on a date.

Walt: Caroline, are you planning on going to the football game this week?

Caroline: I'm not sure.

Walt: Well, would you like to go with me?

Caroline: Walt, I appreciate your invitation, but I am not interested at this time. I need to study.

Walt: Oh, come on! You can study another time!

Caroline: Walt, I appreciate your invitation, but I am not interested at this time.

Walt: Sure, you say that now, but I know you'll change your mind by Saturday.

Caroline: Walt, I appreciate your invitation, but I am not interested at this time.

Walt: Hum. Okay. Maybe another time . . .

Notice that Caroline maintains her assertive stance through the repetition of the same words. She does not utter a negative word, but repeats the same words over and over. Additionally, Caroline does not feel the need to explain herself further than the need to study and that she is not interested. By declining Walt's invitation with assertiveness, Caroline is able to control the situation without insulting or offending Walt. (It must be noted, however, should Walt's actions escalate in aggressiveness, it is time to call Campus Security or the local police.)

In order to respond assertively, rather than react aggressively, you will want to learn a few simple strategies. The founder of these techniques is Manuel J. Smith, PhD, who authored the book When I Say No, I Feel Guilty (1975). His ideas are considered standard by most communications scholars and include:

Broken Record: (the name is a metaphor for a broken vinyl record) " . . . to be persistent and to keep saying what you want over and over again without getting angry, irritated or loud" (74). This was Caroline's response to Walt's persistence.

Fogging: When you feel someone is being critical of you, "agree with the truth . . . or principle" (105). This does not mean you are agreeing with breadth of the criticism. For example, agreeing by restating the criticism such as, "You're right. I do sound, act, respond, . . . like a . . . " forces the critic to hear their assertions.

Negative Assertion: Stating something that sounds negative about yourself without altering your demand or request.

I-Statements: Stating your feeling and reactions with an "I" statement (I feel . . . about . . .) without the use of judgmental or blaming words.

Of course, Smith's assertiveness training requires mental and verbal practice, so you will learn to automatically defer to them when you feel guilty or that you are being criticized. One final point about Smith's theory is that he includes an "Assertive Bill of Rights." These are as follows:

I. You have the right to judge your own behavior, thoughts, and emotions, and to take the responsibility for their initiation and consequences upon yourself.
II. You have the right to offer no reasons or excuses for justifying your behavior.
III. You have the right to judge if you are responsible for finding solutions to other people's problems.
IV. You have the right to change your mind.
V. You have the right to make mistakes—and be responsible for them.
VI. You have the right to say, "I don't know."
VII. You have the right to be independent of the goodwill of others before coping with them.
VIII. You have the right to be illogical in making decisions.
IX. You have the right to say, "I don't understand."
X. You have the right to say, "I don't care."

These ten rights when combined with Smith's assertiveness techniques will help you learn to stand your ground without becoming aggressive. As a result, you will be an assertive person who can communicate your wants and needs with respect of others as well as personal respect.

Learning to communicate with assertiveness is one of many ways to minimize your aggressive behaviors. The first step in diffusing aggressiveness is to pause by counting to ten, as a form of distraction, before responding to the threat you are experiencing. Remember, your body is entering "fight or flight" mode and you must try to limit the amount of adrenaline pumping through your body. Taking slow, deep breaths while counting will help return your body to its normal state. This should allow time for you to clear you head and think about how to constructively handle your aggressive response. Then, apply the following tips from Aronson, Wilson, and Akert's book, Social Psychology (2006), to constructively cope with aggressive behaviors.

Venting versus self-awareness: Learn to identify when you feel the need to vent. Then, redirect this behavior by expressing your feelings in a non-violent, nonjudgmental way. Also, it is best to seek the help of a third party to help you cope with your aggressive tendencies. (Aronson, 2003)

Apologize: Yes, a simple apology and promise to not behave in this way going forward is constructive.

Empathize: See the source of your aggressive behavior as a human being and try to understand how this person feels. When people act on aggression they tend to dehumanize the victim. By turning this dehumanization process around it allows you to see the person and their perspective.

REFLECTION 6.B:

There is an expression "we will just agree to disagree." What does this statement mean to you and when would it apply?

____

____

____

____

Obviously, if you struggle with deep-seeded aggression, these tips will be a step in the right direction. If you are unable to cope with your aggressiveness in a healthy constructive manner, seek help from the highly-qualified counselors on your campus.

OBJECTIVE 3: Understand How to Develop Healthy Relationships in College and Careers

Developing healthy relationships in college as well as in your career will have a variety of benefits. Establishing positive relationships in college means you create mutually respectful relationships with peers, professors and other campus employees. Peer relationships encompass students in your classes, student organizations in which you participate, or students with whom you establish interactive relationships in social settings. Learning to communicate your ideas in a non-threatening way while respecting the opinions of your peers will improve your self-esteem and increase respect from others.

Establishing positive relationships with your professors is critical to your academic success and very often your career. Professors generally welcome the opportunity to help you with the course work in their class. Sometimes, professors will offer advice on courses you should take or careers to consider. Overall, your professors teach because they are committed to your learning and success. (For practical ways to accomplish this, see "Section 6.2: Relating to the Professor.")

Finally, the third group of people you should establish positive relationships with are the employees at your college or university. This group includes everyone from the college president to those who maintain the beauty of your college facility. Each of these levels of college employment is important because you will need to work with them to accomplish your academic goals to complete your degree. Basically, learning to work well with your peers, professors, and campus employees means you are learning to collaborate in the same way you will work in your choice of career.

COURSE CONNECTIONS

Actively Participating in Your Mathematics Class

Many mathematics classes are no longer "lecture" or "chalk and talk." They have become more interactive, requiring students to participate more. This participation may be in the form of going to the board, working in groups, or working one-on-one with another student. As a result, being prepared for class is essential. In addition, it is crucial that you actively participate in your class.

- Write down the Objectives of the day's lesson.
- Write out the meaning of all newly introduced vocabulary words.
- Take notes. Consider your preferred learning style. (This will be covered more thoroughly in a later chapter.)
- Listen carefully.
- Ask questions when something is not clear to you. Try to be specific about what you are having difficulty with. Avoid "I don't understand."
- Volunteer to work a problem at the board.
- Raise your hand to answer any questions your instructor asks during class.
- Contribute to the assignment if you are working in a group.

© Wittayayut/Shutterstock.com

Your instructor writes five problems on the board and asks for volunteers of two students each to go to the board, work one of the problems, and then explain the solution to the class when all groups are finished. The rest of the class works in groups of four on all five problems. You do not usually volunteer to go to the board because you are unsure of your ability to work the problems, but you also have difficulty working in groups because of your shyness.

Which would you choose and why: work with one other student at the board on one problem or work in a group on all five problems?

Learning to communicate in college will be the catalyst for a lifetime of successes. While effective communication skills may feel unfamiliar or even unnecessary, the effort you invest in them will pay off. In the business world the term "Return on Investment" refers to the rate of payoff of an investment over time. Similarly, investing in your ability to communicate today will have a high margin of payoff in the end.

6.2 RELATING TO THE PROFESSOR

OBJECTIVE 4: Understand the Need to Connect with Each Professor

While you may not realize it today, investing in strong relationships with your professors will have a high rate of return on investment (ROI). This means you are relating to your professors, acknowledging the need or cost of connecting by investing your resources wisely. One benefit of investing time with your professor during class, and throughout the term, is learning from your professor, who can teach you pertinent accumulated knowledge and assist you with additional learning techniques. The most obvious of these is the ability to learn course content from a highly informed individual.

Perhaps a less obvious way to invest in connecting with your professor is the opportunity to learn from your instructor's journey through academia. Because your professors have learned to successfully navigate the halls of higher education, they can offer you a perspective on what they did to earn two or three degrees. Use your professor as a resource for your navigation of college as often as they will permit. For example, when you are given a group project to complete, you can learn team work, problem solving, critical thinking, writing, and speaking. These are only five of the needs identified as skills needed in the workplace but more could be applied in your learning environment. By investing in building a relationship with your professors, you are going to experience a high yield of your ROI.

Consider for a moment what a class looks like from the perspective of a professor during a lecture. The instructor sees a sea of faces staring back at him or her. Often, learning students' names is challenging due to the combined number of students in their classes. This being said, your professor looks out and sees some students who are slouched in a chair dressed as if they just rolled out of bed and other students sitting up straight in their chair, reviewing the chapter which was read prior to arriving in class, and dressed in a way communicating an air of professionalism. Staring at the faces in the class, the professor is more naturally drawn to the latter group. Perhaps the students in the first group are prepared to be actively engaged in the class, but their body language does not communicate this message accurately to the professor.

Exactly how can a student communicate to a professor that he is willing to invest in learning from them? Non-verbal communications may speak louder than verbal communications in this instance. When you are in a classroom, what do your non-verbal signals communicate to your professor? Remember, your professor is working tirelessly to teach you often highly complex information, so you can succeed in the class and your future career. From the front of the room professors are reading your non-verbal cues to gauge your comprehension and interest in the topic. Thus, your behaviors communicate even when you are often unaware of the message you are sending. Kendra Cherry, author of *Everything Psychology* (2010), offers the foundation for pointers on how to more accurately communicate in a classroom:

1. **Self-monitor your non-verbal communication signals.** Eye contact, gestures, posture, body movements, and tone of voice are the types of non-verbal signals you use to communicate. Self-monitor the messages your body is sending to your professors
2. **Align the verbal and non-verbal signals.** Make sure you match your verbal and non-verbal communications to communicate a stronger message. An example of this may be seen in the student who says they want to learn and earn an "A" in a class but are texting and talking throughout the lecture.

© Syda Productions/Shuttersock.com

3. **Pay attention to the tone of your voice when you speak.** Expressing enthusiasm or disdain through the tone of your voice can increase or diminish your connections with professors as well as fellow learners. If your tone communicates disdain while you are stating even the most positive of words, your tone will be what you communicate. Additionally, communicating respect through your tone is vital in increasing your connections with people.

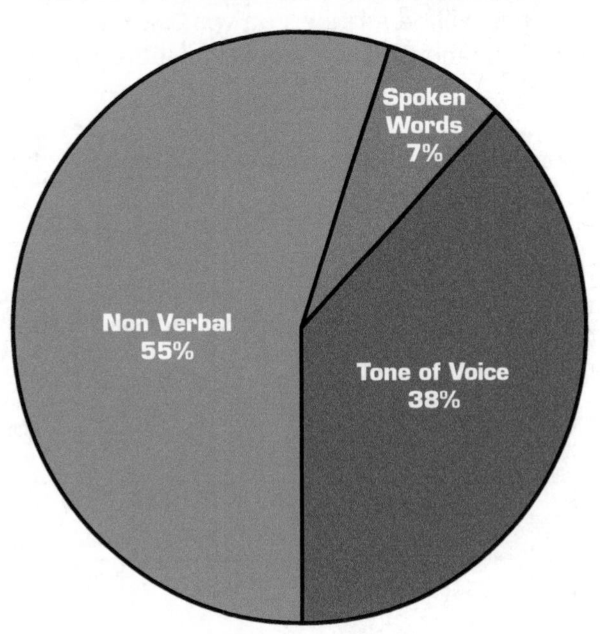

4. **Exercise good eye contact.** The balance between too much or too little eye contact can signal your level of interest and learning to your professor. Too little eye contact may communicate a lack of learning, while too much eye contact may communicate an aggressive posture. Thus, a balance between the two ranges of eye contact is advised.
5. **Ask questions for clarification.** When you are confused or lack understanding in a classroom, politely raise your hand and ask your question when called upon. Raising your hand extends a level of respect to your professor. If you need to make an appointment and visit your professor, it is best not to do so during the class lecture.
6. **Use non-verbal cues to communicate your understanding of the material presented.** When you are listening to a lecture and taking notes, periodically you may nod or smile to communicate to your professor you are listening and understanding the material. Of course, when you furrow your brow, frown, or look perplexed you are communicating a lack of understanding. Use your non-verbal communication cues to tell your professor what you comprehend.
7. **Learn to read the non-verbal cues from your professor and classmates.** Pay attention to the non-verbal cues given to you and learn to read them accurately. For example, if a professor seems to ignore your question by not addressing it in class, do not assume they are disinterested in helping you learn. Follow up with the professor to make sure they received your question and to determine why it was not addressed. Similarly, be careful when reading anyone's non-verbal cues. Read the classroom's signals to reinforce your own perceptions.
8. **Remember the context in which you are communicating and adjust accordingly.** A college classroom should have a more formal communication stance than you have with your peers. Additionally, emailing a professor should reflect this level of respect by including your course, section, and your full name as well as clearly constructed messages or requests. Remember, your professor can easily have upwards of 150 students, and taking time to decipher your message may not communicate your message in the most positive manner.
9. **Understand that signals may not be clearly communicated, so monitor them.** Closely monitor the words you use, and the non-verbal messages you communicate, to ensure they align with the situation.
10. **Practice, practice, practice!** Learn to use your non-verbal cues to reinforce your verbal message. This means practice will be required on your part. Practice reading your professors accurately, too. Practice by building a self-awareness of the signals you send and receive in and out of the classroom.

Learning to communicate your eagerness to learn to a professor may take time, so there is no time like the present to begin!

EXERCISE 6.4: Communication Skills

Complete the following self-evaluation of your non-verbal messages sent in each of the classes you are currently taking.

Courses in which I am enrolled	My non-verbal stance	Ways to improve my non verbal communication

Courses in which I am enrolled	My non-verbal stance	Ways to improve my non verbal communication

EXERCISE 6.5: Non-Verbal Communications

How would you rate your overall non-verbal stance in a classroom? Do you think the areas you have listed above for improvement will yield a high ROI? If so, why? If not, why?

____

____

____

____

What do you think will be the future of your relationships with your professors? After you have completed their course requirements, do you think you may follow up with them in the future semesters of your education? Frequently, you will want to ask a professor for a letter of recommendation for a job, volunteerism, or an internship. Most professors are inclined to write these recommendation letters for students with whom they have established a positive rapport. A general guide for most professors is they will not write a letter for a student they do not remember having taught. For this reason, you will want to make yourself memorable! Be the student who is remembered for your ability to communicate effectively with your professors and peers.

OBJECTIVE 5: Understand Writing Arrangement and Style of an Email Communication

Since much of your personal communication with your professors will be in the form of an email, understanding the written arrangement and style of email or electronic communications will increase your connections with a professor. An email is comprised of three parts: message *envelope*, the message *header*, and the message *body*. The envelope is similar to a traditional mailing envelope in that it secures the information being sent. The header includes information concerning the recent, sender, subject, date, and time. The body of the message includes the elements you want to communicate in the form of sentences.

As with any form of communication, it is critical to consider the audience, purpose, and tone. When your audience is your professor, be sure to communicate with clear and concise writing, easy for your professor to understand the nature of your message. Based on what you need, you will consider the purpose of your writing. Typically, the purpose is going to be one of the following: inform, instruct, or persuade. Tone, the attitude of the message, is critical to consider prior to sending because

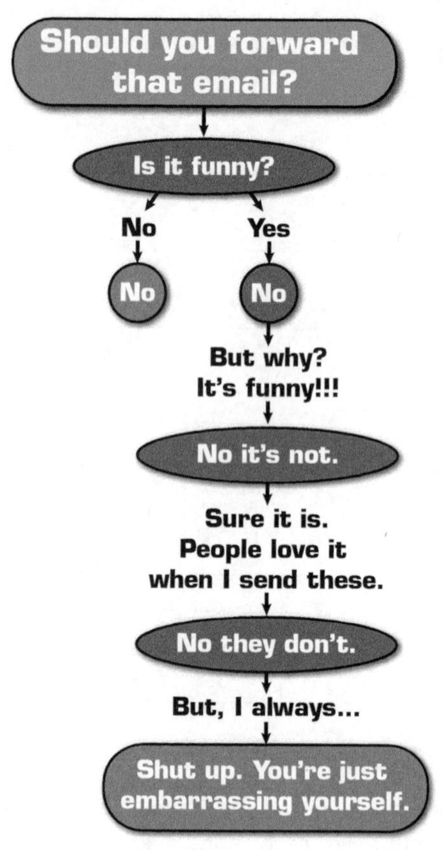

Gary Dudak Nov 07, 2013

it is represented in your word choice, font size or case, and the thoroughness of the message. Jeremy F. Hyman and Lynn F. Jacobs authors of *A Professors Guide* have created "Etiquette Tips for E-mailing Your Professor" in which they offer some sound advice on emailing your professors.

1. **Email is forever.** Once you send it off, you can't get it back. Once your professor has it, he or she owns it and can save it or, in the worst case, use it as evidence of your uncooperative or negative attitude.
2. **Email goes where it's told.** Check—and double check—to see that the correct address appears in the "To" line. Just because your mom and your professor are both named "Lynn" is no reason to send all your love to Professor Lynn. Also be careful not to "reply all" when it is not appropriate.
3. **Professors might not be using the university email system.** So send it to the address they actually use, not the one on the university directory. (Check the syllabus or assignment sheet for clues.)
4. **Professors generally do not open mail sent from accounts they do not recognize because of threats of viruses or hacking.** Always use your college email address when communicating with an instructor.
5. **Subject lines are for subjects.** Put a brief explanation of the nature of the email (like "question about paper") in the subject line. Never include demands such as "urgent request— immediate response needed."
6. **Salutations matter.** The safest way to start is with "Dear Professor So and So" (using their last name). That way you will not be getting into the issue of whether the professor has a PhD or not, and you won't seem sexist when you address your female professor as "Ms." or, worse yet, "Mrs. This and That."
7. **Clear and concise is best.** Your professor might get 25 or 30 emails a day [from students in multiple course sections], so it is best if you ask your questions in as focused and succinct way as possible. (Hint: it's often good to number your questions).

   If your question is very elaborate or multifaceted, it is best to visit your professor in person office hour.

   Extra Pointer. Before sending a draft of a paper to a professor as an attachment, check to see that he or she is willing to accept such longer documents. If not, see if he or she will look over a page or even a central paragraph of your work incorporated into the body of the email. And be sure to "cc" yourself any time you send a piece of work.

   5-Star Tip. Never email your paper as an attachment in a bizarre format. You might think .odt is really cool since you did not have to pay for Open Office. But what happens when the professor discovers it takes him or her 20 minutes to find the plug-in that does not work, then another half hour to download Open Office (which ties up all too much space on his computer). What was supposed to be a 15-minute grading job on your paper is now taking over an hour. And then the professor has to assign your grade? Stick to [Microsoft] Word or [rich text format] RTF.

8. **Always acknowledge.** If your professor decides to answer—or send you the handout or reference you asked for—be sure to tell him or her that you received it. That way he or she will know the email was delivered.
9. **THIS IS NOT A SHOUTING MATCH.** Don't write in all uppercase letters, which is an email convention for anger or other strong emotions. No one likes yelling. Do not be surprised if you are asked to resend your email in a more acceptable "tone."
10. **No one really likes emoticons and smileys.** Trust us on this one. :)
11. **This is not Facebook.** Don't write the professor in the way you'd write on your friend's wall.

    5-StarTip. It's never a good idea to "poke" your professor on Facebook, no matter how funny it seems at the time.
12. **This is not IM-ing.** So pls dun wrte yor profeSR llk ur txtN. uz abbrz @ yor own rsk. coRec me f Im wrng. (Translation thanks to www.transl8it.com, which features a neat little Facebook widget.)
13. **This is not College Humor.** Resist the temptation to talk about the "bad ass" paper you need help with, your "loser" TA who didn't teach you what you needed to know, or the "crappy" grade you just got on the midterm.
14. **This is not RateMyProfessors.com.** The professor does not want your comments about his or her performance in the class. Save those for the end-of-term evaluations, where you will be able to say what you wish anonymously.
15. **Spelling mistakes make you look lazy.** Always use the spell check and proofread your email.
16. **Signoffs and signatures count.** Always end by thanking the professor for his or her time, and closing with "Best wishes" or "Regards" (or some other relatively formal, but friendly, closing). And always sign with your (entire) real name.
17. **Your professor doesn't want to hear your philosophy of life.** Skip the cute quotes or statements of your religious or political views at the bottom of your email. You never know what offends.
18. **Don't lay it on too thick.** It's one thing to be polite and friendly in your email; it's another thing to wind up with a brown nose.

EXERCISE 6.6: Email Communication with Professors

Based on the information you just read about emails, write an email to your professor requesting instructions on your most recent homework assignment.

From:

To:

Subject:

Traditional emails may be the primary means of communicating, but some professors are communicating via social networking such as texting or Tweeting®. What are the distinctions of these communication forms?

Email: Electronic messages sent to one or more recipients through the Internet with delayed time. This is highly respected in most businesses as a secure means of communication within standards of professionalism.

Text Message or Texting: Short Message Service (SMS) created on a cell phone, or other portable device, in which people send brief messages and/or pictures to one or more people at a time. Typically, it is used to send messages to replace a phone call.

Tweet®: Real time communications comprised of no more than 140 characters may be sent from a cell phone or portable device to a number of followers at one time.

In a recent study promoted by the National Association of Engineering of the National Academies entitled "Text Messaging as a Tool for Enhancing Student-Instructor Interactions" conducted at Michigan State University by S. Patrick Walton, texting between professors and students has the potential to increase course communications. This study compared face-to-face, phone, texting, online chat, and email communications between professors and their students. Most students indicated a strong preference toward meeting with a professor in a face-to-face setting. The second most preferred method of communication was emailing a professor. Phone conversations, online chat, and text messaging where equally the third option selected by the students. It is suggested in this study that over time students may become more inclined to text or chat online with professors. Do not be surprised if your instructor does not allow texting to his or her private phone.

This being said, some of your professors will encourage you to use text messaging or Twitter as a means of staying active and engaged in your course. The general rule for you to follow in communicating with these less traditional means is to follow the lead of the professor. Professors who want you follow their Twitter feed or interact through texting will extend an invitation to do so. For you to assume tweeting or texting are acceptable means of communication may send an implied message that you perceive your professor to be a peer rather than a professional. If you are not sure, refer to the syllabus. Typically, emailing your professor is always a safe means of communication.

The use of the word "safe" in this textbook refers to a secure and private means of communication between you and the person with whom you are communicating. You are probably aware of recent scandals in the media in which a person sent a text or tweet only to have it become an embarrassing public situation. While it is unlikely you are intentionally sending inappropriate messages to your professor, have you ever inadvertently texted a message to the "wrong" person? It is easy to accidently send a casual message intended for a friend to another person, so avoid this type of embarrassing situation with your professors by avoiding texting.

The most secure way to communicate with your professor is through the use of your college email account. Then, be sure you are sending the email messages to the college's secured email server by using the email including the college name. By sending your message through the college server, you are less likely to have your email hacked by an outsider. Email accounts from providers such as Google, Yahoo, or Hotmail are not secure, and if they are hacked, limited attention to catching the perpetrator will be invested because you have used a free email provider. Primarily, the free accounts do not have the number of personnel needed to research and follow up with you in the event of a hacking. Play it safe and use your college email account ALWAYS! Most professors will not answer an email sent by a student unless the student uses their college email account.

PERSON to PERSON

In this exercise, you will be focusing on email communication. Let's discuss the possible inappropriateness of certain content!

© Rawpixel.com/Shutterstock.com

An instructor received the following email communication:

last night i just found out my grandmother had passed. so we are on our way to Denver right now. It won't let me go and do my quiz and im freaking out over here!! I didn't even take it yet and IDK WHATT TO DO. PLEASE HELP ME! i wass= unable to take the quiz Omg. help! This totally sucks. Everything sucks today haha. is there an option for me to take it.
Thanks for being so... umm... I dont know, I guess like, helpful and what not.

Based on this description, rank the following as to the issues or concerns with the email with 1 being the greatest concern.

Clarity ____ Tone ____ Punctuation ____ Grammar ____ Timing ____

Here is some additional information.

- The syllabus clearly states emails must be written following Standard American English rules of grammar.
- The instructor received this email two hours later from the same student: "did u receive my email? Please reply soon soon soon!"
- The instructor's gender is female and the student's gender is male.

Based on all the information you now know, rank them again as to what you believe is the most important issue with the email. Has your ranking changed?

Clarity ____ Tone ____ Punctuation ____ Grammar ____ Timing ____

1. What pieces of new information do you think should influence the email response?

____

____

____

continued

2. What pieces of new information do you think should not influence the email response?

____

____

____

Here are your last pieces of information.

- The syllabus clearly states the instructor will respond to email within 48 hours.
- The class is English as a Second Language.

Based on all the information you have about this situation, select which of these actions you think the instructor should take or suggest an alternative.

1. Instructor should ignore both emails ______
2. Instructor should ask the student to rewrite and resubmit. ______
3. Instructor should respond with permission to take the quiz late. ______
4. Instructor should respond with ______________________________
5. Any other suggestion? ______________________________

1. What pieces of new information would you still like to know about the situation?

____

____

____

2. Are there any pieces of information that could influence the instructor's response?

____

____

____

6.3 RELATING TO GROUPS

Relating to peers in groups can be a positive or negative learning experience.

Dominique offers an example of the group dynamics that challenged her on many levels. She was assigned a group project and encouraged to find group members with whom to work for the academic term. Since the assignment was given in the first week of class, Dominique chose to work with the people who sat near her in class, but she did not know them prior to that academic term. Initially, everyone seemed to get along and work well with each other, but after three weeks the group's cooperation seemed to slowly fall apart. Two of the four members started dating each other and forgot about the rest of the group. They rarely showed up for the preparation meetings, and when they did, they did not have their work ready. That meant Dominique and the other group member felt the burden to complete the project without the two distracted members. As a result, negative feelings were expressed in an aggressive way, which crippled the group's productivity to the point they did not speak. By midterm, the group was experiencing more problems when the couple decided to break up. On the day of the presentation of the group's project, one member did not show up, which meant their portion of the project could not be presented. The three group members, who did show up, presented their parts independent of each other. In the end, everyone's grade suffered because the group dynamics were weak. As a result of this challenging experience, Dominique dreaded working with a group for the duration of her college career.

Perhaps you have experienced working in a similar group for a class project. Do you think a little knowledge of group dynamics would have benefited Dominique's group or your own?

EXERCISE 6.7: Working in Groups

Describe a time when you have worked in a group that did NOT work well together to complete a single project. Evaluate the reasons you believe the group did not work.

____

____

____

____

Describe a time when you have worked in a group that did work well together to complete a single project. Evaluate the reasons you believe the group did work.

____

____

____

____

REFLECTION 6.C:

Evaluate YOUR participation in working with the groups you described above. Did your involvement hinder or enhance the project?

____

____

____

____

Keep this information in mind as you begin the next section of the chapter.

OBJECTIVE 6: Understand the Stages of Group Dynamics

Group dynamics describes the way in which people in a group relate to one another. It explains the roles ascribed by members of a group and the effect the individual's role has on the group. Since everyone is connected by a common goal, the project, it is the individual personalities and their reactions to the group's goal that can make or break a group. There are five predictable **stages of group dynamics** offering you a means of working more productively when you are in a group. B. Tuckman is credited with defining the five stages: forming, storming, norming, performing, and winding down.

Stage one is *forming*. In this stage group members are literally forming opinions about one another. Through the process of orientation and initiation, group members begin to identify one another's unique personality traits and talents. There is little trust, heightened anxiety, and minimal conflict at this stage.

The second stage of group dynamics is termed *storming* because it is at this point dynamics may become stormy. Group members are more comfortable with each other because they are beginning to trust each other. Anxiety, which was high in the forming stage, is subsiding because on a very basic level the members are seeing themselves as a group that makes adjustments for the group member's idiosyncrasies. It is at this point minor power struggles begin to occur, but members are reluctant to verbally discuss them. Members are more concerned with expressing their own opinion or perspective and want to minimize any anxiety within the group. In this stage, group members define their roles, yield or compete for power, and various motivational levels are revealed.

Norming, the third stage in group dynamics, is also identified as the stage in which rules are set by a group. Agreement on how the group members will negotiate and operate is more established; and, while formal norms are established, so are informal norms. The latter is often more influential than formal or stated rules. At this stage trust and sharing more than just the work devoted to the project occurs. This results in a more cohesive group actively building skills necessary to complete the project's work. Since the group has established some rules, anxiety is diminished. Conflicts are managed by the group because they have an agreed plan for self-management.

Getting the job done, *performing*, is the fourth stage of group dynamics. The focus at this point is on completing the shared task. Trust levels in the group are very high, but anxiety over completing the task may emerge. Overall, the performance of the group members is very high and conflicts are subdued in order to increase productivity in the group.

Stage five is called winding down or *adjourning* because the group's task has been accomplished. It is at this point where the students part ways. Of course, if group members have become friends, they may have the opportunity to remain friends.

As you can see, group dynamics have predictable stages that can increase your ability to work professionally and productively. Additionally, working in groups is not a unique experience for college as you will work in groups throughout your career. Team work is one of the skills identified in Bill Coplin's book, *10 Things Employers Want You to Learn in College: The Know-How You Need to Succeed* (2003). Understanding the dynamics of a group can help you successfully negotiate to produce exemplary work.

TABLE 6.1

Theory: Five Stages of Group Dynamics		**Practical Focus**	
Stages	**Characteristics**	**Focus**	**Strategies**
Forming	Minimal *trust.* Heightened *anxiety.* No evidence of *conflict.*	Deal with anxiety about the unknown. Identifying the complementary skills of the group members as they relate to the goals of the group.	■ Clarify goals. ■ Allow uncertainties and concerns to be voiced. ■ Establish and agree on procedures to guide meeting behavior. ■ Be supportive of all contributions.
Storming	*Trust* is developing. *Anxiety* lessened because the group members are beginning to see themselves as part of a group, but anxiety may still exist as adjustments are made to each other. *Conflicts* may manifest as power struggles emerge, but it usually is dismissed. Individuals may be concerned with having their opinions heard, but they do not want to create more anxiety.	Keep focus on positive outcomes. Ask yourself: What is the purpose and goals of the group? Which group member has the skills suited to complete the task? Exercise your active listening skills.	■ Encourage expression of feelings even if task is temporarily interrupted. ■ Accept negative feedback about process or progress. ■ Use reflective and interpretive feedback to ensure all views are heard. ■ Encourage all group members to participate in resolving issues. ■ Facilitate resolution of conflict by synthesizing opinions and identifying consensus views. ■ As conflicts are resolved, remind group of agreed procedures and if necessary, reorient group toward goals.
Norming	***Trust*** is more stable and members are learning to connect beyond their work. Thus, cohesion is developed, and they build skills necessary for productivity. ***Anxiety*** is minimized among most members because the rules of behavior are clearly defined. ***Conflict*** is self-managed by the group members. An agreed upon plan for managing conflict is recognized by the group.	How can I contribute to the completion of our group goals? If conflict occurs, determine the most expeditious means of resolving it, so the group can be productive.	■ Encourage all group members to take on task and maintenance functions. ■ Encourage and allow leadership to shift from member to member. ■ Accept and air suggestions for alternate approaches or revised procedural rules. ■ Encourage and assist systematic planning for task achievement.
Performing	Heightened **trust**. **Anxiety** is primarily focused on completing the task may resurface but productivity and performance is high. In order to heighten performance, **conflict** is submerged.	What is my part in the performance/ presentation? How can I support fellow group members in their performance?	■ Periodically group members need reminders of any criteria against which performance will be judged or graded. ■ Be aware of time and resource constraints.
Adjourning	Bid farewell and congratulate one another on a job well done.	Debrief, evaluate, and celebrate.	■ Is there a reflection or group evaluation due upon completion? ■ Celebrate the group's accomplishments!

EXERCISE 6.8: Implementing Five Stages of Group Dynamics

Analyze a small group meeting and how that experience could have improved through knowledge of the five stages.

____

____

____

____

____

REFLECTION 6.D:

After a group project, as part of the final grade, many instructors have each member evaluate (anonymously, of course) all other members' input into the project, as well as their own. Unfortunately, most students rate all other members highly, as well as themselves, regardless of everyone's participation, for fear their group members will rate them negatively.

Develop a way in which these evaluations can provide the instructor with a more accurate account of participation without fear of reprisal from the rest of the group.

____

____

____

____

OBJECTIVE 7: Understand Conflict-Resolution Strategies

Even the most organized and well-intentioned groups may have conflicts. Resolution of these conflicts requires a set of skills aiding in the group's productivity, increased understanding of group members, and improved self-knowledge. For these reasons, a few strategies to negotiate a resolution to conflicts are of great benefit. According to Mind Tools, the basic steps for ***conflict resolution*** include:

- Set the scene.
- Gather information.
- Agree on the problem.
- Brainstorm solutions.
- Negotiate solutions.

Setting the scene requires you to listen actively and exercise your assertiveness skills. When you state your perspective, be sure to state it is your opinion of the conflict. Once you have stated your perspective, listen to all the opinions expressed without emotion. Then, tell the group or individual what you understood them to say. By restating, rephrasing, or summarizing the situation you are employing active listening. When you are speaking, be sure to exercise assertive tones and non-verbal messages rather than aggressive ones.

In gathering information, you will want to follow the advice of Stephen Covey's book entitled *Seven Habits of Highly Effective People*. In it Covey encourages people to "Seek first to understand and then to be understood." This means listening and seeking to understand the motives or goals of others will aid in your ability to be objective.

After listening to the various informative components of the conflict, try to agree with the group or individual on the conflict. This allows common grounds for resolving the conflict. If this stage is omitted it, the individuals may be working on resolution of their personal perception of the conflict which may differ from that of the group.

Once everyone understands the source of the problem or conflict, the group can brainstorm for solutions. All of the members contributing toward the resolution better ensures investment in the process of reconciliation. Additionally, everyone in the group has unique ideas for the solution, so someone else may have the more creative problem solving strategy.

The final stage for conflict resolution is negotiating solutions. Consider all of the ideas generated in the brainstorming session and identify the one, or a combination of ideas, the group sees as the best solution. Often, the group may have resolved the conflict by this point because they have worked together to identify, listen, and communicate the concerns as a group. It is important to recognize each member's opinion in this final stage to generate a win-win solution. Win-win means everyone leaves the conflict resolution session feeling as if they won the negotiation. In contrast, win-lose situations means one side of the negotiation table feels as if they lost something significant. If win-lose negotiations occur, it is unlikely the group dynamics will be productive or even civil in extreme situations.

The primary need in negotiating resolutions to conflicts is the willingness of your group to work together. If you determine the conflict cannot be resolved after working through the previously stated steps for resolution, you may want to meet with your professor. If you identify a serious concern such as aggressive tendencies, you may want to seek assistance from your professor or the counseling center on your campus. Working in a group does not mean you should ever feel intimidated or threatened so if you do feel this way nip the aggression or destructive behavior in the bud quickly.

OBJECTIVE 8: Understand Synergy as it Relates to Group Dynamics

Having focused on the worst case scenario of group dynamics, you may be led to believe there is no way you can work amicably within a group. This is not the intention of this textbook nor is it typically the situation you will experience during group work.

Synergy is the best case scenario for group dynamics and is the result of active participation by all group members. According to R. Buckminster Fuller, the originator of the term, "Synergy means behavior of integral, aggregate, whole systems, unpredicted by behaviors of any of their components or subassemblies of their components taken separately from the whole" (1979). This complex definition simply stated describes the phenomenon occurring when "the whole is greater than the sum of its parts" (Sholtes 2010) When synergy is applied to group dynamics, it means that all of the member's individual efforts and talents when working together create something that no one could produce on their own.

Synergy in Architecture

© Ted Thai/Getty Images

A visual of synergy is demonstrated in architecture as seen in Epcot Center in Florida. Upon entering the amusement park a round chrome structure welcomes you to spaceship Earth. This structure is comprised of multiple triangles that, when connected, offer structural integrity that a triangle alone does not. When the triangles are fixed in such a way as to share the load of the structure, the triangles generate synergy because they create a better product by joining their energy.

Getting a group to synergy means all of the members recognize and respect the skills of each individual member. Additionally, the group understands the need to work collaboratively toward a common goal. This means if one person is skilled in speaking; let him work with the group to share this skill. Then, when the presentation occurs everyone can perform as a skilled speaker. Too often groups attempt to work by fragmenting the skills of its members. Synergy requires everyone to work toward achieving a product none of the members could produce in isolation. By understanding group dynamics, while stated in a linear process, actually work better when the common goal is synergy, you will be on your way to working synergistically. Finally, by employing the strategies suggested for conflict resolution, such as active listening and assertiveness, prior to any conflicts, you will begin with a stronger foundation.

COURSE CONNECTIONS:

Study Groups in Hard and Soft Sciences

Study Groups in General

- Find people with whom you believe you can work.
- Try to keep the group to four or less.
- Set a specific time, duration, and place to meet.
- Try to meet at least once a week.
- Meet in a quiet, study-conducive area or possibly an online chat room set up by your instructor. Most colleges have study rooms in the library which can accommodate up to six to eight people.
- Do not allow your study time to be used for idle chatter, but set up specific tasks as well as time for a break.
- Try to ensure everyone contributes.
- Decide beforehand what each member will focus on for the study session.

Hard Sciences

- Focus on procedures and concepts.
- Focus on technical vocabulary.
- Create flash cards for vocabulary.
- Create a flash card for each type of problem or concept.

- Use different types of instructions to ask the same question. This is especially important for mathematics courses.
- Be specific about any area in which you are having difficulty.

Soft Sciences

- Focus on discipline specific vocabulary.
- Focus on processes (e.g., writing, research studies).
- Anticipate topics on which you might be asked to discuss in class or on a test. Then, generate responses from the course materials.
- Explain concepts to one another aloud.
- Practice using vocabulary words in sentences.
- Focus on any area in which you are having difficulty.
- Analyze the assignments you have completed in class to anticipate assessment or test questions.

If you could create the perfect study group from the students in your mathematics or science class, which three would you select (first names or initials only) and why? Be specific about your evaluation of each student's strengths.

____

____

____

____

If you could create the perfect study group from the students in one of your soft science classes, which three would you select (first names or initials only) and why? Be specific about your evaluation of each student's strengths.

____

____

____

____

Did you use the same criteria for selecting the students for your mathematics or science class than you did for the soft science class? If yes, explain what criteria you used, and if not, how was the criteria different?

____

____

____

____

6.4 COLLABORATING OUTSIDE OF CLASS

OBJECTIVE 9: Learn How to Identify a Study Partner

Have you ever heard the phrase "collaborate to graduate?" Graduating from college is a journey that when shared with fellow learners can increase your odds of earning your degree. Just as synergy generates structures supporting individual components that are strengthened when joined, **collaboration** with your peers can strengthen your learning and success toward graduation.

Collaborating outside of class with a study partner or group offers another opportunity to learn and connect with students in your courses. Identifying a partner with whom to work means you will need to look for students who are equally or more motivated than you are. Enthusiasm breeds enthusiasm, so find the student in your class who is eager to talk about the subject you are learning. Watch for the students who take notes in class as an indication of someone with whom you will want to study. Also, observe the students who are earning a good grade in the class as potential study partners. These elements comprise the study partner who will encourage you to perform at your optimum level in learning.

When you meet to study with the person you think is going to create a more synergistic learning environment, come prepared to study. This may mean creating assignments prior to meeting. For example, if you are meeting to discuss the last three weeks of class, make sure you arrive with:

- a textbook or other written resources,
- chapter notes,
- class notes,
- lab notes,
- and/or questions you have generated as a result of processing the information presented and read.

You may want to prepare essay questions you feel certain are going to be on the test as well. This may be in the form of an outline, but needs to be written down. Discuss the possible answers to the essay questions with your study partner. In a mathematics class, be sure you have worked and understand the process of each problem. The more complex problems may need to be written on a dry-erase board in a study room within the college library. In a science class, be certain to study all the diagrams. Many times, the pictures help illustrate the interactions of the topic being presented. Then, you and your study partner can freely discuss the solution.

The most important component to bring to your study session is respect and a positive attitude. Even if you have all the preparation for studying completed prior to meeting, if you show up with a negative attitude, you will limit your learning as well as that of your partner. Come prepared to learn mentally and physically.

Concerning the time dedicated to studying with your partner, establish a beginning and ending time for your sessions. Begin promptly and end at the designated time out of respect for one another's schedules. If you fail to end your sessions in a timely manner, you may be reluctant to meet again.

OBJECTIVE 10: Understand the Role of Diversity

Diversity is part of learning in college as well. There has been no other time in America when so many cultures are represented in the college classroom. ***Culture*** refers to a set of practices, customs, principles, codes, and traditions within an organization. Students enter the classroom with a set of practices and beliefs acquired from the various groups and organizations where they have participated. It is from this background knowledge that students view the world and their learning. Therefore, it is the diversity of cultures in college classes that make the learning richer and relevant. By understanding the various perspectives in a class, you will enrich your appreciation for the unique qualities in your classmates. Additionally, you will find the information shared by everyone offers a more realistic view of America today.

Demonstrating respect for diversity in your classes means explicitly acting in ways serving as a catalyst for shared understanding. This means you may need to monitor your thoughts and actions to limit offensive, albeit unintentional, words or behaviors. Developing sensitivity to everyone's beliefs will increase your ability to self-monitor your actions and language. Be slow to categorize people by their appearance or language. Just because a person looks as if they are from a specific region of the world does not mean they are from that area. In other words, try not to make assumptions or judgments based solely on looks. In order to successfully self-monitor your actions and words, you will want to recognize your personal bias and preconceptions. College will be a time of growth through the acceptance and value of diversity.

The values of embracing the diversity in your courses are many and varied. American students can learn about the world without leaving our shores when they open the door to those from around the globe. Learning about the customs through dance, religion, and discussions increases global perspective. Diversity expands horizons as you increase your social groups. How boring is life when everyone is the same? Learning about the various people and cultures in your college classroom expands your knowledge of the world. Some of the practices in other countries are actually very similar to American customs, so you will get to learn how humans are basically the same. Additionally, diversity in the classroom means you are learning to problem solve more creatively. Observing the moral and ***ethical dilemmas*** cultural diversity offers presents, you will expand the appreciation of your beliefs and background, while increasing your creative thinking. After reviewing the value of diversity in your classrooms, you will be prepared to work alongside your peers more constructively.

Diversity is the new norm! You are experiencing real world dynamics by learning to work with people who have different cultures, beliefs, and appearances. College provides a microcosm of our world, so seek opportunities to learn and grow.

OBJECTIVE 11: Understand Strategies to Connect with Others In and Out of Class

Once you acknowledge the role diversity plays in your education, you can collaborate with your peers. According to Jeremy S. Hyman and Lynn F. Jacobs article "Why Does Diversity Matter at College Anyway?" (2009) the value in your education is as stated:

> Diversity **enriches the multiple perspectives** developed by a liberal arts education. Diversity magnifies the power of a general education by helping to liberate you from the tunnel vision of an ethnocentric and egocentric viewpoint. By moving beyond yourself, you gain a panoramic perspective of the world around you and a more complete view of your place in it.

Issues of diversity play a role in how students and teachers view the importance of the classroom and what should happen there. Students may perceive that they do not "belong" in the classroom setting—a feeling that can lead to decreased participation, feelings of inadequacy, and other distractions. When you have the opportunity to collaborate with students with diverse backgrounds, you are actually learning more than any textbook can offer. Being **ethnocentric**, evaluating other peoples and cultures according to the standards of one's own culture, limits your education and the expansion of your ideas. In contrast, being **egocentric**, or self-centered, limits your education with a narrow view of the world. The diversity offers the opportunity to see the solutions to problems you will work through in class from an expanded perspective. This means collaboration and synergy are more likely to occur.

You may want to seek opportunities to connect with diversity beyond the classroom, too. With the number of student organizations with specific populations they serve, you do not need to look very far to find occasions to interact outside of class. The friendships you will establish as a result of getting to know people of diversity in a more causal setting will provide memories throughout your life and establish lasting relationships.

In the workplace you will be collaborating with all types of people, so the more you learn in college, the better prepared you will be for your career challenges. Since the diversity you encounter in your college classes closely resembles the work place, you are gaining insights into establishing connections between college and your career. In contrast, failing to focus on extending your personal understanding and appreciation for diversity in college may hinder your initial success in the workplace. Beginning early to expand your understandings of others will give you a competitive edge once you begin your career.

Collaborative work will either contribute to or subtract from a feeling of self-worth. Obviously, successful connections and collaborations will boost your self-worth, while conflict-ridden collaborative attempts will do the opposite. Fortunately, you will have the skills necessary to negotiate the tumultuous terrains of less-successful groups with your knowledge of the stages in group dynamics and conflict resolution. Imagine the boost your self-esteem will experience when working through the challenges in less productive groups. Knowing you have successfully worked out conflicts in a constructive manner will aid in your ability to generate synergistic relationships on a frequent basis.

Career Connection

In college, peer interaction in and out of the classroom requires active listening and the ability to relate to others in a healthy way. The ability to properly communicate with your instructors and other college personnel is necessary for your success. The ability to also effectively communicate with others and successfully resolve conflicts are skills highly valued in the workplace.

CHAPTER SUMMARY

In summary, communication skills are critical to your college success as well as your future relationships. In this chapter you have learned various ways to communicate in a constructive manner. The ultimate goal of communications with other people is to seek synergistic connections.

Active listening includes several behaviors. First, an active listener must focus on the meaning of the words uttered by speaker and watch for non-verbal cues of the speaker. Secondly, you will use your nonverbal cues to communicate you are listening and understanding the words being spoken. Third, and perhaps most importantly, do not allow your personal bias to create misunderstandings. If you are listening to a person and it sounds like they are being critical of you or have an opposite opinion than you, ask follow up questions for clarification. The fourth step to active listening is to allow the speaker to communicate their idea without interruption; the likelihood of them listening to you poses a question is unlikely. The final and fifth step to active communication is to respond with appropriate words.

Aggressive and assertive behaviors and communication techniques were covered in this chapter. There are many ways to learn to communicate assertively. A few from Smith are broken record, fogging, negative assertions, and "I" statements.

There are strategies to extinguish aggressive behavior and a few discussed in this chapter are counting to ten, venting versus self-awareness, apologizing, and empathizing. If a person struggles to control aggressive communication or behaviors, he or she should seek the help of a professional counselor. Fortunately, most college campuses have highly qualified counselors to help understand and diffuse aggressive behaviors.

Learning to work well with your peers, professors, and campus employees means you are learning to collaborate in the same way you will work in your choice of career. Establishing positive relationships in college means you create mutually respectful relationships with peers, professors, and anyone who works on the campus. Peer relationships encompass students in your classes, student organizations in which you participate, or students with whom you establish interactive relationships in social settings.

Understanding the written arrangement and style of email or electronic communications will increase your connections with a professor. Group dynamics describes the way in which people in a group relate to one another. It explains the roles ascribed by members of a group and the effect of the individual's role has on the group.

Synergy is the best case scenario for group dynamics and is the result of active participation by all group members. Collaborating outside of class with a study partner or group offers another opportunity to learn and connect with students in your courses. Diversity is part of learning in college as well. There has been no other time in America when so many cultures are represented in the college classroom. *Culture* refers to a set of practices, customs, principles, codes and traditions within an organization. By embracing diversity you are enriching your understanding of other perspectives and opinions.

CHAPTER 6: Self-Check

Vocabulary: Define the following:

1. active listening
2. non-verbal communication
3. assertive behavior
4. aggressive behavior
5. email
6. tweet®
7. text messaging
8. social networking
9. synergy
10. diversity

Concepts:

11. Describe signs of active listening and contrast this to hearing.
12. Explain two strategies to increase active listening.
13. Evaluate your personal ability to listen actively.

14. Explain the difference between assertive and aggressive behavior.
15. Identify three strategies to become more assertive in a learning environment.
16. Identify two strategies to minimize aggressive behavior.
17. Define a positive relationship as it relates to college.
18. Describe three relationships in college that must be established.
19. What are Bill Coplin's ten skills that should be learned in college, so you can succeed in your career? (*10 Things Employers Want You to Learn in College: The Know-How You Need to Succeed,* [2003])
20. Compare and contrast Coplin's Top Ten Criteria regarding career preparation.
21. Identify your primary need to connect with each professor.
22. Identify ten behaviors that communicate learning to a professor.
23. Devise a plan for connecting in class by learning and communicating through behaviors.
24. Discuss the purpose of recommendation letters and the criteria for a good letter.
25. Explain your understanding of legal and ethical boundaries.
26. Formulate a well-written student-to-professor email.
27. Describe the elements of writing arrangement and style of an email communication.
28. List and explain the stages of group dynamics.
29. Summarize three conflict-resolution strategies and the conditions necessary for resolution.
30. Explain synergy as it relates to group dynamics and strategies for increasing synergy.
31. Identify and elaborate on characteristics students should use in identifying a study partner.
32. Explain the role of diversity in college.
33. Describe two strategies students can use to connect with others in and out of class.
34. Describe how collaborative work can contribute to or subtract from a feeling of self-worth.
35. Create three note cards, the first with a true-false test question, the second with a multiple choice test question, and the third with an essay question.

CHAPTER 7
Taking Notes

T.I.P.S.—(Tactical Information that Promotes Success)

Write down everything the instructor writes on the board, including charts, graphs, and figures.

REPEAT TO REMEMBER . . .

© Rawpixel.com/Shutterstock.com

To take better notes, come to class prepared.

What this means is to **pre-read** the material being discussed. Familiarity with the concepts will assist you with your note taking!

© wavebreakmedia/Shutterstock.com

Once a set of notes is written, the serious learning can begin. As you know, **repetition** is critical to learning. In math and sciences be certain to practice a few exercises or procedures directly after class, if possible. Doing so will **reinforce** your learning and clarify your notes.

© chrisdorney/Shutterstock.com

Reading and writing provide the necessary **repetitions** to reinforce learning when done at the same time.

Write down *everything* your instructor thinks is significant enough to write on the board. This means learning to write the most important points and how to use abbreviations. At times, it will require you to speed up or slow down based on the speaker.

If you prefer to use a laptop or tablet, be certain to ask your instructor if this is allowed. For classes having a lot of symbols or graphs, handwritten notes may be quicker. It is too time consuming to find the symbols on a computer.

In **mathematics and lab science classes**, be certain to include all figures, graphs, and illustrations accompanying the detailed work. This will provide a complete set of notes from which you can begin to study and reinforce the information provided during class. Consider this situation. Your instructor puts a problem on the board, drawing a triangle and the labeling the sides. She asks you to find the perimeter. If your notes only contain the equation but not the figure, the review of your notes at a future time will not identify the conceptual details.

Reading and writing are blended when students take notes on the reading materials. This allows for deeper processing to occur in learning new or unfamiliar materials.

In **Education,** students observe teachers and children by taking notes. These consist of descriptions of what a teacher or child is doing or saying. These notes assist in discovering specific behaviors in that teacher or child.

CHAPTER 7: OBJECTIVES

7.1 Taking Notes in a Lecture Course

Objective 1 Understand the Purpose and Value of Taking Notes during a Lecture

Objective 2 Understand Techniques to Outline a Lecture

Objective 3 Recognize the Key Points in a Lecture

Objective 4 Use Two Columns to Organize Notes

7.2 Taking Notes Using Electronic Devices

Objective 5 Understand When and What Device to Use for Recording a Lecture

Objective 6 Discuss the Relationship between Learning Preferences and Recording

7.3 Learning with Your Notes

Objective 7 Understand How Visual Notes and Graphic Organizers Enhance Note-Taking

Objective 8 Understand How Using Bloom's Taxonomy Promotes Recursive Learning

Objective 9 Apply Learning Style Preferences to Note-Taking

CHAPTER CONCEPTS:

Some or all of the following terms may be new to you. Place a check mark in the column reflecting your knowledge of each term.

	Know	Don't know	Not sure	Page # where first found		Know	Don't know	Not sure	Page # where first found
Comprehension					Self-Quiz				
Cornell Notes					Modified Self-Quiz				
Studying Productively					Using Note Cards				
Two column Notes					Graphic Organizers				
Recursive Learning									

7.1 TAKING NOTES IN A LECTURE COURSE

Imagine sitting in a new course on the first day of class. You're ready to take notes, because you are used to this tool from high school. However, you soon discover you cannot keep up with what the instructor is saying and you begin to wonder if you've made a mistake about signing up for this course.

© Andresr/Shutterstock.com

You are not alone. Your instructor can speak at 100–125 words per minute while you can only write down information at 35–40 words per minute. Additionally, you can think at around 300 words per minute and there is the problem. How do you deal with all the differences in speeds? This is what this chapter will help you manage.

OBJECTIVE 1: Understand the Purpose and Value of Taking Notes during a Lecture

How does the previous scenario relate to taking notes in a class? Hearing and memory recall is tough even when you are highly motivated to remember the information. Sitting in your class listening to your instructor or a student speaker requires information to be heard and recalled later. When distractions, or even time elapses, get in the way of your ability to store information in your brain's long-term memory, forgetting occurs. Because your brain needs support when it comes to processing short term memory, memory aids are critical for recall. In this chapter you are going to learn the value of note-taking, several ways to organize your notes, and how to personalize your notes based on your particular learning preferences.

If you are trying to remember a critical piece of information, you will need to make sure it is stored in your long-term memory. Take a minute to review the memory process illustrated in Figure 7.1, specifically long-term memory covered in Chapter 3. As you think about this process of acquiring information for long-term memory, where in this model do you think note-taking fits?

FIGURE 7.1 Memory Process

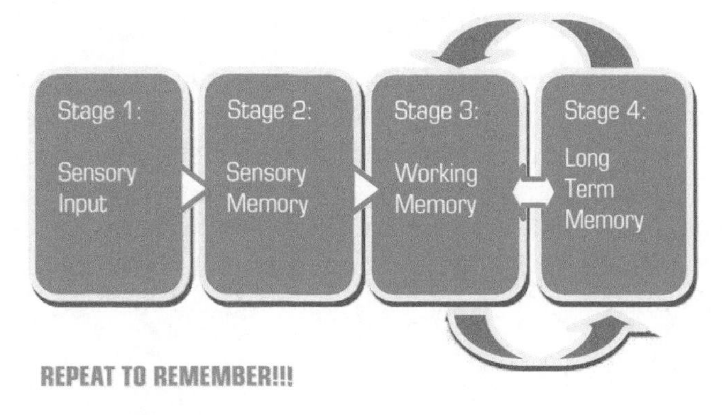

Repeat to Remember

If you said it was in the sensory memory, you are correct. Listening to a lecture is engaging the auditory senses. Then, when you record the words on the page, you are creating another sensory image. Remember, you have less than three seconds to process sensory information before it is lost. Processing the information from sensory memory while taking notes means you are engaging your working memory to determine which piece of information is most important for inclusion in your notes. Again, the time limitation in working memory of less than thirty seconds means writing down the information is essential if you want to process it to your long-term memory. Throughout the first three processes of memory making, you are engaging your long-term memory to determine the schema you have stored that relates to the concepts and to which you can attach the new information for more permanent long-term storage. Once the new information is stored in your long-term memory, it is there for an unlimited amount of time. Of course, you will need to work on recalling or recognizing the information later.

Note-taking increases your opportunities to learn and retrieve information. Imagine test preparation, after not taking notes during a lecture, and having limited memories of class to learn the concepts. Knowing your working memory lasts thirty seconds or less, how can you expect to remember the information for up to a month? Most college classes cover a body of material for about four to five weeks before you take a test. The probability of remembering something you have not taken notes on for this amount of time is minimal.

Note-taking has several advantages, with the most obvious being writing down information during a lecture means you will be able to review it later. More specifically, taking notes will increase your:

- focus and attention,
- comprehension,
- recall and recognition,
- review of concepts,
- and connections between ideas/courses.

These five benefits of note-taking will allow you to learn more productively and permanently. According to the New American Heritage Dictionary, productivity "is the quality, state, or fact of being able to generate, create, enhance, or bring forth goods and services."[1] ***Studying productively*** means you will be able to generate, create, enhance, or bring forth information from your memory more easily and automatically. As you have previously read in Chapter 3, the memory process requires repetition to make the information more easily recalled or recognized.

When you are taking notes during class, your focus and attention are dedicated to listening and learning. However, there will be days you will not be as focused due to illness or personal distractions. This is normal and to be expected on occasion. The solution is to check with another student in the class to fill in the gaps of information you missed. Minimizing distractions in your life will also help, although forcing yourself to listen, take notes and focus on the most important concepts; you may find your other distractions have moved to a "back burner." By taking notes you are an engaged active learner who is processing the information through listening, thinking, and writing.

---

[1] "productivity." *The American Heritage® New Dictionary of Cultural Literacy, Third Edition.* Houghton Mifflin Company, 2005. 5 Nov. 2013.

REFLECTION 7.A:

One benefit from taking notes which has not been mentioned is you will inevitably write down something the instructor said you do not understand. In this situation, what is the value of taking notes and how do you handle it?

____

____

____

Comprehension, the processing of information for greater understanding, is the byproduct of taking notes during class. As you listen and think, you are processing the meaning of the spoken words and recording the information as you understand it. Taking notes will allow you to contemplate the information on a deeper level as you are exposed to supporting information.

Recall and recognition are the critical stages of memory that will help you succeed in college and beyond. Taking good notes while listening means you will have the information preeminently recorded, so you can incorporate ongoing review of the course materials. This means you will need to review your notes periodically. Repeated review of your notes will aid in your ability to store the concepts in your long-term memory. Constant review of the information for confirmation will guarantee you arrive for your test with increased confidence.

Connecting ideas in your courses increases your ability to remember specific points throughout the academic term, year, or your career. As was previously discussed in Chapter 3, learning facts in isolation is an ineffective way to study. Learning to connect ideas between courses you are taking or have taken will increase your long-term memory.

EXERCISE 7.1: Self-Assessment of Note Taking

Take a minute to reflect on how you are currently taking notes.

Rate your current note-taking methods on a scale of 1 to 5.

I use complete sentences when taking notes during a lecture.
Never Always
1 . . . . 2 . . . . 3 . . . . 4 5

I do not use any common format, but tend to write in block paragraphs.
Never Always
1 . . . . 2 . . . . 3 . . . . 4 5

I capture the main points and most of the supporting points in a lecture.
Never Always
1 . . . . 2 . . . . 3 . . . . 4 5

I use abbreviations and shorter words when taking notes.
Never Always
1 . . . . 2 . . . . 3 . . . . 4 5

I use my notes for reviewing and learning quickly after taking them.
Never Always
1 . . . . 2 . . . . 3 . . . . 4 5

So far in this chapter you have:

- established the reasons for taking notes and
- evaluated how you are currently taking notes.

Would you like to know a way to take better notes the first time for the most efficient use of your time and energy? Two methods of note-taking will offer you this valuable tool:

- ***Cornell Notes***
- Outlining

Each note-taking system has unique features, which distinguish it from other note-taking forms, but both are highly useful. In all honesty, using either one of these two methods will save you time in the long run and boost your memory quickly.

© Lewis Liu/Shutterstock.com

Historically, the Cornell note-taking system has demonstrated a strong appeal for students and professors alike. Cornell note-taking was created by Walter Paulk in the 1950s. Since its origin, this systematic format for taking notes has supported many college students through learning successfully.

Basically, this system employs the use of a two-column format with space left at the bottom of the page for a brief summary of the information included on the bottom of the page. This means you will need to allow about two inches on the left side of your notebook page for one of the columns (the main ideas). The remaining six inches will create the other column (supporting information for the main ideas). See Figure 7.2 on the next page for a visual on the format of this method.

Notice the white space on the page. The open space on the paper communicates to your brain that the information written on the page is importance because the contrast is emphasizing the words on the page. Be sure to leave space between the concepts you are taking notes on for this reason.

Summarization is a critical component of Cornell note-taking. By writing a brief summary at the bottom of the page you are forcing yourself to recite and record information which will increase your learning. It is best to write the summary as soon after the lecture as possible rather than trying to generate a summary during the lecture which could distract you from something important. Reflecting on the information once you leave the room will provide another chance to review the materials. The summary will be a valuable tool when you prepare for a test.

Once you have created your notes using the Cornell system, you have also generated a wonderful review tool. By taking a blank sheet of paper and covering the right side of your two-column notes, you can quiz yourself. Ask the question or cues you have written on the left side, recite an answer, and move the paper to check your accuracy. You will have immediate feedback as to your understanding of the concept. If you come across a concept you are unsure of, create an additional study tool (i.e., note card, graphic organizer, visual cue, etc.) to help remember the material. All in all, the Cornell note-taking method saves you time and increases your ability to learn more accurately.

FIGURE 7.2 Cornell Note Taking Example

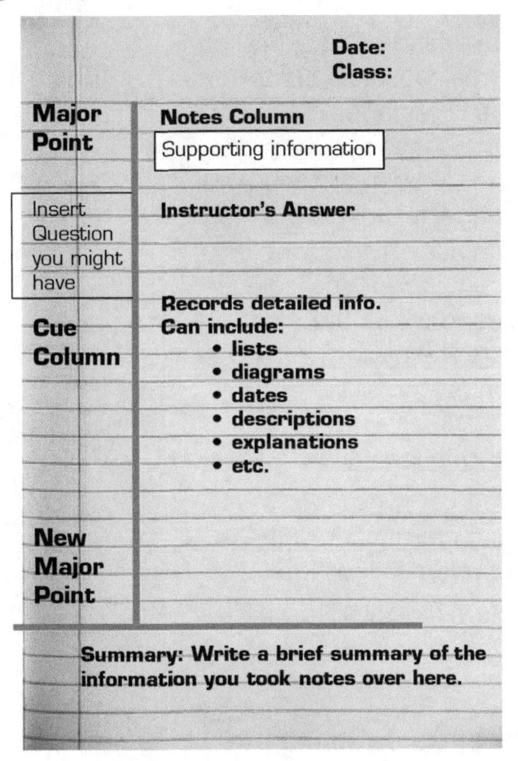

EXERCISE 7.2: Taking Cornell Notes

Create a set of Cornell notes for an upcoming lecture. Your professor will give you time to work with a group of students in your class to compare your notes. As you evaluate your notes, and notes from fellow learners, discuss the following:

1. Did you draw your page in the Cornell style?

2. Did you list the major points on the left and supporting information on the right?

3. Did you list question in the left column and have them answered by your instructor with answers in the right column?

4. Did you summarize your lesson at the bottom of the page?

5. Now that you have created this note page, discuss three ways you can use it for learning course materials.

OBJECTIVE 2: Understand Techniques to Outline a Lecture

Using the outline method of note-taking offers you a format for taking notes, which creates connections between the ideas presented. This is not a formal outline process, so you need not stress over the rules you may have learned concerning outlines. Generally, the use of dashes, stars, or other symbols to represent different levels within the outline will work fine for most subjects. The exception for using symbols is in some science, mathematics, or physics classes in which the symbols already have a specific meaning. The general format of creating an outline for note-taking is:

1. Write the most general information on the left margin of your paper.
2. Write the similar supporting information with the general topic under it and indent to the right.
3. The relationship of the facts is indicated through the indentions.

FIGURE 7.3 Example of outline note-taking

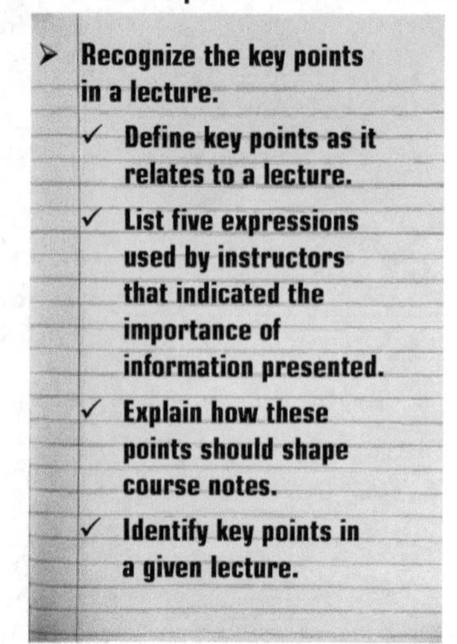

EXERCISE 7.3: Taking Notes by Outlining

Create a set of outline notes for an upcoming lecture. Your professor will give you time to work with a group of students in your class to compare your notes. As you evaluate your notes, and notes from fellow learners, discuss the following:

1. Is the most general point above the supporting details?
2. Do the indentions of the information connect information?
3. How did you emphasize important details from the lecture?
4. Now that you have created this outline, discuss three ways you can use it for learning course materials

OBJECTIVE 3: Recognize the Key Points in a Lecture

In order to record the information in the accurate column for Cornell notes or in an outline system, you will need to listen for cues from the instructor or student speaker as to what the main idea is or supporting details. There are a few ways to determine the importance and logical development of the ideas given. Watch and listen for:

- Pauses prior to or after a point is made (generally to give you time to write it down!)
- Repeated or emphasized points
- Key concept introductory phrases ("A key element of," "The primary cause," etc.)
- Information written on the board

These cues are ways of understanding the information given to you during the class. If you are using the Cornell note-taking method, you will record the main idea in the left cue column and the supporting details in the right notes column.

REFLECTION 7.B:

You have attended many classes at this point in the semester as well as in your previous learning environment, thus, you have experienced many instructor's methods of teaching. The four suggestions above for identifying important material is not a complete list. You, assuredly, have experienced other ways of identifying important material. Write at least two other methods you have used and explain how they helped you improve your note-taking.

____

____

____

____

Writing with an abbreviated method rather than full sentences or words is a valuable time saving technique to employ while taking notes. Remember the first part of the chapter and the different speeds of actions? A word of caution concerning the abbreviation of your notes is to be sure to record enough information so as to increase your understanding of the lecture. Using abbreviated methods for taking notes does not mean you are supposed to take brief notes. Below are a few examples of how you can write in a more cryptic style during the lecture but maintain the meaning:

FIGURE 7.4

Symbol(s)	Meaning
&, +	and, plus, positive
=	equals
–	minus, negative
#	number
x	times
>	greater than, more, larger
<	less than, smaller, fewer than
w/	with
w/o	without
w/in	within
↓	decrease
↑	increase
/ for	per
∴	therefore

Of course, you may have some symbols you already employ not on the list from above. Write some of the ways you already abbreviate text. (Hint: text messaging)

Abbreviation	Meaning

As you listen to your instructor, you may realize he speaks too fast or too slow. When a speaker's pace is too fast to write everything down, try to get the main ideas and leave room to fill in the missing information with a classmate after class. Of course, you can visit the professor to get the missing information occasionally. Having a speaker whose pace is too slow can be equally challenging. When this occurs, write your notes and then listen. Sometimes your professor will stop and tell a seemingly irrelevant story. Be sure to jot a note or two about the story because if the professor seems to feel this information relates to the topic, it typically does. Sometimes it can seem challenging to pace your note-taking with the speaker's pace, but learning to do so will increase you note-taking accuracy.

FIGURE 7.5

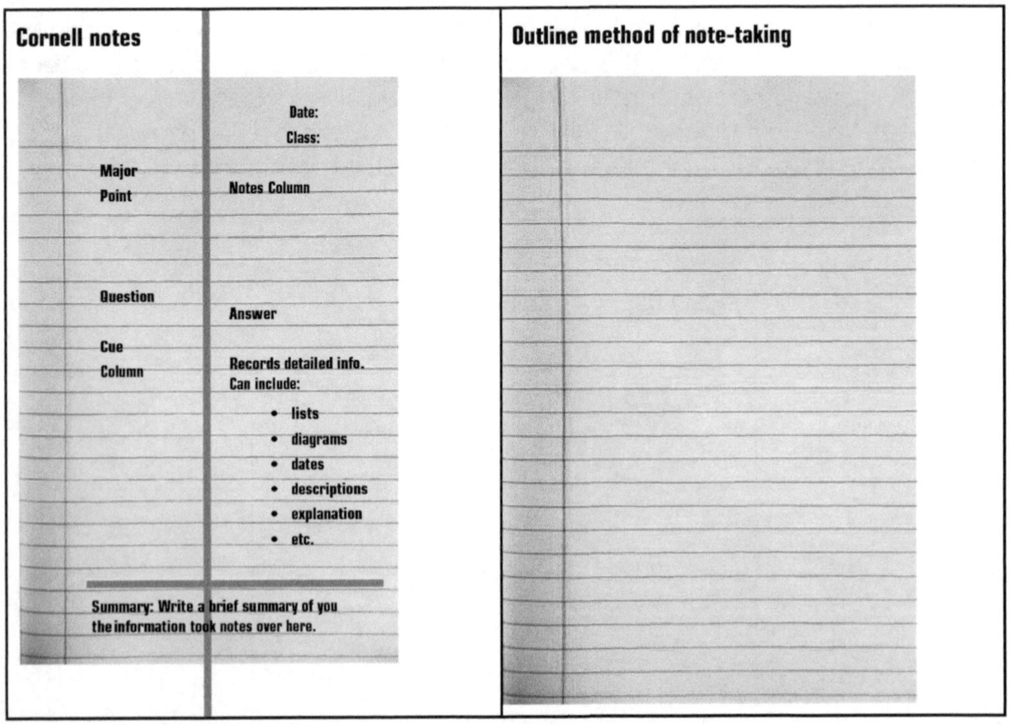

Cornell notes

Date:
Class:

Major Point — Notes Column

Question — Answer

Cue Column — Records detailed info. Can include:

- lists
- diagrams
- dates
- descriptions
- explanation
- etc.

Summary: Write a brief summary of you the information took notes over here.

Outline method of note-taking

Having learned how to use the Cornell and outline note-taking systems, you may see how they are similar. Both systems require you to process information from listening to words on a page. By performing this act, you are increasing the probability of successfully recalling the information you heard. Another similarity between the Cornell and outlining note-taking systems is they both require you to identify the main idea and supporting details. Then, as you take notes, you will record the information in way that connects the spoken ideas. In the Cornell system, you record this information in two-columns and in outlining you indent information for emphasis.

Notice that the same information is recorded on your notes, just arranged slightly differently. See Figure 7. 5 on the previous page.

EXERCISE 7.4: Similarities and Differences between Cornell and Outlining Note

Complete this Venn diagram, in Figure 7.6 on the similarities and differences between Cornell and outlining methods of note-taking.

FIGURE 7.6

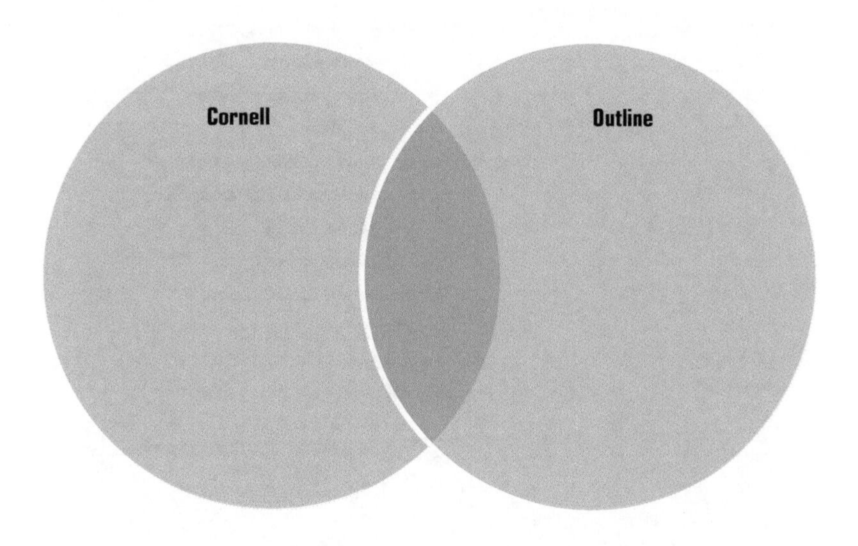

EXERCISE 7.5: Benefits of using Cornell and Outlining Notes

Explain the benefits of using Cornell and outlining methods of note-taking.

____

____

____

____

____

____

OBJECTIVE 4: Use Two Columns to Organize Notes

Another way to take notes is to modify the Cornell and outlining methods and create a two-column system. The uniqueness of this method is the omission of a summary at the bottom of the page as is expected in the Cornell method. You would choose to use this method when you are primarily concerned with the recording the two points in a lecture. For example, your microbiology professor might be explaining a topic with several new vocabulary words. By taking notes and placing the words and definitions in each column, it will create a quick and easy-to-use vocabulary study guide. Another helpful way to use your two-column notes is to use the left side for the label or title of a chart or graph and the right side to sketch the chart or graph.

FIGURE 7.7 Two-Column Notes

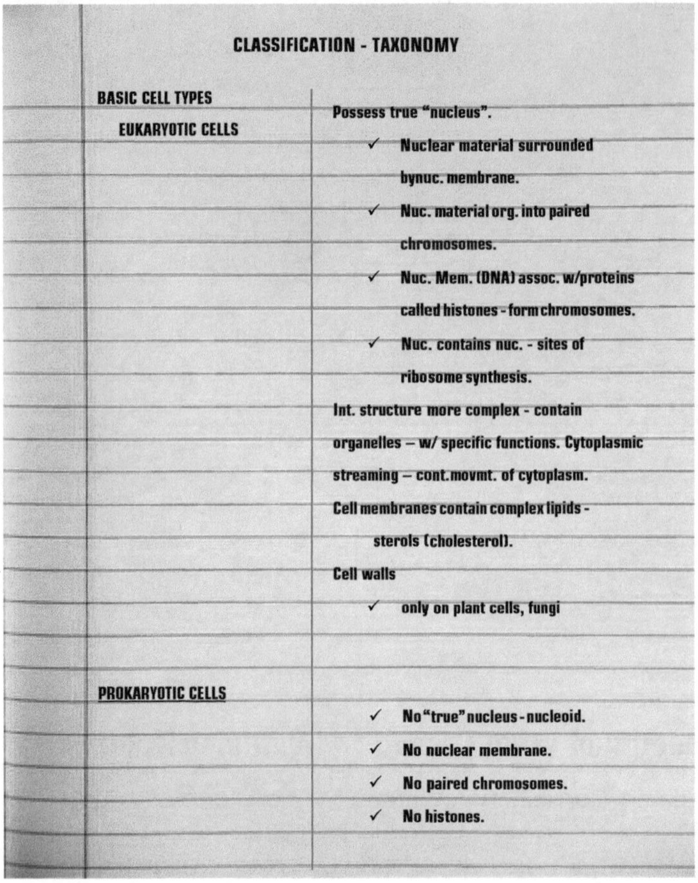

CLASSIFICATION - TAXONOMY

BASIC CELL TYPES	
EUKARYOTIC CELLS	Possess true "nucleus". ✓ Nuclear material surrounded bynuc. membrane. ✓ Nuc. material org. into paired chromosomes. ✓ Nuc. Mem. (DNA) assoc. w/proteins called histones - form chromosomes. ✓ Nuc. contains nuc. - sites of ribosome synthesis. Int. structure more complex - contain organelles – w/ specific functions. Cytoplasmic streaming – cont. movmt. of cytoplasm. Cell membranes contain complex lipids - sterols (cholesterol). Cell walls ✓ only on plant cells, fungi
PROKARYOTIC CELLS	✓ No "true" nucleus - nucleoid. ✓ No nuclear membrane. ✓ No paired chromosomes. ✓ No histones.

EXERCISE 7.6: Note-Taking Methods

Based on your understanding of taking notes by employing the two-column, Cornell, and outlining note-taking methods, how would you say it compares to what you have done previously?

Be sure to refer back to your self-assessment of note-taking methods you recorded in Exercise 7.1.

How will you use this information to improve your note-taking methods?

After taking a set of well-written notes, how will you use them as a study tool? There are many ways to use the arrangement of the information in this format. Three of them are:

1. ***Self-quiz:*** Take a sheet of clean notebook paper and cover up the right side of the page. Read aloud the question or cue on the left and test your knowledge by not looking at the notes on the right. After you state your answer, move the paper down to see if you were right. Continue doing this until you have completed your self-review of the course notes.
2. ***Modified self-quiz:*** If you take notes on single sheets of paper, fold the page on the dividing line between the cue and answer columns. Read the cue column and see how many answers you get right. This process can be reversed as you read the note-taking column to determine if you know the cue, vocabulary word, question, etc.
3. ***Use a set of note cards*** from your two columns by recording the cue information on one side and the note-taking column on the other side. Then, you can quiz yourself on the information for ongoing review.

Another suggestion for taking notes is to only write on one side of the page. This allows the back of your pages to remain blank. When you read or have diagrams, connect to the information you have included in your notes; you can write it on the blank (back) adjacent to the notes, as illustrated in Figure 7.8 below.

FIGURE 7.8

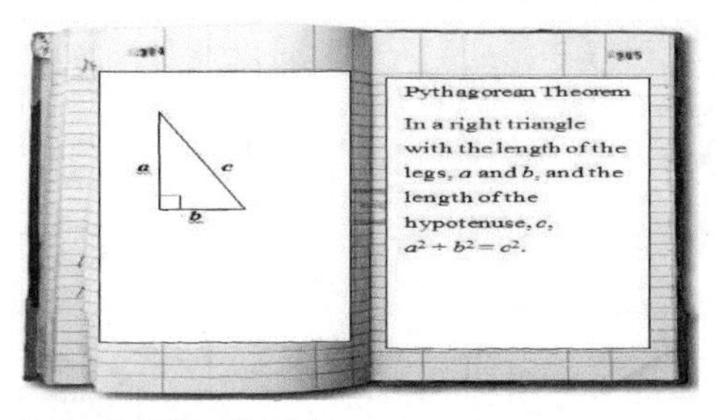

If you have written the summary at the bottom of the Cornell note-taking method pages, you can consolidate them into one summary of the materials. Then, when you prepare for your mid-terms and final exams, you will have the benefit of your summary for test preparation.

Each of these techniques is useful in most classes, but there are a few classes you will take where neither of these methods fits best. For example, an effective way to take notes in a math class is found in the Course Connection on the next page.

Course Connections:
Taking Notes in Mathematics Classes

<table>
<tr><td>You're trying to take notes in class but your instructor is talking faster than you can write. You need to know what is important and how you can reflect this in your notes.
When reading, most students use a highlighter to identify what is important. In a mathematics class, consider using two different colored inks to clarify the procedures.</td><td></td><td></td></tr>
<tr><td>In each blank at the right, write why you think a different color is used.
In your reading-intensive courses, notes are generally presented from left-to-right, whereas in mathematics, problems can be worked vertically. This can pose a challenge in identifying what is important in each problem.
Mathematicians use a red color change to emphasize any processes employed to complete the exercise. The black font shows: the results of the processes and what has not changed.</td><td>Solve the equation:
$5x - 9 = 3(x + 3)$
$5x - 9 = 3(x + 3)$
$5x - 9 = 3x + 9$
$-3x \quad -3x$
$2x - 9 = \quad 9$
$+9 \quad +9$
$2x \quad = 18$
$2 \quad\quad 2$
$x \quad = 9$</td><td>Read the Instructions
Original example

(why the red arrows?)

(why the red -3x?)

(why the red +9?)

(why the red division by 2?)</td></tr>
<tr><td colspan="3">Even if your instructor does not use these methods when explaining problems in class, you can use the techniques for yourself.</td></tr>
<tr><td colspan="3">Given the equation $2x - 6(x + 1) = 2$, solve it using the two color method and state your reason for using the 2nd color on any step on which you use it.</td></tr>
<tr><td colspan="3">__________ __________
__________ __________
__________ __________
__________ __________
__________ __________
__________ __________</td></tr>
<tr><td colspan="3">Describe how the two-color method might help you through the problem. Identify any difficulties you had in using the two colors (if any).
____
____
____
__________</td></tr>
</table>

7.2 TAKING NOTES USING ELECTRONIC DEVICES

Are you one of those people who take pictures of everything with your phone? Do you ever intend to print any of the pictures you take? If you are like most people, you take many pictures but very few, if any, are printed. Using technologies to take notes can end up just like your unprinted photos—fading away into darkness. Ironically, the notes you may take with technology, but fail to look at, are like your brain's ability to hold onto the information if it is never reviewed. The key to taking notes in any method is to review them often for extended periods of time.

OBJECTIVE 5: Understand When and What Device to Use for Recording a Lecture

One important point to consider prior to using technology when taking notes is the time required to set up your device. Some schools have you log into their Wi-Fi system, which may be slower than you are accustomed. Also, testing the device prior to beginning a lecture will save you frustrations if you are not prepared to begin when class starts. If you are not ready, you may lose valuable information while you trouble-shoot your technology. If you plan on using technology to take notes, be sure you understand how to use your device before ever attempting it in class. A "quick run-through" the night before might be a good idea.

Another area for serious consideration prior to using a computer or digital device to take notes is to ask yourself how easily are you distracted? Are you going to be tempted to check your social networking sites, go shopping, or text a message during the lecture? If you are easily distracted you may want to opt out of taking notes with your digital devices.

There are numerous technological tools available to use for note-taking. Some of the technology-based note-taking methods will provide more flexibility than others. The important guiding principle for using technology is to use it as one of many repetitions in learning the course materials. Some tools for technological note-taking tools include:

- Notebook computer
- iPad™ or similar device
- Smartpen

Many college students use their notebook computer to take notes. If you are going to use this device,

- learn keyboarding
- and how to use the outline format in Microsoft Word.

This device can help you keep up with your instructor's speed of speech (remember, about 110–125 wpm) because you can probably type almost twice (50–60 wpm) as your writing by hand (30–35 wpm).

Using an iPad®, or something similar, allows you to write on the pad just as if you were using a pen to make this procedure easier. A special pen is needed for this and it costs extra. You will still be taking notes around 30–35 wpm with this device.

A Smartpen, which is used with specialized "dot" paper, records the lecture as you take notes. (This is also expensive as the special paper can only be used one time and cannot be erased.) When you are ready to study, you can select a section of notes and listen to your professor's lecture at this same point. This pen has a microphone in the top that allows this function to work. Using this writing tool, you can create well-written notes with Cornell or outlining methods as well as record the lecture simultaneously. Using this device will help identify any areas of incorrect notes because you will see your notes as you hear your instructor's presentation. (Seek permission from your professor prior to recording his or her lecture.)

After you have taken your notes with the Smartpen, you can upload them to your computer. More information on these technologies can be found at:

http://www.livescribe.com/en-us/smartpen/

http://www.apple.com/ipad/

http://www.sas.calpoly.edu/asc/ssl/lecturenotes.html

There are other ways to capture a recording of your professor's lectures such as voice recordings on smartphones, iPads, and notebook computers. It is critical you seek permission from your professor prior to any recording. You may wonder why a student would want to record a lecture.

Basically, students who learn best from hearing the information might want to employ this method, so they can listen to it repeatedly. Sometimes, students will listen to the lecture for ongoing review as they commute to campus. The key is to use the recording for learning. Too often students record lectures only to have them forgotten. The only way recording actually helps to learn is to use it! Just because you are recording the lecture does not mean you do not need to take notes as well. The recording is an additional tool, not a replacement for taking notes.

Another "note-taking" method used by smartphone owners is to take a snapshot of the board or the PowerPoint presentation during class. This method may be especially helpful if there are multiple diagrams or complicated mathematical material. If you are taking a picture in addition to taking notes, be sure to note on your written page to refer to the picture you took.

EXERCISE 7.7: Comparing Technological Devices

Go online and learn about the weight, size, and cost of each of the technological devices mentioned thus far. Record the information in the space below. Then, determine which offers the most value for taking college lecture notes.

	Smartphone	**Notebook Computer**	**Smartpen**
dimensions			
weight			
cost range			
ease of use			

Describe the one device you think offers the most value for taking college lecture notes. Be sure to support your answer with the information you discovered during your online inquiry.

____

____

____

____

____

____

____

____

In addition to the devices mentioned thus far, there are online resources for note-taking you may want to consider.

FIGURE 7.9

Resource	Cost	Storage	Printable	Hints
Evernotes https://evernote.com/ Allows users to create notes, save pictures, share documents, and store research findings in one place.	Free (additional resources available with paid membership)	Cloud and PC	Yes, if you save them first	There is an app for this program.
Google Drive "Google Docs is an online word processor that lets you create and format text documents and collaborate with other people in real time."	Free (individual account necessary to access this application)	Cloud and PC	Yes	
ReadWriteThink Notetaker http://www.readwritethink.org/classroom-resources/student-interactives/readwritethink-notetaker-30055.html "This hierarchical outlining tool allows students to organize up to five levels of information for reading and writing activities. [. . .]The *Notetaker* creates an HTML file of students' outlines, which can be printed or saved and edited later in any HTML editor."	Free	Only way to save is a screen shot	yes	Turn off the sound on your computer, because it has the stroke clicking sounds.
übernotes http://www.ubernote.com/webnote/pages/default.aspx Includes note-taking system and file storage.	Free	Cloud	yes	
Zoho Notebook "Create, edit, share & publish your documents online with our word processor."	Free (5 GB)	Cloud	yes	

EXERCISE 7.8: Comparing Internet Note-Taking Resources

Go to the Internet and review the previous note-taking resources. Write a brief description of the one you believe is the best note-taking system on this list and explain why you feel this way.

As you have probably noticed, it is important to speak with your professor before you record (auditory or visual) a lecture. This is due to a few very important reasons such as:

- Intellectual copyrights
- Copyrighted materials
- Attendance in class
- Family Educational Rights and Privacy Act (FERPA)

The first reason is a professor retains "intellectual property rights" to their original lectures or teaching techniques. If you record a lecture and then share it with others, you are violating the instructor's rights and you could be subject to litigation.

The second reason is the copyright laws on how materials are used in class. Publishing companies and some websites offer free use of materials by professors *if they are used for use only*. If you take pictures of the materials, this could violate the terms of the instructor's agreement *classroom* with the publishing company.

The third reason is some professors feel recording lectures may encourage low attendance in their class. For example, if you record the lecture and share it with a student who is absent, absenteeism may increase. While this is not necessarily the case with all students who are recording lectures and sharing it with fellow learners, the professor has the right to refuse you the recording device in class. Of course, students who are working with student services and have permission to use the device will want to communicate this to their professor on the first day of class.

The final reason is, and perhaps the most overlooked by students, it is illegal for professors to reveal who is enrolled in their classes per the Family Educational Rights and Privacy Act (FERPA).

> The Family Educational Rights and Privacy Act (FERPA) (20 U.S.C. § 1232g; 34 CFR Part 99) is a Federal law that protects the privacy of student education records. The law applies to all schools that receive funds under an applicable program of the U.S. Department of

> Education.[. . .] When a student turns 18 years old, or enters a postsecondary institution at any age, the rights under FERPA transfer from the parents to the student ("eligible student").

This means information concerning your identity, grades, or financial information, are bound by the Federal laws. Prior to turning 18 years of age, the rights and responsibilities of your records were placed on your parents, but now that you are over 18 years of age you are given this responsibility. As such, colleges, including professors, are not allowed to disclose any information concerning your identity or grades to anyone. This is for your personal protection and is the right of every student sitting in a classroom. Video recordings may violate the rights of every student in the class, so make sure you speak to your professor before recording anything.

OBJECTIVE 6: Discuss the Relationship between Learning Preferences and Recording

As you know from Chapter 3, learning preferences take the form of aural, visual, or kinesthetic. It seems obvious to assume the auditory learner will be the student who can most benefit from an audio recording of the lecture.

Does this mean the student will not need to take notes during a lecture? Yes or no. Why?

____

____

____

Because lessons are presented through speeches and examples, the auditory learner will prefer this method of course delivery. Taking notes in this class is equally important. Even though students who prefer auditory learning may be able to hear and understand the lecture, it does not mean hearing the lecture once leads to learning the course materials. Additionally, as you read and learned in Chapter 3, it is important all of the senses are used to learn to your maximum potential. This means the auditory learner will want to use visual and kinesthetic pathways for processing the information in class as much as they may depend on their auditory learning preference.

Similarly, do you think the visual learner is the prime candidate for learning from videos or snapshots of the board? Obviously, if all students need to employ all of their senses to learn, then all students will benefit equally from the video recordings of the lectures. Understanding the need to employ your senses during the learning process means you may have stronger preferences for one type of information delivery over another, but learning in college requires you to use all of your learning modalities.

The kinesthetic learner may prefer to type the notes as the instructor speaks because this is a different way of using the body. Notes will still be taken and he or she will be using multiple senses.

In the end, all students will benefit from audio and video recordings of the lecture materials presented in class. Students who actually use the resources will be the ones who benefit the most. If you want to learn through the use of audio and video recordings you will need to invest the time outside of class using them. Too often, students will obtain permission to record the lecture and record it, only to let it sit unused. Just as the photos in your phone fade away into darkness because they are not viewed, your recorded lecture materials can also fade away.

SOMETHING TO THINK ABOUT

1. Take a minute to compare and contrast the two pictures below. Do you think the students are listening carefully?

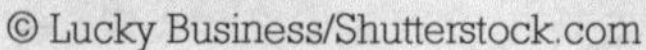

© Lucky Business/Shutterstock.com

© Dragon Images/Shutterstock.com

2. How would your group discussion be different if you knew

- the class on the right had English language learners?
- the class on the left was an education class?
- the female in the front row of the picture on the right is hearing impaired?

3. Discuss the photographs again from the perspective of communication skills.

- After the discussion, write a paragraph, three to five complete sentences, about the photographs as they relate to taking notes.

7.3 LEARNING WITH YOUR NOTES

There are many methods for learning with your notes. This section will discuss the creation and use of visual notes and other graphic organizers to improve note-taking techniques. Understanding your learning style preference will enhance the effectiveness of these strategies.

In addition, recursive learning will be discussed to demonstrate the use of Bloom's Taxonomy during note-taking, reading, and active listening.

OBJECTIVE 7: Understand How Visual Notes and Graphic Organizers Enhance Note-Taking

Finally, you will want to learn to create visual notes from your lecture notes for ongoing review and study. A picture really is worth a thousand words! Our brains will remember pictures and color more often than notes comprised of just words on a page. Visual note-taking with ***graphic organizers*** incorporates the use of pictures, text, and arrangement of the information for evaluation, synthesis, or analysis.

In case you are thinking drawing pictures works for little children who use crayons, take a look at a recent research study demonstrating the effectiveness of taking visual notes with graphic organizers. Martin Eppler's article entitled "A Comparison between Concept Maps, Mind Maps, Conceptual Diagrams, and Visual Metaphors as Complementary Tools for Knowledge Construction and Sharing" (2006), describes the study in which he analyzed the effects on students who used visual notes to learn. His outcomes are as stated:

> The results provide first indications that the different visualization formats can be used in complementary ways to enhance motivation, attention, understanding and recall.[2]

Basically, Eppler's study demonstrates how using visual notes increases your ability to visualize the information being taught with specific increases in recall and recognition. This is one of many research outcomes demonstrate the need to use graphic organizers, illustrated in Figure 7.10 on the next page, as visual note-taking methods for your improved learning.

In general, the foundation of your visual notes will be the well-written lecture notes you have already created because it is challenging to create visual notes while listening. This stems from the need to listen closely to the lecture. If you are distracted by processing the information on a deeper level during the lecture, you will miss important points from your professor. The true value of creating visual notes is the opportunity to process the information you are learning on the deeper level of making connections and associations. While it may seem as if you are merely doodling, you are actually wiring and firing the information into your long-term memory.

As you know from this textbook, repetition of your learning material is the key to making an "A" in your classes. Repeat to remember! Visual note-taking is how you repeat your lecture materials to remember the concepts as well as make critical connections between concepts.

Since repetition and application are critical keys to your learning, it is time to apply the information from this section in learning how to create visual notes.

EXERCISE 7.9: Comparing Graphic Organizers

Select two of the graphic organizers in the table provided and generate a visual set of notes from your most resent lecture in this class. Be prepared to share this with your fellow learners.

---

[2]Eppler, Martin J. "A Comparison between Concept Maps, Mind Maps, Conceptual Diagrams, and Visual Metaphors as Complementary Tools for Knowledge Construction and Sharing." *Information Visualization*: PalgraveMacmillan Ltd. 2006.

FIGURE 7.10 Formats of visual note-taking methods are:

	Concept Map	Mind map	Comparison map	Visual Metaphor	Matrix
Picture	Notetaking; Traditional; Visual; linear; logical; pictures		[Text] [Text] [Text]	[Text] [Text]	Topic 1, Topic 2; Item 1; Item 2
Description	top-down diagram demonstrating the connections between ideas in a hierarchical form, commonly used in organization charts	multicolored and image-centered, diagram represents a concept and/or connections between portions of learned material in order of rank or priority	circular shaped image in which information is written on two or more concepts to show the relationships between them	graphic structure that uses the shape and elements of a familiar artifact to organize content meaningfully and use the associations with the metaphor to convey additional meaning about the content	Two or more categories of objects are arranged in a table-like format to create connections between or among them.
Value	Visually see connections between the information				
Application	A chapter in a math book, containing sections of instruction, each section containing subsections of objectives, text, illustrations, practice problems, review and self-check questions.	Take a typical day and break it into the activities where a student spends time. Take each activity and record the amount of time spent, its priority, and associated actions that could be increased or decreased to enhance study effectiveness.	Writing an essay comparing and contrasting the benefits and dangers of using genetically modified seeds for the production of food crops.	An illustration of a balance, where the number of human silhouettes on each side of the scale represents the relative populations of two countries. Two figures on one side and ten on the other could imply a population of five times greater.	On a group presentation project, the participant names are placed in the column headings, and the various pieces of the presentation are listed in the row headings. The intersection of a rows and columns indicate the one or more persons who will work on that part. As more parts of the presentation are added, the rows can be increased.
Guide lines	a visual form of outlining, where a primary concept is separated into its constituent parts, and each part is then further divided; this continues as far as necessary to describe the makeup of each component	Begin in the center with the primary concept. Add radiating lines to show categories of subjects that can then be further divided into related ideas. Use color to quickly recognize specific subjects and classify the concepts.	Use this to compare and contrast ideas. The primary idea is in the larger circle and the smaller circles contain the points to be made, both for and against the main idea.	Used extensively in advertising and political cartoons where a comparison is made of a person, place or idea to another concept through the use of images that show or imply similarities.	Typically, the two categories are arranged so one (fewer object numbers) becomes the column headings (participants), while the more variable category becomes the row headings (presentation parts).

OBJECTIVE 8: Understand How Using Bloom's Taxonomy Promotes Recursive Learning

Recursive learning, a term you may not be familiar with, is something you may already be doing while studying. Simply, ***recursive learning*** is learning through repeated experience or exposure to a concept. This means prior experiences and expectations play a major role in your ability to learn new information. For example, if you have taken notes in a particular way in other learning environments with favorable success, you will continue to use the same method when you enter a college classroom. If this note-taking method does not work as effectively, you will be more motivated to look for a new approach. In the end, if you stick to the old method just because you have always done it that way, you may hinder the learning process.

When this concept of repeated learning is applied to note-taking, it will be beneficial to review Blooms Taxonomy as discussed in Chapter 4. Remember, the higher-order thinking skills (evaluate, synthesize, and analysis) are the goal of learning for college. This means you will want to learn to recreate your classroom lecture notes in a way that extends your learning to the higher-order thinking skills.

EXERCISE 7.10: Using Note-Taking to Improve Higher-Order Thinking

Review the information you have learned on ways to recreate your lecture notes and explain how these methods increase the use of your higher order thinking skills.

Evaluation

Synthesis

Analysis

Through the application of recursive learning toward your note-taking learning strategies you will experience

- increased learning,
- increased connections between course materials,
- increased long-term retention,
- and better grades!

© Justin Sullivan/Getty Images

There is a GI Joe® advertising slogan that states "You now know, and knowing is half the battle." GI Joe cartoon episodes end with a Public Service Announcement (PSA) in which GI Joe learns and teaches kids how to do the "right" thing. In the first episode, the action figure character Alpine poses the question, "What do you do when you're lost?" He proceeds to explain, "Stay calm. Think. Where did you see him last? Go back there."[3]

---

[3]"Knowing is Half the Battle Episode Endings." *The Ultimate G.I. Joe Cartoon Website.* 27 May 2005. Web. 1 Nov. 2013.

What does this mean when applied to offer recursive learning and note-taking strategies? When learning through taking notes in class, "Stay calm. Think!" Then, after class review your notes to go back and really learn the information. You now know a wide variety of ways to take notes and you will need to find a variety of ways to create novel study aids from them. Repeating to remember is critical to your successful learning from your notes, so allow ample time for this process to take place.

OBJECTIVE 9: Apply Learning Style Preferences to Note-Taking

Take a moment to review your learning preferences as discovered in Chapter 3. Did you demonstrate a preference for learning visually, aurally, or kinesthetically? How does your learning preference affect your note-taking?

FIGURE 7.11

VISUAL	AUDITORY	KINESTHETIC
Initially, using Cornell or ***two column notes*** and visual note-taking for recursive learning.	Initially, using any of the note- taking strategies and then coupling them with a digital recording device so you can hear them again. Speaking to a classmate as a review of the course materials will be of tremendous benefit for this type of learner.	Initially, using any of the note- taking strategies and add keyboarding, so you can feel the movement in your hands as you learn. Getting up and moving around as you read your notes aloud will be of great benefit because you are engaging your bodily movement while processing the information.

EXERCISE 7.11: Note-Taking and Learning Preferences

Explain how note-taking addresses the learning preference for a visual, auditory, and kinesthetic learner. Describe how you will apply this information to your personal learning strategies.

Taking notes during a lecture is the beginning of learning the course materials. In order to fully understand and be able to remember the information, you will want to extend the learning through recursive learning that incorporates your whole brain. As was discussed in Chapter 3, learning is not a partial-brain activity, but rather a whole-brain activity. You will want to experiment with all three of these learning modalities to process information for maximum learning. Creating a set of well-written notes is the foundation and will be used for reading and re-writing notes for deeper learning.

EXERCISE 7.12: Note-Taking and Whole-Brain Learning

Explain how each of the following note-taking strategies can be a whole brain learning process.

Note-Taking strategy	How can the strategy be explained as a whole brain learning process?
Traditional paragraphs	
Cornell	
Two-Column	
Outline	
Note-Taking While Using Electronic Devices	
Concept Mapping	
Mind Mapping	
Visual Metaphor	
Matrix	

Obviously, note-taking is more than just listening to your professor speak and recording the spoken words. Active learning includes the extension of your engagement with the material delivered in a lecture in your study sessions. The sooner you can process the information, the more likely you will learn it and store it in your long-term memory.

REFLECTION 7.C:

Explain how viewing this process (three different ways) might help strengthen your ability to understand concepts in other situations.

____

____

____

____

____

PERSON to PERSON

In this exercise, you will be introduced to a student in a class with 250 students. Let's discuss note-taking and accessing information!

© Shutterstock.com

Carl is enrolled in a freshman class. About 80% of the students bring laptops to class. Carl is considering the advantages and disadvantages to taking notes by hand, laptop, or video recording.

The instructor encourages the use of any supportive learning electronic device.

Based on the description, rank the steps Carl should take to improve his note taking.

Read the section prior to class ______

Sit close to the instructor ______

Take notes on a computer ______

Take notes by hand ______

Here is some additional information.

- The instructor uses PowerPoint presentations, which can be downloaded prior to class.
- There is a mandatory one-hour per week lab session for tutoring and quizzes.

Based on all the information you now know about these three students, rank them again as to who you believe will be most successful this academic term. Has your ranking changed?

Read the section prior to class ______

Sit close to the instructor ______

Take notes on a computer ______

Take notes by hand ______

1. What pieces of new information do you consider to be a positive influence on note-taking?

____

____

2. What pieces of new information do you consider to be a negative influence on note-taking?

____

____

Here is your last piece of information.

- This is a College Algebra class.
- Carl notices other students surfing the Internet during class.

Based on all the information you have about this classroom does your advice change?

Read the section prior to class ______

Sit close to the instructor ______

Take notes on a computer ______

Take notes by hand ______

1. Would your decision be influenced if you knew Carl's learning preference?

____

____

2. Are there any pieces of information that could be seen as both positive and negative influences on note- taking?

____

____

Career Connection:

© Robert Kneschke/
Shutterstock.com

Whatever field you choose to pursue after college, taking notes will probably be a critical component for your position. From the ability to take correct orders over the telephone to gathering information on an ill patient, taking witness statements after a car accident, or listening to the information on your company's roll-out of a new product, the ability to listen attentively and concentrate on the information being delivered are skills you will need to be successful in college.

CHAPTER SUMMARY

Note-taking and long-term memory work to increase your capacity to learn and retrieve information. Taking notes during the course lecture affords you the chance to increase your long-term memory and retrieval, which are essential for college success.

Note-taking has several advantages with the most obvious being writing down information during a lecture means you will be able to review it later.

There are a variety of ways to create a set of well-written notes. Some of these are:

- Cornell Note-Taking
- Two-Column
- Outline
- Traditional paragraphs

Taking notes with the use of digital or electronic devices has both advantages and disadvantages. The notes you may take with technology, but fail to look at, are like your brain's ability to hold onto the information if it is never reviewed. The key to taking notes in any method is to review them often for extended periods of time.

Once you have determined the use of technology to be a support in your learning, you will want to consider which device to use. There are many note-taking applications and websites to consider in this decision. Using technology, just because it is novel, does not necessarily mean you will use it later.

Finally, you will want to learn to create visual notes from your lecture notes for ongoing review and study. Visual note-taking with graphic organizers incorporates the use of pictures, text, and arrangement of the information for critical thinking. Repeat to remember! Visual note-taking is how you repeat your lecture materials to remember the concepts as well as make critical connections between them.

Ultimately, you will determine which note-taking strategy is best suited for your learning preference and how you can use it to increase your higher order thinking skills. Beginning with a set of well-written notes from your class lecture is the foundation of your learning. Recursive learning will allow you the opportunity to learn from your experiences and repetition. Because, you need to repeat to remember and notes afford you this learning advantage.

CHAPTER 7: Self-Check

Vocabulary: Define the following:

1. recursive learning
2. comprehension
3. graphic organizers
4. Cornell notes

Concepts:

5. Explain the advantages to note-taking.
6. Describe the connections between note-taking and long-term memory.
7. List five reasons to take notes in class.
8. Describe the process of Cornell note-taking.
9. Describe the process of creating an outline.
10. Recognize verbal cues are ways of understanding lecture information.

11. Utilize abbreviations to increase rate of writing.
12. Use two columns to organize notes.
13. Compare the column approach to other note-taking options.
14. Illustrate three ways to review course lecture notes through the use of column organization.
15. Evaluate when audio recordings are appropriate.
16. Evaluate online note-taking applications and programs.
17. Explain guidelines for copyrighted materials.
18. Explain guidelines for recording instructor's lectures.
19. Discuss Family Educational Rights and Privacy Act (FERPA).
20. Explain the characteristics and features of visual notes and graphic organizers.
21. Explain the value of using visual notes and graphic organizers. Types: mind mapping, concept map, matrix, visual metaphor.
22. Explain how to use visual notes for study tool.
23. Create a set of notes from your lecture notes in this class.
24. Synthesize recursive learning and Blooms Taxonomy.
25. Discuss two strategies for engaging taxonomy during note-taking.
26. Explain how note-taking addresses the learning preference for a visual, auditory, and kinesthetic learner.
27. Describe how to make learning through note-taking a whole brain learning activity through visual/mind mapping.

---

1. Create three note cards for this chapter, the first with a true-false test question, the second with a multiple choice test question, and the third with an essay question.
2. Complete this chart to understand the overview of various note-taking options.

TYPE OF NOTES	TRADITIONAL	CORNELL	TWO-COLUMN	OUTLINE	CONCEPT MAP	MATRIX	MAPPING
Uses							
Benefits							
Attentiveness							
Lecture Rate							
Process							
Format							
Other:							

CHAPTER 8
Reading

T.I.P.S. (Tactical Information that Promotes Success)

When you read a college textbook, EXAMINE the pictures for vocabulary reinforcement!

STUDY the pictures carefully for vocabulary and process reinforcement when you read a college textbook!

© Dmitry Meinikov/Shutterstock.com

Charts and graphs can actually save you from reading several paragraphs, if not several pages. They are concise and can save you from reading a significant number of pages.

© Davizro Photography/Shutterstock.com

You have probably heard the adage "a picture is worth a 1,000 words." How is this true when reading a textbook? Can you skim the pictures to save time?

While many books have pictures, mathematics books have graphs and charts and biology books have diagrams or illustrations. These are a critical component to reading effectively and efficiently.

Mathematics and science textbook pictures contain significant information. Diagrams in mathematics and science textbooks should be studied carefully to enhance reading comprehension. They will actually save you TIME! You could read the paragraphs, but many times the information will make more sense as a series of interconnected pictures. For example, studying the diagrams about cells, ribosomes, and mitochondria will help you to understand the written explanation of their interconnectedness. Graphs show how each part correlates to the others, either in science or mathematics.

In all **reading** situations, comprehension is greatly increased when time is invested in slowing down to understand the pictures, charts, and graphs. Remember, these visual aids act similarly to a summary of a large body of work. To support the original report, reading the visual aids offers a recap of the research findings, cause and effect correlations, or other pieces of vital information.

In **writing**, using the right word can make the difference between communicating clearly or not. When appropriate, use a thesaurus to locate the best word to express your idea. While most computer software programs used in writing have a limited thesaurus, it is best to use one with more options.

In **education**, acronyms are used in text to refer to organizations, concepts, observations and conditions. Knowing how to correctly "translate" the meaning of "word" can either provide a clear understanding and clarity or create confusion and frustration to the material read.

CHAPTER 8: OBJECTIVES

8.1 Reading Course Materials

Objective 1 Understand Active Reading Strategies

Objective 2 Understand How to Activate Schemata during Pre-Reading

Objective 3 Understand How to Develop Vocabulary Learning Tools

Objective 4 Understand How to Apply Morphology as a Strategy for Reading Textbooks

Objective 5 Identify the Main Idea and Supporting Details for Increased Reading Comprehension

Objective 6 Understand How to Annotate and Highlight the Main Idea and Supporting Details of a Paragraph

Objective 7 Understand Strategies for Reading Works of Narrative Fiction

Objective 8 Understand Strategies for Reading Procedural and Declarative Documents

8.2 Taking Notes While Reading

Objective 9 Understand How to Use SQ4R While Reading

Objective 10 Understand Combining SQ4R and Cornell Note-Taking

CHAPTER CONCEPTS:

Some or all of the following terms may be new to you. Place a check mark in the column reflecting your knowledge of each term.

	Know	Don't know	Not sure	Page # where first found		Know	Don't know	Not sure	Page # where first found
Active Reading					suffix				
Passive Reading					Prefix				
Pre-Reading					Root				
During Reading					annotating				
Post Reading					highlighting				
schema					Declarative				
morphology					Procedural				
Morpheme					Figurative language				
					Expository				

8.1 READING COURSE MATERIALS

Reading is a skill requiring practice and specific strategies. This is not a new revelation, but is a worthwhile reminder. To better understand the importance of reading, consider the person who wants to scuba dive. Anna was so intrigued by scuba diving, she watched videos on the technique, read books on famous dives, purchased the necessary gear, and even went out on a boat in Cozumel, Mexico to observe scuba divers. After investing her time and money on her interest of scuba diving, Anna had never learned nor practiced the skill of scuba diving. When she returned home from Mexico, Anna's brother Jonathan asked how it felt to be 90 feet deep in the sea and what did the ocean's sea life look like. All of the sudden, Anna realized she was not a scuba diver!

Coastline view of Cozumel

© Darryl Brooks/Shutterstock.com

This "ah-ha" moment motivated Anna to begin learning the skills necessary to actually scuba dive. She enrolled in scuba diving classes to learn how to:

- perform pre-diving gear check,
- use the gear correctly,
- control her body or trim position,
- utilize safe ascent techniques,
- and communicate underwater with the appropriate signals.

As a class, everyone learned in the pool, but once the skills were secured they dove at a local lake. Eventually, Anna learned to scuba dive, so she returned to Cozumel, Mexico. This time, rather than watching other people scuba dive while she sat on the boat, Anna plunged from the boat into the crystal blue waters and descended down. Anna was mesmerized by the colorful fish, sea turtles, amazing coral, and the warmth of the water. What was most surprising to Anna was her appreciation for the beauty beneath the surface of the water. She thought to herself, *If I'd never learned to scuba dive, I'd never have known the incredible tranquility and beauty below. All of the time and energy I spent on learning to scuba dive was worth it!*

© Brian Lasenby/Shutterstock.com

Reading is very similar to learning to scuba dive: developing an appreciation of reading and the skills necessary to be an active reader offer you the opportunity to read with comprehension. If you only purchase a book for a class but do not read it, you will never discover the knowledge, beauty, or tranquility awaiting you. Additionally, taking time to learn active reading strategies will increase your comprehension of the material, which will help you discover the treasures of learning. A few of these are:

- increased long-term memory storage and easier retrieval of material,
- increased vocabulary,
- higher grades in your courses,
- and ability to connect information you are reading in one class to another class.

Reading is participant sport, so dive in!

OBJECTIVE 1: Understand Active Reading Strategies

Just as Anna had to take a class to learn the skill of scuba diving, you will want to learn a wide variety of reading strategies to do well in your classes. ***Active reading*** strategies are the techniques you use while reading to increase your comprehension of the text. Perhaps you have learned to highlight, annotate, or take notes while reading. All of these are strategies to read actively, so you may already know a few techniques. Just as Anna knew the theory of scuba diving but not how to actually participate in the sport, you may have learned the theory of annotation, highlighting, or note-taking without actively using them.

Many times students are ***passive readers***, reading a chapter without engaging their mind by connecting with the words on the page. ***Passive reading*** is similar to driving and texting (although less dangerous!) because our brain can only focus on one thing at a time. For example, either the driver will attend to the road or the message he or she is texting. Similarly, readers will be able to focus on the text only if the brain is able to focus on it. Active readers need strategies that will aid in maintaining the mind's attention on the words in a book, so they glean the most information from it while reading.

Preparation of your brain is essential for active reading because the brain processes the information. Before you begin to read deeply, you will want to include a ***pre-reading*** warm-up. This may be as simple as skimming the material to ascertain the gist of the content and then asking questions about what you anticipate the material to be addressing. After you have prepared with the pre-reading warm-up, you are ready to read! Active reading includes ***during reading*** skills such as annotating, highlighting, note-taking, and summarization. You will increase your comprehension significantly by asking questions as you read, too. After you have read and employed one or more of the previously listed *during reading* skills, you will benefit from a ***post reading*** strategy such as writing the answers to the questions you generated, discussing the concepts with a fellow learner or within your class, and analyzing the concepts more deeply. Throughout the active reading process, you will increase your comprehension, learning recall and recognition, and make connections between the text and yourself.

EXERCISE 8.1: Active Reading Skills

Identify the skills utilized during each of the active reading processes.

1. pre-reading

2. during reading

3. post reading

EXERCISE 8.2: Active Reading Strategy

Comprehension Processes

Having some understanding of how we comprehend helps underscore the relevance—or irrelevance—of common and/or recommended comprehension instructional strategies. To comprehend, current theory says we employ both our knowledge of langue and our knowledge of the world (latter often referred to simply as background information). We employ this knowledge to use propositions, schemata, and mental models. We also use inferences that are based on the text, as well as our prior knowledge, to help with these processes. Propositions are the smallest units of text information that can stand separately and be tested as true or false (Kintsch, 1074). They are ideas, not the words themselves (McNamara, Miller, and Bransford, 1991).

To learn more, visit: http://www.lynchburg.edu/wp-content/uploads/volume-4-2009/BeyerJ-Strategies-Helping-Struggling-Readers-Expository-Text.pdf and read "Strategies for Helping Struggling Readers Comprehend Expository Text", by Julie Beyer.

© michaeljung/Shutterstock.com

© mavo/Shutterstock.com

Step 1—Pre-Reading: Survey the passage for: bold, italicized, or color text

Answer, who or what is this about?
Answer, what is the author's point?
Answer, what do I already know about this topic?
Answer, what are some questions I have about this topic?

Step 2—During Reading:

Locate answers to the previously generated questions in Step 1.
Highlight the author's main ideas.
Write a question mark in the margin for any questions you have while reading.
Write a check in the margin for any information you agree with.

Step 3—Post Reading: After you have read this passage:

Write a brief summary.
Record the answers to the questions you generated in Step 1 and located in Step 2.
Explain how you can use the information in the passage in your classes.

EXERCISE 8.3: Reactions to Active Reading Strategies

Write your reactions after having used the strategies in the previous passage.

How much time did it take you to complete this passage while using the three phases?

Do you think your comprehension was increased as a result of the active reading strategies? Why?

Do you see yourself using the strategies in your textbook readings in college?

Explain your understanding of schema.

REFLECTION 8.A:

Explain how you would use the active reading principles for a section in an education, mathematics, or lab-science course.

1. pre reading
2. during reading
3. post reading

Discuss how the application of these skills is different for an education, mathematics, or lab-science course than for a section of a psychology or political science class.

OBJECTIVE 2: Understand How to Activate Schema During Pre-Reading

Rather than tell you about the benefits of activating prior knowledge, you will experience how prior knowledge helps with reading.

EXERCISE 8.4: Main Idea

Read the following passage to determine the main idea.

> The procedure is actually quite simple. First, you arrange things into different groups. Of course, one pile may be sufficient depending on how much there is to do. If you have to go somewhere else due to lack of facilities, that is the next step; otherwise, you are pretty well set. It is important not to overdo things. That is, it is better to do too few things at once than too many. In the short run, this may not seem important, but complications can easily arise. A mistake can be expensive, as well. At first, the whole procedure will seem complicated.
>
> Soon, however, it will become just another facet of life. It is difficult to foresee any end to the necessity for this task in the immediate future, but one never can tell. After the procedure is completed, one arranges the materials into different groups again. Then they can be put into their appropriate places. Eventually, they will be used once more and the whole cycle will then have to be repeated. However, that is part of life.

Record the topic of this passage. ______________________________

Are you at a loss as to what the passage is about? Most people are confused by this passage because their schema or prior knowledge has not been activated prior to reading. There are eight words that will increase your understanding. This is all about how to do laundry![1] Now, review the passage with this little piece of information and see if it makes more sense.

The "How To Do Laundry" passage was used in a famous experiment conducted by JD Bransford and MK Johnson in 1972. The participants in the study were divided into groups. The first group was given the topic of the paragraph prior to reading. The second group was not given the topic of the paragraph until after having read the passage. As you personally experienced the passage reading similar to those who were members of the second group, you know how the study participants felt: confused! Lack of information prior to reading resulted in limited success, if any, in determining the topic of the passage. Then, when the participants in the study were told the topic, the passage made complete sense. The study participants in the first group experienced significant increases in comprehension of the topic reading due to the activation of prior knowledge at the beginning of the reading process. Bransford and Johnson's research offers insight into the critical role of pre-reading in determining your reading comprehension.

In case you do not recall the definition of **schema** (Chapter 3) as was included in the reading passage on Exercise 8.1, it is "a device for representing knowledge of a concept, along with specifications for relating it to an appropriate network of connections that seem to hold all components of that particular

[1] A video of this is at: http://www.youtube.com/watch?v=mzbRpMlEHzM

concept" (Porter 2003). Simply stated, a schema is prior knowledge you have acquired since your earliest memories. These include memories such as:

- the smell of your favorite meal cooked by your mother.
- the touch of your feet on the cool bathroom tiles after a bath.
- seeing the sun rise or set in your favorite place.
- hearing your favorite song on the radio.
- tasting *Juicy Fruit* gum for the first time.

You may be thinking: *Those are all sensations. How do I use these to read better?* When you read about a sunrise, in your brain you have to see a picture of a sunrise in order to comprehend it. Similarly, visualizing the topic you are going to read prior to reading in detail will increase your comprehension.

There are many ways to activate prior knowledge or schema when you are beginning to read; these include:

Surveying: A detailed overview of the material where you read the title, the headings, the first and last paragraphs, all of the visual aids (charts, graphs, pictures, etc.), and questions at the end of the chapter.

Skimming: A broad overview of the materials, where you quickly pick out the important details, with a surface-level understanding of the topic.

Scanning: A narrow overview of the materials, where you preview the reading materials for specific information.

Once you have invested the five to ten minutes in activating your prior knowledge through one of these strategies, you have set yourself up for increasing your comprehension of the materials by almost 70%, according to Branford and Johnson. Imagine it! In the few minutes it takes to activate your prior knowledge, you are significantly increasing your ability to comprehend your textbook reading.

In addition to surveying, skimming, and scanning your reading materials to increase your comprehension, you will want to predict or anticipate what you will learn from the reading materials. After you survey, skim, or scan the materials you are going to read, ask yourself: *What do I anticipate or expect to learn from this reading material?* This single question helps you communicate to your brain your purpose for reading. Understanding this purpose helps you focus your active reading skills.

REFLECTION 8.B:

Explain how you can connect the skills of surveying, skimming, and scanning to the reading of a section in your education, mathematics, or lab science course. Explain how their use is different in applying them than when reading a passage from an English or history section.

OBJECTIVE 3: Understand How to Develop Vocabulary Learning Tools

© Milos Batinic/Shutterstock.com

When you are surveying, skimming, or scanning reading materials, you may identify some words unfamiliar to you or used in a new way. It is important you take time to understand these two; you will limit your reading comprehension if you fail to realize their meaning. One way to quickly learn the definition of unknown or unfamiliar words is to use the glossary in your textbook. Traditionally, the glossary is located in the back of a textbook, but more recently a glossary may be on the companion website for a textbook.

EXERCISE 8.5: Glossary Location and Use

Take a minute to find where this book's glossary is located.

Where is the glossary for this textbook located? ____________________

How did you locate the information needed to find the glossary? ____________________

____

If you cannot locate an unfamiliar word in the glossary, there are other ways to determine its meaning. For example, list all of the definitions for the word "run" you know:

Run means ____________________

____

How many different definitions for run do you know? ______

In the dictionary there are over forty (40) definitions and phrases with the word "run" in them. Did your list include all forty? ______ If not, you are in good company! Most people do not realize this three-letter word has so many definitions. Each definition is determined by the context of how the word is used. For this reason, learning to determine the meaning of an unfamiliar word in context is a critical skill for increasing reading comprehension.

When reading an education, mathematics or lab-science course section of the book, it may be difficult to understand meanings of words you do not understand through context. Generally this is because the vocabulary used in these courses is not found in ordinary conversation. The glossary will be important for you to understand the meaning of unfamiliar terms. Unfortunately, not all mathematics textbooks include a glossary, so you will need to become familiar with the index at the back of the book. The index identifies the page number on which you will find definitions for certain words, applications, or concepts.

REFLECTION 8.C:

Locate the glossary in the back of your mathematics textbook, if it exists. If not, use the index.

Write the definition of **rhombus**. ____________________

____

Did you use a glossary or the index? ______________________________

If you forget the definition of a word or concept, you can always refer to the ____________ for its location.

Because words illustrate their meanings by their use in a specific context, you will need to learn ways of understanding the word in the context of the discipline or passage you are reading. First, circle unfamiliar words in your textbook. This may occur when you are conducting the pre-reading strategies or during your reading of the passage. Once you identify a new word and have circled it, look for a (an):

Synonym: A synonym offers a clue for the words meaning in context. By finding a word with the same meaning, you can relate this to the unfamiliar word's meaning.

Antonym: If there is not a synonym, you can try to locate an antonym, opposite meaning, to determine the unfamiliar word's use in context.

General Knowledge: If the author does not offer you either of these context clues, use your general knowledge of English grammar, usage, and punctuation. This means you will look for clues concerning the part of speech, ***suffix***, prefix, Latin or Greek roots, or for commas, semicolon, and colons.

Example: If none of the other clues have provided you the meaning of the unfamiliar word in context, look for an example from the author. Often authors will give the definition of the word they are using immediately after the word is introduced into the text with an illustration. The illustration helps the reader make meaning of the word in context.

Basically, this skill will become automatic; you will do it without thinking, as you practice using the clues.

ILLUSTRATION: Process of Determining the Meaning of a Word in Context.

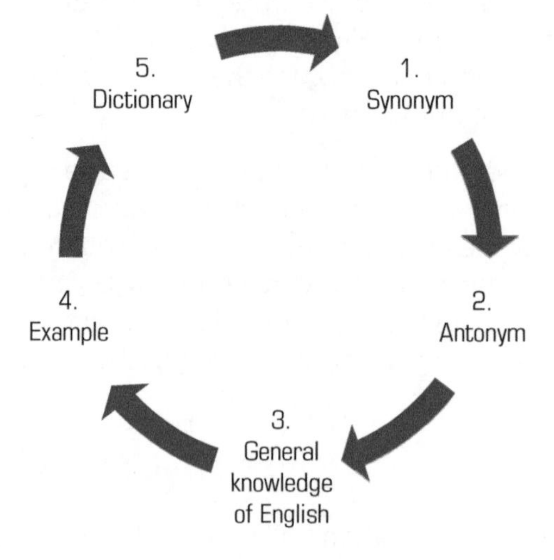

EXERCISE 8.6: Word in Context

Practice determining the meaning of an unfamiliar word in context.

The Pythagorean School

Pythagoras himself did not publish any books; the assumption of his school was that all their knowledge was held in common and veiled from the outside world, and that the glory of any fresh discovery must be referred back to their founder. Thus, Hippasus (circ. 470 BC) is said to have been drowned for violating his oath by publicly boasting that he had added the **dodecahedron** to the number of regular solids enumerated by Pythagoras. Gradually, as the society became more scattered, this custom was abandoned, and treatises containing the substance of their teaching and doctrines were written. The first book of the kind was composed, about 370 BC, by Philolaus, and we are told that Plato secured a copy of it. We may say that during the early part of the fifth century before Christ the Pythagoreans were considerably in advance of their contemporaries, but by the end of that time their more prominent discoveries and doctrines had become known to the outside world, and the center of intellectual activity was transferred to Athens.

Though it is impossible to separate precisely the discoveries of Pythagoras himself from those of his school of a later date, we know from Proclus that it was Pythagoras who gave geometry that rigorous character of deduction it still bears and made it the foundation of a liberal education. There is reason to believe that he was the first to arrange the leading propositions of the subject in a logical order. It, according to Aristoxenus, was also the glory of his school that they raised arithmetic above the needs of merchants. It was their boast that they sought knowledge and not wealth, or in the language of one of their maxims, "a figure and a step forwards, not a figure to gain three oboli."

Pythagoras was primarily a moral reformer and philosopher, but his system of morality and philosophy was built on a mathematical foundation. His mathematical researches were, however, designed to lead up to a system of philosophy whose exposition was the main object of his teaching. The Pythagoreans began by dividing the mathematical subjects with which they dealt into four divisions: numbers absolute or arithmetic, numbers applied or music, magnitudes at rest or geometry, and magnitudes in motion or astronomy. This "quadrivium" was long considered as constituting the necessary and sufficient course of study for a liberal education. Even in the case of geometry and arithmetic (which are founded on inferences unconsciously made and common to all men) the Pythagorean presentation was involved with philosophy; there is no doubt that their teaching of the sciences of astronomy, mechanics, and music (which can rest safely only on the results of conscious observation and experiment) was intermingled with metaphysics even more closely. It will be convenient to begin by describing their treatment of geometry and arithmetic (Rouse, 16-17).

Ball, W. W. Rouse. A Short Account of the History of Mathematics. NY: Dover Publications. 1960

List five words unfamiliar to you from *"The Pythagorean School"* passage and the context clue you used to determine its meaning in context.

Unfamiliar Word	Context clue used to determine meaning
Example: **dodecahedron**	**General knowledge** of Greek roots: "dodeca" = twelve (12), "hedra" = seat or base. May deduce dodecahedron is a twelve sided structure which is three-dimensional.

As you have seen, understanding the vocabulary within context of a chapter and discipline increases your comprehension of the reading materials you will have in college. Perhaps, more importantly, increasing your vocabulary through a wide variety of texts (i.e., novels, textbooks, articles, etc.) is the most effective way to increase your reading and writing comprehension.

EXERCISE 8.7: Vocabulary Strategies

Write a sentence explaining how to use each strategy offered for vocabulary.

Glossary:

____

Vocabulary in Context:

____

OBJECTIVE 4: Understand How to Apply Morphology as a Strategy for Reading Textbooks

In order to help you increase your general understanding of word parts in English, you will want to make sure you have a firm grasp on ***morphology***, the study of the forms of words. A ***morpheme*** is a letter or word which is the smallest meaningful component in the grammar of a language. These include:

Suffixes: a letter or a group of letters added to the ending of a word to change its use or meaning.

Suffix	Definition	Example
-able, -ible	is; can be	affordable, sensible
-al, -ial	having characteristics of	universal, facial
-ed	past tense verbs; adjectives	the dog walked, the walked dog

Suffix	Definition	Example
-en	made of	golden
-er, -or	one who; person connected with	teacher, professor
-er	more	taller
-est	the most	tallest
-ful	full of	helpful
-ic	having characteristics of	poetic
-ing	verb forms; present participles	sleeping
-ion, -tion, -ation, -ition	act; process	submission, motion, Relation, edition
-ity, -ty	state of	activity, society
-ive, -ative, -itive	adjective form of noun	active, comparative, sensitive
-less	without	hopeless, homeless
-ly	how something is	lovely, cleverly
-ment	state of being; act of	contentment, amusement
-ness	state of; condition of	openness, sadness
-ous, -eous, -ious	having qualities of	riotous, courageous, studious
-s, -es	more than one	trains, trenches
-y	characterized by	gloomy, cheery

Prefixes: a letter or a group of letters added to the beginning of a word to change its use or meaning.

Prefix	Definition	Example
anti-	against	anticlimax
de-	opposite	devalue
dis-	not; opposite of	discover, distrust
en-, em-	cause to	enact, empower
fore-	before; front of	foreshadow, forearm
In-, im-	in	income, impulse
in-, im-, il-, ir-	not	indirect, immoral, illiterate, irreverent
inter-	between; among	interrupt, interagency
mid-	middle	midfield, midterm
mis-	wrongly	misspell, misinterpret
non-	not	nonviolent
over-	over; too much	overeat, overzealous
pre-	before	preview, preseason

continued

Prefix	Definition	Example
re-	again	rewrite, redirect
semi-	half; partly; not fully	semifinal
sub-	Under	subway
super-	above; beyond	superhuman
trans-	across	transmit, transoceanic
un-	not; opposite of	unusual
under-	under; too little	underestimate

***Roots*:** a letter or a group of letters with a fixed meaning from Greek or Latin origins. Many Greek roots are associated with words concerning science.

Greek Root	Definition	Example
anthropo	man; human; humanity	anthropologist, philanthropy
auto	self	autobiography, automobile
bio	life	biology, biography
chron	time	chronological, chronic
dyna	power	dynamic, dynamite
dys	bad; hard; unlucky	dysfunctional, dyslexic, dystopia
gram	thing written	epigram, telegram
graph	writing	phonograph, photograph
hetero	different	heteronym, heterogeneous
homo	same	homonym, homogenous
hydr	water	hydration, dehydrate
hyper	over; above; beyond	hyperactive, hyperbole
hypo	below; beneath	hypothermia, hypothetical
logy	study of	biology, psychology
meter/metr	measure	thermometer, perimeter
micro	small	microbe, microscope
mis/miso	hate	misanthrope, misogyny
mono	one	monologue, monotonous
morph	form; shape	morphology, morphing
nym	name	antonym, synonym
phil	love	philanthropist, philosophy
phobia	fear	claustrophobia, phobic
photo/phos	light	photograph, phosphorous
pseudo	false	pseudonym, pseudoscience

Greek Root	Definition	Example
psycho	soul; spirit	psychology, psychic
scope	viewing instrument	microscope, telescope
techno	art; science; skill	technological
tele	far off	television, telephone
therm	heat	thermal, thermometer

Latin roots, many of which are associated with words concerning laws.

Latin Root	Definition	Example
ambi	both	ambiguous, ambidextrous
aqua	water	aquarium, aquamarine
aud	to hear	audience, audition
bene	good	benefit, benevolent
cent	one hundred	century, percent
circum	around	circumference, circumstance
contra/counter	against	counterbalance
dict	to say	dictation, dictator
duc/duct	to lead	conduct, induce
fac	to do; to make	factory, manufacture
form	shape	conform, reform
fort	strength	fortitude, fortress
fract	break	fracture, fraction
ject	throw	projection, rejection
jud	judge	judicial, prejudice
mal	bad	malevolent, malefactor
mater	mother	maternal, maternity
mit	to send	transmit, admit
mort	death	mortal, mortician
multi	many	multimedia, multiple
pater	father	paternal, paternity
port	to carry	portable, transportation
rupt	to break	bankrupt, disruption
scrib/script	to write	inscription, prescribe
sect/sec	to cut	bisect, section
sent	to feel; to send	consent, resent

continued

Latin Root	Definition	Example
spect	to look	inspection, spectator
struct	to build	destruction, restructure
vid/vis	to see	vision, video
voc	voice; to call	vocalize, advocate

EXERCISE 8.8: Morphemes

Review the lists of prefixes, suffixes, and roots and identify a total of ten morphemes new to you.

List the morphemes and their definitions below.

1.
2.
3.
4.
5.
6.
7.
8.
9.
10.

These can be the first of many morphemes for you to learn in order to increase your vocabulary. To gain a perspective on why you would prefer to learn the morphological meaning of English words rather than trying to memorize them, how many words would you guess are in the Oxford English Dictionary? ______ The *Oxford English Dictionary* states, "The Second Edition of the 20-volume Oxford *English Dictionary* contains full entries for 171,476 words in current use, and 47,156 obsolete words." Obviously, it is easier to learn the morphemes than to memorize 171,476 words.

REFLECTION 8.D:

Using only the morphemes listed in this section, write a definition for each word below and then use the word in a sentence.

1. inducted ______________________________

____

2. morphed ______________________________

____

3. thermodynamics ______________________________

____

4. telegraph ______________________________

____

5. immortality ______________________________

____

EXERCISE 8.9: Morphemes and Reading Comprehension

Read and practice the use of morphemes to increase your reading comprehension.

The Amoeba, Cells, and Tissue

We have thus seen how the nutritive material is taken into the animal's system and distributed over its body, and incidentally, we have noted how the resultant products of the creature's activity are removed. The essence of the whole process, as we have already stated, is the decomposition and partial oxidation of certain complex chemical compounds to water, carbon dioxide, a low nitrogenous body, which finally takes the form of urea, and other substances. We may now go on to a more detailed study, the microscopic study, or histology, of the tissues in which metaboly and kataboly occur, but before we do this it will be convenient to glance for a moment at another of our animal types—the Amoeba, the lowest as the rabbit is the highest, in our series.

Wells, H.G. *University Correspondence College Tutorial Series: Text Book of Biology, Part 1: Vertebrata.* Project Gutenberg eBook. 8 June 2007. Web. 13 Oct. 2013.

1. Circle the words with a prefix, suffix, or a root.
2. Choose five words from the text to demonstrate your understanding of how to use morphology to understand the meaning of vocabulary used in a text. Then, predict the meaning of the word through the use of its morphological meaning.

1. ______________________________

2. ______________________________

3. ______________________________

4. ______________________________

5. ______________________________

OBJECTIVE 5: Identify the Main Idea and Supporting Details for Increased Reading Comprehension

© Misunseo/Shutterstock.com

Reading can be compared to working a jigsaw puzzle because you have to figure out the basic patterns and frame of the text before you can construct the center of a puzzle. When working a puzzle, people usually sort through the various shapes and patterns to find the straight edged pieces first. Once the outer edge is constructed, it makes completing the interior picture easier. Think of the topic and main idea of a paragraph as the outer edges of reading comprehension. Once you have these constructed, the supporting details are easier to determine or predict.

How would you apply the previous metaphor of jigsaw puzzles and reading to the reading process? Think of it as listening to someone tell you a story, while the whole time you are asking yourself, "So what's the point of the story?" Trying to read without understanding the author's point is similar to listening to your friend ramble on and on. When reading, this means you are going to need to determine the point the author is actually making about the topic (Who or what is this about?). Then, you can determine the main idea by asking yourself "What is the point the author is making about the topic?"

Once you know the topic and the main idea, it is time to determine the major and minor supporting details. A major supporting detail directly supports the main idea. Think back to the jigsaw puzzle for a moment. If the outer edges that are straight-edged pieces comprise the main idea, then the puzzle pieces directly connected to the outer edges are the major supporting details. A minor supporting detail directly relates to the major supporting detail. If minor supporting details were puzzle pieces, they would directly connect to the major supporting details. Once you have discovered the major and minor details of a paragraph, you will be able to see the picture being painted for you by the author.

EXERCISE 8.10: Main Idea and Details

Read the following paragraphs to determine the main idea, major details, and minor details. Write the words and phrases of these comprehension elements in the space provided on the left.

Notations	Albert Bandura (1925–Present)
	Albert Bandura's social learning theory stressed the importance of observational learning, imitation, and modeling. "Learning would be exceedingly laborious, not to mention hazardous, if people had to rely solely on the effects of their own actions to inform them what to do," Bandura explained in his 1977 book on the subject. His theory integrated a continuous interaction between behaviors, cognitions, and the environment. His most famous experiment was the 1961 Bobo doll study. In the experiment, he made a film in which an adult model was shown beating up a Bobo doll and shouting aggressive words. The film was then shown to a group of children. Afterwards, the children were allowed to play in a room that held a Bobo doll. Those who had seen the film with the violent model were more likely to beat the doll, imitating the actions and words of the adult in the film clip. The study was significant because it departed from behaviorism's insistence that all behavior is directed by reinforcement or rewards. The children received no encouragement or incentives to beat up the doll; they were simply imitating the behavior they had observed. Bandura termed this phenomenon observational learning and characterized the elements of effective observational learning as attention, retention, reciprocation and motivation. (Source: http://stanford.edu/dept/psychology/bandura/bandura-bio-pajares/Albert%20_Bandura%20_Biographical_Sketch.html)

OBJECTIVE 6: Understand How to Annotate and Highlight the Main Idea and Supporting Details of a Paragraph

© Tatiana Popova/Shutterstock.com

Reading without writing in your textbook is like purchasing a car and rarely or never driving it. Did you know cars depreciate in value the minute you drive it off the car dealer's lot? The car still looks brand new even after five years because it is rarely driven, and the textbook looks brand new at the end of the academic term because it was not written in. Did you know books, like cars, lose their original purchase value as soon as you walk out of the book store with it?

Both scenarios in the example above are absurd, yet students often think it is best to abstain from writing in a textbook so he or she can get more money back on the book when the term ends. If the professor is going to use the book in the next term, you may earn a little more for the book when you sell it back to the bookstore. However, if a professor decides to use a different edition of the same book or change books, the buyback price on your textbook will be lower or non-existent. Write in your books because you own them and have little power over the amount the book will earn at the end of the academic term.

Writing in your books during the reading process increases your focus and recall of the materials. Have you ever struggled to recall a fact, but remember you highlighted it in blue on the lower left text on the page? Even the recall of a fact can be aided by a simple act of writing in your books. Highlighting and annotating are the tools used to focus your attention while reading and increase your recall or recognition of information later. ***Highlighting***, as you may know, is marking a book's most important information with a colored pen. In contrast, ***annotating*** is writing notes about what you are reading in the margin of the text. Both serve a very important purpose in reading if completed as an active reading strategy.

Highlighting may be the most overused and abused reading skill in existence today. Many students are highlighting everything in the book which results in colored ink on everything in the book. This is counterproductive to the intention of highlighting because it makes nothing important. Highlighting requires you to think critically with skill and precision. If you highlight 25% of the page, you are probably highlighting the most important information. To test if you have highlighted well, go back and read the information you highlighted to determine if:

- you have highlighted the main ideas and major supporting details of a paragraph.
- the highlighted words and phrases, when read, make sense.
- a short-hand version of the information is represented in your highlighted words and phrases.

If your highlighting reflects the bulleted information, you have a well-highlighted text that will increase your focus and learning.

Highlighting example:

	"Silkworms and Their Work"
Main Idea Supporting Detail	The caterpillars of a few butterflies and of many moths are spinners of fibers similar to silk. Among these last is the beautiful pale-green lunar moth. Spiders spin a lustrous fiber, and it is said that a lover of spiders succeeded, by a good deal of petting and attention, in getting considerable material from a company of them. Silkworms, however, are the only providers of real silk for the world. Once in a while glowing accounts are published about the ease with which they can be raised and the amount of money which can be made from them with very small capital. This business, however, like all other kinds of business, requires close attention and skill if it is to be a success. An expert has said that it needs more time to build a spool of silk than a locomotive. Tappen, Eva March. "Silkworms and Their Work." *The Industrial Readers III: Makers of Many Things.* Cambridge: MA. Riverside Press. (1916) 92. <Project Guttenberg>.

Notice that the main idea and major supporting detail are the only words highlighted. The first two sentences of this paragraph are minor details offering a contrast of ideas to the author's point and major support.

EXERCISE 8.11: Highlighting Application

Use the following passage to highlight important details.

	The silk is taken off the reel, and the skeins are packed up in bales as if it were of no more value than cotton. Indeed, it does not look nearly so pretty and attractive as a lap of pure white cotton, for it is stiff and gummy and has hardly any luster. Now it is sent to the manufacturer. It is soaked in hot soapy water for several hours, and it is drawn between plates so close together that, while they allow the silk to go through, they will not permit the least bit of roughness or dirt to pass. If the thread breaks, a tiny "faller," such as are used in cotton mills, falls down and stops the machine. The silk must now be twisted, subjected to two or three processes to increase its luster, and dyed,— and if you would like to feel as if you were paying a visit to a rainbow, go into a mill and watch the looms with their smooth, brilliant silks of all the colors that can be imagined. After the silk is woven, it is polished on lustering machines, singed to destroy all bits of free fibers or lint, freed of all threads that may project, and scoured if it is of a light color; then sold. (97–8)

Annotation is reading and writing notes on the information in the margin of your textbook. The information annotated includes:

- the main idea,
- the major supporting details,
- questions you have concerning the information in the text,
- connections you are making in the textbook and the class or other classes you are taking or have taken,
- and vocabulary words and their definitions.

It is easier if you develop a symbol system rather than trying to write out every word you want to express in the margin of the book. For example:

- (!) indicates the main idea.
- (+) indicates a major supporting detail.
- (?) indicates this is a point needing more information for clarification.
- (√) indicates this is a point you agree with.
- (○) circle the word to indicate a new vocabulary word
- (∴) (<insert three dots, therefore symbol>) indicates the effect or outcome.
- 1, 2, 3 . . . indicates a list or enumeration of a process.

As you can see, the symbols are easier to jot down than a sentence or group of words. This does not mean you will never need or want to write phrases or sentences in the margin of your book. Exercising frugal use of words while annotating means you will save time while employing this strategy.

Annotation example:

	"Silkworms and Their Work"
+ Feed ① Eat white Mulberry Put on Table ② 2-3 wks. Worms appear Growth rate ③ Fresh Air Need ④ W. eat all the time the grow. W. lose appetite 1-2 days b/f skin falls off. ⑤	The way to begin to raise silkworms is first of all to provide something for them to eat. They are very particular about their bill of fare. The leaf of the osage orange will answer, but they like much better the leaf of the white mulberry. Then send to a reliable dealer for a quarter of an ounce of silkworm eggs. That sounds like a small order, but it will bring you nine or ten thousand eggs, ready to become sturdy little silkworms if all goes well with them. Put them on a table with a top of wire netting covered with brown paper, and keep them comfortably warm. In a week or two, there will appear some little worms about an eighth of an inch long and covered with black hairs. These tiny worms have to become three inches or more in length, and they are expected to accomplish the feat in about a month. If a boy four feet tall should grow at the silkworm's rate for one month, he would become forty-eight feet tall. It is no wonder that the worms have to make a business of eating, or that the keeper has to make a business of providing them with food. They eat most of the time, and have from four to eight meals a day of mulberry leaves. The worms they make a queer little crackling sound while they are about it. They from a quarter of an ounce of eggs begin with one pound a day, and work up to between forty and fifty. Silkworms like plenty of fresh air, and if they are to thrive, their table must be kept clean. A good way to manage this is to put over them paper full of holes large enough for them to climb through. Lay the leaves upon the paper; the worms will come up through the holes to eat, and the litter on their table can be cleared away. As the worms grow larger, the holes must be made larger. It is no wonder that their skins soon become too tight for them. They actually lose their appetite for a day or two, and they slip away to some quiet corner under the leaves, and plainly wish there were no other worms to bother them. Soon the skin comes off, and they make up for lost time so energetically that they have to drop their tight skins three times more before they are fully grown. Wet mulberry leaves must not be given them, or they will become sick and die, and there will be an end of the silkworm business from that quarter-ounce of eggs. They must have plenty of room on their table as well as in their skins. At first a tray or table two feet long and a little more than one foot wide will be large enough; but when they are full-grown, they will need about eighty square feet of table or shelves. At spinning time, even this will not be enough (92–3).

From the previous example, you can see how annotation requires the reader's focus to be on the text in order to accurately annotate. It is clear to see the author is explaining the process of growing silkworms as well as the stages of silkworm's growth. If you were reading this text for a class, this information would offer your instructor the makings of a good test question. Annotation helps create order out of the words on the page to help create meaning and guide the reader's analytical thinking skills.

Some experts say annotating is more active learning than the use of highlighting. Annotation does require the reader to think more critically and analytically while reading. Highlighting can become common place if the reader is not thinking about what and why he or she is highlighting, so the successful way to highlight is through analyzing the meaning of the text, and capturing the main idea and major supporting details only. Annotation allows you to do this and more. You may choose to use one or both of these active reading strategies to increase your comprehension.

EXERCISE 8.12: Annotation Application

Use the following passage to annotate important details.

	After the worms have shed their skins four times and then eaten as much as they possibly can for eight or ten days, they begin to feel as if they had had enough. They now eat very little and really become smaller. They are restless and wander about. Now and then they throw out threads of silk as fine as a spider's web. They know exactly what they want; each little worm wants to make a cocoon, and all they ask of you is to give them the right sort of place to make it in. When they live out of doors in freedom, they fasten their cocoons to twigs; and if you wish to give them what they like best, get plenty of dry twigs and weave them together in arches standing over the shelves. Pretty soon you will see one worm after another climb up the twigs and select a place for its cocoon. Before long it throws out threads from its spinneret, a tiny opening near the mouth, and makes a kind of net to support the cocoon which it is about to weave (94–5).

The most important point to remember about annotation and highlighting is "just do it!" Annotation and highlighting are tools to help you learn. Use them often and with precision to gain the most benefit from them.

OBJECTIVE 7: Understand Strategies for Reading Works of Narrative Fiction

What do you prefer to read, a novel or a textbook? Many people have a strong preference for one over the other. If you enjoy reading novels more than a textbook, you like to read narrative texts. In contrast, if you find pleasure in reading textbooks more than reading a novel, you favor reading an ***expository*** (explaining, informing, describing) text. Both expository and narrative texts will be required reading in college, so learning about the features of each will offer you the understanding of the types of materials found in them.

Primarily, you will be reading expository materials in college. Textbooks, employee handbooks, lab manuals, and newspapers, and some types of magazines are examples of expository text. The structure of an expository text can be:

- description,
- enumeration,
- sequencing,

- cause and effect,
- compare and contrast,
- and problem-solution.

Understanding the structure and types of reading materials that use an expository text structure will help you predict what you will read. Calling upon your schema to aid in your comprehension is part of this process as well.

Additionally, you will read **narrative** or literature-based materials. The most basic understanding of the narrative text's structure is that it has a beginning, middle, and ending. Have you ever read, listened to someone tell you, or have told the story of the "The Three Little Bears?" On a very basic level, this is the structure of a narrative.

Example narrative reading:

A LESSON IN MANNERS

One morning there was a loud knock at Dean Swift's door. The servant opened it. A man who was outside handed her a fine duck that had lately been killed, and said, "Here's a present for the Dean. It's from Mr. Boyle."

Then, without another word, he turned and walked away.

A few days afterward the man came again. This time he brought a partridge. "Here's another bird from Mr. Boyle."

Now, Mr. Boyle was a sporting neighbor who spent a good deal of time in shooting. He was a great admirer of Dean Swift and took pleasure in sending him presents of game.

The third time, the man brought a quail. "Here's something else for the Dean," he said roughly, and tossed it into the servant's arms.

The servant complained to her master. "That fellow has no manners," she said.

"The next time he comes," said the Dean, "let me know, and I will go to the door."

It was not long until the man came with another present. The Dean went to the door.

"Here's a rabbit from Mr. Boyle," said the man.

"See here," said the Dean in a stern voice, "that is not the way to deliver a message here. Just step inside and make believe that you are Dean Swift. I will go out and make believe that I am bringing him a present. I will show you how a messenger ought to behave."

"I'll agree to that," said the man, and he stepped inside. The Dean took the rabbit and went out of the house. He walked up the street to the next block. Then he came back and knocked gently at the door.

The door was opened by the man from Mr. Boyle's. The Dean bowed gracefully and said, "If you please, sir, Mr. Boyle's compliments, and he wishes you to accept of this fine rabbit."

"Oh, thank you," said the man very politely. Then, taking out his purse, he offered the Dean a shilling. "And here is something for your trouble."

The lesson in manners was not forgotten; always after that, the man was very polite when he brought his presents. And the Dean also took the hint, for he always remembered to give the man a tip for his trouble.

Jonathan Swift, often called Dean Swift, was famous as a writer on many subjects. Among other books he wrote "Gulliver's Travels," which you, perhaps, will read some time.

Baldwin, James. *Fifty Famous People: A Book of Short Stories.* The Project Gutenberg EBook. July 2004. eBook. 22 Oct. 2013.

This is brief, but illustrates the beginning, middle, and ending of the narrative.

EXERCISE 8.13: Identifying the Beginning, Middle and End of a Story.

Write the beginning, middle and ending of the story in *"A Lesson in Manners."*

Beginning:
Middle:
Ending:
The primary point of this story is:

While there are volumes of books written about the numerous arrangements of a narrative's structure, one of the most differentiating between a narrative from an expository text is the use of figurative language. Figurative language includes words and phrases with non-literal meanings, which paint pictures in the mind of the listener or reader. Some figures of speech in the English language include:

- **Simile:** comparing two unlike things with "like" or "as." (i.e., She is good as gold.)
- **Metaphor:** comparing two unlike things without "like" or "as." (i.e., It is raining cats and dogs.)
- **Personification:** to give human qualities to nonhuman things. (i.e., His dog is the master of the house.)

As you can see, figures of speech enhance everyday language as well as written words on a page.

EXERCISE 8.14: Figurative Language

Brainstorm with a partner in class or friend outside of class as many examples of figurative language you can recall.

Simile	Metaphor	Personification	Other

Based on the fact ***figurative language*** in narratives offer readers images to understand the whole meaning being communicated, you may wonder if figures of speech are ever used in expository text? Yes! Expository texts often employ figurative language to communicate meaning through images. The best way to recognize this is through the understanding of two more words: connotation and denotation. **Denotation** is the literal meaning of a word as it is found in the dictionary, but **connotation** is the meaning of a word in a specific context. An obvious verbal example of this is when someone walks by and your friend says, "That's a cool jacket." In this context, the use of the word "cool" is not literal. The jacket does not contain actual cooling materials, but is considered to be unique. An example in expository text of connotation is as follows:

> "I can't see how anyone would think that it would be okay to mete out punishment to someone who has been subdued and is not any threat," says John Ralphling, lawyer for the man who was pepper-sprayed by the officers" (Welch, William M. "Some Say Cop Videos Misleading." *USA Today*. Nov. 30, 2006)

Why did Mr. Ralphling use the words "mete out" punishment? "Mete out" means "to give out something such as punishment or justice, especially in a way that seems harsh or unfair." The punishment given to Mr. Ralphling's client was pepper-spray. It seems Mr. Ralphling's use of "mete out" could have been used to incite, provoke, or exaggerate.

EXERCISE 8.15: Connotative Words

Circle the connotative words that might have changed the image painted in the reader's mind if *"mete out"* had been replaced with:

administer *respond with* *react with*

Explain how this might change the image in the reader's mind.

There is, however, more to this story. "Los Angeles Police Chief William Bratton says his officers were using justifiable force in subduing suspects in the Hollywood and Venice Beach incidents, even if the video strikes viewers as disturbing."

In the Venice Beach pepper-spraying, Bratton said county prosecutors examined the video and cleared officers of wrongdoing because the video showed the man was clearly combative.

"Combative" means ready to fight or argue, aggressive, belligerent, confrontational, and antagonistic. The police chief could have ended his comment here, yet he chose to add one more sentence.

> "The officers showed remarkable restraint," Bratton said.

What does the use of the word "restraint" convey to you?

Word choice is critical to writers because each word communicates a message. The literal (denotative) meaning or figurative (connotative) meaning of the words selected is very carefully reviewed. For example, prior to publication, the *USA Today* piece from above was sent to the editor and fact checker. This means professional writers have someone review their words with scrutiny prior to printing them to make certain they communicate accurately. If professional writers use this type of cautious word choice when writing, you will want to carefully consider the author's literal and figurative meanings in the words they use on the page.

OBJECTIVE 8: Understand Strategies for Reading Procedural and Declarative Documents

Determining your purpose for writing is another aspect of reading you should consider in order to maximize your learning. Prior to reading, you should survey the materials, which has been previously discussed. When you survey the book or documents you are going to read, determine your purpose for reading. One way to accomplish this is by asking yourself: What do I want to learn from this reading? What does my professor want me to know after reading this material? There are three basic purposes for reading and each are engaging you on different levels of focus. The purposes for reading are:

TABLE 8.1 How reading purpose alters focus.

Purpose	Focus Level	Types of reading materials
Entertainment	Shallow	Novel, short story, or poem.
Critical	Deep	Textbook, magazine, email, and online materials such as a blog or e-commerce site.
Thorough	Deeper	Research materials such as journal articles, test materials, lab report or outcomes of a study

Based on the purpose of your reading, which is determined prior to reading, you will process information on different levels. As noted in the previous chart, when you read a novel for pleasure the mental processing is shallow and critical reading requires a deep processing stage, which is analyzing the text. The highest level of focus is dedicated to reading thoroughly, which means you are reading to evaluate and synthesize the text. The terms to describe the various levels of focus are aligned with Bloom's Taxonomy (See Chapter 4) because each level progresses to the higher order thinking skills.

The text can be written in a procedural or declarative format. ***Procedural*** materials are those including a process as seen in mathematics and science. These materials require you to attend to the steps or order of operation being explained in the text. ***Declarative*** information is written to inform or instruct you on events or concepts. Typically, declarative information is located in your history, education, science, government, psychology, or anthropology textbooks. The approaches to reading procedural or declarative information differ slightly, so the skills you need will also vary.

TABLE 8.2

Reading stages	Procedural	Declarative
Pre-Reading	**Survey:** headings and subheadings, charts and graphs. **Skim:** determine how the author has organized the materials. **Ask:** What the directions are asking me to do?	**Survey:** headings and subheadings, charts and graphs. **Skim:** determine how the author has organized the materials. **Ask:** What do I already know about this? What do I want/need to learn?

Reading stages	Procedural	Declarative
During Reading	**Highlight:** the verbs in the directions (i.e., do, sums, divide, etc.) **Annotate:** ■ Summarize each of the directions in a way you understand what you are being asked to do. ■ Jot words or phrases that aid in your comprehension of the charts, pictures, or diagrams. ■ Enumerate the steps described in the process. ■ Pause to visualize the steps described. ■ Circle unfamiliar vocabulary. ■ Place a question mark (?) by confusing materials or concepts you do not understand. ■ Seek help with the material where you placed a question mark (?) next to. ■ Predict how challenging the upcoming material will be, based on what you have learned in this chapter.	**Highlight:** the main idea and major supporting details. **Annotate:** ■ Write words or phrases in the margin of the book to indicate: ❑ comprehension (√) or lack of comprehension (?) ❑ connections to other classes or material in this class (+) ■ Jot words or phrases that aid in your comprehension of the charts, pictures, or diagrams. ■ Enumerate chronological ordered events described. ■ Pause to visualize the events described. ■ Circle unfamiliar vocabulary. ■ After reading each section, ask yourself: *Do I understand what I just read?* Then, write a brief summary of each section in the book (subheadings or paragraphs). ■ If you realize you are confused or do not understand a concept, review your annotations to determine where you got lost.
Post Reading	■ Review your summary of the directions to determine if you understand them correctly. ■ Revise your understanding as needed. ■ Perform the tasks, find the solutions, needed to express comprehension of the materials.	■ Summarize the information you read in your own words. ■ Reread passages posing challenges for you. ■ Connect the ideas from the reading to your prior knowledge, to courses you are, or have taken, and to ideas within the class you are in. ■ Evaluate your recall and recognition of the reading materials.

As you can see, reading and learning procedural and declarative information requires two sets of reading skills.

EXERCISE 8.16: Procedural and Declarative information

Take a moment to review the reading materials in your courses. How will you read and learn the materials in your courses for long-term recall and recognition now that you understand the purposes for each?

Course	Procedural	Declarative	Both

Course Connections:
Reading a Mathematics Textbook

You might be asking yourself, "Who reads their math book anyway?" The better question is "Why should I read it?" or "How do I read it?" Why is easy to answer . . . to improve your understanding and, thus, your grade! How is not as easy to answer. It takes practice.

A mathematics textbook is structured differently than texts in other subjects. Usually, each chapter is divided into five to seven sections, consisting of six to ten pages each.

What is the advantage for students to have a section of this length?

____

Not all textbooks are structured exactly the same, but they are similar.

Most sections of a textbook contain the following content components:

Title of the section: This lets you know what you will be covering in this section.

Objectives: Objectives, learning outcomes, or topics list the specific skills you will learn in the section.

Vocabulary: The new mathematical terms necessary for understanding the section will be listed here.

Examples: These are sample problems keyed to the objectives or learning outcomes to explain a process.

Solution: This is the worked out problem generally with the steps listed to let you know how to complete it.

Whether assigned or not, it is good practice to read the section(s) to be covered before class because

1. the objectives will tell you what skills you will be learning in each section;
2. the vocabulary words alert you to watch for, and highlight, their definitions;
3. you will have a better grasp of the vocabulary being used in your instructor's explanation;
4. you may not understand everything you read the first time through, but you can write questions in the margins to ask in class;

When reading your textbook, read any explanation and then read each example carefully, paying close attention to the steps used in the solution to work through the problem.

You want to UNDERSTAND what you are doing! If you get to a point where you do not understand what is written, it is best to stop since mathematics concepts build on one another. Stopping will eliminate any frustrations with the material. Let your instructor explain it when you next go to class.

<table>
<tr><td>AS YOU COMPLETE THE ASSIGNMENT
check your answers. You do not want to work problems incorrectly because unlearning an incorrect process is more difficultly than learning it correctly.</td><td>When beginning the exercises, be sure to read the instructions carefully!
1. What is the perimeter of the figure? ________
2. Calculate the area of the figure. ________
7 in
21 in</td></tr>
<tr><td>The answers to the odd-numbered exercises are probably in the back of the book or they may be available online.
____
Why could this be important to you?
____
________________________</td><td>REFLECTION:
What is the importance of understanding the instructions in the two exercises above?
____
________________________</td></tr>
</table>

8.2 TAKING NOTES WHILE READING

Have you ever invested your time in reading a textbook chapter only to forget everything you just read? This, unfortunately, is more common than you might realize. As discussed in Chapter 3, creating a memory includes the repetition of concepts. Creating connections between your readings for long-term retention will include taking notes while reading, in addition to the annotation and highlighting already discussed in this chapter.

EXERCISE 8.17: Metacognitive Moment:

Take a moment to record the process you use when reading and taking notes.

If you do not have a system, explain why you do not have one.

There are many ways to take notes, as you saw in Chapter 7, but reading and note-taking will require another system. This is the SQ4R system, which is comprised of the following steps:

FIGURE 8.1 Diagram: SQ4R Reading and Note-Taking Process.

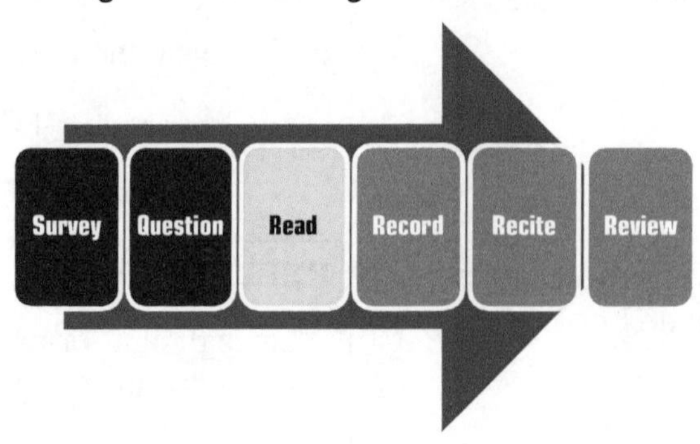

OBJECTIVE 9: Understand How to Use SQ4R While Reading

Now, you have seen an overview of the SQ4R process so, read on to learn what is included in each stage and how you can use each step to increase the opportunities to learn as you read and take notes.

TABLE 8.4

Reading Stages	SQ4R Steps	Action Plan	Learning Cycle
PRE-READING	**SURVEY**	Before you start reading the Chapter or article, prepare your brain to learn and connect your prior knowledge, schemata. **Read the**: ■ introduction ■ conclusion or summary of the chapter ■ the headings ■ subheadings ■ charts, graphs, and visual aids ■ bold, italicized, or colored text **Ask:** ■ What does this look like it will be about? ■ What do I already know? ■ What do I anticipate learning?	Day 1 Time: about five to ten minutes once you learn this system.
	QUESTION	Create questions by turning the headings and subheading into questions using words like: ■ How ■ When ■ Why ■ Who ■ What ■ Which ■ Where These questions establish your purpose for reading, so you can ask questions and seek answers as you are reading.	

Reading Stages	SQ4R Steps	Action Plan	Learning Cycle
DURING READING	**READ**	Read and annotate or highlight the answers to the questions your created.	Day 1: Time: Depending on the length of the chapter and your familiarity with the topic, this may take, at the least, 45 minutes.
AFTER READING	**RECORD**	After you have read the textbook chapter, record the answers to the questions you generated in the pre-reading stage.	Day 1: Time: at the least 30 minutes.
	RECITE	Read your questions and answers out loud and create more study aids as needed.	Days 2–5
	REVIEW	Create a study guide for the chapter by recording the concepts included, in the form of an outline or a table of contents. Try to test your knowledge initially by not using your notes or study aids. After you have exhausted the concepts in your recall memory, review your notes and the book to make sure you have included the most important information. Write a summary of the chapter. Be sure to connect the ideas within the textbook as your read more chapters. Also, connect the ideas to those you are or have learned in other courses. Finally, determine if you have any remaining questions requiring more research or a visit to your professor.	Days 6–7

The SQ4R is a tried and true system of reading and note-taking which works effectively for traditional books and eBooks. Basically, you are approaching your reading systematically with repetition that is naturally built into the strategy. Take a minute to determine how many repetitions there are in the SQ4R system and record your answer here: ____________________.

If you counted five, six, or seven, you are pretty close. These numbers represent the minimum number of repetitions you will encounter with this strategy. The answer is, actually, unknowable because you may need more or less repetitions to learn some of the more challenging material you may cover in your courses. The beauty of the SQ4R reading and note-taking strategy is you will have the opportunity to learn the concepts in the reading material more permanently because you are taking time to absorb them. Remember, the "slow drip" metaphor for learning presented in an earlier chapter? This is how you practice it in a practical way.

EXERCISE 8.18: SQ4R

Complete the SQ4R on the following passage on the next page. This passage on Memory was extracted from a text written to college students in 1921 entitled *How to use Your Mind.* See if some of the information sounds familiar to this textbook.

SQ4R	Second Aids to Memory: Retention, Recall and Recognition
	Our discussion up to this point has centered [*sic*] around the phase of memory called impression. We have described some of the conditions favorable to impression and have seen certain and accurate memory depends upon adherence to them. The next phase of memory—**Retention**—cannot be described in psychological terms. We know we retain facts after they are once impressed, but as to their status in the mind we can say nothing. If you were asked when the Declaration of Independence was signed, you would reply instantly. When asked, however, where that fact was five minutes ago, you could not answer. Somewhere in the recesses of the mind, perhaps, but as to immediate awareness of it, there was none. We may try to think of retention in terms of nerve cells and say that at the time when the material was first impressed there was some modification made in certain nerve cells which persisted. This trait of nerve modifiability is one factor which accounts for greater retentive power in some persons than in others. It must not be concluded, however, that all good memory is due to the inheritance of this trait. It is due partly to observance of proper conditions of impression, and much can be done to overcome or offset innate difficulty of modification by such observance.
	We are now ready to examine the third phase of memory—**Recall**. This is the stage at which material that has been impressed and retained is recalled to serve the purpose for which it was memorized. Recall is thus the goal of memory, and all the devices so far discussed have it for their object. Can we facilitate recall by any other means than by faithful and intelligent impressions? For answer let us examine the state of mind at time of recall.
	We find that it is a unique mental state. It differs from impression in being a period of more active search for facts in the mind accompanied by expression, instead of a concentration upon the external impression. It is also usually accompanied by motor expressions, either talking or writing. Since recall is a unique mental state, you ought to prepare for it by means of a rehearsal. When you are memorizing anything to be recalled, make part of your memorizing a rehearsal of it, if possible, under same conditions as final recall. In memorizing from a book, first make impression, then close the book and practice [*sic*] recall. When memorizing a selection to be given in a public speaking class, intersperse the periods of impression with periods of recall. This is especially necessary in preparation for public speaking, for facing an audience gives rise to a vastly different psychic attitude from that of impression. The sight of an audience may be embarrassing or exciting. Furthermore, unforeseen distractions may arise. Accordingly, create those conditions as nearly as possible in your preparation. Imagine yourself facing the audience. Practise [*sic*] aloud so that you will become accustomed to the sound of your own voice. The importance of the practice of recall as a part of the memory process can hardly be overestimated. One psychologist has advised that in memorizing significant material more than half the time should be spent in practicing [sic] recall.

SQ4R	Second Aids to Memory: Retention, Recall and Recognition
	There still remains a fourth phase of memory—**Recognition**. Whenever a remembered fact is recalled, it is accompanied by a characteristic feeling which we call the feeling of recognition. It has been described as a feeling of familiarity, a glow of warmth, a sense of ownership, a feeling of intimacy. As you walk down the street of a great city you pass hundreds of faces, all of them strange. Suddenly in the crowd you catch sight of someone you know and are instantly suffused with a glow of feeling that is markedly different from your feeling toward the others. [. . .] Thus the feeling of recognition that accompanies recall is responsible for one of the benefits of reviews. At such a time material once memorized becomes tinged with a feelingful [*sic*] color different from that which accompanied it when new. Review, then, not merely to produce additional impressions, but also to take advantage of the feeling of recognition.
	We have now discussed memory in its four phases and have seen clearly that it operates not in a blind, chaotic manner, but according to law. Certain conditions are required and when they are met memory is good. After providing proper conditions for memory, then, trust your memory. An attitude of confidence is very necessary. If, when you are memorizing, you continually tremble for fear that you will not recall at the desired moment, the fixedness of the impression will be greatly hindered. Therefore, after utilizing all your knowledge about the conditions of memorizing, rest content and trust to the laws of Nature. They will not fail you.
	By this time you have seen that memory is not a mysterious mental faculty with which some people are generously endowed, and of which others are deprived. All people of normal intelligence can remember and can improve their ability if they desire. The improvement does not take the form that some people expect, however. No magic wand can transform you into a good memorize[r.] You must work the transformation yourself. Furthermore, it is not an instantaneous process to be accomplished overnight. It will come about only after you have built up a set of habits, according to our conception of study as a process of habit formation.
Kitsen, Harry D. "*How to use Your Mind: A Psychology of study being a Manual for the use of Students and Teachers in the Administration of Supervised Study, 2nd. ed.* The Project Gutenberg EBook. 11 Jan. 2004. Web. 10 Oct. 2013.	

EXERCISE 8.19: Reading and Note-Taking with the SQ4R

After you have completed the reading and note-taking with the SQ4R on the previous passage, take a minute to reflect on your experience.

Survey stage: What did you expect to learn from this passage?

continued

<table>
<tr><td>What did you already know about this topic? Did your prior knowledge aid in your comprehension of this passage?

Since there were no headings or visual aids, did you find this passage more challenging to survey?

List bold or italicized words from this passage:</td></tr>
<tr><td>Questions:

What types of questions that you generated did you find most helpful as you read this passage?</td></tr>
<tr><td>Reading:

Describe the reading process you experienced having completed the Survey and Question stages prior to reading.</td></tr>
<tr><td>Recite:

Did you feel comfortable stating the questions and answers out loud? If not, why? How will this aid in your ability to remember this information?</td></tr>
<tr><td>Review:

Review your summary and connections you have written between this text and other course materials read in this class. Do you think this will be useful if you have a test over this within the next 6 months? Will what you wrote in your summary still make sense to you in six-months? If not, what do you need to do to make your summary a better study tool?</td></tr>
</table>

If this is the first time you have used the SQ4R to take notes while reading, you may think it is too structured. Recall learning to drive and all the skills needed to drive safely. How long did it take for you to feel confident in your ability to drive near your home? Did it take more practice to drive confidently on a highway? Learning to perform well in reading is similar to driving because both require repeated practice in order to build self-confidence. As you use the SQ4R reading strategy more frequently, it will become as natural as driving on a highway.

OBJECTIVE 10: Understand Combining SQ4R and Cornell Note-Taking

In Chapter 7, you were introduced to Cornell note-taking as a strategy to help you as you listen and take notes in a lecture. Take a minute to review the structure and process of Cornell note- taking. Now, you will see how to use them with the SQ4R to increase your learning and recall of course materials.

TABLE 8.5

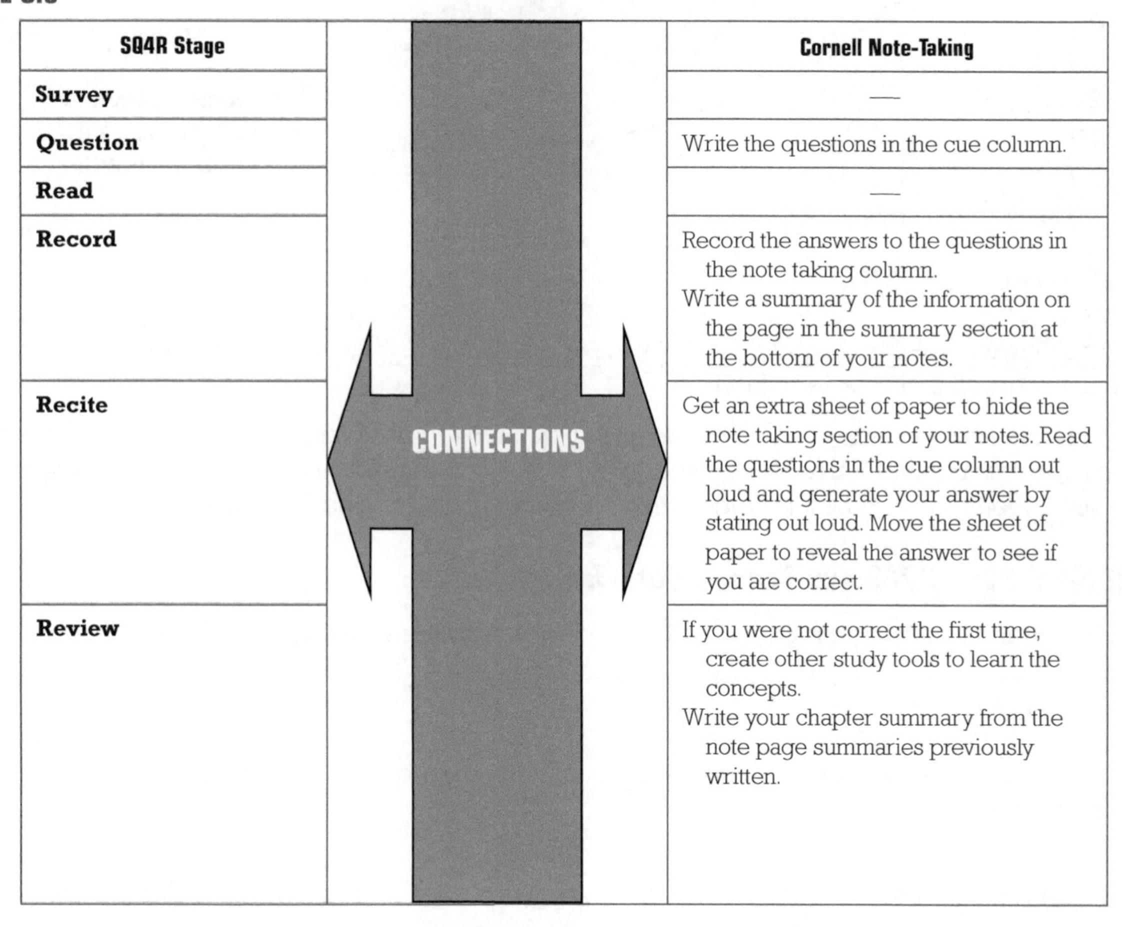

SQ4R Stage		Cornell Note-Taking
Survey		—
Question		Write the questions in the cue column.
Read		—
Record		Record the answers to the questions in the note taking column. Write a summary of the information on the page in the summary section at the bottom of your notes.
Recite	CONNECTIONS	Get an extra sheet of paper to hide the note taking section of your notes. Read the questions in the cue column out loud and generate your answer by stating out loud. Move the sheet of paper to reveal the answer to see if you are correct.
Review		If you were not correct the first time, create other study tools to learn the concepts. Write your chapter summary from the note page summaries previously written.

Blending the two strategies provides the opportunity to strengthen your memory due to the repeated manipulations of the course material you are learning. In Chapter 3 you learned about the memory process and how repeated review created long-term memory. The "Overcoming Curve" demonstrates you need to review the material you are learning for at least four review sessions. Other research suggests up to ten repetitions to learn and retain the information for long-term retention. Combining the SQ4R with Cornell note-taking allows for this type of ongoing review.

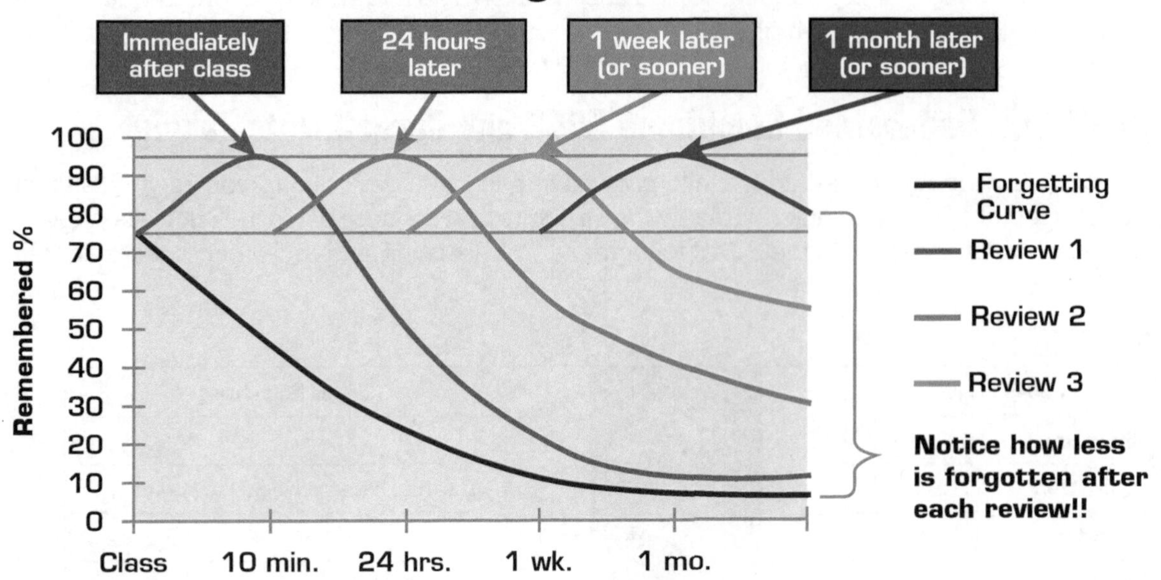

Source: Teichert D.J."Lest They Forget." Brigham Young University: Idaho. 9 Nov. 2010. Web. 29 Oct. 2013.

Go to http://www.schooltube.com/video/003e3144eed144dd9196/ for a good video that demonstrates how to use Cornell notes for repetition.

As you learned about Anna and how her passion was limited to learning about scuba diving at the beginning of this chapter, once she dove into the water and actually experienced scuba diving, she more fully understood it. Now, it is time to dive into using the SQ4R and Cornell note-taking!

EXERCISE 8.20: SQ4R and Cornell Note-Taking

Select a section of this chapter to read and apply the two strategies of SQ4R and Cornell note-taking.

Be sure to include:

- How long did it take you to complete the section you were reading while using these strategies?
- Did this amount of time seem longer than your previous reading and note-taking strategy?
- If you were given a quiz in the next class over the material you read and took notes on, how well do you think you would do?
- How would your current recall of the material compare to your previous reading comprehension?
- Explain how you plan on using these two strategies moving forward.

REFLECTION 8.E:

Select the next section in your mathematics or lab science textbook you have NOT covered and apply the SQ4R note-taking (you may use Cornell if you wish).

Compare and contrast how using the method works for expository writing and procedural writing.

___

___

___

___

Does the procedure described in the Course Connections provide enough guidance for you to review the material prior to class than the SQ4R method? Explain your answer.

___

___

___

___

PERSON to PERSON

In this exercise, you will be introduced to six students, all in an Introductory Biology class. Let's discuss classroom behavior and group dynamics!

Cindi sits in the front row. The subject seems easy to her. She does well on all the exams and is willing to help others, provided they have completed their assignments.	Tomas sits in the back row of the classroom, wears graphic t-shirts, slouched down in his chair, and acts bored with the presentation.	Jim is a recent retiree taking this class for personal growth and enrichment. He is surprised and concerned by the changes in classroom dynamics since his "old college days."

continued

Lesley has multiple body piercings and tattoos and excels in the laboratory component of the class.	Cary is a recent high school graduate who feels he already knows the class information. He spends most of the class time texting under the table while the instructor is speaking.	Eleanor returned to college after her company downsized. She hopes to become a nurse. Her native language is Spanish.

Based on these descriptions, select three members who should be assigned to Group 1 and three for Group 2 to work on a group project.

Cindi ____ Lesley ____ Tomas ____ Cary ____ Jim ____ Eleanor ____

Here is some additional information.

- Cindi is not willing to work with others who are not trying.
- Every time the instructor asks a question no one else answers, Tomas gives the correct response.
- Lesley volunteers at the Animal Center.

Based on all the information you now know about these students, assign them again to two groups as to who you believe will have the best group project experience. Has your ranking changed?

Cindi ____ Lesley ____ Tomas ____ Cary ____ Jim ____ Eleanor ____

1. What pieces of new information do you consider to be a positive influence on group dynamics?

____

____

2. What pieces of new information do you consider to be a negative influence on group dynamics?

____

____

Here are your last pieces of information.

- Cary has already missed 20% of the class sessions.
- Cindi and Cary each work 30 hours a week and spend little time studying.
- Eleanor has an associate's degree in English.

Based on all the information you have about these students, group them one last time as to who you believe will be the most compatible in this group assignment.

Cindi ____ Lesley ____ Tomas ____ Cary ____ Jim ____ Eleanor ____

1. What pieces of new information would you still like to know about each student?

____

____

2. Are there any pieces of information that could be seen as both positive and negative influences on the project results?

____

____

Career Connection:

© Uber Images/Shutterstock.com

In college, reading comprehension is critical to your success. You must be able to read long passages quickly and be able to communicate this information to another.

This skill can be applied to the real-world in everyday tasks such as reading maps, manuals, instructions, or prescription warnings.

In the workplace, you might be required to read business proposals, blueprints, or litigation briefs, or asked to provide research on a topic.

CHAPTER SUMMARY

Reading in college requires you to dive in and experience learning on a deeper level as was seen through Anna the scuba diver. There are hidden treasures awaiting your discovery in the books you will read. A few of these, often hidden treasures, are

- long-term memory storage and retrieval,
- increased vocabulary, higher grades in your courses,
- and the ability to connect the information you are reading about in one class to another class.

Reading is not a spectator sport, so dive in!

Active reading strategies are the techniques you use while reading to increase your comprehension of the text. Active readers need strategies that will aid in the mind's attention on the words in a book, so the reader can glean maximum information from it while reading.

Before you begin to read deeply, you will want to include a ***pre-reading*** warm-up. Active reading includes **during reading** skills such as annotating, highlighting, note-taking, and summarization. After you have read and employed one or more of the previously listed during reading skills, you will benefit from a ***post reading*** strategy such as writing the answers to the questions you generated, discussing the concepts with a fellow learner in your class, and analyzing the concepts more deeply.

Schema Theory helps with pre-reading because it engages prior knowledge. It is prior knowledge you have about this subject. In order to comprehend the text you are reading, prior knowledge and pre-reading aid in your retention of information

Three ways to activate prior knowledge or schema when you are beginning to read include **surveying**, **skimming**, and **scanning.**

Understanding the vocabulary within context of a chapter and discipline increases your comprehension of the reading materials you will have in college. Perhaps, more importantly, increasing your vocabulary through a wide variety of texts (i.e., novels, textbooks, articles, etc.) is the most effective way to increase your reading and writing comprehension.

Because words get their meanings by their use in a specific context, you will need to learn ways of understanding the word in the context of the discipline or passage you are reading. Circle unfamiliar words in your textbook. Once you identify a new word and have circled it, look for synonyms, antonyms, general knowledge, clues concerning the part of speech, suffix, prefix, Latin or Greek roots, or for commas, semicolon, and colons.

Once you know the topic (Who or what is this about?) and the main idea (What is the author's point about the topic?) it is time to determine the major and minor supporting details in the paragraph.

Writing in your books during the reading process increases your focus and recall of the materials. Highlighting and annotating are the tools you can use to focus your attention while reading and to increase your recall or recognition of information later.

Primarily, you will be reading expository (explaining, informing, describing) materials in college. Understanding the structure and types of reading materials using an expository text structure help you predict what you will read.

One of the most contrasting features between a narrative from an expository text is the use of figurative language. Figurative language includes words and phrases with non-literal meanings that paint pictures in the mind of the listener or reader. Some figures of speech in the English language include simile, metaphor, and personification.

The text can be written in a procedural or declarative format. Procedural materials are those including a process as seen in math and science. Declarative information is written to inform or instruct you on events or concepts.

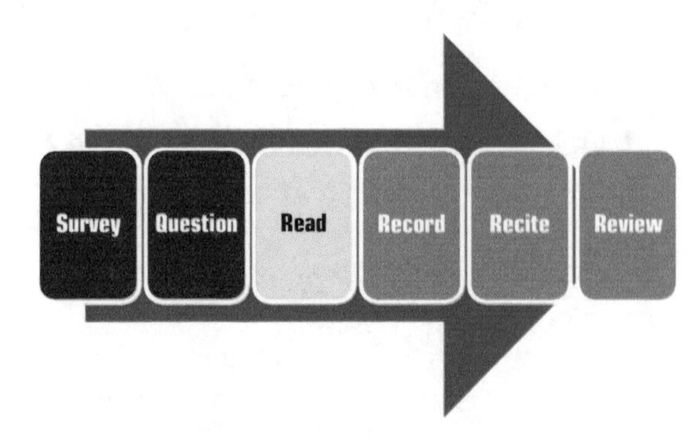

When the SQ4R is added to the Cornell note-taking method, you increase your comprehension as a result of the repetition. Repeated learning is the secret to long-term retention of your course content.

CHAPTER 8: Self-Check

Vocabulary: Define the following:

1. pre-reading
2. during reading
3. post reading
4. schema
5. learning objective
6. declarative reading
7. procedural reading
8. annotation
9. highlighting
10. figurative language
11. expository
12. morphemes
13. prefix
14. suffix
15. root
16. SQ4R

Concepts:

17. How is reading like scuba diving?
18. Explain the three purposes for reading and when you use each of them.
19. Why do you need to activate prior knowledge or schema before reading?
20. Describe three (3) ways to activate prior knowledge.
21. Discuss ways to activate schema prior to reading.
22. What are the values of vocabulary development?
23. How does a reader identify the main idea and major supporting details?
24. Compare and contrast annotation to highlighting. Explain how to use each.
25. Contrast declarative and procedural reading materials and the reading strategies for each.
26. How do you use the SQ4R?
27. How do you combine the SQ4R with Cornell note-taking and why would you want to do this?
28. Compare and contrast active and passive reading strategies.
29. Describe pre-, during, and post reading strategies.
30. Identify new use of word or an unfamiliar word in text and discuss strategies for understanding unfamiliar word in context.
31. State examples of each of the vocabulary learning tools.
32. Explain how knowledge of vocabulary enhances reading comprehension.
33. List, identify, and define ten prefixes, suffixes, and roots.
34. Recognize topic, main idea, and supporting details in a paragraph.
35. Recognize denotative and connotative meanings.
36. Compare and contrast strategies for reading narrative to expository text.
37. Evaluate when to use reading comprehension strategies based on the two types of information.
38. Discuss the best way to study procedural or declarative information for long-term recall and recognition.
39. Compare and contrast the advantages and disadvantages to SQ4R and Cornell note-taking.
40. Discuss how to combine SQ4R and Cornell to improve note-taking.
41. Describe SQ4R and Cornell Notes to increase long-term retention for recall and recognition.

42. Explain how note taking addresses the learning preference for a visual, auditory, and kinesthetic learner.
43. Describe how to make learning through note taking a whole brain learning activity through visual/mind mapping.
44. Identify the key words from learning objectives as a focus tool for learning.
45. Evaluate the accuracy of notes to learning objectives.
46. Describe the process and the uses of outlining.
47. Create three note cards, the first with a true-false test question, the second with a multiple choice test question, and the third with an essay question.

CHAPTER 9
Studying

T.I.P.S.—(Tactical Information that Promotes Success)

Study as long as necessary to learn the material; there is no magic formula for how much time you need in each course to be successful.

Imagine you are playing in a football game in a "4th and goal" situation and your team needs one more touchdown to WIN. You are in the fourth quarter with two minutes left on the clock and within two yards of scoring the touchdown. Do you go through the defensive line, around it, or throw a pass to reach the end zone? If there was more time on the clock, you would have more options. Managing the clock is a critical component of winning the game.

© Hannamariah/Shutterstock.com

Similarly, studying needs to avoid the limitations to winning imposed on the last play only providing two play options. Managing the clock during a game or in the classroom means watching the clock to limit "last minute" cramming.

TOUCHDOWN!

© Pete Saloutos/Shutterstock.com

Deciding how much time to spend studying for each course is critical to your success in college. You will probably need to spend more time on some subjects than others, but effectively managing your study time will limit the need for any last-minute cramming.

In **mathematics**, spiraling the homework is one strategy to improve long-term retention of the concepts. Homework should be started as soon as possible after class. Then, take a break and do additional problems later. Finally, do more problems prior to the next class session. This will reinforce the topics. You will be surprised how much you will remember!

In **reading and writing**, a chapter for long-term memory retrieval requires writing while you read. This can be completed through annotation, summarization, outlining, or mapping. If you are reading, you need to be writing!

In **education**, scaffolding information is a common practice for teachers. This means instructors introduce information with support systems in place to enhance learning. As a student, scaffolding allows you to preview the text and discuss key vocabulary, or chunk the text and read and discuss as you go. The strategies act as scaffolds to support your learning.

CHAPTER 9: OBJECTIVES

9.1 Managing Study Time

Objective 1: Understand Where, When, and the Amount of Time to Study

Objective 2: Understand Strategies for Creating Productive Study Sessions

Objective 3: Understand the Importance of Preparing for Class during Study Sessions

9.2: Rehearsing Classroom Notes

Objective 4: Develop Note Cards

Objective 5: Apply Strategies for Information Recall and Recognition

Objective 6: Understand Strategies to Implement Review Options

9.3 Practicing Strategies for Memory Improvement

Objective 7: Understand the Use of Mnemonic Devices

Objective 8: Understand the Loci Method for Long-Term Learning and Connections

Objective 9: Understand "Deep Processing" as the Key to Learning

CHAPTER CONCEPTS:

Some or all of the following terms may be new to you. Place a check mark in the column reflecting your knowledge of each term.

	Know	Don't know	Not sure	Page # where first found		Know	Don't know	Not sure	Page # where first found
pre-reading					mnemonic device				
deep process learning					key information				
recall					acrostics				
recognition					loci method				

© Africa Studio/Shutterstock.com

It may seem odd to have a chapter dedicated to studying for college students, but as you will see, there are many reasons to take time to reflect on the most productive way to study. As you may have heard, "Work smart, not hard." This means you are taking charge of your time and spaces to learn in ways to maximize your resources. Working smart means you are finding ways to work by limiting wasted time or energy in the process. In fact, **working smart** means you are fully aware of the elements working to make you the best student—the one who earns the "A" and makes it look easy. Do not be deceived! Earning an "A" does require work on your part, but learning to **work smart** will minimize how hard you have to work and how difficult the work may be.

9.1 MANAGING STUDY TIME

OBJECTIVE 1: Understand Where, When, and the Amount of Time to Study

Do you ever look at people who accomplish great things and wonder how they are able to do so much? Is there some secret as to how they are able to do so much with, often, seemingly meager resources? Some people suggest setting goals is the secret to successful productivity. Most of the self-help books you read contain similar advice for achieving your goals as was explained in Chapter 2. Basically, this premise suggests setting your long-term goals and then breaking them down into manageable steps creates short term goals so you will succeed.

You may wonder if this is the only way to achieve greatness. There are as many words of wisdom on this as there are "experts" to tell you what to do, The secret to achieving greatness in college is maintaining the momentum. In other words, endure the distance included in the academic term to accomplish the goals you have established for these four to six months. This means you will need to work daily at checking the priority items off your "to do" list. Some students say it is easier to focus on the demands of the current term rather than looking down the road four to five years from today.

Throughout this textbook you are learning how to manage your time and resources. By following and personalizing the information you have covered so far, you are hopefully seeing some positive results in your classes. As the semester races along, the ending can seem as if it has arrived sooner than anticipated due to the demands and rigor of your learning. Having to manage multiple projects at the same time can feel overwhelming, but slowing down to conduct an inventory of your successes can increase your motivation to persevere. Maintaining an organized work space and study schedule, evaluating the productivity of your study sessions, and the ongoing review for daily course preparation are three ways of maintaining your momentum throughout the semester.

EXERCISE 9.1: Study Time

Take a minute to check out this assessment to better determine your study habit's effectiveness.
http://www.educationplanner.org/students/self-assessments/improving-study-habits.shtml

1. Based on the information learned from the previous self-assessment, at what times are you most likely to experience optimum learning?

 ____

 ____

 ____

 ____

2. How is this information consistent with your current study schedule? How is it different? What changes will need to occur in order to incorporate your optimum learning time in your study sessions?

 ____

 ____

 ____

 ____

3. Discuss the variables of time and place with regard to productive study spaces.

 ____

 ____

 ____

 ____

Studying in an organized space means you have considered the time of day, lighting, and your course schedule to create an environment that can maximize your ability to learn. These variables change based on your learning preferences, but there is an overall need to organize your study space. Some ways to accomplish this are:

Maintain ample office supplies: purchase file folders, pens, pencils, paper, printer ink, three-hole binders with tabs, stapler, tape, scissors, paper clips, highlighters, sticky notes, and other course specific materials. You may want to consider purchasing a small file drawer to organize your course materials. If you are short on cash and space, you may purchase a more portable file folder system.

Select proper seating. Select a chair both comfortable and functional because you are going to be sitting it in for extended periods of time. Additionally, if you are using a computer to study, you will want to make sure the height of the chair allows you to view the computer monitor screen from a distance of 20–30 inches to avoid eye and neck strain. The chair height should also allow for your thighs to be parallel to the floor when seated. Another primary concern of your chair is for your posture to be upright for extended periods of time. The closer your back is to the back of the chair, the more likely you may be to slouch, so you need to adjust your sitting position so there is some distance between your back and the back of your chair.

FIGURE 9.1 Workstation Planner

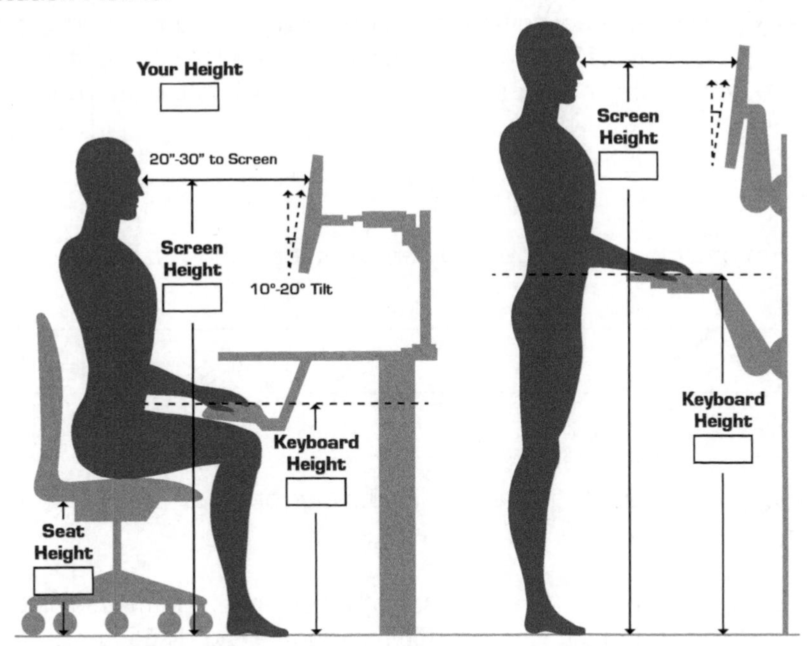

(Source: "Workspace Planner: Find the Right Position for Your Workstation." Ergotron Inc. 2012. Web. 4 Dec. 2013.)

An interactive worksheet for this desk and chair adjustment for your computer work space can be found at that site.

Arrange your desk: As you can see from the diagram above, the computer desk in your work station should fit to your body. This means that your arms should be resting at a natural 90-degree angle with your shoulders facing the computer monitor. If you skip this step, you will find your neck and shoulders will ache after sitting for long periods. By adjusting your desk, chair, and monitor to be just below your eye level, you will reduce strain on your eyes.

Eliminate or reduce noise: Working memory can only process one piece of information at a time when learning. For this reason, minimizing the noises around you when you study will allow you to think and learn more easily. Instrumental music (no lyrics are sung) with 60 beats per minute has been shown to be more effective when studying. All other music used in the research indicates it will distract you from focusing and limit your learning.

Maintain proper lighting: Generally, three sources of light are suggested for a constructive study area. For example, you can use natural light from the window during the day, an overhead light, and a desk lamp. By using three different sources of light, you will avoid eye strain and remain more alert. Also, by avoiding bright or intense lights, you will be able to study more productively over long time periods.

Selecting the right time to study is as important as any of the previous suggestions. When is the best time for your learning potential to be higher? This is personal because you have an internal clock that allows you to wake up or go to sleep. Additionally, your internal clock will have times in which you have greater focus than others. A very general rule for most people is to avoid work requiring high levels of concentration in the middle of the afternoon, around three o'clock. This is the time most brains need to rest or reboot according to Dr. Medina's research on the brain, which can be found in his book *Brain Rules*. Over a period of several days, determine the times of day you feel most energetic and focused and when you are just "beat." These may not be the same times every day, so keep a log. You may even be one of those people where three o'clock in the afternoon is an energy-filled time.

REFLECTION 9.A:

How can your ability to provide an effective study environment help you in the workplace?

___

___

___

For optimum learning, set aside study time each day during your most energetic and focused time. To maximize your study time, follow these recommendations:

- Turn your phone to "airplane" or "do not disturb" mode and turn the television and music (other than slow instrumental) off. This will minimize noise and distractions.
- Work on your most difficult or least favorite subject first. Trying to study one of these at the end of your study session is counterproductive.
- Set a non-intrusive alarm for one hour. Quit studying when the alarm rings.
- Take a ten minute break. It is important you get out of your chair and move around. Play with your dog or cat, walk around, stretch, do a few jumping jacks, eat a nutritious snack (an apple or banana is good) but DO NOT turn on the television, music, or your cell phone.
- Return to your studying and set the alarm again for one hour but change subjects to one you enjoy or one requiring different skills than the first. For example, if you were working mathematics problems, perhaps read your history assignment next.
- When the alarm rings, take another ten minute break as before.
- If you must study more than two hours, take a 30-minute break before beginning your third hour. Take the time to walk outside, eat a light meal, or watch your favorite sitcom.
- Whatever amount of time each day you have to study, divide the time you have by the number of subjects you need to study. Be sure, however, to maintain the ten minute break before moving to another subject. After your study time, turn your phone back on and catch up!

OBJECTIVE 2: Understand Strategies for Creating Productive Study Sessions

Productivity, "a measure of the efficiency of a person, machine, factory, or system in converting inputs into useful outputs" (http://www.businessdictionary.com) offers a framework for understanding how to be more efficient in your study sessions. As stated in the formal definition, productivity means you will "convert inputs into useful outputs." In other words, you will learn to increase how much you learn by comprehending the proper amount of energy and time needed to invest in your study time to yield outputs of success.

FIGURE 9.2 Model: Productivity and Study Sessions

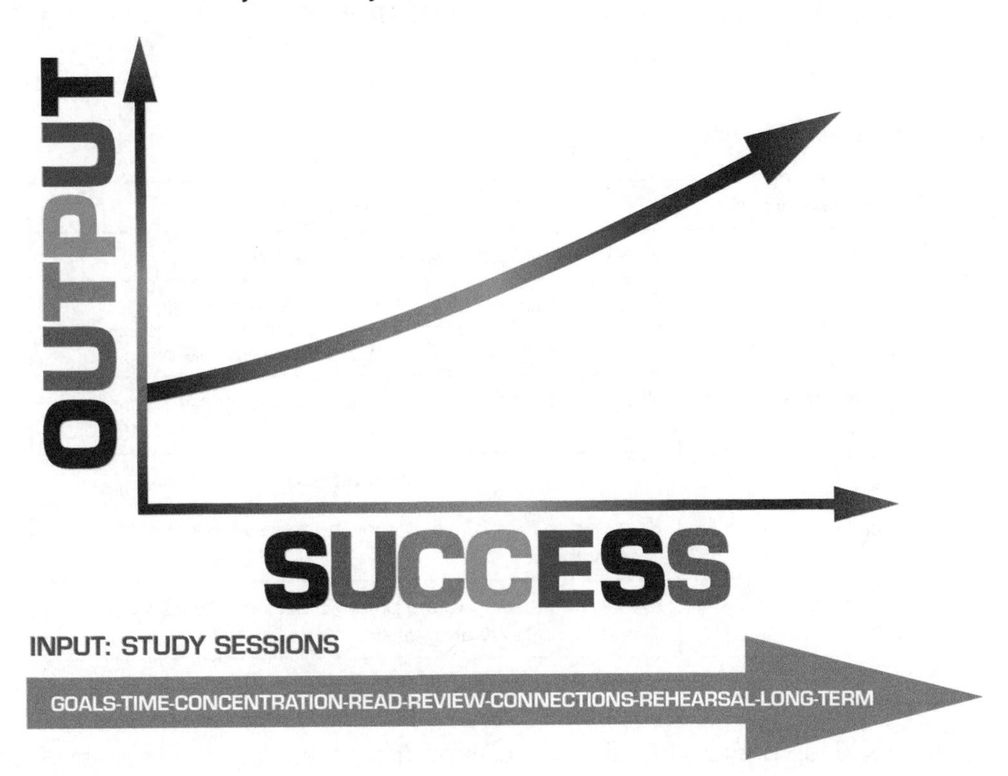

REFLECTION 9.B:

Describe in your own words what the figure above means.

____

____

____

____

____

____

____

Establishing goals for each study session is a valuable tool for measuring the "input" of your study sessions. In so doing, you can determine a realistic amount of information to learn from your course materials. In turn, this increases your productivity of learning because you know what you want to achieve in any given session. Ultimately, this means you will have the tools to measure how well you achieved your study session goal.

Exactly how does a college student identify goals and determine the amount of time needed for deep process learning? Remember, deep process learning includes:

TABLE 9.1 Deep Processing Method

Deep Processing Level	Question (Input)
Elaboration	How does this concept relate to other concepts?
Distinction	How does this concept differ from other concepts?
Personal	How can I relate this information to my personal experience?
Appropriate retrieval and application	How am I expected to use or apply this concept?
	Result (Output)
Automaticity	Practiced to the point that knowledge recall is not a conscious effort.
Overlearning	Extending learning to the point where the information is recalled quickly and easily.

The time required for deep process learning is, perhaps, more than you may have invested in previous learning environments. This input of information means you will increase your productivity and output to create your college success. How much is earning A's in all of your classes' worth to you? The answer you give to this question will determine your output for success.

As for setting a goal during your study session, it is just like setting short term goals as demonstrated in Chapter 2. Recall that the components of a SMARTER goal are:

Specific: What are the specific steps necessary to achieve the goal (i.e., dates, times, events)?

Measurable: How will you measure and track your progress?

Attainable: How likely will you achieve a goal in the time you have stated?

Relevant: What are the related steps or skills necessary to have in order to achieve this goal?

Time: When will you achieve this goal?

Evaluate: How will you determine when you have achieved this goal?

Revise: After working toward achieving goal and evaluating your progress, do you need to revise it?

Goals set for each study session will aid in determining successful output in ways such as being prepared for class and earning an "A" in every class. Creating personal study goals for each session will require a little forethought but will increase your efficiency and productivity while learning.

EXERCISE 9.2: SMARTER Goals

Select one of your upcoming course assignments and write a SMARTER goal for the next study session.

Course: ______________________________

S ______________________________

M ______________________________

A ______________________________

R ______________________________

T ______________________________

E ______________________________

R ______________________________

Written Goal: ______________________________

____

This exercise is intended to be the first few written goals for study sessions of many more to come. Establishing the habit of formulating a goal for each study session will provide the opportunity to increase your learning and success in college.

OBJECTIVE 3: Understand the Importance of Preparing for Class during Study Sessions

Reflect on a social event in which you eagerly anticipated attending. How much time did you spend on preparing for the evening? After showering, doing your hair (and make-up if necessary), you carefully selected something to wear and added the appropriate accessories. Now, compare this to preparing for your class sessions. While the comparison of going out to attending class may seem a bit of a stretch, the similarities are not really too different.

In readying yourself for class the first considerations are:

- **pre-reading** the materials,
- realizing the opportunities resulting from preparation,
- reassessing the relationship between study space, time, goal setting and intentions to preparation,
- and realization of outcomes for students who are prepared.

Did you know that "one of five college students self-report that they frequently come to class without readings or other assignments that were expected to be completed before class time"[1] (*NSSE* 2008)?

Most students intellectually understand the benefits of reading a chapter before attending class. Generally, homework should be completed prior to class. Research conducted on this suggests students might not pre-read because they:

- do not understand how learning in college is different from high school or other learning experiences,
- feel the instructor is going to cover the information in their lecture and reading it themselves would be unneccessary,
- do not have the literacy levels needed to read and comprehend their textbook,
- and/or have instructors who have not clarified the expected outcomes from reading the course materials.

Students who are not sure why or how to read a chapter prior to class are not going to pre-read. Fortunately for you, this book has given you several ways to read a textbook through the active reading strategies recorded in Chapter 8.

Pre-reading your course materials means you read and annotate or highlight with active reading strategies. As you will recall, the SQ4R provides you with a wonderful strategy that produces strong connections between reading comprehension and long-term memory. Additionally, reading with a proven strategy will help you predict the amount of time you need to dedicate to preparing for class by pre-reading.

Just to make a point, remember that one out of five students admitted they did not read or complete the assignments prior to attending class in college. This means that four out of five students (80%) are reading and preparing for class and are ready to learn upon arrival. Which student will you choose to be, one of the 20% students or one of the 80% students?

Of course, the primary reason for pre-reading and preparing for a class is to increase your learning and successful outcome in your class. Additional benefits include an:

- increase in self-confidence,
- increase in ability to interact during class discussions,
- and an increase in the ability to link information within the course as well as to other courses.

Preparing to learn is similar to taking the time to stretch before you run or exercise. The stretching activity tells your brain you are about to do something different or new. Then, as you run, your muscles know exactly how to respond to the situation. Preparation through pre-reading is like stretching your muscles because your brain will be able to accurately respond to the new material you are learning and run it through your memory process more easily.

Entering a class session prepared will help you feel more confident about yourself because of your grasp of the information being presented. Your increased confidence in the material may result in engaging in class discussions. You might even have a few questions to ask your professor, which could impress him or her.

---

[1] "NSSE Annual Results 2008." *National Survey of Student Engagement (NSSE)*. Bloomington, IN: U. of Indiana. (2008).

Perhaps the most important byproduct of preparing to learn prior to class is your ability to connect the newly learned information to previously covered course materials. As you know, this is the ultimate goal in learning! Understanding how new information relates to prior knowledge (schema) increases your long-term retention of the new information.

Additionally, understanding how the course material you are learning relates to the other courses in which you are enrolled or have taken increases your critical thinking. Learning about how to manage your time and resources in ways to "work smart" in combination with "working hard," requires you to act on the information given to you. In this chapter, you have learned about study spaces, time management, goal setting for study sessions, and preparation strategies to use prior to class lectures. Take a few minutes to determine how you can apply this to your personal learning.

EXERCISE 9.3: Study Sessions

Complete the chart.

Application	Study space	Time management	Goal setting for study sessions	Preparation strategies to use prior to class lectures
I have learned . . .				
I will do . . .				
Outcomes of this action will be . . .				

As you previously read in this chapter, twenty percent of all college students admit to arriving in a class unprepared. These students are probably going to have challenges with:

- completing the expected assignments well,
- engaging in classroom discussions,
- extending the learning from rote memorization to deep process learning,
- earning high grades in the courses they are taking,
- understanding why they did not perform well in college,
- and maintaining an exceptional GPA.

Each of the challenges listed demonstrate how this student is not adequately preparing to succeed in college. Academic probation varies between higher educational institutions, but basically, if a student has earned a GPA lower than 2.0 is given a semester to recover. The number of students on academic probation varies as well, but school reports indicate between 15%–40% of first year students will end up on academic probation. Fortunately, the numbers indicate between 59%–90% of academic probationary students recover after only one academic term. This means students earned significantly higher grades in the next term of their academic probation. It is unfortunate so many students learn about the need for preparation in college classes after they experience failure. The good news is most will recover from it and go on to achieve great successes.

Avoiding academic probation at the beginning of a college career will allow a student the opportunity to maintain a higher overall GPA. For example, a student who takes four classes, each three hours credit in one semester, may have a scenario such as:

ENGL1301	C	Semester Grade Point Average 3.0
HIST1301	B	
HUMA1301	B	
MATH1301	A	

In contrast, the student who does not do so well may have a scenario like:

ENGL1301	D	Semester Grade Point Average 1.75
HIST1301	B	
HUMA1301	F	
MATH1301	B	

If the student with the lower grade point average has a successful second semester, such as:

ENGL1301	A	Semester 2 **Overall** Grade Point Average 3.0
FREN1401 (4 hr class)	A	
HUMA1301	A	

Then, when the two semesters' GPAs are combined, the student will have earned an overall GPA of 2.77. Basically, it takes several semesters of outstanding grades to work off the one bad semester's grades. To prevent this from being your story, be prepared to learn in your college classes.

REFLECTION 9.C:

Because many employers are now reviewing college transcripts more than in previous years, how can multiple semesters of poor to average grades affect your ability to obtain a position when you apply after college?

____

____

____

____

____

____

EXERCISE 9.4 BENEFITS IN PREPARATION

Allow ample time to reflect on all you have learned and determine how you will apply the information.

List ten (10) of the benefits you have learned or have had personal experiences with in your preparation for courses:

1. ______________________________
2. ______________________________
3. ______________________________
4. ______________________________
5. ______________________________
6. ______________________________
7. ______________________________
8. ______________________________
9. ______________________________
10. ______________________________

List ten (10) of the disadvantages of not preparing for courses you have learned or have had personal experiences with:

1. ______________________________
2. ______________________________
3. ______________________________
4. ______________________________
5. ______________________________
6. ______________________________
7. ______________________________
8. ______________________________
9. ______________________________
10. ______________________________

Go back over the two lists and place a star beside the items on the list you practice. What does this reveal about your current course preparation?

Identify the two areas you think you need the most improvement on and determine a strategy you have learned in this course to avoid them.

1. ______________________________

2. ______________________________

Review both lists and explain why you think students would choose to ignore course preparation.

____

____

____

____

____

____

9.2 REHEARSING CLASSROOM NOTES

Taking notes in your classes is only the tip of the iceberg in your learning from a lecture. Taking time to review and revise them will increase your learning as well as earn you a higher grade in your classes. If you were convinced rehearsing your classroom notes would prepare you to earn an "A" in all of your classes, would you do it? While there may not be statistical data to support this claim, it is obvious rehearsing your classroom lecture notes will increase the probability of earning an "A."

OBJECTIVE 4: Develop Note Cards

Many students are familiar with how to create a set of note cards for rehearsing and reviewing a set of classroom notes. There are a wide variety of methods you can employ to create your note cards, so find the one that best suits your learning preference and the course materials. For the most part, note cards include information such as:

- topic/concept,
- definition,
- and example.

One side of the note card has one piece of information and the back has an additional component. Students review the information on each side for an extended period of time in an effort to learn. The amount of information as well as the placement of the information may be personalized, but it is important to review your set of well-written lecture notes and include the most important information on the note cards.

Even though you are personalizing the note card information or format, there are a few characteristics of a well-written note card that promotes long-term learning connections. Just the act of creating your note cards is the first step to creating long-term learning of your course materials. Creating a set of note cards will include a few basic steps:

- Write one concept on each card.
- Rewrite the information from your lecture notes on the note cards.
- You may abbreviate with bullets and numbers when appropriate.
- Use pictures for visually oriented disciplines (i.e., science, art, advertising, etc.)

Once you have created a set of well-written note cards, you can easily take them with you and review the course information. If you want, punch a hole in the upper left-hand corner and purchase a round shaped metal clip at an office supply store to carry them. The clip helps maintain the order of your cards in the event you drop them. Also, the clip will easily fit in a three-ring binder clip for better organization of your materials.

FIGURE 9.3 Note Cards On Round-Shaped Metal Ring

The advantages of creating and studying with note cards are:

- Ongoing review is readily available through the use of note cards.
- Creating the cards provides an opportunity to rework the lecture materials.
- Reviewing the note cards extends learning to the point the material can be moved to the long-term memory.
- Ease of transportability means the cards can be used in a variety of settings.

It is critical to remember note cards are just one of many ways to learn course content. If you solely rely on note cards for your learning, you may not be employing deep process learning, which is the primary disadvantage to using note cards. To learn how information connects from one chapter, lecture, course, or experience to another means you are processing the information more deeply. Recall the other critical components of deep-process learning:

Deep Processing Level
Elaboration
Distinction
Personalization
Appropriate retrieval and application
Automaticity
Overlearning

Note cards will not be able to guarantee deep processing will occur, but they will increase your automaticity and overlearning. Both of these are necessary for your success in studying and learning course materials, so there is a tremendous value in creating note cards. Additionally, creating note cards will encourage elaboration and distinction, and personalization will be even more useful for deep processing of information.

EXERCISE 9.5: Deep Processing

Review the elements and questions one should answer for deep processing. Then, create new ways of using them in generating a set of deep-processing note cards.

There are many online applications and resources for creating digital note cards. Many students prefer creating digital note cards because most smart phones will allow you to load them and carry them everywhere you go. Take a few minutes to review the features of digital note cards on the following websites and determine which one you prefer.

EXERCISE 9.6: Note-Taking Applications

Log on to the Internet and review the note-taking applications. Evaluate each application and the features it offers. Then, determine which one(s) you would most likely use and state why.

Application	Does it have a Smart phone app?	How easy is it to use?	Best feature is . . .	Worst feature is . . .
http://www.studyblue.com/				
http://cram.com/				
http://www.flashcardmachine.com/				
http://quizlet.com/				

I would be more likely to use ______________________________ note card creator

because ______________________________.

REFLECTION 9.D:

Consider when note cards could be a valuable resource in a career after college. Record a few considerations.

At this point you may be asking yourself if note cards in every core subject are created the same way. This is a good question! In some courses you will learn procedural knowledge and in other classes you will need to learn declarative knowledge; thus, the note cards may be different. Procedural knowledge will be found in core subjects such as: mathematics, science, and computer programming. Declarative knowledge includes courses such as education, history, government, social sciences, and English. An example of a note card for declarative knowledge is shown in Figure 9.4. An example of a procedural note card is described in the Connecting Courses feature.

FIGURE 9.4 Declarative Knowledge Note Card

Front:

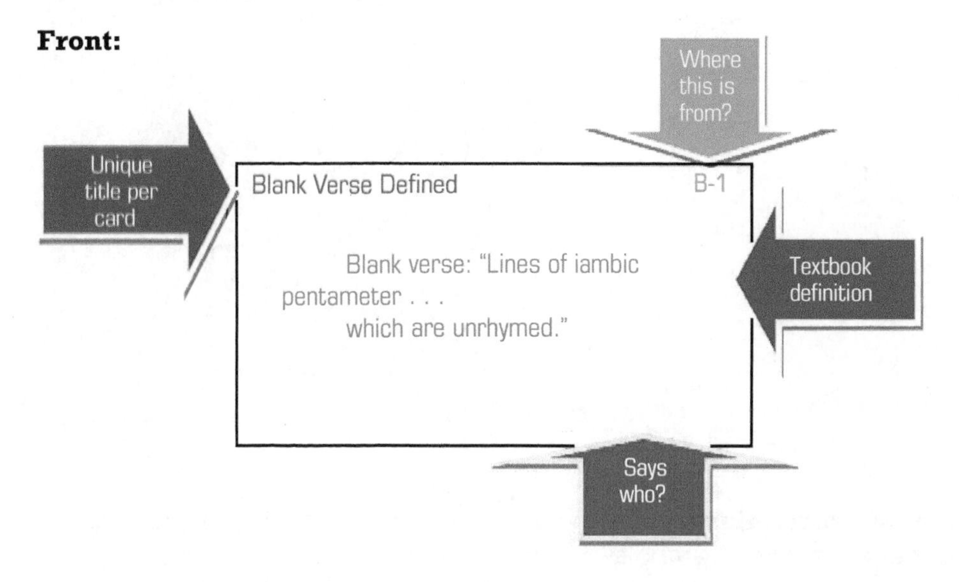

Back:

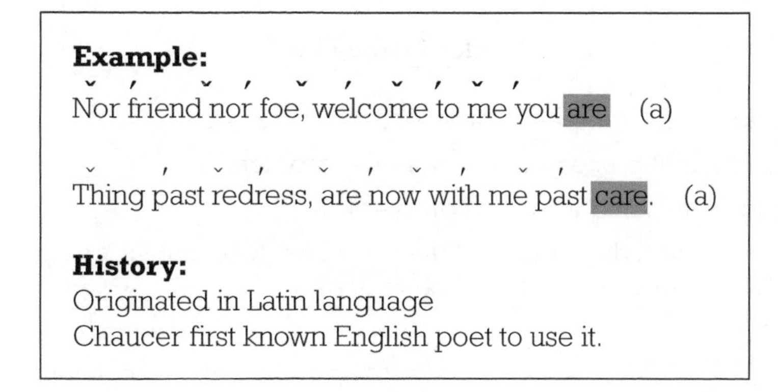

Notice the information on each side of the note card examples is tailored for the subject matter. This type of note card system allows you to customize the information and what you need to include based on the course requirements. The number one criterion in creating your own note card arrangement is to be consistent! Always use the same corner or middle section of the note cards for the same categories of information, so you will not have to tax your working memory while learning.

Note Cards for A Procedural Course

Front of Note Card

1. Write a problem with the instructions given as in the textbook.
2. Be sure to include any vocabulary associated with the problem.

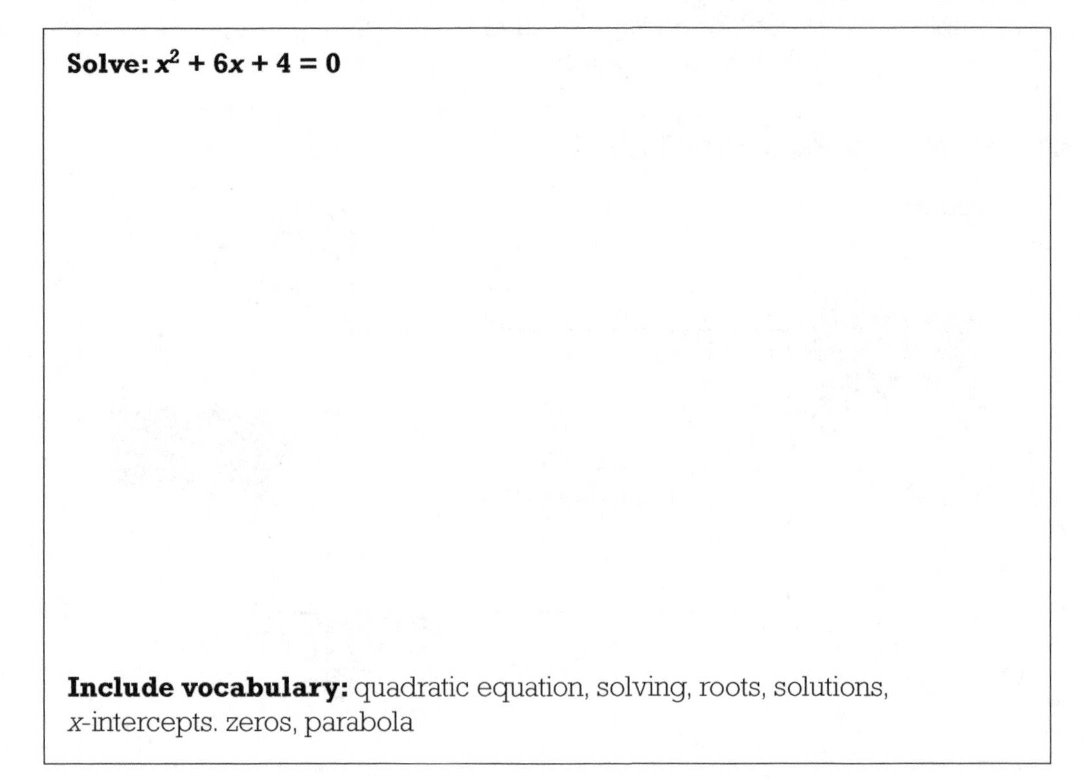

Back of Note Card

1. Match the problem to an example or an objective.
2. Write down your thought process as you work the problem.
3. Make notes of places that might cause a problem.
4. Make a list of any different directions that may be given for a similar problem along with any different forms in which the answers should be written.

Section 10.2, page 709, #25

Solution: $x^2 + 6x + 4 = 0$ Try factoring. The polynomial does not factor.
Use the quadratic formula where $a = 1$, $b = 6$, and $c = 4$.

$$x = \frac{-b \pm \sqrt{b^2 - 4ac}}{2a}$$

$$x = \frac{-6 \pm \sqrt{(6)^2 - 4(1)(4)}}{2(1)}$$

$$x = \frac{-6 \pm \sqrt{20}}{2}$$

$$x = \frac{-6 \pm 2\sqrt{5}}{2}$$

$$x = \frac{2(-3 \pm \sqrt{5})}{2}$$

$$x = -3 \pm \sqrt{5}$$

Alternative directions:
find the roots;
find all solutions;
find all values of x that satisfy . . .

The answer(s) to these instructions must be given as point(s).
find the zeros;
find the x-intercepts

EXERCISE 9.7: Note Cards

Create at least one note card for each of the courses you are currently taking. Then, compare and contrast the arrangement of information.

OBJECTIVE 5: Apply Strategies for Information Recall and Recognition

The natural challenges in learning for most students are realized when they need to recall or recognize information on a test, in a class discussion, or in generating written responses on essay questions. Thus, it is important to understand the format in which the information will be tested to ensure greater likelihood of generating the answers when needed. This information and ongoing review can increase the probability of deep-process learning to occur.

Exactly what does recognition and recall mean when it comes to learning? **Recognition** is simply that: being able to recognize information you covered in your course materials when you see it. This can be in the form of multiple choice, true/false, matching, or any other method of recognizing the correct answer. On the other hand, **recall** means being able to pull information forward when needed. Typically, recall questions on a test will be in the form of short answer, essay, or in questions that require you to work a problem or explain a procedure. Knowing how you will be asked to demonstrate mastery of your course content prior to a test should direct the way in which you prepare for the evaluation.

Manipulating the course information in a variety of ways will increase your long-term retention of it. This is accomplished through repeated practice and categorizing the information in new ways during your review sessions. Note cards provide a system that allows you to review and rearrange information in innovative ways. Since this section focuses on learning for a recall test, it means you are preparing to recognize the correct answer. Keep this in mind as you learn.

There are as many ways to organize the note cards for review as you can generate. For the sake of brevity, three will be offered in this chapter. These include:

1. creating two stacks,
2. creating games,
3. and recitation.

Creating two stacks requires you to determine two categories for placing the cards. The easiest and most obvious categories are "Know" and "Need to Learn." As you initially review the set of note cards, see how many answers you know without pausing. If you pause even briefly, place the card in the "Need to Learn" pile. Every day review the "Need to Learn" stack and place all the cards you know automatically in the "Know" stack. Continue working through the note cards until you have them all in the "Know" stack. This is an easy way to increase the number of exposures you have to the material on which you need more repetitions. Also, it feels great to have all of the cards in the "know" stack before you are required to demonstrate your learning in the form of a recognition test.

Creating games is a way of reviewing your note cards that may sound silly, but it really does help you learn your course content. It may be necessary to create one set of cards with the answers on one side and the topic or word on a separate card. You can place the cards on a flat surface with the only the topic showing. Then, pick up the card with the answer to see if you have selected the right answer. If not, place both cards in the positions in which you originally found them. If you have picked up the two cards with the topic and accurate definition on them, place the cards in a stack. Continue to play the game until you have all the cards matched with the correct answers. If you have a study group, this is a great way to engage everyone. Form two or three teams and play the game. You will be very prepared to recognize the "correct" answer on your upcoming test.

Recitation is reading the information on the cards out loud. As you know, hearing the information allows you to engage more of your senses for learning. This activity allows you to use your visual sense for reading, auditory sense for listening, and kinesthetic sense for picking up and manipulating the cards. When you add in the reading and writing required to create the cards, you will have quadruple-strength learning. This method of note card review is very comprehensive and will more than adequately prepare you to ace your recognition test questions. Use your imagination to come up with more ways to learn from the note cards you have created for your course work. It may seem too elementary or overly time consuming but it will provide numerous opportunities for learning.

Recalling your course materials requires you to process the information on a deeper level. As you know, recalling information means you have to store it accurately in your brain and be able to pull it forward without cues. Generating ways to prepare for this type of assessment will require you to make connections between the course materials. For example, if you were to answer a recall test question in this class over deep-process learning, you would need to memorize the steps of deep processing:

Deep Processing Levels
Elaboration
Distinction
Personalization
Appropriate retrieval and application
Automaticity
Overlearning

Then, you would need to be able to recall each of the process meanings and how it is applied to learning. An example of this is:

Deep Processing Level	Question
Elaboration	How does this concept relate to other concepts?
Distinction	How does this concept differ from other concepts?
Personalization	How can I relate this information to my personal experience?
Appropriate retrieval and application	How am I expected to use or apply this concept?
	Result
Automaticity	Practiced to the point that knowledge recall is not a conscious effort.
Overlearning	Extending learning to the point where the information is recalled quickly and easily.

Just trying to memorize this in isolation may be tough, but if you begin using it in your classes, you will only need to remember what you do to learn in this way. This application method applies well to procedural learning because the repeated use drills the information deeper into your brain. Preparing to demonstrate your expertise of declarative knowledge means you will need to apply the deep-process learning to that information. In so doing, you are creating lasting connections in your brain. In other words, you are "firing" and "wiring" as was discussed in Chapter 2.

EXERCISE 9.8: Learning Strategies

Apply the information you have read about in this section to learning for recognition tests by explaining your understanding of the strategies offered in this chapter.

Strategy	How it works . . .	How it aids in recognition retrieval . . .

Ongoing review means you are reviewing the course materials over a period of time. This requires you to begin as soon as the lecture notes are written and note cards are created. Practice is the key to learning for recall or recognition.

EXERCISE 9.9: Reviewing for Recall and Recognition Retrieval

Describe ongoing review and explain how you are using this for recall and recognition retrieval.

____

____

____

At the risk of sounding like a broken record, recall and recognition are two different cognitive processes that require varying degrees of learning. Recall must be generated purely from memory and necessitates deep-process learning. Recognition requires you to identify the right answer and employs learning with the aid of retrieval cues. Thus, it is important to understand how the professor will be asking you to demonstrate your knowledge of the course materials. Preparing for a recognition test may impair your ability to do well on a recall test. Learning the material as if it were all going to be on the recall level of retrieval will prepare you to succeed on either assessment.

EXERCISE 9.10: Recall and Recognition

Complete the following questions.

How does recall differ from recognition retrieval?

What do these differences suggest concerning learning your course materials?

REFLECTION 9.E:

The bottom of Bloom's Taxonomy contains the levels of recognition and recall. How can improving your recall retrieval improve your higher order thinking skills?

____

____

OBJECTIVE 6: Understand Strategies to Implement Review Options

You have been exposed to many strategies to use while reviewing your lectures in this chapter. Each strategy has benefits for learning a wide variety of information in college courses. Take a moment to personalize the information by completing the following exercises.

EXERCISE 9.11: Key Information

List five strategies for reviewing key information.

Review Strategy	Explain how it helps with reviewing course materials.
1.	
2.	
3.	
4.	
5.	

EXERCISE 9.12: Procedural or Declarative Content

Explain which of the five (5) strategies are best used for procedural or declarative content.

Learning about strategies that will increase your ability to retrieve the course content is only of benefit if you apply them. Preparing to do well in class means that time management for your study sessions will be paramount.

These review strategies will work best if you have created the well-written notes and study materials throughout the semester. For example, preparing for a mid-term exam will be more productive if you have had ongoing reviews with repeated practices. Before you take a comprehensive exam, the Five Day Review strategy is a great way to manage your time and limit the workload on your working memory. Basically, this strategy requires you to view all of the material to be covered on the exam and space the practice review over five days. The first day is used to organize your course materials. The last four days will be a review of 25% of course materials per day.

TABLE 9.2 Five Day Study Review

Day 1	Day 2	Day 3	Day 4	Day 5
Determine which chapters will be included in the exam. (This example covers the entire semester.) Organize notes, note cards, quizzes, or tests.	Focus on chapters one, two, and three. Review the organized materials for these chapters.	Focus on chapters four, five, and six. Review the organized materials for these chapters.	Focus on chapters seven, eight, and nine. Review the organized materials for these chapters.	Focus on chapters ten and eleven. Review the organized materials for these chapters.

Creating a quick overview of daily materials will include:

Check lists: These should include all the formulas, ideas, and text materials covered in a chapter or section of material.

Summary or maps: These should have been created while creating your Cornell notes (bottom of each page) or from the notes you have created maps for in Chapter X.

Quick review: Think about each chapter over which you are preparing to demonstrate your knowledge and write a table of contents of the concepts included. Afterward, check your work against your notes and textbook for accuracy or for information you excluded.

Freewrite: Get a sheet of paper and pen for a low tech way to use this strategy. If you prefer to use your computer, pull up a new Word document, turn OFF you monitor, and place your hands on the "home keys" of your keyboard. Despite whichever you choose to use, you will proceed by writing everything you can think of on a given topic for five minutes. During the five minutes, you are to write or type continuously. DO NOT STOP WRITING! If you run out of ideas, write something like, "Thinking, thinking, thinking. I don't know what to write." Eventually, a new idea will pop into your mind and you can continue writing. After five minutes of CONTINUOUS WRITING, review what you know. This review strategy may feel uncomfortable at first, but it becomes easier with more practice. The value of this strategy is the engagement of your whole brain. This is why you should continue to type or write, even when it seems like you have exhausted your knowledge. Read what you have recorded and be prepared to be impressed! This will reveal all you know about the topic you are preparing to review. Compare this information against the textbook or your notes to see where there are any gaps. You now know what you need to learn.

Working productively with a group means everyone arrives on time prepared to study. It is often best to assign different topics or chapters to each person to present. Then, as your group study session progresses each member will be ready to help each other learn. The assignments may be:

- writing a review,
- mapping out the information,

- answering possible essay questions,
- and/or creating a study game for the group to play.

By clearly defining the purpose of the study session prior to meeting, everyone will be prepared to contribute to the group's learning.

SOMETHING TO THINK ABOUT

1. Take a minute to review the picture below. Do any of the groups reflect effective studying practices? Why or why not? Write a paragraph, three to five complete sentences, about the three groups within the photographs as they relate to *studying.*

© Nejron Photo/Shutterstock.com

2. Would your discussion be influenced if you knew the male on the lower right is taking an online class?

3. Discuss the photograph again from the perspective of critical thinking skills and teamwork.

9.3 PRACTICING STRATEGIES FOR MEMORY IMPROVEMENT

Learning takes time and repeated opportunities to process the information. For these reasons, it is critical to learn to employ active learning strategies for assisting the working memory. As you may recall from Chapter 8, the working memory can manage five to nine pieces of information at a time and lasts for less than one minute. This means it is necessary to learn ways to trick your brain into believing the information is related. One such method for tricking your brain is called mnemonic devices.

OBJECTIVE 7: Understand the Use of Mnemonic Devices

Mnemonic devices are acronyms (letters that create a new word) or **acrostics** (first letter of each word is the memory cue used in a poem or sentence). You may remember the acronym PEMDAS from your mathematics class. It is the memory cue for the acrostic of the order of operations used when simplifying expressions.

> Please Excuse My Dear Aunt Sally.
>
> Parenthesis, Exponents, Multiplication, Division, Addition, Subtraction

This example demonstrates the strength mnemonics have in our long-term memory as most students learned this one in the sixth grade at eleven or twelve years of age. For many reading this, it has been eight to ten years since you learned it, yet you still remember it.

Mnemonic devices are ways to trick your brain into storing and retrieving information that may be too taxing for the working memory to remember in isolation. Chunking information in innovative ways in which the working memory only needs to hang onto five to nine elements will increase retrieval when the information is needed.

In order to create your own mnemonics you will look for information that requires processes, procedures, or practically anything to be retrieved more easily. For example, have you used HOMES to recall the Great Lakes? (Huron, Ontario, Michigan, Erie, and Superior.)

As you can see, employing mnemonic devices increases your ability to learn dense information by tricking your brain into thinking the information is a smaller size. Additionally, taking the time to create these "tricks" to the brain, allows the information to be processed more deeply. Learning with deeper processing will increase your retrieval when it counts most!

Mnemonics can be created for any type of course information too large for the working memory to retain. This means you can use mnemonics in a few of the following ways:

Course	Mnemonic	Concept
Education	SLANT	S= Sit up L= Lean forward A= Ask Questions N= Nod your head T= Track the teacher An appropriate action and/or a position of the body in a desk in a classroom
Mathematics (trigonometry)	SOHCAHTOA	Sine is opposite over (divided by) hypotenuse, cosine is adjacent over (divided by) hypotenuse, tangent is opposite over (divided by) adjacent
Psychology	**P**ink **S**carves **B**elong **E**verywhere, **S**o **A**ccessorize!	PHYSIOLOGICAL, SAFETY, BELONGING, ESTEEM, SELF-ACTUALIZATION from Maslow's Hierarchy of Needs
Art Appreciation	**U**nless **B**ats **V**acate **R**ooms **E**very **M**an **P**auses	Unity, Balance, Variety, Rhythm, Emphasis, Movement, Proportion
Biology	**K**indly **P**lease **C**ome **O**ver for **G**reat **S**paghetti	Kingdom, Phyllum, Class, Order, Genus, Species

Mnemonic devices can be harmful if they are not accurate. For example, PEMDAS actually means Parentheses (**or any grouping symbols)**, Exponents, Multiplication **and** Division (**performed left to right)** and Addition **and** Subtraction (**performed left to right)**. Many students believe they must perform multiplication first regardless of where it occurs in the expression. The same happens with addition. Perhaps a better (although not great) acrostic might be **G**enerals **E**xpect **M**ajors to **D**irect **Left to Right A**nd **S**ignal **Left to Right.**

EXERCISE 9.13: Mnemonic Device

Review your notes and textbook from one of your courses and create two mnemonic devices from them.

1. ______________________________

____

____

2. ______________________________

____

____

OBJECTIVE 8: Understand the Loci Method for Long-Term Learning and Connections

In 350 BC, Aristotle wrote a book entitled *Memory* because of the critical role memory played in the educational training during his era. It is speculated the training of Roman citizens included, among other things, public speaking. The ability to speak well was critical to these educated citizens as they were asked to determine the legal matters with little notice. This training included learning to speak extemporaneously on a wide variety of topics. Aristotle developed this book as a way of understanding the role of memory in this setting. One of the techniques he describes in this book is the **loci method**.

The loci (location) method of memory for easier recall consists of imagining a room or building that houses the information attempting to be learned. Through the act of visualizing the rooms with various artifacts that hold the objects being learned, a person can walk through the room or building and open the doors or drawers to review the knowledge within its contents. Basically, the loci method requires a person to recognize information they want to remember. Then, through the act of visualizing it in the room that is created in one's mind, the information is recovered or recalled. For example, you have a list of random vocabulary words to learn such as: mirage, phenomenon, pig Latin, microbial, alignment, latent, onomatopoeia, borborygomous, hardihood, peculiarly, xenophobia, and exaltation. Most people would not be able to remember more than about five of these words within 24 hours of initially learning them because of the overload it creates in the working memory. Of course, with the use of the loci method, most people will be able to recall these words after 24 hours.

The loci method to learn these words would go something like this:

> *I imagine a large red brick building that looks like it has two stories and one main door in the middle of the building. The trees on the property are large and full of green leaves and the landscape is well kept. I have to walk up three steps and open a large wooden door painted black. Once inside the atrium, I see there are numerous doors leading to different rooms.*
>
> *As I turn to my right, I see a door that looks like a mirage of a Caribbean beach, so I enter the room. This room feels like a fantasy. Once inside, I see white sandy beaches with large red and white striped sun umbrellas for lounging around the beach. I hear the sounds of the ocean as the waves cascade into the beach and there are metal drums in the distance. I can smell the arid sun and taste the salty water. This room is definitely a mirage!*
>
> *As I depart from the mirage room I reenter the main hall and open the next room on the left. As I enter I feel as if I'm walking into the international space center because it is dark outside and I'm unable to feel the gravitational pull back to earth. This phenomenon makes me stop to observe the space station and the incredible technology there is on board. When one of the astronauts speaks to me, I am suddenly pulled toward the door leading back inside the house and I am in the hallway.*
>
> *There was an eerie silence surrounding me as I entered the hall and then I heard the abrupt sounds of pigs squealing! Eventually, I could make out what the sounds were attempting to communicate. They said, "Urryhay upway andway eedfay emay!" Oh! I get it! The pigs are saying, "Hurry up and feed me!" I did so, and left the room immediately.*

You probably have the idea by now of how to create a loci method of memorizing something.

Because you are visualizing associations between the information you want to remember and the rooms, you are more likely to retrieve the information. Additionally, when you develop your loci with your senses, you are activating your sensory memory. This is the beginning of memory, remember? When you feel, taste, smell, touch, and hear with your mind, you trick your body into believing it is real. So, by visualizing information in a specific setting and linking the senses to the information you are trying to learn, you will hang on to the information longer.

The previous example of the loci method is silly. Being silly, when it is related to learning, actually increases the chances of retrieving the information later. You will find creating mnemonics and the loci method odd initially, but when you realize how much you can recall when the information matters most, you will choose to use one of these methods more frequently.

OBJECTIVE 9: Understand "Deep Processing" as the Key to Learning

Deep process learning, as explained throughout this chapter, is learning that incorporates the following elements:

Deep Processing Level	Question (Input)
Elaboration	How does this concept relate to other concepts?
Distinction	How does this concept differ from other concepts?
Personalization	How can I relate this information to my personal experience?
Appropriate retrieval and application	How am I expected to use or apply this concept?
	Result (Output)
Automaticity	Practiced to the point that knowledge recall is not a conscious effort.
Overlearning	Extending learning to the point where the information is recalled quickly and easily.

Learning on this level requires "orienting tasks" or study strategies that encourage deep processing. Simply memorizing facts you have found in a chapter or that seem important from the lecture from note cards will not promote this deep processing. Until you elaborate, find the distinctions, personalize, and determine the appropriate retrieval or application of the information, you will only have shallow learning experiences.

Connections between the information presented in your course lectures each week will allow you to elaborate on, and identify distinctions between, the concepts you are learning. If you define your intentions of learning prior to beginning (i.e., goals) you will be more focused on trying to relate the information between the weekly lectures. Additionally, it is valuable to connect your newly learned information to prior knowledge and/or the courses in which you are currently enrolled. In so doing, you are learning to think like a college student who is on the path to success.

Course Connections:
Mnemonic Devices in Song

You probably do not remember the words to "Pop Goes the Weasel," but you would recognize the melody. It is common in toy Jack in the Box.

The Quadratic Formula: If $ax^2 + bx + c = 0$ then $x = \dfrac{-b \pm \sqrt{b^2 - 4ac}}{2a}$

There is a caution with this song! You must understand your order of operations (use the new mnemonic in this chapter), including simplifying radical expressions and rational expressions in order to apply this formula correctly.

There are several songs searchable on the internet describing the periodic table, other formulas, and other adaptations of the quadratic formula.

PERSON to PERSON

In this exercise, you will be introduced to a student in a Biology class. Let's discuss study practices!

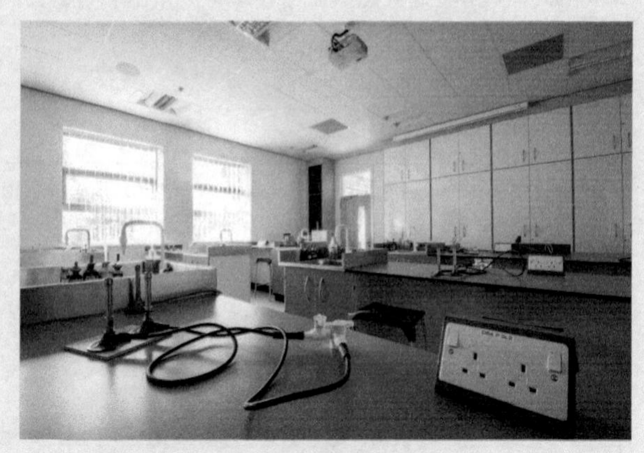

© Robin Stewart/Shutterstock.com

Alona likes attending college. She is enjoying all aspects of college life EXCEPT her biology class. So far, she has not been successful on either of the two exams. After reflection, Alona believes she needs to make some changes in her approach to the course material.

She reviews the syllabus to discover she has a total of four exams and a comprehensive final exam. The lab component is easy for her and she is making an 85% average on the lab work.

Alona has always created vocabulary flash cards for the terminology. Her difficulty is primarily in recalling the information. The portions of the exam that are multiple choice questions are easier for her than the essays and completion.

Based on the description, select the best two options for Alona.

Visit with the professor. ______

Attend the tutoring laboratory. ______

Speak with an advisor regarding withdrawing. ______

Ask a friend to study with her. ______

Change her study habits. ______

Here is some additional information.

- Alona's roommate stays up late and listens to loud music so Alona listens to music via earphones while studying to avoid distractions.
- Alona took high school general biology and earned an A.

Based on all the information you now know about Alona, rank her options again as to which you believe will be the best option for her. Has your ranking changed?

Visit with the professor. ______

Attend the tutoring laboratory. ______

Speak with an advisor regarding withdrawing. ______

Ask a friend to study with her. ______

Change her study habits. ______

1. What pieces of new information do you consider to be a positive influence on success?

____

____

2. What pieces of new information do you consider to be a negative influence on success?

____

____

Here are your last pieces of information.

- Alona is taking this biology class *online*.
- Her schedule includes Calculus, Government I, English Composition, and Spanish.

continued

Based on all the information you have, rank her options one last time as to which you believe will be most beneficial to her this semester.

Visit with the professor. ______

Attend the tutoring laboratory. ______

Speak with an advisor regarding withdrawing. ______

Ask a friend to study with her. ______

Change her study habits. ______

1. What pieces of new information would you still like to know about her?

____

____

2. Are there any pieces of information that could be seen as both positive and negative influences on success?

____

____

Career Connection:

© Sean Locke/Shutterstock.com

When you think of studying, perhaps college and taking exams come to mind. But studying also must be done in the workplace where you are required to continue certifications, keep up with new software packages, or learn a new task. In today's technological world, even learning how to operate the newest version of your smartphone requires a little studying. Good study skills are critical to your college success and may be applied to the real-world in tasks such as passing the exam for a Certified Public School Teacher, to obtain a real-estate license, to advance in rank in the military, or even become a naturalized US citizen.

CHAPTER SUMMARY

Managing your study time will help you learn what time of day or evening you learn best, as well as where you study most productively. Finding a well-organized study space that has three light sources encourages studying. The study environment should be conducive to learning with and without technology and needs to be organized to the point you are most productive.

Understanding strategies for creating productive study sessions includes learning to set study session goals with the SMARTER method. Knowing deep process learning requires ample time; it is important sufficient time is provided.

Preparing to learn in class means students arrive with the assignments completed and the reading comprehended. The benefits of preparing to learn include the advantage students have during class discussions, repeated exposure to the course materials, and deep processing. With the organization of your learning environment, understanding and planning for the necessary time to learn, and setting goals, students are destined for success.

Being prepared and taking notes in class allows for productive rehearsal of the classroom notes. Note cards created with the intention to learn with deep processing will provide learning that is rewarding. There are wide varieties of ways to organize the information on the note card as well as numerous computer applications for creating them. Many smart phones make the applications easily accessible. Because note cards can be easily transported, they allow for ongoing reviews on a regular basis. Additional strategies for reviewing course materials include five day review, quick overview, free writing, and study groups as review options.

Practicing strategies for memory improvement include mnemonic devices. These are strategies for "tricking the brain" into remembering more than the five to nine items working memory typically can manage. By chunking the information into manageable sizes, the working memory will not be overtaxed. Examples of mnemonic devices include: acronyms, acrostics, and loci method. All of these devices offer novel ways of arranging information for long-term memory and ready retrieval.

Finally, deep processing is the key to learning. This type of learning includes elaboration, distinctiveness, personalization, appropriate retrieval cues, automaticity, and over learning. The goal of deep processing is to establish connections between the information you are learning and information you have previously learned. These increase the connections you make among the concepts you are learning.

CHAPTER 9: Self-Check

Vocabulary: Define the following:

1. pre-reading
2. recall and recognition
3. mnemonic device
4. acronyms
5. acrostics
6. the loci method
7. deep processing

Concepts:

8. Describe the characteristics of a well-organized study space.
9. Identify three light sources that encourage studying.
10. Self-identify the most productive time for studying.
11. Discuss the variables of time and place with regard to productive study spaces.
12. Explain how to set study session goals.
13. Identify productive goals and ample time for deep learning.
14. Create a personal study goal that aligns with the SMARTER method.

15. Explain why a student needs to prepare for class and the opportunities that result.
16. Discuss ways to apply information concerning space, time, goals setting, and intention to prepare for learning.
17. Compare and contrast characteristics of students who prepare for learning prior to attending class to those who do not.
18. Explain the elements that comprise note cards for learning.
19. Describe the characteristics of note cards more likely to increase long-term learning connections.
20. Explain the advantages and disadvantages to learning with note cards.
21. Evaluate three online note card apps that are readily available.
22. Create a note card for each core subject.
23. Explain three ways to use note cards to increase recognition and recall.
24. Explain the way one studies for a test primarily requiring recall skills.
25. Explain the way one studies for a test primarily requiring recognition skills.
26. Clarify how ongoing review relates to recall and recognition.
27. Discuss how recall and recognition are on two different levels of learning.
28. List five strategies for reviewing key information.
29. Explain which of the strategies are best used for procedural or declarative content.
30. Describe five day review, quick overview, free writing, and groups as review options.
31. Discuss which study strategy is best for various disciplines.
32. Describe the process by which mnemonic devices are created.
33. Explain how mnemonic devices can increase learning.
34. Identify the types of course materials used in a mnemonic device.
35. Create a mnemonic device for one of your courses.
36. Discuss the origin of the loci method.
37. Describe the process employed in the loci method.
38. Explain how the loci method creates connections within course materials for long-term retention.
39. Explain how elaboration, distinctiveness, personalization, retrieval cues, automaticity, and over learning relate to deep processing.
40. Discuss two review strategies to strengthen cognitive learning.
41. Explain the role of whole brain learning in making connections for deeper processing.
42. Create three note cards for this chapter, the first with a true-false test question, the second with a multiple choice test question, and the third with an essay question.

CHAPTER 10

Writing and Oral Presentations

T.I.P.S. (Tactical Information that Promotes Success)

Writing words to describe step-by-step procedures increases the understanding of mathematics while simultaneously improving reading and writing skills.

By applying the connections between reading and writing to mathematics you will facilitate your learning.

College mathematics is abstract, so it may not fit into a simple equation or formula. Writing mathematics in a manner that others can understand will require similar skills you use for other classes. You still need to follow grammatical rules. For example, $x + 3 = 7$ is a sentence, (read "x plus three equals seven"). The equal sign could be considered a verb!

© Library of Congress

What do reading and writing have to do with math class? Why do I need to read the book and take notes?

Many people believe **mathematics** is NOT writing intensive. However, if you describe (in words) the steps you take to work any problem, you may strengthen your understanding of the mathematics.

Solve:

$2x + 3 = 8$	Original Equation
$2x + 3 - 3 = 8 - 3$	Subtract 3 from both sides.
$2x = 5$	Simplify.
$\frac{2x}{2} = \frac{5}{2}$	Divide both sides by 2.
$x = \frac{5}{2}$	Simplify.

By **reading** your mathematics aloud, you may hear errors that you do not see. It will improve your writing and your understanding of mathematics.

In **writing** the reason that a mathematics problem can be solved in words, there is an increase in learning. This method is particularly effective when reviewing a test you have taken and write the explanation of what you were thinking and what you should have been thinking to correct the missed problems.

In **education**, a stronger emphasis on reading and writing skills in math and science became a federal mandate for instruction in preschool through twelfth grade increasing and sustaining public and youth engagement in STEM education.

CHAPTER 10: OBJECTIVES

10.1 Writing Within Courses

Objective 1 Understand How to Use Summarization and Paraphrasing
Objective 2 Understand How to Write a Personal Response
Objective 3 Understand How to Make Connections to Course Work and Writing

10.2 Developing Writing and Speaking Skills

Objective 4 Understand How to Write a Presentation
Objective 5 Understand How to Outline an Oral Presentation
Objective 6 Understand the Qualities of Speaking

10.3 Developing Research and Library Skills

Objective 7 Understand Methods of Beginning Research
Objective 8 Understand Ways to Access Research Materials in the Library
Objective 9 Understand Strategies to Access Relevant Databases and Research Materials on the Internet

10.4 Evaluating the Validity of Resources

Objective 10 Understand the Reliability and Credibility of a Resource
Objective 11 Understand Methods to Avoid Plagiarism

CHAPTER CONCEPTS

Some or all of the following terms may be new to you. Place a check mark in the column reflecting your knowledge of each term.

	Know	Don't know	Not sure	Page # where first found		Know	Don't know	Not sure	Page # where first found
summarization					points of agreement				
personal response					points of challenge				
paraphrase					transition effects				
reflection					visual theme				
PQRST					primary source				
PED					secondary source				
bibliographies					peer-reviewed journals				
glossophobia									
Boolean Expression									

10.1 WRITING WITHIN COURSES

© LiliGraphie/Shutterstock.com

Flannery O'Connor, a renowned southern American author, once wrote, "I write because I don't know what I think until I read what I say," **which sums up the primary reason professors will ask you to respond to the course content. Most people do not know what they think or feel about a topic until they write about it!**

Writing in college courses will require a wide variety of skills and strategies. Because you have taken or will complete one or more composition courses, this chapter's primary focus will be on how to create the various writing assignments you will be expected to perform within your college courses. Bear in mind, you will need to be able to clearly communicate in writing for almost any profession you choose, so writing is a critical component of your life-long success.

OBJECTIVE 1: Understand How to Use Summarization and Paraphrasing

Two of the more widely used forms of writing you will perform in your classes are:

- ***Summarization***: A brief overview of the most important points of a reading or speech.
- ***Personal response***: Your reaction to the information you read or heard.

It may surprise you to know the number one writing assignment in college classes is to write a personal response to the concepts you learn in class. Most people think the essay is the most assigned form of writing, but in reality the personal response is most often assigned.

In order to write a comprehensive summary of the reading materials in your class, you will need to understand a summary is a condensed version of the information you read. This means you will want to include ONLY the most important details in your comprehensive summary. For example, when summarizing a paragraph, include the main idea and the major supporting details. This can be visualized in the following way. Have you ever hand washed your car on a beautiful sunny day? Perhaps you go to a local discount center and purchase a bucket, soap, and a large sponge. Then, you fill the bucket with water and soap to create a sudsy solution. When you slosh your large sponge in the water solution, it becomes full of the water and soap to the point it allows you to wash the exterior of the car with ease. This sponge is so full it can transport the water from the bucket to the car so you can clean off the dirt more quickly.

Imagine the saturated sponge is the information you read in a chapter or an article. The reading material is heavy with information found in the book or article, but not critical to the primary focus of the reading materials. Returning to the car wash analogy, let us say you want to detail the interior of your car with this same sponge. You have to wring it out until you barely feel the water on it. This damp sponge is like a summary because it only contains the minimally important substance of your readings. Reading college materials may make your brain feel like a heavy, soapy, unmanageable sponge, so be sure to wring out the sponge and write a summary like the damp sponge. In so doing, you will be composing a well-written, comprehensive summary.

REFLECTION 10.A:

Compare the strategies of summarizing a paragraph to those of annotating or highlighting when reading a section in a textbook.

____

____

____

____

Some students think summarization and paraphrasing is the same thing, but they are not. As stated previously, a summary is a condensed version of the reading assignment only including the most important information. In other words, you will restate the essence of the text with as few words as is possible. In contrast, paraphrasing is expressing the original author's meaning by rewriting the sentence or phrases, replacing each word in the sentences, in your own words. Basically, you will want to use synonyms to replace words new or unfamiliar in a sentence. Take the first line of Abraham Lincoln's *Gettysburg Address* as an example of how a ***paraphrase*** is different from a summary.

TABLE 10.1

Gettysburg Address	Paraphrase	Summary
"Four score and seven years ago our fathers brought forth on this continent, a new nation, conceived in Liberty, and dedicated to the proposition all men are created equal."	Eighty-seven years ago in 1776, the men who established the New American nation, which was created from their own free-choice, were committed to the intention that all men are created the same.	The founding fathers of America in 1776 declared all men were created equal by the US Constitution.

Notice the paraphrase is actually a little bit longer than the original text and the summary is shorter than the original and paraphrased texts.

EXERCISE 10.1: Similarities and Contrasts Between Summaries and Paraphrasing

Complete the following Venn diagram on the similarities and contrasts between a summary and a paraphrase.

FIGURE 10.1

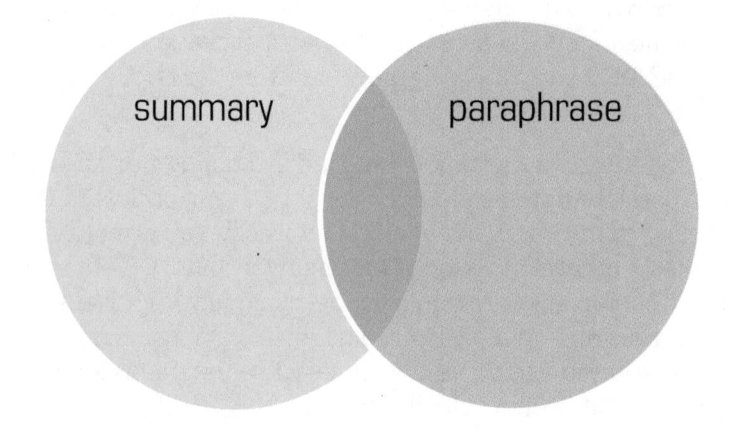

Write one sentence reviewing what you discovered about summarization and paraphrasing.

___

___

___

Read the following excerpt from Chapter 1 of *The Humbugs of the World* written by PT Barnum of Barnum and Bailey Circus in 1866:

CHAPTER I.

GENERAL VIEW OF THE SUBJECT.—HUMBUG UNIVERSAL.—IN RELIGION.—IN POLITICS.—IN BUSINESS.—IN SCIENCE.—IN MEDICINE.—HOW IS IT TO CEASE.—THE GREATEST HUMBUG OF ALL.

A little ***reflection*** will show that humbug is an astonishingly wide-spread phenomenon—in fact almost universal. And this is true, although we exclude crimes and arrant swindles from the definition of it, according to the somewhat careful explanation which is given in the beginning of the chapter succeeding this one.

Medicine is the means by which we poor feeble creatures try to keep from dying or aching. In a world so full of pain it would seem as if people could not be so foolish, or practitioners so knavish, as to sport with men's and women's and children's lives by their professional humbugs. Yet there are many brave M. D.'s who, if there is nobody to hear, and if they speak their minds, will tell you plainly that the whole practice of medicine is in one sense a humbug. One of its features is certainly a humbug, though so innocent and even useful that it seems difficult to think of any objection to it. This is the practice of giving a *placebo*; that is, a bread pill or a dose of colored water, to keep the patient's mind easy while imagination helps nature to perfect a cure. As for the quacks, patent medicines and universal remedies, I need only mention their names. Prince Hohenlohe, Valentine Greatrakes, John St. John Long, Doctor Graham and his wonderful bed, Mesmer and his tub, Perkins' metallic tractors—these are half a dozen. Modern history knows of hundreds of such.

It would almost seem as if human delusions became more unreasoning and abject in proportion as their subject is of greater importance. A machine, a story, an animal skeleton, are not so very important. But the humbugs which have prevailed about that wondrous machine, the human body, its ailments and its cures, about the unspeakable mystery of human life, and still more about the far greater and more awful mysteries of the life beyond the grave, and the endless happiness and misery believed to exist there, the humbugs about these have been infinitely more absurd, more shocking, more unreasonable, more inhuman, more destructive.

(Source: Barnum, P. T. "The Humbugs of the World." *The Project Gutenberg eBook*. Ed. Julia Miller. Project Gutenberg, 18 Sept. 2008. Web. 30 Dec. 2013. Path: http://www.gutenberg.org/files/26640/26640-h/26640-h.htm#CHAPTER_I.)

EXERCISE 10.2: Summary of a Book Excerpt

On a separate sheet of paper, write a brief summary of the above expository.

EXERCISE 10.3: Paraphrase of a Book Excerpt

On a separate sheet of paper, write a paraphrase of the following excerpt taken from PT Barnum's book entitled *The Humbugs of the World.*

> Science is another important field of human effort. Science is the pursuit of pure truth, and the systematizing of it. In such an employment as that, one might reasonably hope to find all things done in honesty and sincerity. Not at all, my ardent and inquiring friends, there is a scientific humbug just as large as any other. We have all heard of the Moon Hoax. Do none of you remember the Hydrarchos Sillimannii, that awful Alabama snake? It was only a little while ago that a grave account appeared in a newspaper of a whole new business of compressing ice. Perpetual motion has been the dream of scientific visionaries, and a pretended but cheating realization of it has been exhibited by scamp after scamp. I understand that one is at this moment being invented over in Jersey City. I have purchased more than one "perpetual motion" myself. Many persons will remember Mr. Paine—"The Great Shot-at" as he was called, from his story that people were constantly trying to kill him—and his water-gas. There have been other water gases too, which were each going to show us how to set the North River on fire, but something or other has always broken down just at the wrong moment. Nobody seems to reflect, when these water gases come up, that if water could really be made to burn, the right conditions would surely have happened at some one of the thousands of city fires, and that the very stuff with which our stout firemen were extinguishing the flames, would have itself caught and exterminated the whole brave wet crowd!

Now that you understand how to write a comprehensive summary, you may be wondering when and how to use one for studying your course materials. Take a moment to review the memory process in Chapter 4. Notice in order for you to retain information in your long-term memory, repetition is required. Thus, summarizing provides a process to record the essence of the material you are learning with the most important points to be included. This will stimulate your brain to process the information a few more times to ensure your long-term retention. You will be reviewing the information you are learning that encompasses one round of repetition. Then, you will employ your higher-order thinking skills to determine what information is most critical to include in the summary.

There are many ways to use summarization as a study strategy, including Cornell note-taking, PQRST, and PED. You may have familiarity with a few of these strategies, but more are still being introduced. All of these tools used consistently will provide you with increases in retention and recall of your course materials.

The Cornell note-taking system incorporates summarization on the bottom of each page of notes. If you are taking notes from reading materials or from a lecture, the summary at the bottom of the page will help you process the information more completely. After you have taken your notes, get a fresh sheet of paper and record all of the summaries you wrote. Take a moment to review them, making sure they offer the meaning of the material with supportive information. If you realize there are gaps in your summary, gather the remaining major details to complete the chapter or lecture summary. Then, when it is time to prepare for a test, you have a study aid that will assist in your learning.

PQRST is similar to the SQ4R discussed in Chapter 8. Use the following steps to guide your learning:

1. **Preview:** Preview the major headings of the chapter, lecture, or other resource you will read.
2. **Question:** Formulate questions from those headings. It is helpful to know how you are going to be demonstrating your knowledge for a grade prior to writing the questions. For example, an

essay test question is worded a bit differently than an objective test question. More on this will be discussed later, but it is helpful to be aware of this when drafting your questions.

3. **Read:** Read the set of well-written notes or the chapter information looking for the answers to your questions.
4. **Summarize:** Write a summary of the information you have read, being sure to include the most important points from the original source.
5. **Test:** Now, go back to the questions you wrote in step two and write your answers. Check them for accuracy. Review the answers you have identified as being weak.

This method of learning will take time, so begin early!

Three of the principles of deep processing are personalization, elaboration, and distinctions; that is what ***PED*** represents. After having written your summarizations, go back and try to locate information that can be personalized. This is best achieved by responding to Dr. Chew's prompt:

> *How can I relate this concept to my own personal experience? Relating concepts to your personal experience helps increase meaningfulness, elaboration and distinctiveness.*

Then, you can extend the information you wrote in your summary by elaborating on it with the following Dr. Chew prompt:

> *How does this concept relate to other concepts? Elaboration means making meaningful associations between the concept you are studying and related concepts.*

Finally, you will want to review your original summary and add distinctions within the concepts. Once again, Dr. Chew's prompt is a great guide for accomplishing this task. He suggests you complete the following:

> *How is this concept different from other concepts? Distinctiveness means you have to make clear contrasts between the concept you are studying and other concepts.*

The PED strategy will most certainly enhance your deep processing learning, increasing the possibility you can ace the test, be prepared for the class discussions, and learn your course material in a way that it will be with you for most of your life.

REFLECTION 10.B:

For each of the prompts given by Dr. Chew, state how you would apply them to the mathematical example below. (The PEDs written in the second column do not correspond with any step in the example.)

Solve:		***P:***
$2x + 3 = 8$	Original Equation	
$2x + 3 - 3 = 8 - 3$	Subtract 3 from both sides.	
$2x = 5$	Simplify.	***E:***
$\frac{2x}{2} = \frac{5}{2}$	Divide both sides by 2.	
$x = \frac{5}{2}$	Simplify.	***D:***

OBJECTIVE 2: Understand How to Write a Personal Response

In order to write a response you will want to have established a firm understanding of the materials. This means you will want to read, annotate, and summarize the materials before trying to respond. It may be beneficial to use a symbol as you write when you feel a strong reaction to the information. For example, use a (+) plus sign when you agree and a (–) minus sign when you disagree. Then, you can more easily review the reading to begin generating your response. Three elements that may be the foundation of your written response assignment are:

1. analysis or critique of the reading,
2. personal opinions or views,
3. and a combination of these.

Often, completing the analysis means you will need to read and question the information rather than taking the statements as truth. In other words, doubt the author as you read in order to critically evaluate the piece. Conducting the second element based on your personal opinions or views, means you will:

- understand the instructor expects you to present personal views on topic.
- support your challenges of writer's views.
- raise new questions.
- add your voice to the conversation.
- ***Points of agreement*:** support the author's arguments, but supply additional reasons or evidence, extend the argument
- ***Points of challenge*:** challenge all or part of the author's argument, raise doubts regarding audience, show flaws in reasoning

EXERCISE 10.4: Response Paper

Read the excerpt previously used from *Humbugs*. When you have formulated your personal perspective on it, write your response by incorporating both analysis and personal views.

Take a moment to reflect on the personal response you completed. Rate your response by using the following evaluation tool.

Criteria	Below Average	Average	Above Average
Analysis of the material is thoughtful, relevant, and offers at least one innovative idea toward this concept.			
Personal opinions of the concepts presented in the original text relate to the topic and extend the understanding of the concept.			
Equal balance between analysis and personal opinion is evident.			

Typically, a response to any reading assignment will be individualized, so no two students will have the same information in their responses. Obviously, the personalization of the information will be unique. Your prior knowledge will offer you the foundation for this response. There may be some similarity between student's analyses, since the information in the class may be the same. Because student's written responses in the assignment are personalized, professors appreciate your work as a way to encourage your critical thinking.

EXERCISE 10.5: Comparisons of a Summary and a Response

In Exercise 10.1 you were asked to write a summary of excerpts from **Humbugs**. Take a moment to compare that summary with the response you wrote. Complete the following chart by listing ways these two forms of writing are different

Summary	Response

Then, write one sentence explaining the similarity between them.

____

____

Perhaps the last step in Exercise 10.5 perplexed you. If so, you are in good company! There is little if any similarity between writing a response and a summary of a written text or lecture. The purpose of each minimizes any similarity between them. A summary, as you recall, gives the nuance of the information with the inclusion of the major points. In contrast, a response is personal and analytical. Thus, the two offer opportunities to learn the same information on two different levels of learning, with the response being the deeper of the two.

Course Connections

Laboratory Reports

Just because you are not in writing class does not mean you will not have to write summaries and response papers!

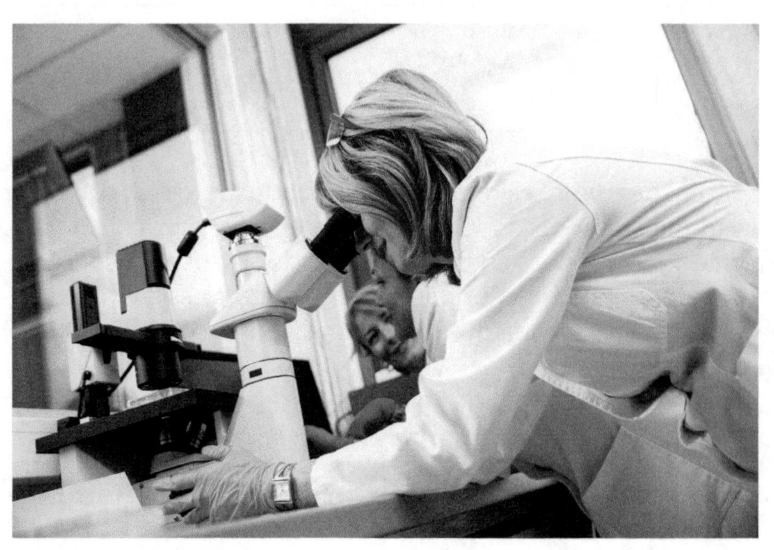

© PointImages/Shutterstock.com

In your lab classes, you may be required to write BOTH summaries and responses within the same paper. The write up of the experiment constitutes the "summary" part and your observation of the outcome of the experiment will be your "response."

REFLECTION 10.C:

How will your ability to write summary papers and response papers help in your lab science courses?

____

____

____

How could your ability to write summary and response papers be an advantage in your mathematics classes?

____

____

____

OBJECTIVE 3: Understand How to Make Connections to Course Work and Writing

Writing essays will be an important means of communicating your ideas to your professors and peers in class. As such, you will take at least two writing courses in your college plan. This being said, there are a few important points to review in writing an effective college essay.

When writing a college essay it is best to adhere to the writing process. The writing process includes:

- idea formulation,
- organization,
- draft process,
- review and revise,
- and edit.

Begin by reading the assignment given to you very closely. You may want to underline or highlight verbs within the assignment, so you are able to directly address your professor's expectations. Then, brainstorm for ideas through free writing, list making, or other creative processes. Once you have an idea, begin organizing your thoughts by writing a thesis statement and formulating an outline. The outline may be written as a map if this helps you express your ideas more precisely. Write the first draft of the essay. Share this draft with as many people you know who understand the demands of writing and listen to their comments and feedback. Then, revise the areas you agree need more work or to be moved around for clarity. Finally, review your essay for standard English usage of punctuation and grammar. Make the final corrections and you are ready to submit your essay!

This brief overview may simplify the process to the point you think writing an essay is so easy it can be completed the night before it is due. Erase this thought from you mind because writing is a process that takes time—hours, days, even up to a month or more! To plan your time well for writing an essay, see the information in Chapter 3 concerning "backward planning." Allowing time for your essay to develop will create an essay that is more interesting, connected to the prompt, and may earn you an "A."

Remember, you are writing to a person or audience. Be sure to address the topic in such a way as to address their interests and concerns. Another point concerning writing is to tell the reader what you are going to tell them in the beginning. This may be written in the form a thesis statement for the entire essay or a topic sentence for a single paragraph. Next, tell the reader what you told them you were going to write. In other words, explain your thesis and topic sentences with relevant supporting details. Finally, be sure to tell the reader what you told them by adding a concluding sentence in each paragraph and a final paragraph that accomplishes this goal for your essay. By following this simple advice, you will write a more cohesive essay focusing on the thesis statement. Leading the reader to the points you are making will make your essay clearer and easier to read.

EXERCISE 10.6: Writing an Essay

Your instructor assigns an essay on *Punishment for Cruelty to Animals.* Corporal Punishment in Schools.

1. Write a thesis sentence:

____

____

2. Write two or three statements supporting your thesis sentence.

____

____

Writing in college demands you to look at big ideas and explain, evaluate, analyze, or synthesize them. What does this mean to you? You are going to have fun because you are not limited to writing a 5-paragraph essay. You will need to build upon the knowledge you have learned in other classrooms to increase your writing skills. In college writing assignments you will be asked to summarize, respond to, and write elaborative essays. In other words, when you write in college you are being asked to evaluate your position on a topic and then defend it. This is a process that takes time due to the revisions and editing involved in communicating your ideas to the intended audience as clearly as possible. Thinking and writing about your position concerning the big ideas in your history class will mean you are thinking critically. This, ironically, is a skill you will need in the work place, too.

10.2 DEVELOPING WRITING AND SPEAKING SKILLS

Very often in your college career you will be asked to make presentations in class. The preparation for this type of oral presentation requires you to write the presentation, understand when to use technology, ways to organize your information, and how to succeed in public speaking. While this may come easily for some people, it is estimated 75% of people, when asked to speak to a group, experience anxiety, avoid public speaking all together, and/or have physiological symptoms such as nausea or panic. For those who have never experienced this phobia, ***glossophobia***, it is hard to imagine this deep-seated fear, but for the majority of those who have glossophobia, it is all too real.

Former President Franklin D. Roosevelt (1933–1945) said in his 1933 Inaugural Speech, "We have nothing to fear but fear itself." He was telling the American people that fears should be boldly approached and successfully overcome. All speakers, particularly those who are paralyzed by this fear, will need to face it head on. Yes, all public speakers experience some level of anxiety. The sooner you start working on conquering this fear, the sooner you will find the joy in public speaking.

OBJECTIVE 4: Understand How to Write a Presentation

One of the best ways to learn the joy of public speaking is to carefully and thoughtfully write your presentation. Consider who will be in the audience and how the information will be received. With the prolific use of technology in public speaking, determine which form of technology is the best for your presentation. Of course, there is always the option to forgo the use of technology, too. Knowing you are learning the best way to formulate a public presentation of your ideas in a college class is the way to prepare for your future career.

There are many ways in which you can present your information to make it entertaining, informative, and persuasive. But the first rule you need to remember is the "Rule of Three." Tell the audience what you are going to tell them, actually tell them, and then tell the audience what you just told them. In other words, provide an overview followed by the content and conclude with a summary. Informative presentations are those telling the audience new information on a topic. Persuasive presentations are those appealing to the audience to accept, do, or act on the information presented. Most college presentations, as well as professional presentations, will require you to inform and persuade the audience. Typically, this requires presenters to have completed an in-depth research on the topic, in order to know the nuances within the topic's presentation. Think back to the times when you have prepared a speech. Did this require you to write a paper or some other type of artifact for submission? Most professors will tie the topic to the course work you are completing. Even if the topic does not seem to encourage course connections in your opinion, you should attempt to connect the topic to the course work. Making the oral presentation informative and persuasive will engage your audience. There are three things to consider when presenting your knowledge of the subject:

- Know your topic matter well.
- Practice your speech prior to delivery.
- Remember to converse with your audience.

Be familiar with your topic. It is helpful to actually have multiple conversations with someone who will listen to you, and provide feedback, prior to your presentation. Because the method of delivery is speaking, this technique will help you hear what you are saying before you say it in your speech. Practice through repeated rehearsal. Write the speech and practice, so you will not sound as if you are merely repeating rote information to your audience. Have you, as an audience member, ever felt like the person speaking was robotic? This is what happens if a speaker does not really know how to deliver with a natural tone. When practicing your speech, watch yourself in a mirror. This means you will need to find a private place in which you can carefully study your facial expressions. Your eyes, when speaking, matter, so be sure to train your eyes when to communicate for emphasis. Also, recruit friends to watch you speak prior to your formal delivery. The more practice you have before you speak, the more relaxed and natural you will appear. This may sound like a lot of work on how to look and speak naturally. It is, but it will help you focus on the topic of the speech rather than getting overly anxious.

Remember, public speaking is merely having a conversation with a group. By engaging in the conversations with multiple people prior to the big day, you will be equipped to extend the conversation to your class members. Take your time and try to enjoy the moment! If you get nervous, you are normal. At times, people will have trouble controlling their breath when speaking publicly. If this happens, STOP talking! (If you have a glass of water available, take a small swallow.) Take a deep breath and continue. Do not say "I'm sorry," "Please forgive me!" or "I am nervous!" The audience already understands your emotional state and is there to support you. Typically, when you regain your breath control, you will return to the speech with greater confidence.

Exactly who is the audience for whom you are preparing to present your findings? If you are working on a class presentation, then the audience will be your peers and the professor. This means you will want to grab and hold the attention of the audience by anticipating:

- what they already know,
- what they want to know,
- and their stance on the issue or topic.

If your audience is less informed on your topic, include the basic information necessary to understand your point(s). Be sure to define new terms or concepts and stay away from technical jargon. This means you will want to offer the essential information in a clear way, so your audience will understand your ideas. Additionally, repeat the new or unfamiliar terms throughout the presentation as needed. Remember the rule of three, mention the information you want to communicate three times within the presentation and it is more likely you will communicate. If an audience is given too much unfamiliar information in an oral presentation, it is likely they will quit listening to you. However, if this is a presentation on new material for a class, your classmates should be taking notes!

If you are speaking on a topic that the audience has some knowledge, dedicate your time to the extension of their familiarity. Tell the audience what you learned new or more recently on this topic. If you are speaking to an audience that includes a wide range of prior knowledge on your topic, or some know more than others; try to focus on the foundations. You will want to mention that some people in the audience already know a great deal about your topic, but you are going to review the basic information and progress to newer information. This will help the people who are familiar with the foundational information to continue listening with the anticipation you are going to address new information in the second part of the presentation.

Sometimes you will present controversial information in which the audience may either strongly agree or disagree. When organizing your oral presentation ideas, keep the level of agreement foremost in your thoughts. Anticipate the disagreement and be prepared to respond in your presentation to these points. For example, if you are speaking on the ethical use of embryonic stem cells, you can anticipate some of the audience will agree while others disagree their use is ethical. Knowing this, present both sides of the argument initially. Then, follow up with reasons their use is ethical by using reliable, relevant, and valid sources. This means you will need to think about which points will be questionable and presenting them in your speech. Ignoring them will only antagonize the audience members who disagree with you.

After you have a firm grasp on the topic of the presentation and audience to whom you will address, determine how much technology will enhance the presentation. Remember, vision trumps all of the senses you possess, so if you can find a way to incorporate it with ease and emphasis, do so. Perhaps answering the reverse question, "When can technology hinder or distract my audience?" is the easier question to address. Most students consider PowerPoint® presentations as the easiest form of technology to use in a presentation. This is a fine medium, as long as it adheres to the assignment and is well-written.

As a point of caution, any time you use technology, it should only serve as a support to your presentation. Unfortunately, if you have created the PowerPoint® as the primary element of your presentation, and encounter a problem with the technology, you may be unable to effectively present your information. The visual aids in your oral presentation are just aids, not the presentation itself!

Most students have a general understanding of how to create PowerPoint® presentations. Many will benefit from understanding a few basics on how to best create a PowerPoint® slide show. When creating the visual aid of a PowerPoint® one should know:

- **Less is more!** Try to determine the primary points of your presentation and create the PowerPoint® presentation in such a way as to constantly serve as a reminder of the points for your audience. Thus, fewer slides and minimal text will be more engaging for the audience.
- **Limit information provided per slide**: Because the slides are there to aid in the audience's understanding of your topic, do not write your presentation word-for-word on the slides; you

may be tempted to read it rather than deliver your speech. It is better to find a picture or graph to reinforce your verbal delivery. If you must use text, use it with discretion.

- **Limit *transition effects* (animation):** Transitions from one slide to another should be as simple as possible. 'Swirling' the contents can be distracting and, actually annoying to some people. Animation, on the other hand is very useful in presenting the points you want to make when you want to make them. Animation allows you to "hide" the material until you 'click' to move to the new information. This keeps your audience from reading ahead and missing what you might be saying.
- **Maintain *visual theme:* Determine one background theme for all** of the slides to add uniformity to the presentation. The default "white" is more challenging on the viewer. To reduce eye strain, find a dark background and use white font.
- **Employ appropriate charts:** While more on this is forthcoming, suffice it to say that charts, numbers, and statistics are difficult for the audience to process during your presentation. Use them with discernment and allow time during the presentation for the audience to "do the math."
- **Beware! Color and FONT communicate.**[1]
  - Color evokes emotions, so use colors that motivate!
    - Cool (such as blue and green) colors work best for background.
    - Warm (such as orange and red) colors work best for text.
    - Most popular combination? Blue background and yellow font.
  - Fonts
    - Sans Serif fonts are easier to read on PowerPoint®.
    - Titles should be font size 44.
    - Subtitles should be in a bold font between font size of 28 to 34.
    - A general rule of thumb for font size is:
      - A one-inch letter is readable from 10 feet.
      - A two-inch letter is readable from 20 feet.
      - A three-inch letter is readable from 30 feet.
    - Use contrast: light on dark or dark on light.

Word

Art

- If you really feel it necessary to incorporate WORDART to communicate, use it sparingly.
- **Look at the "big picture."** After creating the PowerPoint® presentation, review it in the slide sorter. Look at the order of the information you are presenting. Is it in a logical sequence? In other words:
  - Are you showing the audience information that builds upon itself to create the primary point(s) of your message?
  - Does each slide connect to the previous one in such a way as the audience can follow the informational flow with ease?
  - Are you allowing ample time for each principle to be processed by the audience?

[1]"Tips for Creating and Delivering an Effective Presentation." *Microsoft Corp.* 2014. Web. 3 Jan. 2014.

Now that you understand the essence of creating an easy-to-follow PowerPoint® presentation, take a few minutes to learn the ways in which images can most enhance your presentation. Use high resolution photographs rather than cartoonish pictures because the audience will better relate to real pictures.

EXERCISE 10.7: Professional-Looking Slides

Which slide looks more professional?

A. © Yayayoyo/Shutterstock.com

B. © Goran Djukanovic/Shutterstock.com

Write the words that best describe the impression you have of each slide:

Slide A	Slide B

What does this tell you about the use of human photos?

____

____

____

____

What is your assumption about the person who created each slide?

____

____

____

____

Another way to use photographs in your PowerPoint® presentations is to filter the image when the words are the primary emphasis of your point. This allows you to use the image, but guides the audience to the words.

A.

B.

Notice how the colors are similar? The picture of the student in "B" is blurred and the thought bubble is brighter with bold and italicized text. The revisions are only slight, but the emphasis is on the text in "B." In creating your slides, determine if you want the picture or your text to communicate your message.

Graphs and charts are intended to provide an enhancement of your presentation. The question you will want to answer in using them, as well as your pictures, is "How much detail do I need to give my audience for them to understand my point?" A common error in using graphs and charts is overloading your audience with details that do not reinforce the point(s) you are making. Be selective. The purpose of graphs and charts is to demonstrate a trend through contrasts and comparisons. Thus, be sure to use them to inform the audience of the trends you have found.

Charts and Graphs

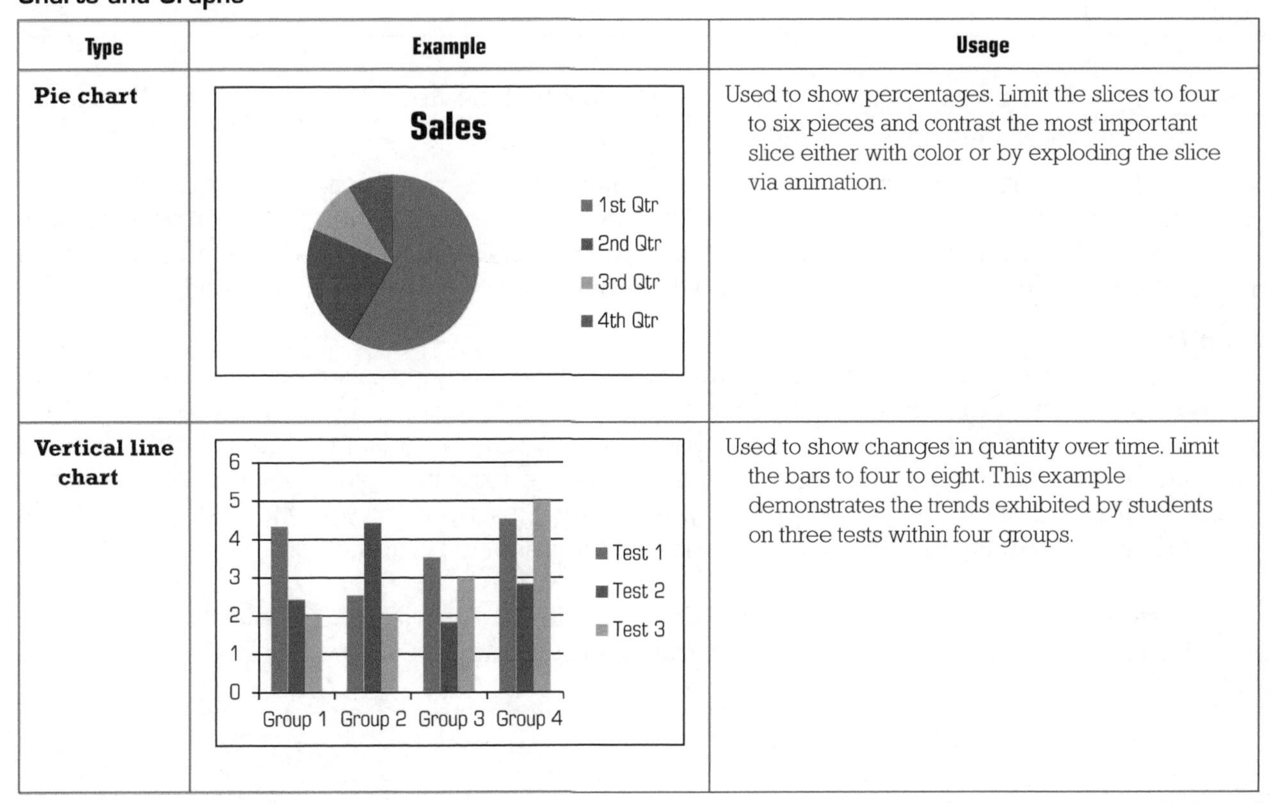

Type	Example	Usage
Pie chart	Sales 1st Qtr 2nd Qtr 3rd Qtr 4th Qtr	Used to show percentages. Limit the slices to four to six pieces and contrast the most important slice either with color or by exploding the slice via animation.
Vertical line chart	0 1 2 3 4 5 6 Group 1 Group 2 Group 3 Group 4 Test 1 Test 2 Test 3	Used to show changes in quantity over time. Limit the bars to four to eight. This example demonstrates the trends exhibited by students on three tests within four groups.

continued

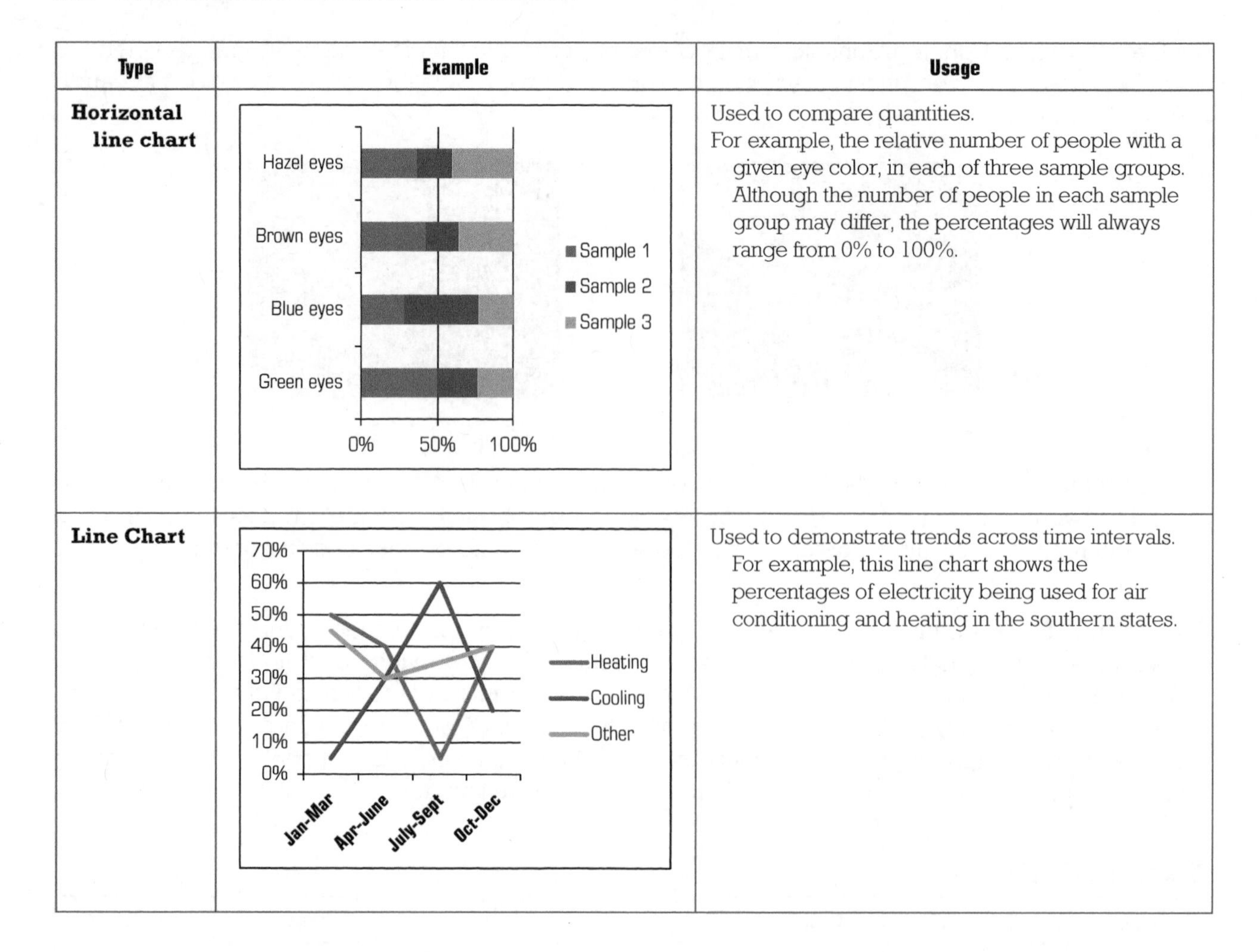

Type	Example	Usage
Horizontal line chart		Used to compare quantities. For example, the relative number of people with a given eye color, in each of three sample groups. Although the number of people in each sample group may differ, the percentages will always range from 0% to 100%.
Line Chart		Used to demonstrate trends across time intervals. For example, this line chart shows the percentages of electricity being used for air conditioning and heating in the southern states.

When using charts, be sure you can explain them with a high degree of accuracy. This will help you demonstrate your knowledge of the topic with confidence.

First and foremost, read and understand the information you are going to present. Until you fully understand it, you will not be able to organize your materials to maximize your presentation. Once you comprehend the material, you are ready to arrange the materials you will present. Determine the type of visual aids that will be an enhancement and the order in which you will present the ideas.

Step 1:

Begin by reviewing your thesis statement you wrote for the essay on this topic. If you were not required to write an essay, construct a thesis statement. A thesis statement informs the audience of the overall point you are going to make in your presentation. You may recall the components of a thesis statement from your English class as a complete sentence explaining your point on a given topic. Then, determine three to four primary points you discovered supporting your thesis statement. If you are working with a controversial topic, the thesis statement should be arguable.

> Example: "While many people believe slavery ended in America in the 1860s, it is clear slavery is currently alive and well within America in the form of human trafficking."

Three major points I would want my audience to know about my stance on human trafficking are:

- How and where human trafficking is taking place in America today.
- Who is responsible for allowing this form of slavery.
- Why and how all bear responsibility for ending human trafficking in America.

Step 2:
Now, what I want to communicate is clearer and I can begin crafting my presentation for the audience. How much does the audience know about this topic? See the information presented above on how to address the various levels of knowledge and how to adjust your presentation accordingly.

Step 3:
The choice of using visual aids is the next step. Determine if the use of one or more of the following is best for your presentation:

PowerPoint Presentation: Slides as described above that enhance the information presented.

Board: Use of board or easel to write your points for the audience.

Poster: Pre-made poster that offers a visual representation of the information in your presentation.

Handout: (e.g., outline, brochure, flyer) Notes over the information you are presenting for the audience to take with them as a reminder of your message.

Step 4:
Actively engage in conversations with peers and professors on your presentation topic.

Step 5:
Read current news publications for more information in current events around the world on your topic. Add this to your presentation as you see fit.

When creating your presentation materials, look for the types of professions involved in the events or actions. For example, the human trafficking topic lends itself to the inclusion of information from the following professions:

- law enforcement
- immigration law civil rights
- sociology
- psychology
- child protective custodial services
- child or adult advocacy

This particular topic, like many you will explore in classes, lends itself to many different types of professions. Thus, it may be impossible to incorporate all of them in your work. However, you can include one or two with ease. This will help you understand how professionals need to educate the public on a topic.

There are very few professions exempt from public speaking as it provides the opportunity to inform and persuade within the job market. Opportunities to inform fellow workers on changes in policy, safety, income projections, and goals, and a wide variety of systemic changes await college graduates. However, that will require public speaking techniques. As a matter of fact, it has recently been noted that students who graduate with degrees in science, technology, engineering, and math will be promoted to management within five years of entering the job force. This means most of the people, who may not even see themselves in this type of position today, will be required to present information to large groups and implement the strategies for successful public speaking. While the majority of America's college degrees are not awarded to people in science, technology, engineering, and math, most liberal arts majors will be expected to present as well.

Consider the following scenario in light of the need to present within your profession. You are working and see a way to save the district money. In order to motivate everyone to participate in the idea, you have to present it to your supervisor. After doing so, your supervisor is in agreement and wants you to present it at the next departmental meeting. This is a typical work place scenario, so learning to present today may influence your achievement in your future career.

OBJECTIVE 5: Understand How to Outline an Oral Presentation

After you have read, comprehended, and organized with the five steps above, you will want to determine the best way to organize your oral presentation notes. Typically, the duration time for a presentation will be between five to twenty minutes. This is determined by your professor's assignment sheet, so be sure to find this information. You are familiar with your topic and the points you want to highlight, but you will not be able to memorize the entire speech. For this reason, you will want to generate a set of notes written in outline form from the information you wrote in your essay or have determined to be critical information.

The outline of the speech will be written on 3x5 note cards so you can easily manipulate the cards as you work through the presentation. Write the outlined information large enough for you to easily read from a respectable distance. Then, when you are in front of the audience, you can appear more natural and conversational.

Your outline should include the thesis statement and three to four points you are making to the audience. This is a brief format and will not be written in complete sentences because sentences are too long for the note cards. Additionally, if you write sentences, it may be easy to fall prey to reading them. The purpose of the outline is to allow you enough information to articulate your ideas in a natural way. This will require you to be overly familiar with the information you are presenting.

If you are confident with your presentation, it is less likely you will become nervous. In the event you should become nervous, having a brief prompt on a notecard to remind you of the speech's focus will allow you to more quickly get back on track and eliminate your nervousness.

An oral presentation is different from a written essay in many ways. As you have seen, a presentation requires a set of oral processing skills not necessary for writing. Skills that are recognized as essential for presentations include:

- Over familiarity with the topic of the presentation
- Ability to restate information as a summarization of ideas
- Briefly written points for outline and for the audience in the form of visual aids
- Rehearsal of the delivery
- Time to create the visual aids

- Technology needed to generate visual aid(s)
- Clear understanding of the audience and their knowledge on your topic
- Confidence in public speaking
- Nonverbal communication skills
- Voice and breath control

In, addition to the above, some of the skills essential for writing an essay can enhance a presentation:

- Ability to write summarizations and paraphrase
- Well-written sentences and paragraphs
- Logical development of ideas in sequential manner
- Understanding of writing structures (compare, contrast, cause-effect, etc.)
- Understanding of writing conventions such as spelling, grammar, punctuation, etc.
- Multiple drafts and revisions

Both presentations and essays require the following:

- Information on a topic
- Persuasive point on an arguable topic
- Organization and management of sources
- Constructive criticism from reviewers
- Understand the audience's stance on your topic
- Address the audience's prior knowledge and extend it

It is clear these skills are complimentary, yet different. For this reason, many of your college assignments will require you to write an essay prior to presenting in class. The recommendations for organizing your oral presentation are similar to writing an essay. Because you are addressing an audience for the purpose of informing and persuading them, as you do in an essay, use what you know about writing in organizing your speech. For example, you need a thesis statement and three or four major points to demonstrate it. Then, just as you would begin an essay with an introductory paragraph; begin your speech topic with a brief introduction. Bear in mind the audience wants to know these additional points:

- Who are you?
- What are you going to talk about?
- Why should I listen?

This means you will want to grab the audience's attention with an anecdote, joke, quote, cartoon, statistic, or other type of awareness building technique. If the situation warrants it, explain why you are a credible speaker on this topic. Then, provide a short list of the topics you will be covering. By explaining this to them initially, it is more likely their attention will be focused throughout the presentation.

The topics list will be the point of reference throughout your speech. Audiences are listening for information they can use to follow your points. Examples of these types of words are: *first, second, third, subsequently, therefore, furthermore, before, then,* and *next.* As previously noted, define unfamiliar terms and demonstrate them with visual pictures, if necessary, that provide memorable examples. Explicitly point out the key points you are making to your audience and provide summaries of what you have covered periodically. This will help your audience keep the connections between points much clearer.

Once you have clearly presented your information, signal you are wrapping up the presentation with words or phrases like *finally* and *In conclusion.* Be sure to save these types of words and phrases for the conclusion of your presentation so the audience will understand you are indeed finishing. It is a good idea to end with a memorable quotation, decisive statement, or issue a challenge to the audience. Then, pause for a second or two in silence. End the speech with a grateful "thank you," and move away from the podium.

OBJECTIVE 6: Understand the Qualities of Speaking

The organization of the speech is critical to your success in public speaking. Of course, just as writing depends on a different set of skills than speaking; organizing the speech is different from delivering the speech. There are numerous qualities of speakers who engage their audience through spoken words. Some use humor, some have personal interactions with audience members, some use personal stories, and some just have a way of pulling you into their speech as if the speaker were talking just with you. Additionally, there are great speakers who can serve as your role models. The need to practice refining the qualities and emulating a role model cannot be overstated. It is with these elements that this section will proceed.

Learning the qualities of effective public speakers will allow you to increase your verbal eloquence. As an aside, this may sound similar to the elements founded in the *Elocutionary Movement* that took place between 1800–1865 in England and America. In this movement men and women sought out the help of elocutionists, instructors in the art of public speaking, to enhance their speech making ability. This was in part due to the rise of the middle class in which people were trying to sound like educated and financially stable citizens. The trends included exhaustive body positions for the speaker to learn for greater emphasis while speaking publicly. Fortunately, this movement was eventually simplified. The Elocutionary Movement paved the way for speech classes you take today.

Elocution picture in the 1880s concerning placement of hands.

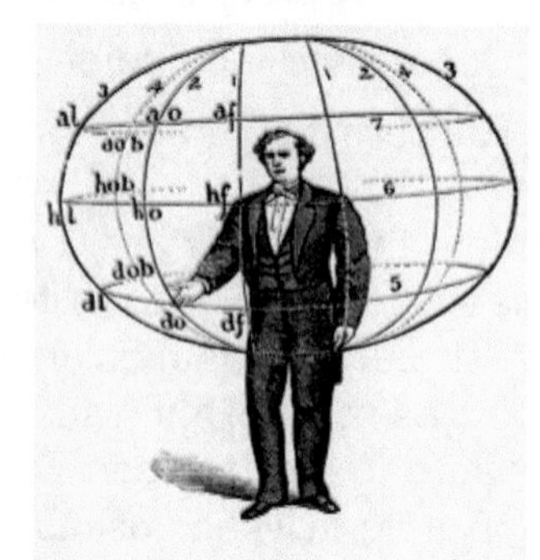

Source: Golden, James L, et al. *The Rhetoric of Western Thought.* N.p.: Kendall Hunt (2003) 198.

Take a look at some of the more highly regarded qualities of effective public speakers. Did you know that most of the presidents had speech writers and that the presidents tried to copy the effective oral delivery methods demonstrated by other presidents? Consider Steve Jobs' presentation when a new Apple® product was launched. Everything he did was purposely designed to convey confidence, authority, and desirability for the new product. It was not uncommon for him to practice his speech twenty-five times until he got it exactly the way he wanted it.

According to the "Four Qualities of Amazing Public Speakers" as written by Desiree Moore, "Learning about the essential qualities of other great presenters is an easy way to become one yourself." In this article, Moore offers insights on how to become more like the amazing public speakers you admire. These techniques "will ensure you are delivering presentations that will influence, inspire, and make a meaningful impact on your audience" (Moore).

The first quality to acquire on your mission to be an amazing speaker may surprise you. While most people tend to explain how to modulate your voice, hold your hands, or establish eye contact, Moore suggests the first step is that "you must first understand who you are as a speaker—and as a person." This requires you to determine your strengths in your interpersonal communication skills. Do you converse easily with people? Do you prefer to tell stories to your friends? Are you effective in motivating people to change? Moore suggests a practical way to accomplish this assessment is by "making a list of your best traits and the areas in which you excel." She then recommends you contemplate how these skills are related to public speaking. Learning who you are and how to use your natural abilities are the foundation of effective speech delivery.

The second quality outlined by Moore is the art of storytelling. These ancient traditions of sharing experiences within a community offer the opportunity to connect with one another emotionally. Telling about your emotional engagement through storytelling is much easier than explaining to someone how to make something. As a result, Moore suggests beginning with a story is the best way to engage your audience.

Moore's third quality of amazing speech makers is generosity. She offers Simon Sinek as an example of a speaker who demonstrates this. In his TED talk, "How Great Leaders Inspire Action," he is noted as saying "Start with why. Tell people *why* you do what you do before you tell them what you do or how you do it." This means you will want to share openly and honestly about your passion on the topic. What motivated you to research this topic and offer a presentation of your findings? Moore says it is equally important to know your audience so you can appeal to them more exactingly. You will want to understand if the group responds better to high-energy speakers or a more low-keyed delivery. The more you know about the audience, the more precise you can be in your oral delivery.

Ironically, confidence is the fourth quality Moore lists. As was previously stated, the majority of people are shy and reluctant public speakers. Yet, what type of speaker are you more likely to listen and learn from—one who is shy or one who is confident? Most would follow the confident speaker, so how do you become that confident person? Moore accurately states,

> "Your nerves do not show. What you're feeling is primarily internal, and others can't sense your fear if you don't let on. Also, your audience is rooting for you—they want a great presentation, so they want you to succeed. Finally, and most importantly, you are in control of your nerves."

The primary way to circumvent this anxiety is to over rehearse your speech prior to giving it publicly. This is a secret many great speakers have employed and continue to do so today. Another way to avoid the nervousness while speaking publicly is to visualize your success prior to giving the speech. Close your eyes, see yourself succeeding, and hear the applause surround you upon completion! A final pointer from Moore is to learn to breathe deeply and stretch your muscles prior to speaking.

In summary, the "Four Qualities of Amazing Public Speakers" as written by Desiree Moore are:

1. Know your strengths and use them while speaking.
2. Begin your speech with an engaging, emotional story.
3. Be generous in satiating your audience's curiosity of you and your topic.
4. Learn to use your nervousness in a productive way that leads to confident speaking.

A college student can employ the "Four Qualities of Amazing Public Speakers" as written by Desiree Moore with ease and enjoyment. Take a moment to contemplate your personal strengths and how these strengths can be used to enhance your speaking ability.

EXERCISE 10.8: Areas In Which You Excel

Write a list of your best traits and the areas in which you excel.

Traits/areas in which I excel	How are each of these traits expressed when speaking or presenting in front of others?

Are there any areas of weakness in your natural traits that with a little focus on improvement, will contribute to your public speaking skills? What are they? How will you work to increase the skill?

___

___

___

© BlueSkyImage/Shutterstock.com

© oneinchpunch/Shutterstock.com

© Stephanie Bidouze/Shutterstock.com

PhotoStock10/Shutterstock.com

EXERCISE 10.9: Storytelling

When was the last time you heard a good story? Take a moment to listen to a story from "story leaders" at: www.storyleaders.com. While you are listening, identify the following elements demonstrated by the storyteller.

Introduction:
Emotion:
Connections to life:
Conclusion:
Confidence:
Generosity:

What did you learn about storytelling from the exercise? How will you use this information?

____

____

____

____

Watch Simon Sinek's TED talk at: "How Great Leaders Inspire Action." Then, write a response to his demonstration of generosity as outlined by Moore.

____

____

____

____

____

Review the information in this chapter on ways to overcome glossophobia. Describe how you will use three of the suggestions in an attempt to build greater confidence in speech delivery.

1. ______________________________

2. ______________________________

3. ______________________________

As you know by now, becoming an effective public speaker takes time and focus.

Remember, practicing the speech delivery will be your best ally toward succeeding! Try to find as many ways as you can to practice your speech:

- To your friends and roommates
- Watch yourself in the mirror to rehearse your facial expressions
- Speak to your professor, conversationally
- Through the visualization of yourself succeeding
- Rehearse with your visual aids
- Use your note card outline as another round of practice

A very important point concerning practice of your speech is to arrive at the room in which you will speak early. Check the technological equipment prior to your speech time to make sure it works. If you have worked on the visual aids and practiced your speech to perfection multiple times, you want to make sure everything works for the big day!

10.3 DEVELOPING RESEARCH AND LIBRARY SKILLS

Library buildings are not confined to brick and mortar buildings because most require internet access. This shift in location requires a shift in the skills needed to navigate your college online-based library resources. Reading online versus a traditional book is an opportunity to learn using the latest technologies available. There are some college professors and students who are joining newer technologies of informational reading reluctantly. In contrast, many students prefer reading from the Internet or a digital reader. There are advantages and disadvantages to both forms.

Some researchers believe reading online can be more distracting. For example, if you are reading on your computer and pop-ups appear, the distraction can cost you valuable study time. Take a minute to think about how often you stop to check email, Facebook®, or other social media while trying to study. It has been reported from business that employees move from one online task to another every three minutes. Eventually, these workers return to their original task, but they lose about twenty-three minutes on each task. Our brain is not wired for multitasking, so the constant interruptions limit the amount of critical thinking and deep thinking a student can achieve. Knowing the ease of distraction working on a computer presents, it is up to the student to determine if working online or reading with a digital device is the best way to read and comprehend information.

The flipside of reading online accurately claims reading online is common in today's society and will become even more "normal" over time. As Sandra Aamodt, a former editor in chief of Nature Neuroscience, stated:

> Reading on a screen requires slightly more effort and thus is more tiring, but the differences are small and probably matter only for difficult tasks. Paper retains substantial advantages, though, for types of reading that require flipping back and forth between pages, such as articles with end notes or figures.

Acknowledging the limitations of reading online or with a digital reader (e.g., Kindle, Nook, iPad) offers a balanced understanding of how to best employ these technologies.

The information highway is actually a super highway of perplexing scope because "we create as much information in two days now as we did from the dawn of man through 2003" (Schmidt). The author of the previous quote is Eric Schmidt, the Executive Chairman of Google®. What exactly does this amount of information look like on a daily basis? Based on information found on www.EducationDatabase.com in 2012 the basic breakdown of a 24-hour day is as follows:

- Over 210 billion emails are sent daily
- 3 million images are added to Flicr® daily
- 43,339, 547 gigabytes are sent across mobile phones globally each day which equals 1.7 million blue ray discs, 9.2 million DVDs, 63.9 trillion 3.5" diskettes
- 70 million new users to Facebook® are added daily
- 5 million tweets are sent through Twitter® each day
- 900,000 new blogger articles are posted daily

All of this uploading of information means that reading online or via a digital device is absolutely necessary and will continue to increase over time. The sheer magnitude of reading and learning available online means students will need to constantly hone active reading skills to adapt to our emerging technologies.

Early research reported by Jakob Neilson suggested online reading rates were slower by twenty-five percent than the traditional text on a page. Yet, the reasons for the decreased speed were never fully defined. What is known about how people read online is that seventy-nine percent of us tend to skim and scan rather than read from sentence-to-sentence. Another suggested reason for the slower reading rates online is that the text needs to be clearer. Microsoft® created "clear type" to reconcile readability concern in 2006 and included in WindowsXP. Finally, it is informative to know the Kindle® and iPad® studied the reading rates on their devices and found readers were still slower on these digital readers than in printed texts. Fortunately, it was about half as slow as Neilson's study on reading with a PC. Thus, reading is slower when using a digital device, but technology vendors are working to minimize the differences between products. If you are a slow reader, it may better to locate a printed book for your class and the research you need to conduct.

As you may already know, the way text is arranged on websites is very different from traditional books. Typically, websites offer brief, bulleted information, often colorful and engaging. Reading from the Internet requires one's ability to critically analyze information to determine the validity and reliability of the sources. Validity means the reader is looking for information that is accurate and can be confirmed. It is often said, "Believe half of what you hear and nothing you read." Question everything and believe nothing you hear or read! In other words, confirm the information provided is valid. To confirm the reliability of the information given on the Internet means the reader needs to determine the trustworthiness or dependability of the information and their sources. This will require the researcher to ask questions of inquiry such as:

- Who is this author?
- What organization is saying this?
- On what date was this resource written and updated?

EXERCISE 10.10: Evaluating a Website for Authenticity

Visit the following websites and determine if the information on each would be something you would include in an essay or presentation on *Establishing Term Limits for US Congress.* Explain your reasons.

1. http://www.balancedpolitics.org/ ____

____

____

2. https://wichitaliberty.org/politics/arguments-term-limits/ ________________________

____

____

3. https://www.cato.org/publications/congressional-testimony/congressional-term-limits ________

____

____

This type of inquiry requires guided practice, so spend some time analyzing a website. In the end, reading and researching online requires students to employ critical inquiry, and logical searches for knowledge. By employing questions, such as those in active reading, research sources can be carefully analyzed for validity, credibility, and relevance to your topic. Ultimately, finding the solution to the research problem you are concerned with will require these analytical skills.

OBJECTIVE 7: Understand Methods of Beginning Research

Learning a few basic research methods will help you write effective essays and reports in your courses. Traditionally, research begins in the first semester of a student's college career, and does not end until the attainment of a degree. There are many reasons research plays such a critical role in achieving a degree: professors have been, and may still be, required to conduct research, the research process incorporates all of the critical thinking skills previously discussed, and the skills required in writing an organized, well-thought out essay demonstrate a level of knowledge. The rigors of research will be a vital component is achieving your dream of a degree.

Research is a critical component to obtaining a college degree. It entails a systematic approach of gathering information to answer a question. You are conducting research throughout your everyday life when you ask friends what the best running shoes are or if they prefer to eat pizza from one restaurant over another in town. Once you gather your findings to these "real life" questions, you evaluate the responses against your personal knowledge, and make a decision. Of course, this is informal research.

Formal research is similar to your informal methods in that you are seeking answers to a question, evaluating the information, and writing your essay on your findings. Unlike the casual method of research you used in your personal decision, you will learn to formally:

- gather information,
- analyze, synthesize, and evaluate the information you have gathered,
- and write an academic essay that includes in-text citations of your sources.

The overriding principle of research is to seek the answers to questions about which you are curious.

To begin the research process means you have already determined your topic of research. Your topic may be assigned by your professor or an area of personal interest. One way to determine your topic will generate more personal interest is to identify a problem. Then, research solutions other people have considered. This type of reading for solutions will require you to employ your active reading skills as previously discussed in Chapter 8. It is important you read the research findings with critical reading skills in order to question the solutions. By doing this, researchers are aware of the previously proposed solutions that may have worked, but may need adjusting in a new environment. For example, immigration to America is not a new problem. There have been immigrants arriving here since 1630 when the Puritans set their feet on the eastern shoreline. By studying what other solutions have been tried with success or failure, there may be a solution to our current concerns. So, it is imperative to find a problem to solve when you are conducting research.

Let us take the example of researching solutions to America's current immigration concerns a step further. Where can you look for solutions proposed previously? Are there any primary sources, or will you need to use secondary sources? Will you need to conduct a survey or interviews? Obviously, there are many options on how to find a solution to an identified problem.

Scholarly research consists of reading articles from peer-reviewed journals, reference books, ***bibliographies***, and conducting personal survey. All of these resources may be relatively familiar to you because you have been writing research papers since you learned to write! Of course, the tools in college may be significantly different from your previous learning environments; they are easily accessible and highly informed librarians await your inquiry for help.

In addition to understanding the various resources for your systematic research, it is important to understand there are primary and secondary sources you will need to consider in your research. A ***primary source*** is one written or spoken by an original source. For example, a speech is a primary source because it is a record of the words spoken by a person. Primary sources may include online interviews, email correspondence, and a personal interview between you and an expert. A ***secondary source*** is one containing information or interpretation of an original source. The latter will be found in encyclopedias, magazine articles, newspaper reports, television programs, or websites. The serious researcher is looking for primary sources, but will need to employ secondary sources due to the time necessary to gather primary sources, artifacts, or data.

If you are going to look for previously proposed solutions, you will need to use published materials, many of which are going to be located in peer-reviewed journals. A ***peer-reviewed journal*** is a scholarly journal that focuses on a discipline and publishes the research within it. Before an article can be published in an academic journal, the article is read and reviewed by experts in the field. This insures the information is accurate and credible, believable. Once the article has been approved by the peers with expertise in the area of inquiry, the article is printed. This process usually takes about two-years to be completed. Fortunately, the peer-reviewed journals are readily available to college students in the databases found on the library's website. More information on this will be in the section of this chapter entitled "Identifying Relevant Databases."

Using **bibliographies** as a point of research means you will locate answers to your questions in the dissertation, thesis, or peer-reviewed articles with bibliographies at the end. Basically, this means you will locate a work in the various databases in your campus library. Read and review them for answers to your research question. When you locate one closely related to your topic, look at the bibliography at the end of the paper. Then, use the sources from this dissertation, thesis, or article to locate their primary sources. Why would you want to do this? Well, it is an example of how to stand on the shoulders of those who came before you with the same or similar question. Their expertise, which may have taken innumerable years to achieve, will help you more quickly locate information. As always, keep copious notes on the sources you have used, so you will save time when it comes to creating your "Works Cited" or "Bibliography."

One primary resource for research is conducting **surveys or interviews** to generate your own primary sources. Some courses encourage this type of research to help students better understand a topic. An illustration of this type of research would be in a speech class focused on interpersonal relationships, specifically long-distance relationships. By creating a questionnaire, students could survey college students on campus to gather information. This information could include topics such as:

- the number of students involved in a long-distance relationship,
- how often the couples get to see each other,
- the level of satisfaction of those involved in a long-distance relationship,
- and/or the level of commitment of those in a long-distance relationship.

Once the questionnaire is created, students will generate information from those on the campus. Then, a careful review of the data will demonstrate some similarities and differences. From this information, conclusions can be drawn and written about in the research paper.

Getting started on research by determining where a problem is in need of a solution will help generate your topic. Once you have the topic, you will need to determine the best method of research to find a solution. Various forms of research will be required such as peer-reviewed journals, primary or secondary resources, or original surveys or interviews. Whatever option you determine to be your best choice for research, remember to take notes as an active reader.

Backward planning is a system of working toward a goal with incremental stages being clearly stated and completed. For example, when writing a research paper, you will begin with the date the assignment is to be submitted to your professor. Then, count back at least four weeks and write clearly stated goals necessary to complete for your paper to be well-written and completed on time. For example, your backward planning for an essay due in four weeks should look something like:

Week 1:

- Determine my topic and write a thesis statement.
- Generate a working outline for my essay.
- Begin research on the college library databases.

Week 2:

- Continue my research with reliable valid website databases. Add this to my draft. Complete Draft 1 of my essay and submit it to the campus Writing Center for review.

Week 3:

- Revise, based on the feedback from the Writing Center.
- Polish my draft.

Week 4:

- Review my polished draft and finish revising.
- Submit the essay!

The beauty of Backward Planning is you will not be waiting until the last minute to write your essay. Since a term paper traditionally accounts for about 25% of your semester grade, finishing it with confidence in the final product will ease your stress during the semester's crunch time.

OBJECTIVE 8: Understand Ways to Access Research Materials in the Library

Within the databases of your library's resources, you will find peer-reviewed journals, primary and secondary research, and many other resources. The librarians (all of them, not just the ones on your campus) have cataloged the information in ways that have predictable results, so you are more likely to find what you need. (In contrast, Internet search engines use algorithms that change as frequently as thirty days, so you are not always guaranteed the same results each time you use them.) Since documenting your sources with citations is essential to research, using the library-based databases will help you manage your findings.

What is a "library-based" database? Because you can access the college databases through the Internet, you may not always need to be within the building called the "library." This means the information you are going to search through is electronically stored.

How do I access a database? You may go to your library and use the computers dedicated to research on site or use your online catalog, in which the materials are indexed, to access your databases. Because each college uses a different pathway to access the online databases, you will need to research the way your college system is organized.

Where can I go for assistance with databases on my campus? Go to your library's website to learn the ways in which you can contact your college librarian.

If researching with databases sounds like it takes time, it does. The rule of thumb is to determine how long you think it will take you, and then double the number. This means starting early will have a great payoff for you. While researching, be sure to take copious notes and record the sources for each article when you find them. There is nothing more frustrating than having your report or paper written and then realize you have to locate all of your sources to write the works cited or bibliography. One suggestion to avoid this is to create an annotated bibliography. This is, basically, writing the citation information and a summary of the article. Often students find that the summary of the article can be inserted into their research paper with little, if any, revision.

1. Describe the process of obtaining access to your college library's databases.
2. Evaluate the best "key word" search for a particular topic.

One you have determined the topic or question you are researching, you will learn to use "keyword" (also called "descriptors" or "identifiers") to conduct your searches within the databases. These keywords are the primary word in the title or the words used within the articles.

If you are struggling to locate relevant articles, use the guided word searches within the databases. Guided word searches are also termed "advance searches" in a database or search engine. This type of search requires you to set up information concerning the date or range of dates of publication, language preference (e.g., English), and format of the document (e.g., book, article, etc.). Another way to search the databases for information relating to your research question is through a ***"Boolean expression."*** This allows you to narrow or broaden your search with the use of three words: AND, NOT, OR. For example, you may want information on "distractions from texting and driving." You can insert the Boolean expression of "distractions texting" AND "driving" NOT "drinking" to narrow your search. These pointers on finding articles in your college's library-based database take a little practice, but will save you time when you learn how to use them.

EXERCISE 10.11: Practice Conducting Research

Now it is time for you to practice conducting research in your college library-based databases. Using the keyword term **"artificial intelligence,"** search for articles that relate to your keyword in two different databases. There are many from which to choose, but a few librarians recommend are:

EBSCO
Academic Search Premier
LexisNexis Academic
ProQuest
Web of Science.

You are free to use any two you select for this exercise.

	Name of database: ______________	**Name of database:** ______________
Number of Results?		
Number in Boolean search results with "'not' computers?		
Number in Boolean search results with "'or' computers?		
How many appear to relate to your keyword?		
Other observations		

The results of the previous exercise will vary based on the database you use and the holdings within your library subscriptions. In general, the use of the Boolean "not" in the search should narrow your results and the use of the Boolean "or" should expand the results. Why does this matter? The more specific you can be in the search and keywords, the more quickly and accurately the research results will be.

REFLECTION 10.D:

Consider the results you obtained in the previous Exercise 10.11. How did the results of the search vary based on the "topic"? Create a list of the subjects you got when you typed in just the basic topic. How did this compare to the subjects you found when you typed in "&" (and). Describe the search outcome subjects you got when you typed in "not." Explain what you learned about research on databases as a result of this activity.

Finally, the purpose of each database varies as does the usefulness. Many databases are very specific for disciplines and research, which means you may not get any results from a keyword search from one database, but get too many results to read in another. If you have a problem searching through the college library-based databases, go visit your college librarian.

OBJECTIVE 9: Understand Strategies to Access Relevant Databases and Research Materials on the Internet

By using your college library-based database, you are more likely to find relevant information more easily. Relevant means that a piece of information relates to your topic as well as the claim by the author relates to the information provided. This means that when you are searching for articles or books to use as support of your thesis statement, you will want to find relevant information.

You may be more familiar and even have a greater sense of comfort when you are using the Internet. First, it is important to understand a Uniform Resource Locator (URL) is the address for the website you may be searching for. Thus it communicates where you are going on the Internet. Typical URLs look like:

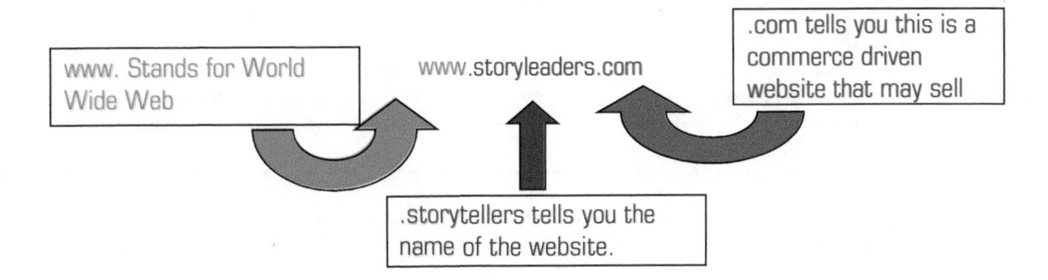

Notice your college's URL probably ends with .edu. This communicates the location of the information is from an educational source. As you probably know, there are many other ways to understand a URL, but this is the most basic information you need to begin searching the Internet for related articles to your research question.

The most important point concerning the URL is how to access different search engines such as Google, Bing, or Yahoo! These search engines, as well any other Internet search engine, are programs designed to search out sources from the Internet that include the keyword you used in the search.

Commonly used search engines for research:

Search Engine	URL (address)
Bing	www.bing.com
Excite	www.Excite.com
Lycos	www.Lycos.com
Yahoo!	www.Yahoo.com
Ask	www.Ask.com
Google	www.Google.com
Dogpile	www.Dogpile.com

Be aware most of the commerce (.com) websites on the Internet are trying to sell you something. As a result, through very sophisticated algorithms within the search engine, companies create web pages that will be in the top ten results of a search engine. Most people on the Internet only click on these top few sites because they show up first. The fact they are first is the result of your keywords does not mean they are the most informative or accurate. The order of appearance only indicates they have manipulated the properties of the search engine. Remember this the next time you are looking for a solution to a research problem because coming in first on the search engine results will not impress your professor if the information is inaccurate.

Once you determine which search engine you are using, enter the keyword search representing your topic. If you are searching for information concerning "artificial intelligence," as was used in the library-based databases, you will discover how a search engine works. A point to consider when entering your keyword searches is that the databases on the Internet are created to find matches to the words you have given it.

EXERCISE 10.12: Results of Search Engines

If you enter a key word search for "artificial intelligence" what are the results on the three major Search Engines?

Search Engine	Key word	Number of Results
Google	artificial intelligence	
Bing	artificial intelligence	
Yahoo	artificial intelligence	

Which search engine generated the most hits? ______________________

Record the first URL for each search engine:

Google: ______________________

Bing: ______________________

Yahoo: ______________________

Click on the first URL for each site and analyze it.

Which one seems to offer the best website for research and why?

Explain what you have discovered about search engines as a result of this exercise:

____

____

____

____

Knowing website developers on the Internet are clamoring to get your attention should inform you of how to conduct research on the Internet. Be aware of the types of websites, the authors, or sources of the website, and how it influences the information published.

Now that you have worked on the Internet search engines and the library-based online databases, you should have a better understanding of how they are similar and different. The most important piece of information you need to know is that the keyword search will work for both databases. The results you get from the two databases will be different. This is due to the fact that the college library-based database will use the keywords the librarians have designated appropriate due to its relevance and reliability. In contrast, the keyword you enter on a search engine, even if it is the same key word, is not organized by anyone but is located by the algorithm for commerce purposes. You may be skilled at using the search engines online for finding the "cheat codes" for your favorite video game because someone is probably trying to sell you something (even in a pop-up ad), but locating scholarly articles is less commerce driven. For this reason, locating credible, reliable sources with a search engine may take more time and offer fewer scholarly worthy results.

Overall, it is better to use the library-based online databases to locate the type of sources your professor is anticipating. While there may be a slight learning curve initially, learning the college system will save you valuable time over the next few years of your academic career.

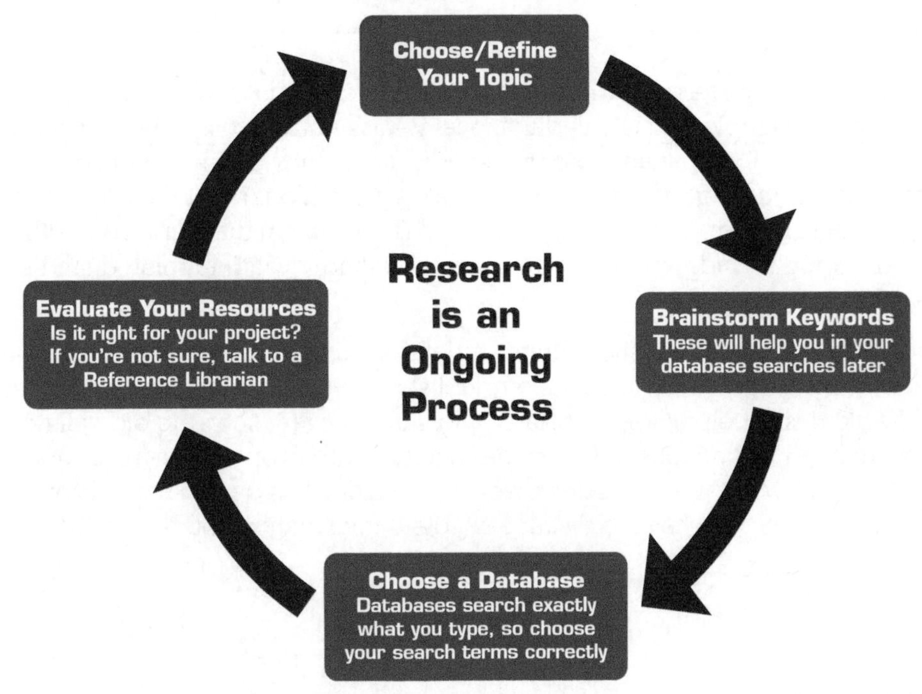

(Photo Source: UBC Learning Commons. "Library_Research Infographic." *Flikr*. 3 May 2013Web. 1/3/2016.)

10.4 EVALUATING THE VALIDITY OF RESOURCES

Now that you know where to go to find the library-based databases, take a moment to understand the best way to use the Internet-based databases. Many instructors will not allow you to use resources from the Internet for a variety of reasons. The primary reason most professors disapprove of Internet resources is because the information reported on most websites is not valid, reliable, or relevant. In order for information found on the Internet to be valid, it must be reviewed very carefully as if you are an expert. Unfortunately, expert opinions concerning the validity or reliability of online website information is not the practice for most websites. As a result, the information on most websites will not prove to be the best way to conduct scholarly research.

In order to use an article or information on a website, if this is approved by your professor, you will need to read critically to evaluate the:

- reliability (How accurate is the information?)
- credibility (How believable is the information)
- relevance (How does it relate to my research question?)

First, it is important to understand the different types of websites on the Internet. What do the ending of following URL's indicate about the website?

www.collin.edu: ______________________________

www.TADE.org: ______________________________

https://go.usa.gov/: ______________________________

www.mod.uk: ______________________________

www.mindmapping.com: ______________________________

www.studygs.net/: ______________________________

Hopefully, you were able to determine that the last part of the URL is the type of website it represents. For example, the www.example.edu is an educational website and https://go.usa.gov is sponsored by the American government. The .net and .org websites indicate they are non-profit organization (which may include schools and college-related professional organizations), but they may only present one side of the argument. For this reason, finding unbiased (information that supports both sides of an issue) is more challenging to find. The best way to avoid getting invalid, unrelated, and unbiased information is to use the college databases.

Another means of evaluating information found in databases is to review the date it was published. Even the college databases include information published over ten years before you are conducting your research. While this is helpful for historians, information over ten years old will not be accepted by most professors in education, business, or hard sciences. To avoid this error in your research, ask your professor if they allow database articles over ten years old. It is best to find this out before you get too deep into your research and have to discard obsolete information you had gathered.

OBJECTIVE 10: Understand the Reliability and Credibility of a Resource

According to the website, Wikipedia defines itself in the following way:

> **Wikipedia** (*WIK-i-PEE-dee-ə*) is a collaboratively edited, multilingual, free Internet encyclopedia that the non-profit Wikimedia Foundation supports. Volunteers worldwide collaboratively write Wikipedia's 30 million articles in 287 languages, including over 4.4 million in the English Wikipedia. **Anyone who can access the site can edit almost any of its articles.**[4]] Unlike traditional encyclopedias, Wikipedia allows outside editing: except in particularly sensitive and/or vandalism-prone pages that are "protected" to some degree, **even without an account readers can edit text without permission**.

This means, the people who edit and revise the pages can do so without even having an account with Wikipedia. Again, this is information taken from Wikipedia's website, not someone who is trying to convince you not to use it!

Another popular website for students to use is YouTube.com. Most students understand this is not a scholarly place to locate information, but they do so any way. According to YouTube.com they are a video exchange site, as stated below:

> Founded in February 2005, YouTube allows billions of people to discover, watch and share originally-created videos. YouTube provides a forum for people to connect, inform, and inspire others across the globe and acts as a distribution platform for original content creators and advertisers large and small.

Do you see any mention of scholarship or academic research? Perhaps this should be the point that inspires you to use more reliable, credible, and relevant sources for your college research.

Based on the definitions provided from Wikipedia and YouTube, their purpose is gather information from anyone who wants to submit. This means the information may or may not be monitored for accuracy. While Wikipedia's credibility has increased in the last few years, it is still not as reliable as the websites whose URL ends with .edu. Another way to use these ever popular websites might be to read or watch a video that explains the basics of your topic. Then, you can branch out from there to conduct your more serious research.

The primary purpose of a college library-based database is to share the findings that have, and continue to, add to the body of research among the scholarly disciplines. In contrast, Wikipedia and YouTube are primary purposed for personal expression and commerce. It seems logical that using the college library-based database for your research is easier, faster, and more productive. Of course, Wikipedia and YouTube are, perhaps, more fun!

Evaluating websites is necessary if you use Internet sites for your research. This means that reading critically is going to be essential in determining if the information on a website is credible, valid, and relevant. By asking a few questions about the information on the website you will be able to determine if information within the site can be used for your research.

- **How complete is the information?** Look for all sides of the issue or research report. If only half of the information is reported on the website, don't use it because it demonstrates the opinion of those who created the website.

- **Is the information accurate or valid?** Even if a website claims to have found the answer to a problem, review the study to make sure the research design, interpretation results, and computer generated information are free of errors.
- **Is the source an expert?** Does the information presented on the website reflect the opinion of an expert in the field? An expert is someone who has mastered a body of research. Most Internet sites are created by non-experts, so be cautious. Additionally, be aware that some websites claim authority over a topic, but lack it. Watch for misinformation as you read critically.
- **What is the bias of the website?** Are they for something or against something? These types of websites should be avoided, because they have inserted their opinion rather than reporting without a bias. Remember, the last letters of a URL (i.e., .com, .org, .edu) may be an indication of bias as well.

By employing these questions to the website you encounter, you will not waste valuable time on useless information. If you think there is some validity to a website, seek another source to confirm its validity. By comparing information on several credible websites, you may discover that the information is accurate. If you are in question as to the validity of the information, ask a librarian.

EXERCISE 10.13: Establishing Reliability

Complete the following chart on the keyword "artificial intelligence."

	URL: ______	Name of Library-Based Database ______	Wikipedia URL: ______
RELIABILITY (How accurate is the information?)			
CREDIBILITY (How believable is the information?)			
RELEVANCE (How does it relate to my research question?)			
Why is this best to use or omit?			

REFLECTION 10.E:

Explain what you would tell a friend who only uses Google to conduct their college research. Be sure to describe what you have learned about the type of information you obtain from the three research tools you used.

______

______

______

OBJECTIVE 11: Understand Methods to Avoid Plagiarism

Be aware that copying information directly from the Internet search engines or college library-based databases without giving proper credit to the original writer is called plagiarism. Basically, doing this is stealing the ideas another person generated. Professors take academic integrity very seriously, so be sure to cite your sources accurately.

Plagiarism is represented when a student writes a paper using another person's words. This is not to suggest you cannot use words written by someone else. You may use another person's words when you give proper citation and reference to the original author. This typically is provided in the form of in-text citations and end-of-paper lists of your sources. Failure to give credit to the original author is plagiarism, which has serious consequences in college. Intellectual dishonesty can lead to, at a very minimum, a failing grade on an essay to, at the maximum, expulsion from college. Thus, it is critical you learn to use proper in-text citation and end-of-paper lists. The latter is often referred to as "Works Cited" or "Bibliography." There are volumes of books written on this topic where you may seek help.

Remember that your paraphrasing and summarization skills presented in the beginning of this chapter are necessary when writing research papers. If you are offering the major points of a source with a summary or are restating the author's words with paraphrasing, you must tell the reader of your paper where you originally found the information. There are numerous books and websites that can help you avoid sounding as if you discovered the original information by conducting an experiment or completing a dissertation. Additionally, the librarian in your college library will be a willing source for your assistance as needed.

Course Connections:

Educational Videos and Online Tutoring

Just because YouTube and other websites offer free educational videos and online help, be careful what you believe! Be sure to work with your professor if you find a questionable point . . . even on a credible website!

Most likely, your education textbook is bundled with an online version of the book as well as videos and additional explanations over the various topics covered. Many offer free tutoring online.

REFLECTION 10.F:

Where can you go to get help on determining which internet sites are safe for you to view correct videos?

____

____

How could you tell if an internet site is giving you incorrect information?

____

____

PERSON to PERSON

In this exercise, you will be introduced to a student in a psychology class. Let's discuss ways for you to increase ethical researching and writing skills!

The first week of class, Kendra noticed the syllabus has a term project that counts 20% of her grade. She was nervous because she did not understand the requirements and expectations of the term project, but the instructor said it will be discussed in detail later in the semester. However, since she was a full-time student, she quickly forgot about the assignment and did not ask about it.

Midway through the term, the instructor briefly mentioned the project to the class and suggested the students develop and submit an outline of their project within the next two weeks.

Kendra began panicking because she did not even have a topic!

Based on this description, select the resources that may help Kendra in developing a topic.

Social media friends ______ Internet search engine ______ Family ______ Peers ______

Meeting with her professor ______ Campus Writing Center ______

Here is some additional information.

- The term project is a presentation, not a written report.
- The specific grading criteria are:
  - Content
  - Style
  - Creativity
  - Complying with the time allotted for presentation (ten minutes.)

Which of the following concerns should primarily influence Kendra's selection of a topic for the term project?

Format ______ Individual project or group ______

Are research sources required? Y or N If so, how many? ______

Syllabus topics ______ Textbook chapter titles ______ Lecture notes ______

Topic selected by the student sitting next to her in class ______

1. What pieces of new information do you consider to be important for topic development?

____

____

____

2. What other information does Kendra need to develop the topic?

____

____

____

Here are your last pieces of information.

- Kendra has a sister who has taken this class.
- Kendra's sister already has an outline she developed for the assignment, but never used when she took the class.

If Kendra used her sister's outline, which of the following apply?

Plagiarism ______ Unethical ______ Family Sharing ______

Academic Dishonesty ______

1. What pieces of information would you still like to know about Kendra or the project?

____

____

____

2. Are there any pieces of information that could be seen as both positive and negative influences on success?

____

____

____

3. What advice would you offer Kendra to help her successfully navigate this situation?

____

____

____

Career Connection:

© lightpoet/Shutterstock.com

The ability to write clearly and present effectively are skills you will learn in college. While you may believe "I won't be writing papers after college," think about possible careers. Lawyers are required to write briefs to persuade a judge to include (or exclude) pieces of information. Political staffers write papers on policy making while environmental scientists write reports regarding the conditions of a site. Teachers may write notes or articles for professional journals and researchers generally write up the results of their research. After these papers are written, some may present their results at a local or national meeting or conference. Therefore, being able to write an essay in an English class is just the beginning of what could be a life-long career in writing.

CHAPTER SUMMARY

Writing is a vital part of your college career and knowing how to write well will advance your career. Thus you will need to learn to write summaries, paraphrases, and personal responses to successfully complete the rigors of a college writing assignment. Ultimately, the writing skills you learn in college may help you advance in the workplace for the majority of your life.

Learning to be an effective public speaker has immediate benefits in college as well as long-term dividends in your career. Writing the presentation requires you to be overly familiar with the topic. Rehearsal of the speech will lessen the anxiety the majority of people experience when asked to speak publicly. The use of an outline written on note cards will also allow you to focus on the points you are attempting to communicate with greater confidence. Becoming an effective public speaker requires you to look at your strengths in communicating with others, learning the art of storytelling, generously sharing of yourself and the information you have, and learning to appear confident.

The ability to conduct research in the current age of online resources requires students to learn how to determine the best source for their topic. This entails the ability to determine the reliability, credibility, and relevance of each source. Using the library-based databases may require students to overcome a slight learning curve, but will be a skill that increases their college success. Using online search engines, Wikipedia, or YouTube, may be of benefit as well. Of course, these require students to learn the skill of critical thinking, as you will need to analyze the information with greater scrutiny.

In the end, research conducted in a systematic way, which includes organizing the sources, will allow you to avoid plagiarism. Knowing where the information originated and citing it within the text and at the end of your end-of-paper, will eradicate the chances of plagiarism. Since the consequences of committing plagiarism are serious, you will want to learn ways to circumvent it.

CHAPTER 10: Self-Check

Vocabulary: Define the following:

1. summarization
2. glossophobia
3. research
4. relevant databases
5. Wikipedia
6. YouTube
7. reliability and credibility
8. plagiarism
9. Boolean expression

Concepts:

10. List the information required to write a comprehensive summary.
11. Explain how to paraphrase.
12. Compare and contrast summary formation to paraphrasing.
13. Formulate well-written summaries and paraphrasing.
14. Clarify when to write a summary for long-term memory recall.
15. Explain three ways to use a summary for study reviews.
16. Discuss strategies to connect course work and writing.
17. Explain the components of a personal response.
18. Describe a personal response.
19. Compare and contrast summarization and personal response.
20. Write a personal response to a given excerpt.
21. Clarify when to write a summary for long-term memory recall.
22. Explain three ways to use a summary for study reviews.
23. Generate a well-written summary from a college textbook chapter.
24. Discuss strategies to connect course work and writing.
25. List three ways to conduct an effective presentation.
26. Predict the best way to address the audience in a presentation.
27. Clarify when technology can enhance or hinder a presentation.
28. Describe when to use visuals and the best types of images to use in a presentation.
29. Explain the role of charts and graphs in a presentation.
30. Describe the process of organizing and building content for the presentation.
31. Connect the information in a presentation to professions.
32. Describe criteria for outlining an oral presentation.
33. Contrast an oral presentation to a written essay.
34. Identify the best way to organize an oral presentation.
35. List five qualities of effective public speakers.
36. Explain how a student can employ the five qualities of effective public speakers.
37. Demonstrate the five qualities of effective speakers in an oral presentation.
38. Describe the benefits of practicing speeches.

39. List three methods for conducting scholarly research.
40. Explain how to use backward planning to predict the completion of a research project.
41. List three databases accessible through a college library database.
42. Describe the process of obtaining access to a college library's databases.
43. Evaluate the best "key word" search for a particular topic.
44. Compare and contrast two databases for purpose and usefulness.
45. Describe how to access other college databases.
46. List two online search tools.
47. Describe how to use an online search engine.
48. Compare and contrast the types of information in the college databases to the online search engine.
49. Explain when to use an online search engine rather than using the college library's database for research.
50. Describe the information available on Wikipedia and YouTube.
51. Contrast the information sources in Wikipedia and YouTube to the college databases.
52. Explain when to use Wikipedia and YouTube in college research projects.
53. Explain how to determine the reliability of a research resource.
54. Explain how to determine the credibility of a research source.
55. Demonstrate the ability to analyze a website, database, and a print resource for reliability and credibility.
56. Explain how to cite a source for parenthetical citations and works cited.
57. Identify plagiarism.
58. Rewrite a passage using paraphrasing and summarization as well as proper citation.
59. Discuss the consequences of committing plagiarism and academic dishonesty.
60. Create three note cards for this chapter, the first with a true-false test question, the second with a multiple choice test question, and the third with an essay question.

CHAPTER 11
Preparing for and Taking a Test

T.I.P.S. (Tactical Information that Promotes Success)

Start studying for each exam the day the unit begins and schedule daily review.

© michaeljung/Shutterstock.com

Preparation is key to a successful ***examination***. Be certain to attend your instructor's review class. Many times, this is where hints are given regarding the exam and the important topics are emphasized.

Reduce anxiety and increase focus to increase performance.

© Library of Congress

Edgar Allan Poe (1809–1849) turned literature upside down when he suggested that a writer should "begin with the conclusion" when writing a story. He obviously did something right, so think about how this works with a test.

Preparation for the exam (and the Final Exam) begins the first day of class; pay attention, take good notes, and study each day. Do NOT cram for an exam. Without proper rest, you may find it difficult to focus.

In **mathematics**, complete homework assignments, pre-read the next sections, and consider forming a study group to help prepare for an exam. On the day of the exam, if a calculator is allowed, be certain to have fresh batteries or a power plug. Once you receive the exam, perform a "memory dump" of all necessary formulas.

In **reading,** beginning early means determining the length of a reading to predict how long it will take you to read it with the highest level of comprehension. It might be useful to time yourself when you read for one minute to see how many words per minute you can read. Count the words to see how fluent you are and use this to predict the time necessary to read the assignment. It is advisable to do this for the textbooks you will read within each discipline because the words per minute will vary. Your familiarity with the topic will also play a critical role in your fluency. The more background knowledge you have, the faster you can read and remember the information.

In **education**, certification tests are common for teachers to take. Often practice tests and resources are available prior to taking the test. Familiarize yourself with the tool available for a successful result. Your entrance and advancement in this profession depends on your passing the test!

Remember, professors typically give three (3) or four (4) tests in a semester. This means you have to remember the information you have read for several weeks before you are asked to demonstrate your knowledge.

The best way to prepare for the taxing demands on the brain is through **writing**. Write a summary of the chapter and/or information in the class, including any salient points. Then, before the test, read the summary. By doing this, you will not need to read and reread the chapters. Find ten (10) ways to read and write the information you need to know for the test and you will make an "A" in the class!

CHAPTER 11: OBJECTIVES

11.1 Preparing for Any Test

Objective 1 Understand How to Use a Course Syllabus and Lecture "Hints"

Objective 2 Understand Format and *Requisite Knowledge* Level of Test Questions

11.2 Taking the Test

Objective 3 Understand the Physical Preparation Needed to Test Well

Objective 4 Recognize Strategies for Managing Time During the Exam

Objective 5 Recognize Strategies for Short-Answer Questions

Objective 6 Understand Strategies for Writing Essay Responses

Objective 7 Understand Educated-Guessing Strategies for Multiple Choice Questions

11.3 Analyzing Test Performance

Objective 8 Understand Causes of Test Anxiety and Strategies for Managing It

Objective 9 Understand Levels of Preparedness

Objective 10 Understand *Post-Exam Strategies*

CHAPTER CONCEPTS:

Some or all of the following terms may be new to you. Place a check mark in the column reflecting your knowledge of each term.

	Know	Don't know	Not sure	Page # where first found		Know	Don't know	Not sure	Page # where first found
Requisite knowledge					Declarative				
Short-answer Questions					Procedural				
Essay questions					Post-exam strategies				
Multiple choice questions					Examination (Exam)				

11.1 PREPARING FOR ANY TEST

Tests are a way in which you or a professor may measure the level of mastery you have attained over a body of material. It is an opportunity to express your knowledge as well as demonstrate your level of understanding in the course. All too often, this four letter word, "t-e-s-t," can conjure up images that are intimidating, which can create anxiety for students. It is little wonder that many students' attitudes toward test taking are frequently less than optimistic. Yet, most students have been taking tests since they entered formal schooling at the age of five. Testing is a skill that is reinforced for the majority of your learning experiences. Why? With a little focus on the elements you have control over, you can learn to embrace the opportunity to exhibit your knowledge.

OBJECTIVE 1: Understand How to Use a Course Syllabus and Lecture "Hints"

You meet your class and the course syllabus is handed to you. Students often disregard the syllabus.

Test preparation begins on the first daabus as a means of guiding them in a course. Remember to hold on to the syllabus after you print it. It is good to refer to it throughout the semester for terms, concepts, and outcomes that you are to have achieved as they are stated in the document.

Because the professor is the author of the document, wise students will learn to listen for ways that your professor will emphasize the important points to you during class sessions. One, most obvious way, is to listen for the points in the lecture in which the professor is expressing great interest or passion on a topic. When a professor takes time from your class to express personal interests, you will want to pay attention. These will probably be on the test! Another way to listen for hints of test material from your professor is to learn words and phrases such as:

- *The primary . . .*
- *The most important . . .*

- *One of the critical reasons . . .*
- *Without X, the development or improvement of Y would not have happened.*

Listen for student questions and the way that your professor replies to them. Just because it may seem like the class focus is lacking, learning is still occurring. Learn to filter out what is repeated and reviewed by your professor because these types of points will be on the test. Another, more obvious way to pay attention during a lecture class session for potential test material is to write everything the professor writes on the board. When a professor writes on the board, you can expect to see this information on the test.

A less traditional way of learning how to read your professor for potential test questions is to watch for non-verbal cues. For example, when does the professor stand up or move closer to the class? This could be a cue of the importance of the material being discussed.

Periodically, compare your lecture notes, chapter materials, and any other learning materials to the course syllabus. Be sure to organize the various course learning materials by the order of importance they are listed on the course syllabus. The combination of these test preparation materials will help you perform better on the test.

Reviewing the course syllabus for information that will be included on the test is one way to control your focus in preparing to take a test. Remember, the professor who wrote the syllabus is going to expect a level of mastery on the student learning outcomes that are listed on it. Use this document to organize your ideas as you move through the course. You may want to take time to add notes to flesh-out the syllabus information as you progress through the course materials. Use the syllabus as a guide for understanding the course materials. Ask: "What concepts are mentioned in the syllabus as being important to the course?" The main material you cover on each test you take will be mentioned in the syllabus.

Lists are a great source for test material, so you will want to increase your awareness of vocabulary in a list format. Consider asking the following questions:

- What words create a list on the syllabus?
- How is the list organized in the course syllabus?
- What information in the list relates to the material where you will be tested?
- What are the points of each item in the list and how can they be elaborated?

Being prepared for a test means you have memorized the list information and know how to apply each concept to the course materials. Merely memorizing a list for a college test or exam is not sufficient for earning an "A" on an assessment. Remember . . . a test is your opportunity to demonstrate how much you have learned!

EXERCISE 11.1: Syllabus Hints

Explain in two sentences how to use the hints from a syllabus to prepare for a test.

____

____

____

____

OBJECTIVE 2: Understand Format and *Requisite Knowledge* Level of Test Questions

Declarative knowledge is expressing that something is true or is the case. Knowing that the tibia and fibula are the two bones in the lower leg is declarative information. For example; information in a psychology, anthropology, or history class is generally factual information. In contrast, ***procedural*** knowledge is knowing and expressing how you do something. Remember, declarative explains *what* you learn, and procedural explains *how* to do or create something.

Understanding whether you are employing declarative knowledge or procedural knowledge will help you determine the best way to prepare for a test. If you are going to take a test where declarative knowledge is assessed, it is best to learn the information and make connections through deeper learning processes. Generally, professors who teach declarative knowledge will test you with multiple choice, matching, true-false, short answer essay, and longer ***essay questions***. Courses that are procedurally driven will typically ask that you demonstrate your ability to use the procedure in solving a mathematical equation or something similar. This means that when you study, you will want to keep in mind the type of knowledge you are learning, and how your professor will assess it.

The following chart will help you study for each type of knowledge driven assessment.

<table>
<tr><th>Declarative Knowledge</th><th>Procedural Knowledge</th></tr>
<tr><td colspan="2">Read and understand the major points
Elaborate: How does this concept relate to other concepts?
Distinctiveness: How is this concept different from other concepts?
Personalize: How can I relate to this concept on a personal level?</td></tr>
<tr><td>Appropriate Retrieval: How will my professor ask questions on this concept?
Practice writing and outlining concepts, review your Cornell notes with questions and answers, and review the vocabulary that is unique to this concept.</td><td>Appropriate Retrieval: How will my professor ask questions on this concept?
Practice working problems you have covered in class and those in your textbook; learn all formulas and procedures for solving problems; be able to identify different parts of a scientific diagram; know all relevant vocabulary.</td></tr>
</table>

As shown in the previous chart, "appropriate retrieval" determines the way that you practice for the actual test. Face it, if you do not practice with the "appropriate retrieval" method, you will not perform well on the test when you need to do your best. Similarly, practicing the expression of declarative knowledge through outlines, vocabulary, and memorization of basic information will help you make connections in the essay questions. If you have only memorized formulas for procedural knowledge or rehearsed memorizing concepts for declarative knowledge based tests, you will not perform well on any test. Knowing how you will be tested over the knowledge will lay a strong foundation for your test-taking successes.

Preparing to take a test means that you are processing the information from your working memory to your long-term memory. Rehearsal, recitation, rewriting, revising, are all ways to review the course materials. Ongoing review requires you to conduct these activities weekly. "Repeat to remember!" is a common expression for students. The better way to learn is to, "Repeat often, in order to remember automatically!" The more automatic you are in the retrieval of information, the better you will be able to perform on a test.

You may remember the term "slow-drip" learning. This was the image of learning that occurs over time to being similar to a drip of water on large boulder. Over time, the water penetrates the solid substance in the boulder and creates a hole. The water is soluble, yet it creates a hole in an insoluble substance with a steady rhythmic drop of water. Learning through ongoing review is like the slow drip of water on a rock . . . (Not to suggest that your brain is as hard to penetrate!) If water can slice through rock, surely ongoing review will create long-term memories of your college materials.

Creating questions for ongoing review will require you to look for the most important information that can be stated as a question. This is often found in the form of a heading or subheading in your textbook. Of course, it is logical to assume that any of the bold, italicized, or color text is a potential question. Be aware of lists in your textbooks, as these are great test questions for your professor to consider. As you know, listen to the lecture for repeated information or ideas that your professor demonstrates a passion toward. These are probably going to be on the test! The syllabus is another document you will want to use to predict test questions because it is the foundation of the course structure.

COURSE CONNECTIONS:
Test Preparation for Procedural and Declarative Knowledge

Test Preparation for Procedural Knowledge	Test Preparation for Declarative Knowledge
Because hard sciences are generally skill-based, test preparations should include: ■ attending class every day ■ taking good notes ■ asking questions in class ■ doing assignments every day and on time ■ reviewing material at least every other day ■ memorizing important formulas and vocabulary ■ memorizing specialized terminology for lab science courses ■ understand the various parts of scientific diagrams and illustrations ■ reviewing note cards involving skills ■ practicing working problems out of order and with varying instructions	Because soft sciences are generally information-based, test preparation should include: ■ attending class every day ■ taking good notes ■ reviewing notes—especially those that have been summarized ■ keeping up with the reading ■ turning in all assignments on time ■ preparing possible "essay" prompts ■ memorizing important dates, persons, and events ■ practice true/false problems ■ preparing possible reflection prompts ■ reviewing material at least every other day

©YanLev/Shutterstock.com

REFLECTION 11.A:

How are the preparations similar in both cases?

___

___

Which of the tools in the procedural list do you believe to be most important and why?

___

___

Which of the tools in the declarative list do you believe to be most important and why?

___

___

11.2 TAKING THE TEST

OBJECTIVE 3: Understand the Physical Preparation Needed to Test Well

© Layne Murdoch/Getty Images

Athletes are aware of the connections between taking care of their body and increasing their performance during competition. Professional NBA player Tim Duncan is considered by many as one of the best powered forwards in NBA history. Few college students may be aware that Duncan earned a degree in psychology from Wake Forest University in Winston-Salem, North Carolina. Many may think that Duncan, being a professional athlete, would only be concerned with his performance on the court, but his leadership on and off the court demonstrate his commitment to teaching healthy principles to those in his sphere of influence. As the founder of the Tim Duncan Foundation, he promotes "health awareness research and education and recreation in order to positively impact his community."[1] He is serious about preparing others, as well as himself, to be the best competitor on and off the court. When asked what he does during the off-season, Duncan stated,

> "I normally take about two to three weeks off after the season ends. During that time I don't really do any training, but after that I start going back into the gym to lift weights and do some light running and shooting. In August, I am in the gym three or four times per week. Once September comes, it is normally a lot like the season, in the gym everyday lifting and doing running and shooting drills and playing pick-up games."[2]

---

[1] "About Tim." *Slamduncan.com*. 2012. Web. 25 January 2014.
[2] "21 Questions with Tim Duncan." *Slamduncan.com*. 2012. Web. 25 January 2014.

The basic training cycle Duncan has described includes a balance of down time and focused time. It is the balance he demonstrates that offers insight into training and maintaining one's "edge" for long-term success. This same strategy can be applied to academics and test taking.

Duncan's off-season training offers a great model for preparing to compete in a college classroom. For example, he states that he takes three to three weeks off after the grueling mental and physical competition of an NBA season that lasts for nine months and includes 82 games. Of course, if Tim Duncan is in the playoffs, he plays at least seven more games. Obviously, he is spent by the completion of the NBA season and post-season. Taking time to recharge is vital for his long-term success. Taking time to recharge is equally vital for your long-term college success.

Notice that Duncan does not sit around waiting for the coach to remind him to go work out after he has taken a brief break. Duncan is going to the gym three to four times per week by August. Then, by September he is ready to work as if the season has begun. The activities he states as his training include weight lifting, aerobic activity, and practice with fellow athletes. College students may not actually go the gym to work on their strength and conditioning, but each of Duncan's activities can be connected to study skills. Weight lifting is similar to on-going review because both gradually increase the amount of information stored in a muscle, the memory muscle for college students. Aerobic activity is like creating long-term memory from the information you are learning in class. Just as Duncan runs to increase the amount of time he can maintain his energy on the court, college students' review and practice learning for more automatic memories to be retrieved. Finally, by practicing with fellow players, Duncan increases his ability to play the game with greater strategies and accuracy by practicing specific plays needed during game time. Similarly, college students who study with partners will increase the ability to learn through implementing successful strategies, practicing general and specific concepts, and demonstrating their knowledge more accurately. All of these "exercises" will create better outcomes for you. You will earn the "A" in the classes!

The need for sleep may be the easiest exercise to increase your cognitive skills, but it is often the most neglected by college students. Most college students attend a nine month schedule of courses. This would include two long semesters, one each in the fall and spring. The stress of two successive semesters of study is taxing on students. This means you will want to plan to have some down time. Daily planning to get at least eight hours of sleep will help you perform well in the college classes you are taking. Research on getting adequate sleep can make your cognitive functions operate more efficiently during the day. This is not to say that getting the eight hours of sleep will make you smarter, especially if you have not adequately prepared for the material that will be on the test, but getting sleep will allow your brain to function better, even under the stress of test-taking.

The topic of eating a healthy diet was previously discussed, but it warrants some additional attention as it relates to food consumption prior to taking a test. Energy is taken into our bodies in the form of carbohydrates, fats and protein. Basically, carbohydrates offer our bodies short term energy boosts.[3] Unfortunately, if we take in too many carbohydrates at one time, we will feel sluggish and the oxygen cannot flow in our brains as well, because the stomach is using it to process the excess carbohydrates. Fats are another form of energy which offers long-term storage of energy. Proteins offer the body immediate energy as well as sustained energy over a longer time frame than carbohydrates. Eating a balanced diet is essential for your overall well-being. Eating protein prior to taking a test will give you the energy needed to remain focused during a long exam.

---

[3] "Carbohydrates, lipids and proteins." *IB Guides: Biology*. 2012. Web. 1/25/2014. http://ibguides.com/biology/notes/carbohydrates-lipids-proteins

High protein foods, rich in **omega-3 fatty acids**, that aid in your test-taking abilities include: dairy (products like cheese, milk, and yogurt), eggs, edamame, wild rice, walnuts, beans, and sea food. Eating these regularly will provide greater cognitive function overall, but make sure to eat some or one prior to taking a test. These foods may be combined with carbohydrates and fats, but the bulk of your pre-test diet should be high proteins that are rich in omega-3 fatty acids.

In addition to getting your sleep and eating a high protein meal prior to a test, you will want to be sure to drink plenty of water. The brain is primarily comprised of water. Often people express that they are thirsty because they sense the need to rehydrate. This is actually the brain signaling to you that your brain needs water to function at its optimum level. It is a good idea to carry a bottle of water into the testing situation (if allowed), so you can rehydrate during the exam.

What Does Water do for You?

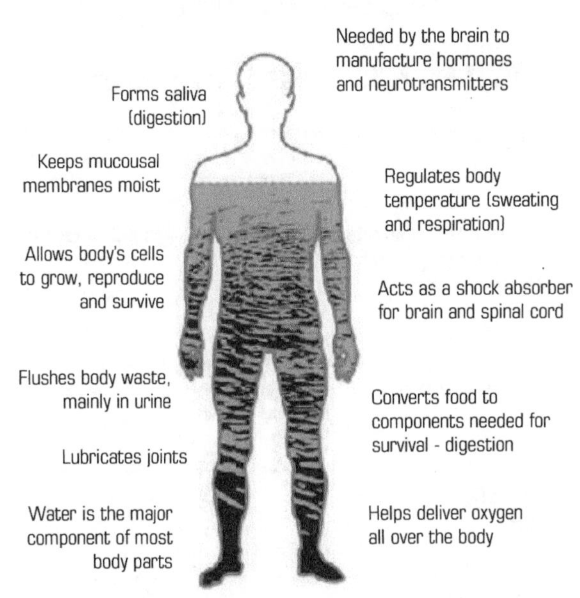

Source: "The Water in You." *United States Department of the Interior | U.S. Geological Survey.* 09 Aug 2013. Web. 1/15/2014.

Due to the typical stress a person experiences during a testing situation, deep breathing can help relieve the stress in a variety of ways. Deep breathing is explained in a variety of ways, but the basics always include:

1. Inhale through your nose for five to ten counts, making sure your diaphragm is expanded.
2. Hold the breath and count to five to ten.
3. Exhale through your mouth, slowly releasing the air for ten to twenty counts.

Proper Breathing

Inhale — **Belly expands to take in air**

Exhale — **Belly contracts to expel air**

Source: Norton, Beau. "Deep Breathing for Anxiety Relief." *Self-Development for the Journey to Success.* 14 Dec. 2013. Web. 1/25/2014.

Since breathing occurs without a person's ability to think about it, when we slow it down deliberately, it creates awareness that change is occurring in your brain and your thoughts can be reignited. When this interruption occurs at the moment of stress, it causes the brain to become more aware as our body becomes more relaxed. The oxygen necessary to allow your cognitive functions to operate at maximum potential require you to breathe deeply and to exhale over repeated times. Taking a few moments prior to beginning a test to deep breathe will allow you to begin the test in a more relaxed state. During the test, should anxiety begin, taking time to breathe deeply will help settle your nerves and increase the flow of oxygen to your brain.

Obviously, the previous suggestions for managing sleep, nutrition, hydration, and breathing, implies that you have dedicated ample time for the learning to occur by creating long-term memories.

EXERCISE 11.2: Test-Taking Strategies

Complete the following review over the habits that increase your success in test-taking.

Describe the following habits as they are applied to test-taking:	Explain how each of the habits lead to greater test-taking success:
sleep	
high protein diet	
exercise	
hydration	
deep breathing	

REFLECTION 11.B:

Explain how deep breathing can be used in a stressful situation in your personal life.

____

____

OBJECTIVE 4: Recognize Strategies for Managing Time During the Exam

Perhaps you are an armchair quarterback and there is a big game on television. The time is running out on the clock and your team still has one time-out on the clock. Are you yelling at the coach, "Call a time-out!" Many times the game is won or lost by the ability of the coach to manage the time during the game. Although you do not have and actual time-out during test-taking situations, the ability to manage your time is critical. *Tick. Tock. Tick. Tock.* The time is flying by as you are taking a test, but how can you use time to improve your test performance? This depends on what type of test you are taking.

Objective tests require you to manage time, so you can get the best answer on each question. If you have a question that you are struggling to answer, after a minute or so, put a dot next to it or write the item number down, so you can come back to it later. Answer the questions you know with confidence first, then return to the test items that stumped you. This allows you to go back and use the remaining time on the challenging questions. Why would you want to waste so much time on the few you do not know, and risk missing the ones you do know?

When you are given the test, stop and read the directions to all parts of the exam. Then, peruse the test questions to see how many you have to answer and in what form they are written. Remember, you do not have to start with item one on the exam! If you are better at writing essay answers, start there. If there is some information you do not know, look for the answer as you complete the rest of the test and go back to answer those items. Knowing all of this before you begin the test will help you manage your time wisely.

Additionally, be sure to jot down any of your mnemonics or formulas you have from the course materials first. This will save you time as you progress through the test as you only need to look at them. Trying to recall the information while you are working a problem or trying to generate a list, taxes the brain. You may actually know the answer, but lack the ability to retrieve it if stress grips your brain during the test. Writing down the mnemonics and formulas as soon as you receive the test will **allow you to think more accurately and automatically**.

Review the number of points you can earn on each test question. If there are items with significantly more weight than others, you may want to start with them. Dedicating the bulk of your time to the heavily-weighted items will allow you to finish the lesser-weighted items with more relaxation. This means you are going to need to manage the clock, so you maximize the time allowed. Be sure to review the test for these bigger-valued questions and predict how long you can spend on each of them. If you see that it is taking longer to complete them than you thought, use an outline or other brief writing system to work on them. Then, move on. Also, be sure to allow time to review you answers.

When you have finished answering the questions on the test, go back over your answers. Make sure you have the correct answers on the answer sheet or Scantron®. Also, before you leave the room, make sure you have answered all of the questions. Occasionally, students will think they are finished, but there are more questions on the back of the final exam page. Don't lose valuable points due to this type of oversight.

EXERCISE 11.3: Managing Test-Taking Time

Explain how you can better manage your time during an exam or test.

____

____

____

____

____

____

REFLECTION 11.C:

In the workplace and as a teacher you may be given a project that includes a deadline. It may be as short as a few hours or take days or weeks. How would you use the skills mentioned above to make sure you complete your project correctly and on time?

___

___

___

___

We must mention here that many of the strategies listed above may not be options while taking an online test. Many instructors will set up their exams where you can see the entire test. This will allow you to skip questions and move through the test at your own pace. Many times you may get a hint of an answer to an earlier problem in a question later in the test. However, there are some instructors that will structure the test so that you see one question at a time and you will not be able to return to that question once your answer is submitted. These types of tests can be very stressful because they are generally timed and trying to manage that time is more difficult.

OBJECTIVE 5: Recognize Strategies for Short-Answer Questions

Short-answer questions are simply ones that require three to five sentences or a list of items to complete. You are not expected to write much, but be sure your answer responds to the question.

The three elements of a short-answer essay include:

1. reading and understanding the question parts,
2. writing clearly with language that is used in the course,
3. and being concise and precise.

First, read the question, watching for words such as list, describe, define or explain. These words are directing you to what type of response your professor will use to grade the information you provide. If you are asked to list the information, this means you can generate a 1, 2, 3, etc. answer. In contrast, if you are asked to define a term or concept, offer a brief but complete definition of the term. The greatest error that most students commit when writing a short-answer response is not addressing the prompt accurately. Slow down and read the words carefully. Secondly, use the language from the course to explain the concepts you are learning. This allows the professor to see that you are using the expected words from the discipline. Finally, write exactly what the prompt asks for in a precise way. Professors will grade these questions while looking for the terms from the class. If professors have to stop and try to figure out what you are trying to say because your answer is vague, you will probably miss the points on your grade.

As you can see, writing short-answer and essay answers on a test means you will approach them a bit differently. Just as the question type is entitled "short" answer, your answers need to be short. You may even be able to write incomplete sentences on these, as long as the professor can understand your point. In contrast, the essay responses require you to literally write an essay! Yes, you will need to write at least five paragraphs that are crafted around a well-stated thesis statement, clearly stated points, and standard English usage. This will take more time than a short-answer question, but essays typically are more heavily weighted on the test.

There are many similarities between a short-answer and essay responses. Obviously, both require you to have studied the materials from the course to the point that you can automatically write about them with precision. Additionally, addressing the prompts with information that demonstrates your knowledge of the course materials is necessary. This means that you will need to write to the point and include relevant information with the vocabulary of the discipline. This allows your professor to see that you have mastered the course materials.

EXERCISE 11.4:

Go back to the previous section on "short answer essay" tips. Then, compare and contrast how the prompt and response in a short answer essay is different than a long essay. Initially, you may need to rely on your understanding of an essay as your source for this section. After reading the next section, see how well you did!

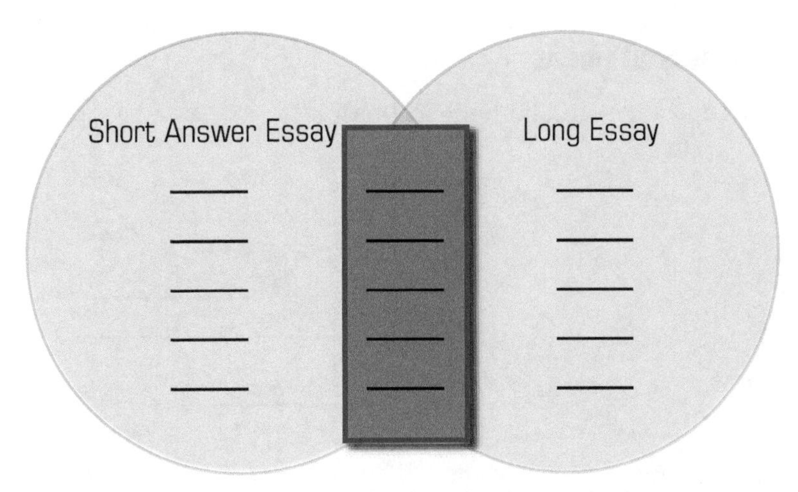

OBJECTIVE 6: Understand Strategies for Writing Essay Responses

When you are taking an essay test, unlike writing a paper or assigned essay, managing the clock means taking time to write a thesis statement and outline the points you are including in your answer. This may seem like it would take too much time to slow down and organize your thoughts, but it actually allows you to write with more "flow" of thoughts. It increases cohesiveness, and is your guide throughout the writing process. Knowing what you are going to write allows you to write automatically, which increases your flow. Since you know what you want to say, you can do so with more accuracy and connectivity. Most importantly, slowing down to generate a thesis statement and outline helps to establish the framework of your answer. Imagine a house that was built without plans or a frame. It could crack at the first strong wind. This is what will happen to your answer if you fail to establish the proper framework. Additionally, if you run out of time to finish the entire essay, your professor will probably give you credit for the thesis and outline. Should this occur, write something like, "Ran out of time, but here is how I would have answered it" next to your thesis and outline.

Writing a thesis statement requires you to have a firm grasp on the information being presented in your course. It is particularly beneficial to have written mock thesis statements and outlines for the items you know or think will be presented on your exam. Basically, the thesis statement is the overriding guide for writing the essay response. As such, it tells your professor:

- how you are interpreting the topic in question with significant points from your course materials,
- what you are writing about,
- how you are directly answering the question concerning the topic of the discussion,
- and what claim you will be proving in the paragraphs to follow.

The thesis statement is usually the last sentence in the first paragraph of the essay. Your professor should be able to read your thesis statement and know the measure of your knowledge on the topic.

After writing your thesis statement, create an outline of the answer you will write. Remember, the thesis statement is the primary point you are making, so every support of the claim should align with your thesis. Thus, the entire response to the question you are asked can be seen in the thesis statement and outline.

EXERCISE 11.5: Thesis Statement

List the four basic points that a thesis statement addresses.

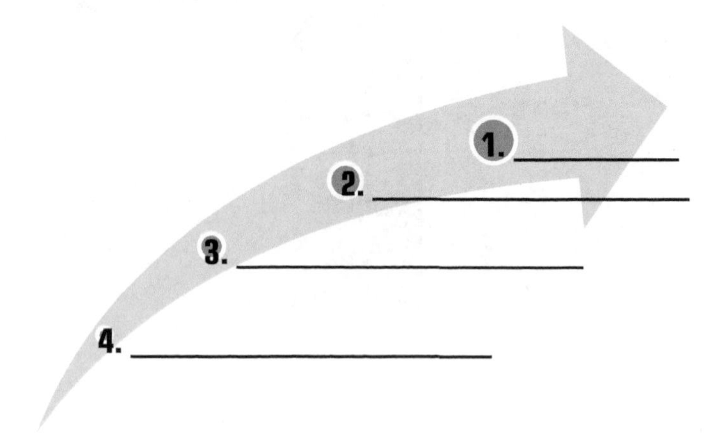

Once you have the thesis statement and the outline clearly written, you are ready to write the remaining parts of the essay. As you may know, an essay is comprised of an introduction, body, and conclusion. Each paragraph provides a vital function in demonstrating your knowledge of the course content. The rudimentary elements of writing are to:

1. tell the reader what you are going to tell them,
2. tell them,
3. and then tell the reader what you just told them.

This translates into (1) the introduction, (2) the body paragraphs, and (3) the conclusion. Be sure to write the information you told the professor in the thesis statement you were going to write. It is always prudent to reread your essay and ask "Does this prove my thesis statement?" If so, I will earn all the points on this question!

Finally, you will want to understand whether you are answering an open-ended or closed prompt. An open-ended prompt may sound like your professor is asking your opinion because there are many "right" answers. For example, an open-ended question for this course might be written as, "Describe the most effective note-taking system you have used this semester and explain why you have such a high opinion of it." The first point is to notice that this is a two part question.

> Part 1: Describe the most effective note-taking system you have used this semester.
>
> Part 2: Explain why you have such a high opinion of it.

Part 1 offers you the opportunity to describe in detail one of the note-taking systems you have learned in the course and one that you have used. Part 2 offers you the chance to explain why you feel as you do about the system, your evaluation of the practical use of the note-taking system. Thus, everyone in the class will answer this question differently. The common element throughout the room will be the description of a note-taking system learned in the class and the evaluation of that system. In contrast, a closed question will only have a limited number of responses because it tests your declarative knowledge of the topic. For example, in this class you might see a closed question such as, "Discuss habits that promote healthier approaches to test preparation." The answer to this question is clearly stated in the beginning of section 2 of this Chapter.

EXERCISE 11.6: Open and Closed Essay Questions

Contrast open and closed essay questions and the types of answers each one requires.

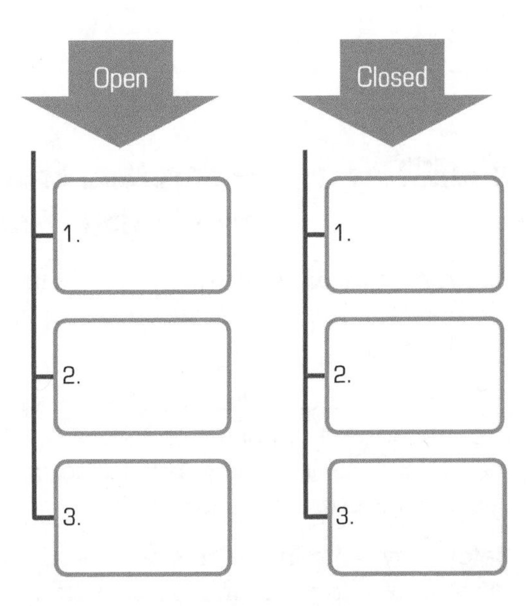

Compare open and closed questions.

Both types of questions share:

• ______________________________

Both types of questions share:

• ______________________________

Both types of questions share:

• ______________________________

REFLECTION 11.D:

Essay writing is a skill that may be required on job applications. Write an essay explaining why you should be selected for the position of a management trainee for a large sportswear company.

____

____

____

____

____

____

____

____

____

OBJECTIVE 7: Understand Educated-Guessing Strategies for Multiple-Choice Questions

There may be times when you are taking a test and are struggling to recall the answer or maybe you did not learn it. If this happens, do not panic! There are ways to successfully navigate around the lapse in memory.

Objective tests offer the test taker the opportunity to see the correct answer as it is interspersed between incorrect options. The means that the brain needs to recognize the correct answer or the one that most accurately responds to the question. Typically, the format of objective tests includes: true/false, multiple choice, and matching.

Before any more information is offered on test-taking, it is critical to pause and understand the importance of reading over the test and the questions to understand exactly what you are supposed to do. Read and reread until you fully understand. There is a "trick" test that you may have seen that tells students to complete five or six questions of the seven. Then, the last question states that the student should write their name on the paper and not complete the rest of the test. More often than not, students will spend excessive time completing the first six items with precision. Then, they respond in aggravation or laughter when they read the last question. While this may seem like a silly example, it demonstrates the need to read the test ALWAYS prior to beginning to take it.

True/false questions require the test taker to select the best choice or determine the factual information as true or false.

Example: True/False 1. Students who sleep eight hours the night before a test will "ace" the test. FALSE. Sleeping eight hours the night before the test will help IF you have studied and prepared prior to sleeping. Remember, **ONLY** select true if everything in the sentence is accurate.

Multiple choice questions offer several options from which you are to select the best answer. Traditionally, these answers follow the question with A, B, C, or D type choices.

Example: 1. A student who is preparing to take a test requiring procedural knowledge should:

A. Memorize random facts in isolation.
B. Rework the problems in the book and those that the professor worked in class.
C. Find the lists of formulas and memorize them.

Answer: B is the best choice even though lists of formulas will be required. Practice of the procedure is the best way to prepare for such a test.

Matching questions are instructing the test taker to select the best answer from several choices. For example, select the best description for each of the following testing formats:

A. Multiple Choice Format	1. Test taker is asked to select the best answer from several choices.
B. True/False Format	2. Test questions that offer 3–4+ answers in the form of A, B, C, . . .
C. Matching Format	3. Test questions that ask the test taker to determine if all or information is true or if it is false.
D. Objective Format	4. Test format that requires the test taker to select the best choice or determine the factual information as true or false.

On the rare occasion that you need to guess the best answer, use a strategy in which to guess more accurately—educated guessing.

#1

One way to do this on a multiple choice test is to read the answers as if they are true/false questions. For example, read the stem (what the question is asking) with the options. Only select the test answer item that is 100% accurate.

Example: Short answer essays include all but one of the following.

A. Thesis statement
B. Bulleted information
C. Three to five sentences
D. Drawing or a diagram

This means you should read the stem "Short answer essay questions do not include" followed by the options. The correct answer to this example is "A" because a thesis statement is not included in a short answer essay. This means that items B, C, and D are true, but A is false.

#2

Additionally, students who are guessing on a multiple choice test can eliminate the ones that merely distract you from the correct answer. Tests are created to include answers that can mislead the test taker who is inadequately prepared. This includes creating answers that are similar to the correct answer, opposite, or just preposterous, in addition to the correct answer. To use this information for educated guessing you will want to try to find the two answers that are most similar. This means you have identified a 50/50 situation. Then, read the stem and turn it into a true/false statement. The answer that is best should be the one that is true.

Example: People with an internal locus of control:

a) See themselves as playing an active role in their decisions
b) See events in their lives as a matter of luck, fate, and other influences
c) Tend to have low self esteem
D) Don't give themselves enough credit for their successes

Step 1: Notice how "a" and "b" even start with the same word! When this appears on a test and you need to guess, narrow it to these two choices and create a 50/50 situation. Then, go with the one answer that that can be correctly answered as a true statement.

Step 2: True/False

People with an internal locus of control see themselves as a playing an active role in their decisions

People with an internal locus of control see events in their lives as a matter of luck, fate, or other influences.

Choice: The first one, option a, is the true statement and will be the best answer.

#3

An educated guess for a multiple choice test that includes answers in the form of numbers is to eliminate the highest and the lowest numbers. Then, choose the number that seems most logical.

Example: The tallest building in the world is:

A. 4,396 ft.
B. 3, 227 ft.
C. 2,722 ft.
D. 1,909 ft.

The answer is found by eliminating the highest and lowest numbers. Of course, this technique does not always work.

Example: The tallest building in the world is:

~~**A.** 4,396 ft.~~
B. 3, 227 ft.
C. 2,722 ft.
~~**D.** 1,909 ft.~~

Then, review what you know about tall buildings and the number of feet in them. Sears Tower in Chicago is 1,451 feet, which was the tallest building in 1973. (This is the one seen in Spiderman movies.) Over the last 40-years there have been many taller buildings built. Perhaps you are thinking that the tallest building in the world is the one seen in the James Bond movie, Skyfall, which is located in Shanghai, China. If so, you would be wrong because it is only 2,073 feet. Due to the competitive nature of the claim on the tallest building, this honor is constantly being challenged and changing.

© Shahid Khan/Shutterstock.com

The tallest building in the world, Burj Khalifa, is located in Dubai, United Arab Emirates is 2,722 ft.

#4

Another educated guessing technique to employ on a multiple choice test is to select the longest answer when none of the other techniques works. This may seem too obvious, but usually the longest answer includes the most information and is correct.

Example: Using the hints on the syllabus for test questions means:

A. You have a printed copy of the syllabus.
B. You have studied the syllabus and recorded concepts as they were covered in class as potential questions.
C. You compare your lecture notes and any other learning materials to the course syllabus.
D. You listen for the professor to reference the syllabus in the lecture.

"B" is the best answer as well as the longest one!

#5

Finally, when taking a multiple choice test with educated guessing strategies, choose "C" when all else fails to help you. There is no magic in choosing "C" other than the statistical advantage that choosing the same letter offers the chance of getting more guesses right.

The most important thing to understand when using educated guessing techniques is to NOT use them as your primary test taking strategy. "Educated guessing" works accurately, more often than not, but it cannot be relied upon to earn you a college degree. Since the information on most of the tests you will take relate to what you hope to work in as a profession, it makes sense to learn the information rather than use educated guessing.

At times you may find you are nearing the end of the time to take the test but have many unanswered questions. Employ the educated guessing strategies with careful consideration if time permits. If the time has expired, but you have a few left to answer select "C."

11.3 ANALYZING TEST PERFORMANCE

Okay, you have taken the test. Now, what? Most students are unaware that learning continues after you have completed the test. Take a moment to remember how anxious you were upon entering the testing situation. Anxiety can wreak havoc on your test performance, so understanding ways to curb it will benefit you in future testing situations. Also, consider how prepared you were to recall or recognize the facts covered on the test. Perhaps you studied many hours for the test, but did not understand or focus on the materials the instructor emphasized on the test. Learning from this helps you in the future.

In most of the college classes, especially those related to your major, you are learning information to make you the best in your profession. This means that learning the materials is essential for your career. Taking time to understand how you performed on the test will teach you what you still need to learn, what you are confused by, and what you know well. Learning from assessment means addressing your confused materials first. Then, go on to learn the information you did not know.

OBJECTIVE 8: Understand Causes of Test Anxiety and Strategies for Managing It

Test anxiety is the term used to describe the negative physical and psychological reactions students often have when taking a test. Some students complain that this condition can cause them to fail or perform poorly on a test.

Anxiety is real. It is palpable. It causes some serious consequences in people's lives. It is also preventable. Anxiety can take on many physiological symptoms such as:

- sweating,
- shortness of breath,
- increased heart beat,
- nausea,
- trembling,

- irritability,
- and lack of focus.

These are serious distractions in a testing situation, so learning to conquer them will help you perform at your optimum level in college as well as in life.

First, it helps to understand what causes the anxiety brought on by a test. Identified contributors that aggravate test anxiety include:

- weak or insufficient study habits
- weak past test performances
- a history of anxiety problems

The first two contributors to anxiety are within your personal management. Learning how to prepare properly for a test can help to increase your confidence and success. The second contributor that can paralyze a student when taking a test is a history of poor performance or failure. Positive self-talk, which was previously addressed in Chapter 5, is the best way to communicate to your brain that you are going to succeed. Our brain believes what we tell it. Be sure to tell your brain, through verbalization of positive self-talk, you are smart, prepared, and more mature than in the past. A famous football coach of the Dallas Cowboys, Tom Landry, once said that the original team he was trying to motivate needed to use positive self-talk to overcome fumbling the ball or missing the action on the play. Coach Landry said he trained his players, after making an error, to say, "That's not like me." As the story goes, Landry's team won their first Super Bowl soon after learning to use this constructive self-talk. Be sure to incorporate this type of positive self-talk to your test-taking history. It may be four little words with a Super Bowl impact on your tests!

The third contributor to anxiety, a history of anxiety problems, may require the assistance of a professional counselor on your campus to overcome. If you experience the listed symptoms as well as extreme manifestations of anxiety, go get help. Trying to self-manage psychologically based concerns is not effective. Watch for the frequency and the duration of your symptoms to determine when you need to seek help. For the most part, every student has or will experience test anxiety from time to time. Most students can employ the deep breathing exercises listed in this chapter to help you relax.

Avoid visiting with your fellow learners prior to taking a test because they may, unintentionally, increase your anxiety. For example, if you are casually reviewing prior to the test and someone blurts out, "Does anyone know the answer to . . . ?" If you did not study that concept and do not know the answer, you might begin to feel anxious even before you get to take the test. Avoid this situation and potential stress by engaging in your own focused personal review.

Take a brisk ten to fifteen minute walk prior to entering the testing room. Walking increases your oxygen flow to the brain which will allow you think more clearly. Additionally, walking releases endorphins, hormones that when released can elevate your emotional state. This means you will enter the testing environment with an increased sense of well-being.

Dress comfortably. If you are wearing shoes or clothing that is binding, you will be thinking about how uncomfortable you are. In contrast, dressing yourself in comfortable clothing allows you to focus on the test. Also, be sure to carry a light jacket or dress in layers, so you can add or remove a layer when you become hot or cold. You have the opportunity to guarantee you are neither hot nor cold in a room whose thermostat is controlled by a computer.

The number one way to curb your anxiety levels in a testing situation is to prepare thoroughly and accurately for the test. This may sound too obvious to be taken seriously, but consider the flip side. How much anxiety do you think you encounter upon entering a room to take a test for which you did not prepare? Extreme anxiety is the response from most college students. Thus, adequate time and energy expended prior to the test will offer the calm confidence needed to perform at your optimum level during the test.

Prepare to take your tests through ongoing review that incorporates deep processing in your learning. When you develop the discipline of learning deeply (as stated in this chapter), you are preparing to pass most any type of test. Knowing the type of questions you are going to be given helps you process and rehearse the information in the way you may be asked to reproduce it for your professor. This may require you to ask your professor about the type of test you are going to be given.

Knowing if the information is declarative or procedural will offer you the opportunity to anticipate these types of questions. Declarative will ask you to affirm your knowledge. Procedural will ask you to apply your understanding of the procedures in solving a mathematical equation or analytical question.

When you take a test, a level of anxiety is to be expected. Recognize the symptoms of anxiety and learn to channel the nervous energy into a positive focus. Through deep breathing and positive self-talk you can create the calm confidence necessary to perform at your optimum level.

OBJECTIVE 9: Understand Levels of Preparedness

When a student prepares through repeated and ongoing review of the course materials, it is beneficial to understand the four levels of cognitive response. There are four levels of response to test questions that students employ when taking a test. These are illustrated in the chart below:

Level	Defined	Response on Objective Tests
Immediate	You recognize or recall the answer with automaticity.	Read your answer carefully. Read the stem with your chosen answer to confirm it is a "true" statement. If so, record it.
Delayed	You recognize or recall the answer with a momentary pause of reflection.	Read the choices as true/false statements to confirm the correct answer. In so doing you will recognize the answer definitively.
Assisted	You can recognize the correct answer in another prompt or question on the test.	You note the question with a dot or check mark, move on, and read the remaining test questions. The answer may be embedded in the test as another question or another question will ignite your recall of the correct answer.
Educated Guess	You have no idea of the correct answer.	You employ the educated guessing strategies you have learned.

Notice that this is a gradual process that you can use to complete the test questions. Basically, you can view the levels of response as four strategies for taking a test. While the process is clearly defined for objective tests, the information necessary to demonstrate your knowledge in a short or long answer essay is similar.

Often professors will embed the answers to other questions within another prompt. For example, if you are uncertain as to how to answer a question, place a dot or check mark next to it and move on. As you work through the remaining questions, the answer to the question you dotted or checked may be recognized in another prompt. Additionally, the answers to the essay and short answer essay are more than likely in the objective portion of the test. As you work through the test, use the test to take the test.

EXERCISE 11.7: Prepared and Unprepared Test Taking Habits

Compare and contrast prepared test-taking habits to unprepared test taking habits.

Unprepared Test Prep	Similarity	Prepared Test Prep

After completing the compare and contrast exercise above, write a brief summary of your findings below.

____

____

____

____

____

REFLECTION 11.E:

Explain how this information on preparedness will alter your preparation strategies in the future.

____

____

____

____

Hopefully, you are fully aware of and understand how to prepare for a test. The most important point you need to act on is to follow through with the dedication to ongoing review that promotes deep process learning.

OBJECTIVE 10: Understand *Post-Exam Strategies*

Consider taking time to review the answers you missed on a previous test before attempting to take another one. This allows you the chance to analyze if the previous attempt was altered due to the:

- **Question type:** Did you miss one type of question more frequently than another? Did you miss most of the points on the essay questions? How can you strengthen your ability to do better next time?
- **Information gaps:** Do you notice that you missed all the questions relating to one type of informational source? Were you absent on the day this information was presented? How can you be more prepared for this going forward?
- **Organization of test:** Do you seem to miss more questions at the beginning, middle, or end of the test? What does this say about your clarity of thought when taking a test? Does this imply something about your time management during the test session?
- **Physical conditions:** Can you recall your physical state while taking the test? Did it distract you from performing at your optimum levels of learning? What changes will you make in the future to prevent this type of event from reoccurring?
- **Emotional conditions:** Remember if you were upset due to a personal conflict with someone you care for prior to taking the test. Is there a way to circumvent this type of altercation prior to taking a test in the future?

By taking a few minutes to review your previous test performance, you will know how to set yourself up for success moving forward. Be sure to exercise your locus of control when analyzing the test, so you know how to maintain the power over your personal successes.

Now that you have learned more on test taking strategies and have personalized them for your success, you are ready to improve your grades on future tests. While a brief mention of mental preparation was touched on in this chapter, the need to reinforce it is critical. Positive self-talk really does work for athletes, students, business people, or people in any walk of life. Learn to feed your brain with positive messages as well. Read inspirational materials daily. Because there is a plethora of negative messages bombarding your brain daily, the need for positive messages need your deliberate attention. Medical doctors tell cancer patients to meditate daily to manage the complications they are experiencing when dealing with the disease. If the medical profession is "prescribing" the need to pause and think on positive messages to cancer patients, it will work for college students as well.

Finally, have you ever heard the phrase, "Success breeds success"? These three little words are packed with a powerfully positive message. It means that when people experience success in their life, they are more likely to experience more success. Why do you think this is true? The first time you complete a task, the second time you are more efficient and skilled to replicate what you learned in round one. Remember the book shelf that needed to be assembled in Chapter 1? The first time you assemble it, it will take more time and energy, but each time you assemble a bookshelf afterward you will improve the time that it requires. Eventually, you will become so skilled that you will not even have to reference the instructions! Test-taking successes breed test-taking success. Work on building the success with repeated practice provided in preparation. This will guarantee you the opportunity to demonstrate your mastery of the course materials on a test while performing at you optimum level.

COURSE CONNECTIONS:

Analyzing Test Performance in Hard and Soft Sciences

Analyzing Test Performance in "Hard Sciences"	Analyzing Test Performance in "Soft Sciences"
Because hard sciences are generally skill-based, analyzing your performance on a test should include questions such as: ■ did I perform the "formula dump" before starting the test? ■ did I know the vocabulary and terminology? ■ did I make minor errors or just did not know how to work the problem? ■ did I use all the time I was allotted? ■ was I able to answer the application problems? ■ could I work the problems I missed after I got home?	Because soft sciences are generally information-based, analyzing your performance on a test should include questions such as did I: ■ outline my thoughts before answering the essay questions? ■ know the important dates, persons, and events? ■ understand the questions that were asked? ■ make spelling and/or grammar errors? ■ use all the time I was allotted? ■ remember answers as soon as I got in my car?

How are the assessments similar in both cases?

____

____

____

____

What changes do you need to make in your study habits before the next test?

____

____

____

____

What changes WILL YOU make in your study habits before the next test?

____

____

____

____

PERSON to PERSON

In this exercise, you will be introduced to a student in a freshman orientation class. Let's discuss preparing and taking a test!

© XiXinXing/Shutterstock.com

Kyle has been unsuccessfully attempting college classes for two semesters. He decided it was time to take a College Success class that is part of the optional first-year orientation. Although financial aid will not reimburse for this type of class, Kyle feels it is worth the additional charge.

His high school had a policy that allowed students to retest if they did not score 70% or above for each exam. Most of the time, Kyle took advantage of this opportunity and retested for each exam.

However, his college classes are not offering this retest option. In particular, Kyle is frustrated because his College Success instructor does not allow retests. How is he to learn testing strategies if the instructor does not provide practice exams (his view of the first exam)?

Based on these descriptions, select the statements that might apply.

- ____ Kyle is not used to preparing for exams because he has always relied on the ability to retest.
- ____ High school and college policies should better align to improve student success.
- ____ The College Success instructor is trying to increase test preparation strategies.
- ____ Kyle's parents are paying tuition which makes Kyle less worried about passing his classes.

Here is some additional information.

- Kyle was diagnosed with ADHD when he was in elementary school.
- The College Success teacher has requested each student create a practice exam.

Based on all the information you now know about this student, rank the strategies you believe will help Kyle be most successful this semester.

- ____ Visit with each of his instructors regarding testing concerns.
- ____ Apply some of the study strategies he learned in an earlier chapter such as creating note cards.
- ____ Create a practice exam for all of his classes.
- ____ Visit with the Accommodations area to see if he qualifies for special testing arrangements.

1. What pieces of new information do you consider to be a positive influence on success?

____

____

2. What pieces of new information do you consider to be a negative influence on success?

____

____

Here is your last piece of information.

- Kyle's mother is a learning specialist at the college he attends.

Based on all the information you have about this student, rank the following statements as to which you believe will be help Kyle to be the most successful this semester.

- ____ Visit with each instructor regarding testing concerns.
- ____ Apply some of the study strategies he learned in an earlier chapter such as creating note cards.
- ____ Create a practice exam for all of his classes.
- ____ Visit with the Accommodations area to see if he qualifies for special testing arrangements.

1. What pieces of new information would you still like to know about Kyle?

____

____

2. Are there any pieces of information that could be seen as both positive and negative influences on his success?

____

____

Career Connection:

© bikeriderlondon/Shutterstock.com

Successfully taking tests is a skill you will learn and practice frequently in college. It is also a skill that you may use throughout your career. Many professions require certification: Public School Teachers, Certified Public Accountants, Environmental Assessors, Realtors, etc. and re-certification if they change areas of specification or relocate to a new state. Even teachers and lawyers may need to take exams if they relocate. Knowing how to prepare and to apply test-taking techniques while taking an exam can improve the chances of passing it!

© Stephen Coburn/Shutterstock.com

CHAPTER SUMMARY

Tests are an opportunity to demonstrate your knowledge of the course materials. Preparing for any test requires a certain level knowledge of the course syllabus, reading of test questions, and preparation for tests. A course syllabus and lecture "hints" are a good place to begin learning what the course and instructor will expect on test day. READ the syllabus and reference it often throughout the class. Also, the format and required knowledge of the level of test questions you will see on the test is vital. Using this to prepare for the test will help you perform at your optimum level.

The process for test preparation includes the physical, mental, and cognitive domains. Physical preparation means taking care of your body with healthy meals, hydration, exercise, and sleep. Mental preparation includes positive self-talk and mental pauses to process the course materials. Cognitive preparation requires the mental processing of the materials to be in the form of declarative or procedural knowledge. Knowing the types of test questions, objective or essay, will drive your preparation, as well.

When taking a test, time management is critical. Just as a coach can be fired for not using the time on the clock to beat an opponent, students can fail a test by not managing the clock to express their intelligence. It is best to work through the objective portion of the test as quickly and accurately as you can. Then, invest the bulk of your time in writing the short answer and long essay questions.

There are four levels of response to a test question: immediate, delayed, assisted, and educated guessing. Students will use the four levels of recall and recognition to respond to the questions on an objective test. Educated guessing is employed only as a last resort.

Tests that are completed may be used to learn how to take tests. Analyzing test performance takes a few minutes to reflect on the variables that affected your performance, but is highly beneficial. One cause of frustration for students is the level of anxiety they experience in test taking. There are constructive ways to manage this or even ways to use it as a source of positive energy.

CHAPTER 11: Self-Check

Vocabulary: Define the following:

1. declarative and procedural knowledge
2. short-answer questions
3. multiple choice questions
4. test anxiety
5. levels of preparedness

Concepts:

6. List words and sections that are included in a course syllabus that offer hints as to most important information to learn when preparing for a test.
7. List words and sections that are included in a course lecture that offer hints as to most information to learn when preparing for a test.
8. Explain how to use the hints from a syllabus or lecture to prepare for a test.
9. Compare the way one studies for a declarative test to a procedural test.
10. Explain why the type of knowledge on a test alters test preparation.
11. Explain the benefits of ongoing review.
12. Compare and contrast the last minute studying to "slow-drip" learning.
13. Identify methods for creating questions to use in a review.
14. Describe the following and explain how they lead to greater test taking success: sleep, high protein diet, exercise, hydration, and deep breathing.
15. Discuss habits that promote healthier approaches to test preparation.
16. Identify three strategies for time management.
17. Discuss how to manage time for an essay test.
18. Discuss how to manage time for an Objective test.
19. List two time management strategies when beginning the exam.
20. List one time management strategy during the exam.
21. List one time management strategy at the end of the exam.
22. Recognize the three elements of a short answer essay question.
23. Compare and contrast a short answer essay with an essay prompt.
24. Understand that the writing process in timed writing is different than writing a term paper.
25. Explain how to write a thesis statement and outline a response to a test prompt.
26. Recognize the elements of an essay answer: thesis statement, introduction, body, and conclusion.
27. Explain an open-ended prompt and how to respond.
28. Discuss educated guessing.
29. List two time management strategies for multiple choice questions.
30. Discuss causes of test anxiety.
31. Describe two strategies for managing test anxiety.
32. Discuss the value of preparation in eliminating test anxiety.
33. Explain the four levels of responses in recall and recognition.

34. Discuss how to use recognition as a recall strategy.
35. Compare and contrast prepared test taking habits to unprepared test taking habits.
36. Discuss post-exam strategies.
37. Explain how to use post-exam evaluation as a tool for preparing for the next test.
38. Analyze prior tests to determining tendencies of accuracy regarding formats.
39. Discuss ways to begin with the end in mind that create greater testing success.
40. Create three note cards for this chapter, the first with a true-false test question, the second with a multiple choice test question, and the third with an essay question.

CHAPTER 12

Planning Academically

T.I.P.S. (Tactical Information that Promotes Success)

Understand WHY you are attending college.

THE WHOLE IS GREATER THAN THE SUM OF ITS PARTS. **IT TAKES 10,000 HOURS TO BECOME AN EXPERT IN A FIELD.** **THIS MEANS** **LEARNING TAKES** **TIME . . .** **TO COMBINE,** **COLLABORATE,** **AND CONNECT** **ALL OF THE PARTS.**	Have you ever heard the phrase, "collaborate to graduate"? It is used to encourage students, professors, and student services. Similarly, Aristotle's philosophies influenced his teaching. The fifth century philosopher said, "The whole is greater than the sum of its parts." How does this look in college? Each class is one part of the sum that is called a college education. By working with advisors, professors, administrators, and peers you obtain a quality education. Thus each individual works to support the success of each individual student. Additionally, knowing **WHY** you are attending college contributes to your graduation. Knowing the answer to this question helps coordinate all the parts of your goals. In **mathematics and lab sciences**, your success in these courses can increase your options for selections of an area of study. **Reading** is a life-long skill that will be essential in all of your college courses. Although there are many parts to reading, the ability to read and comprehend the whole chapter is greater than the sum of its parts. Taking notes, outlining, and summarizing are all good parts, but if they are not combined for more powerful learning each part will be inadequate to meet the challenges of college. All of them combined are more powerful than any one of them practiced in isolation. **Writing** is another life-long skill needed for college success. The writing process includes: invention, arrangement, drafts, revision, and editing. There are many parts that contribute to the whole when writing an essay. Writers become better when several people read your work and offer suggestions. Peer reviews or the use of the campus writing center are ways to do this. Thus, the parts of drafting and revision benefit from the various contributions of a variety of sources. Ultimately, writing the best paper you can means the final draft (the sum of the whole) is greater than the sum of its parts (getting several to review the essay). In **education**, the parts in each class equal the final goal. Speak to an advisor who will assist you in enrolling in courses that count towards your degree and will transfer to another college or university. Students who decide on their own what courses to take frequently spend time and money on non-transferable courses. To avoid this potentially wasted time and money, seek guidance from an informed advisor.

CHAPTER 12: OBJECTIVES

12.1 Looking Ahead to Next Semester

Objective 1 Understand Criteria for Selection of Course Load

Objective 2 Understand the Relationship of Academic Plans and Degrees

Objective 3 Understand Criteria for Course Selection

Objective 4 Understand How Transferring Schools Modifies Degree Requirements

12.2 Considering Delivery Formats

Objective 5 Understand Delivery Format Options for Courses

Objective 6 Understand the Advantages and Disadvantages of the Online Format

Objective 7 Understand the Best Format for Learning Preferences

12.3 Selecting a Major

Objective 8 Understand the Process and Options for Determining a Major

Objective 9 Understand Resources to Support the Selection of a Major

12.4 Choosing a Career

Objective 10 Understand How the Choice of Major Influences Career Choice

Objective 11 Understand Reasons for Career Changes

CHAPTER CONCEPTS:

Some or all of the following terms may be new to you. Place a check mark in the column reflecting your knowledge of each term.

	Know	Don't know	Not sure	Page # where first found		Know	Don't know	Not sure	Page # where first found
hybrid class					major				
blended class					course catalog				
learning communities					degree plan				
flipped classroom					electives				
fast-track					minor				
values									

In a way, college is like getting back into shape after a number of years of a sedentary lifestyle. You enroll in a fitness center. There are many machines and you need to learn how to use them correctly. You enlist the help of a physical trainer to explain all this and to help you meet your goals. You begin to lose weight and develop muscle strength. There is hard work involved and it is going to take time to see the results of your efforts. There will be achievements and even setbacks, but if you keep at it, you will eventually obtain the good health you would like.

Similarly, you finished your first semester of college with the guidance and support of staff, professors, friends, and family. Now, it is time to move on to the next challenge and your college goal—the next semester, ultimately leading to graduation!

12.1 LOOKING AHEAD TO NEXT SEMESTER

It is time to begin planning for next semester's classes. There are questions concerning your next step, such as:

- How many courses should I take?
- How do I know which courses to take next?
- How do I know if the classes I take will count toward my degree?
- Will the courses I take transfer to the college or university where I will complete my degree?

As discussed in Chapter 1, reading and following the directions before assembling a bookshelf will result in a well-assembled bookcase. The questions listed above will assist you in establishing a well-planned college career. Taking the time to seriously consider your next semester can result in less frustration, better grades, and a more efficient route to your desired degree.

OBJECTIVE 1: Understand Criteria for Selection of Course Load

Building your course schedule for next semester will require you to determine the number of class hours you will be able to successfully manage. Review this semester's calendar to help with this decision by considering your commitments holistically. Remember to include the study time ratios recommended in Chapter 2: include two hours for every one hour you are in a face-to-face class and three hours for every one hour you are in an online class. If you are not working, it is possible you want to take additional course hours. For example, in a 16-week academic term, a 12–15 hour credit load is considered "full-time." If you are working, a recommended balance for work and school is to enroll in no more than 12 hours and work 15 hours per week. As you know, 12 credit hours require at least 36 hours of actual class attendance and course preparation. Trying to work more than 15 hours per week while taking 12 semester hours could sabotage your college success.

Additionally, evaluate your success in this semester's courses, your average study time per week, your current responsibilities and the stress level you experienced to help you select an academic load that will continue to support the balance in life you established this semester. If this review indicates that you need to lighten your academic load next term to increase your opportunity for success, consider the decision as a proactive measure. Failing to take this step could result in academic probation or the loss of the entire academic term.

Compare the investment of your course and study time to a financial investment. If you knew there was a way to invest in an opportunity that would never lose money, but would significantly increase your initial investment, would you do whatever you could to put your money in it? Of course you would! As you know from Chapter 2, this is called a high return on your investment (ROI) by the business schools. You will have a higher ROI when you plan proactively to succeed by balancing your time and courses in college.

© Iakov Filimonov/Shutterstock.com

Harvesting a crop implies the time was invested in planting, watering, and tending. Similarly, a college degree implies a significant amount of time and effort were invested in earning it.

EXERCISE 12.1: Course Load

Review this semester's load and use it to establish next semester's.

THIS TERM

1. How many credit hours did you enroll in this semester? ________
2. How many courses (if any) did you withdraw (or withdrawn) from or drop? ________
3. How many courses will you PASS with a "C" or better? ________
4. Did you utilize (if necessary) the math or writing centers? ________
5. On a scale of 1–5 with 1 representing "Never Studied" and 5 representing "Regularly Scheduled Study Time," how would you rate your overall study habits? ________
6. How many times did you miss a class because of some "unexpected" event? (This does NOT include "skipping class.") ________
7. How many times DID you skip class? ________
8. On a scale of 1–5 with 1 representing "Not stressful" and 5 representing "Stressed Out Most of the Time," how would you rate your overall stress level? ________

PLAN FOR NEXT TERM

Considering your answers to the questions above, what changes (if any) will you make to ensure a successful semester? You must be honest with yourself in answering these questions.

1. How many credit hours do you PLAN to enroll in NEXT semester? ________
2. How many courses do you PLAN to PASS with a "C" or better? ________
3. Do you PLAN to utilize (if necessary) the math or writing centers? ________
4. On a scale of 1–5 with 1 representing "Never Studied" and 5 representing "Regularly Scheduled Study Time," how would you rate your PLAN for NEXT SEMESTER'S overall study habits? ________
5. Have you made plans to try to avoid "unexpected" events? ____________________
6. On a scale of 1–5 with 1 representing "Not stressful" and 5 representing "Stressed Out Most of the Time," how would you rate your PLAN for NEXT SEMESTER'S overall stress level? ________

REFLECTION 12.A:

How would you have approached enrolling for classes next semester had you not completed this course and this exercise?

____

____

____

OBJECTIVE 2: Understand the Relationship of Academic Plans and Degrees

You may have heard of a man named Steve Jobs. Perhaps the better way to state that is to say, who has not heard of Steve Jobs, the inventor of Apple Computers and the iPhone, iPad, and numerous other computer applications? He attended college but dropped out during his first semester. He did not earn a degree, but took courses that were of personal interest to him. One of these courses was calligraphy, the art of producing elegant handwriting with a pen or brush. As he worked to create the Apple computer, this course was instrumental in his insistence that a large selection of fonts would be available to the user. Other courses inspired additional developments in the computer, but the choice of fonts is the one that people would recognize. Most people are not as fortunate as Steve Jobs to have achieved such great success without a college degree. As such, stay in school and complete your degree.

Earning a degree means you have fulfilled the course requirements for a chosen major. A **major** is a field of study in which you choose to focus your learning. Most of the time a major is determined by a profession or career goal. For example, if you want to work as a high school English teacher, you may major in education with an emphasis in English. If, on the other hand, you want to teach English in college, you will need a Masters or doctoral degree in a specific area of English (composition, English literature, 19th Century English literature, etc.). Similarly, if you want to be a toxicologist (a person who studies poisons or other substances that are a threat to humans) you will need to major in biochemistry or biology. (Most toxicologists have a Masters or doctorate in addition to the undergraduate degree.) Whatever your choice of major, you will need a plan in order to complete your degree in a reasonable amount of time.

An academic plan is an overview of the courses you will need to complete to earn a degree. Most will include categories of course requirements such as core curriculum (covered in Chapter 1), general educational requirements, mathematics, degree specific courses, science, foreign language, etc. Within each category there will be courses that are required to earn the degree. Each degree will have its own requirements, although the core curriculum will be the same for all degrees at each school.

You will want to learn how to use your **course catalog** in planning your academic future. For example, if you are going to major in physics, which courses do you need to take? Is there a sequence in which the courses need to be taken? Will you be earning a Bachelor of Science or Bachelor of Arts, or, in some cases, both? These are things that are included in your college course catalog, so take time to acquaint yourself with this vital tool. The catalog may be available in print form but is usually available on your college website. Advisors should be consulted if you have any questions.

Within the Course Catalog you will find a list of all degrees offered by the college—generally by "school" for undergraduate degrees and "college" for graduate degrees. For example, you may find a degree in physics under the School of Science and Mathematics or possibly the College of Arts and Sciences, depending on how your college is organized. In addition to all the degrees, and their requirements, you will find a list of all courses the college offers, a brief description of each, the number of credit hours, and any prerequisites (courses or other criteria you must meet in order to take the listed course). This means you need to look very closely at what you will take over several semesters to be sure you are able to complete your degree in a timely manner. Some colleges actually lay out a "plan" for each semester to help you balance your courses so that you are not overloaded.

EXERCISE 12.2: Prerequisites

Locate three courses in the **physics** department which have a prerequisite.

List the courses and their prerequisites.

Course Number	Course Name	Prerequisite Course Number	Prerequisite Course Name

REFLECTION 12.B:

For a degree that you *might* be interested in, locate three courses, as above, which have a prerequisite. Name the department from which you found these courses.

Course Number	Course Name	Prerequisite Course Number	Prerequisite Course Name

Once you have determined to invest in your education, be sure to use your academic plan to file an official **degree plan** at your school. The procedure to do this is available from your advisor as well as online. *The importance of filing a degree plan cannot be over emphasized.* For example, students often take classes over many semesters with the assumption that they are working toward a degree, but realize later they have not taken what is required in the degree that they seek. In the end, this means wasted time, money, and energy. You will be allowed some courses categorized as "electives" that would help offset some of this waste but it is better to plan at the beginning of your college years.

Some colleges and universities require a subject-area professor to serve as an advisor in the field to help create degree plans to avoid situations where you take courses that do not count toward degree. In addition, some colleges require students to have this professor advisor "sign-off" on the student's schedule each semester to ensure the student stays "on track." If your school does not provide such guidance, it will be your responsibility to make sure you follow your degree plan.

Once you file your degree plan, at most schools, you have "locked in" the requirements of the degree. What this means is if the college changes any of the degree requirements within the next few years, your responsibility is only that which is on your filed degree plan. In other words, "the rules cannot be changed in the middle of the game." If, however, you did not file your degree plan earlier, your plan will have to follow the new requirements.

EXERCISE 12.3: Degree Requirements

Review the courses that you would need to take for a degree in **Education** (If your college does not have an Education department, use **SPEECH or COMMUNICATION**.) Print a copy of the degree plan to evaluate it.

Circle the degree you would be earning:

1. Associate of Science   Associate of Arts   Associate of Applied Arts and Science
   Bachelor of Science   Bachelor of Arts   Bachelor of Science and Arts
2. How many TOTAL credit hours are required? ________
3. Explain the difference between the BS and BA degree plans:

____

____

____

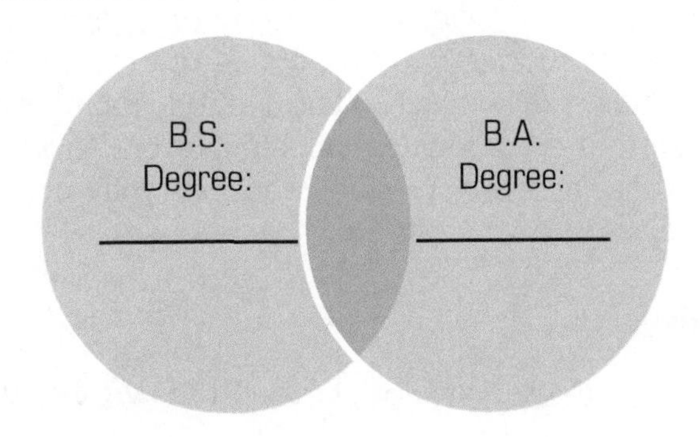

4. How many years are allowed to complete this degree plan? ________

5. What happens if you do not complete this degree in the time allotted by the awarding college?

____

____

____

6. What is the minimum grade point average (GPA) you must maintain to graduate? ________
7. Is there a difference between the GPA for Journalism (Speech or Communication) and the other courses? (If yes, list the GPAs)

____

____

____

8. Is there a foreign language requirement? If so, how is this requirement met?

____

____

____

9. How many upper-division (junior/senior) hours are required from a university to earn an Education (Speech or Communication) degree from them? ________

Electives are courses required in other disciplines than your major but with flexibility in choice of courses. Most include classes in liberal arts such as humanities, theater arts, and sociology. These courses are designed to offer you a balanced education in liberal arts and the sciences. There are some electives that pair better with some degrees than others. Rather than just taking the "easy" classes, think about the long-term applications of your electives and determine how they may be useful in your career. For example, an engineering student will be required to communicate clearly with the various partners in the work place. Knowing this, engineering majors might do well to enroll in communications and technical writing classes. Some colleges recommend the electives that will blend well with different majors, so you might not have to be concerned about these selections. The information in these courses may aid in landing a job in the competitive work place.

Another perspective on elective courses for you to consider is, "how can I take a class that will boost my GPA?" This is not intended to suggest you take the "easy" classes, but to help you in determining what courses to take in a semester. If you have a large amount of highly technical classes in a semester, you may want to consider taking a course that is fun, or one in which you know you will do well. This will help break the tediousness of your study sessions with something that will help you relax. Also, getting an "A" in any class will boost your self-confidence.

EXERCISE 12.4: Electives

Review the college degree plan in EXERCISE 12.3 and locate the electives you need to take (or choose from).

How many elective hours are required? ________

On what level (i.e., freshman, sophomore, junior, senior) do the required elective courses need to be?

___

Where would a student need to go to find the list of electives?

___

REFLECTION 12.C:

1. State a degree that you *might* be interested in. ___
2. What are the electives that your college recommends for this degree (or state NONE if none are listed).

   ___

   ___

   ___

   ___
3. Evaluate these electives and determine if you agree that they would be beneficial for your degree. ___
4. If not, what electives would you rather see that would help with your future career?

   ___

   ___

   ___

   ___

Now that you understand the courses needed for each of the degrees in the previous activities, it is clear that each degree is very specific to a given field of study. While it may seem like there are too many degrees to consider for your college major, it is possible to work on the core subjects for a semester or two while you determine where your interests lie for a career. One way you may work toward this decision is to take one semester of entry level courses in a wide variety of disciplines that interest you. After you complete the semester, you will have a better understanding of each discipline you have studied and may be able to identify the ones that appeal to you. The classes you have taken will probably count toward your electives, so the hours completed are not wasted. The key is *planning*!

OBJECTIVE 3: Understand Criteria for Course Selection

The first step in selecting your course schedule for next term is to review the courses necessary to complete your college or university's core courses—as discussed earlier in the book—as well as those designated for your degree (if you already have a degree plan). Some colleges or universities may require first-year students to enroll in core courses only. Be sure to check with your advisor for any such restrictions. If mathematics is difficult for you, consider taking any required course in the next semester. Taking your mathematics and science course(s) early in your college career allows you to "relax" and know that the requirement has been completed or, should you need to retake the course, there is plenty of time to accomplish this. Many students leave their difficult requirements until their last semester (remember avoidance?). This puts a LOT of pressure on a student whose skills in those areas are not strong, and the semester becomes extremely stressful because of the need to pass the course in order to graduate.

The next step is to consider the number of hours in each course, since a lab or other course may count for more (ceramics, for example) or less (golf, for example) than the typical three (3) credit hours. The number of hours should act as a guide for which classes you consider. Being proactive in your semester course selections will increase your self-confidence, GPA, and course satisfaction.

Knowing when your college's course schedule is available for student registration, how to access it and search for courses will mean you need to do some leg work. Take a few minutes to research how to access your course schedule either online or on campus.

EXERCISE 12.5: Locating the Course Schedule

Explain where you located the course schedule.

____

____

Explain when the course schedule for the upcoming semester is available for review. Is everyone allowed to register at the same time, i.e., the first day it opens, or are there any restrictions to register?

____

____

Now that you know where the course schedule is located as well as the courses in the course catalog, you can now consider the specific courses you want to take next semester.

EXERCISE 12.6: Selecting Courses

List six or seven courses you need to complete for your core requirements, degree requirements (if you have completed a degree plan), or courses of interest.

1. ____
2. ____
3. ____
4. ____
5. ____
6. ____
7. ____

Research these courses to determine when they are offered and select five you would be able to fit into a weekly schedule that includes any work hours, scheduled study time, family responsibilities, and any other recurring activities, and still maintain a balanced lifestyle.

List the name of the course, day, time and duration it meets, and include any labs.

1. ______________________________
2. ______________________________
3. ______________________________
4. ______________________________
5. ______________________________

Repeat Policy

Unfortunately, there may be times when you earn a lower grade than what is needed to count toward your degree. At times, there are situations in which students may fail a class. Your college repeat policy may be used in this situation as well. Often students will repeat a class to earn a higher grade. For example, a student earned a "C" in a science class, but needs to earn an "A" for admission to a particular program. Most colleges allow students to repeat it to earn this desirable grade. The highest grade will then be calculated into the overall GPA. This practice is widely evident in programs that require a high GPA in the lower division courses in order to enter the upper-division classes. For example, if you are working on entering a nursing program, graduate school, or any in the professions to become a doctor or lawyer, you may find yourself practicing this type of repetition of courses. Of course, the best, most efficient way to graduate on time and move forward in your career is to earn the highest possible grade when taking any class the first time.

© ann_saowaluk/Shutterstock.com

Some colleges limit the number of times you may repeat a class. Take a minute to locate the rules in your college concerning repeating courses.

EXERCISE 12.7: Repeat Policy

Write the repeat policy practiced at your college here:

____

____

____

____

REFLECTION 12.D:

Suppose you are only allowed to repeat a course one time at your college, but you fail (or withdraw from) two different classes a second time.

Explain how this will affect your GPA. ______________________________

Explain the consequences of having to go to another college to take these courses in terms of

time ______________________________________

money ______________________________________

motivation __________________________________

attitude ____________________________________

A **minor** in a college or university setting is a secondary field of study or specialization that has clearly laid out courses and hours needed for completion. The hours required to earn a minor in college varies based on the field of study. For example, a communications student who wants to minor in business may need to take up to 27 hours of business classes. Some minors require fewer hours than others. The purpose of earning a minor is to enhance your understanding in another discipline, create the best candidate for an entry-level position in the work place, or satiate one's personal interests in a field outside their major. Of course, like most everything else, the option to earn a minor is based on the policies within your school.

EXERCISE 12.8: Earning a Minor

Research the options available on your campus to earn a minor and locate the number of hours needed in order to attain it. Write your findings below:

____

____

____

____

OBJECTIVE 4: Understand How Transferring Schools Modifies Degree Requirements

Sometimes, students begin college at one school, but graduate from another. While there are as many reasons for this, it is important to understand how transferring can enhance or hinder your goals.

As was stated, there are many reasons for transferring from one school to another. The most obvious is that students who attend a two-year college must transfer to a four-year college or university in order to earn a Bachelor's degree. Community colleges usually only award Associates degrees or certificates, so you must attend a four-year school to graduate with a BA or BS. Sometimes students begin attending one college or university, but realize the degree they want is not offered there or a "better" program is at another school. Some students "reverse transfer" meaning they transfer from a four-year college or university to a two-year college. Normally, this is due to academic reasons. They spend a semester or more at the two-year college, improve their GPA, and transfer back to their original school. Another reason students transfer is to gain acceptance into a competitive university as a transfer student. An example of this is found at Texas A&M University. Students who do not meet the academic requirements for acceptance into Texas A&M can attend Blinn Community College for two years and, with an appropriate GPA, are automatically accepted into Texas A&M as juniors.

Personal reasons, such as health, family proximity, social adjustments, a relationship with someone at another school, or a bad break-up may result in transference to another college or university, too. Various events encountered by students lead to a college transfer, and it is advantageous to know the differences within the degree requirements between the colleges or universities. There may be differences in the number of mathematics, science, or foreign language course requirements. When choosing to transfer after beginning a program at one school, it is wise to contemplate the additional courses required as a result of the change. Some courses may not be transferable into the degree plan but will probably count toward electives. How much more time and money will the transfer require? Weigh the decision carefully, so you avoid any obstacles to completing your degree.

Some of the considerations to review to determine the advantage or disadvantage of transferring to another school should include the following questions.

- Is the school I am currently attending accredited by a national, state, or professional agency? Will the school I am transferring to be accredited?
- Is my GPA and/or number of hours completed most important to transferring?
- Will all my courses transfer?
- Do they offer a program in the degree that I am seeking?
- What is the campus community like?
- How much is tuition?
- Will I be eligible for financial aid or scholarships?
- Will additional classes be required?
- How much more time and money will I need to allocate?

The answers to these questions will probably lead you to ask follow up questions that will allow you to view your choices from all perspectives. Eventually, you will need to determine the advantages and disadvantages of transferring. When contemplating this change, it might be useful to draw a line down the middle of a sheet of paper and write "Advantages" on one side and "Disadvantages" on the other side. Record the information in the column that applies to the advantages or disadvantages and consider which decision is best concerning transferring.

EXERCISE 12.9: Advantages and Disadvantages of Transferring

Complete the following chart:

Advantages of Transferring to X	Disadvantages of Transferring to X
Live closer to my family	It will take me an additional semester to complete my degree.
Save money on the weekend, since I can go home.	Living close to home may mean I will be pulled into family "issues"

Sometimes, transferring is not an option. Family obligations, sudden financial setbacks, or an abusive situation may require a transfer. In these cases, the disadvantages will not matter.

12.2 CONSIDERING DELIVERY FORMATS

When considering the courses you will take each semester, it is advisable to consider the way in which the course is delivered and how you learn best. Unlike college in the 1970s, when students either sat in a classroom or took courses by "correspondence," there is a wide variety of course delivery options. Today, the traditional classroom still remains, however, there is an emphasis on active learning. Thus, the classes tend to be much more interactive. Options such as online, hybrid, blended, learning communities, "fast track," televised, self-paced, computerized, service-learning based, and paired courses, to name a few, can be found in most college schedules. It can be confusing for students who have not taken a class delivered in these ways, so be aware of the method in which your college lists the classes in the semester schedules. Most importantly, think about who you are and how you learn best when enrolling in a class. Now that you are aware of the variables to consider when designing your schedule, take a look at the specifics in each of the previously mentioned course formats.

OBJECTIVE 5: Understand Delivery Format Options for Courses

Course formats are designed to offer learning experiences that enhance your ability to master the concepts. Some, such as online, hybrid, and blended courses, are designed to aid in managing your time. An ***online class*** means that the class is completed through the mastery of materials that are all online and there are no face-to-face meetings. Sometimes students mistakenly believe this is like a self-paced class, but it is usually not. Most instructors expect you to complete a series of activities and assignments that are delivered to you in the form of learning modules with specific due dates throughout the semester. This type of course is ideal for someone who travels a great deal, has a serious illness, or an expectant or new mother. A ***hybrid class*** is typically one that is delivered through meeting MORE than half of the time on campus and the rest of the time online. This format requires you go to campus, but possibly only one day per week. The remaining work is completed independently, or in groups, online. Another option to consider is a ***blended class*** which meets one or more times on campus, sometimes limited only for testing, but is primarily delivered to you in the online format. More and more colleges and universities are offering online options such as these to help meet the needs of their busy students.

Service learning based, is not a typical format for a class, but rather a new addition to courses. Service learning is offered in many classes to increase students' awareness of ways to give back to the community. According to the American Association of Community Colleges,

> "Service learning combines community service with classroom instruction, focusing on critical, reflective thinking as well as personal and civic responsibility. Service learning programs involve students in activities that address local needs while developing their academic skills and commitment to their community."

Courses that include service learning will have some type of community service to be completed as part of the course requirements. Activities ranging from peer tutoring, working in a nursing home, refurbishing homes with dangerous issues, to building handicap ramps are a part of these classes. The goal of these types of classes is to demonstrate to students how the course materials connect to serving others. Some of the proven benefits of this course delivery, as reported in "At A Glance: What We Know about The Effects of Service-Learning on College Students, Faculty, Institutions and Communities" (2001), include:

- student personal development such as sense of personal efficacy, personal identity, spiritual growth, and moral development
- interpersonal development and the ability to work well with others, leadership and communication skills
- may subvert as well as support course goals of reducing stereotyped thinking and facilitating cultural & racial understanding
- a positive effect on commitment to service
- involvement in community service after graduation
- improves students' ability to apply what they have learned in "the real world"
- service-learning contributes to career development

Additionally, these courses suggest connections to increased college completion, so it is probably a format you might want to consider for one of your future classes. Not all courses will offer a service-learning component and most colleges do not give credit for the additional work. However, the payback is worth it! Sometimes, if the volunteer work is within a field of interest, you have the added advantage of seeing if that work is really of interest to you. For example, if you think you want to be an educator and choose the peer tutoring option, you may discover it is not want you want to do. However, you may love it and thus, it will provide motivation for you to continue your preparation. In addition, it will serve as work experience! Some tutors have actually been hired at a future time!

REFLECTION 12.E:

Identify two courses at your college (if any), that include a service-learning component.

______________________ ______________________

Even though these courses might not fit with your desired degree, consider what type of community service you could perform that would tie in with the content of the courses.

______________________ ______________________

______________________ ______________________

______________________ ______________________

Two or more classes that are combined and offered together are called ***learning communities***. Courses like these are available in institutions of higher education ranging from Ivy League schools to most two-year colleges. There are two different interpretations of the term "learning communities." One such arrangement has one professor delivering his or her course the first part of the time while the other professor teaches his or her part the second half. Students earn credit for each class, but take them with the same instructors. The other interpretation is where two instructors combine their two courses that blend the content of the two into a NEW SINGLE course with a new name but still counting the double credit. These instructors take turns teaching parts of the course and sometimes teach together. Students receive credit for the two separate courses, but should a student fail, he or she fails BOTH courses. This interdisciplinary approach leads to the increased connections in two or more subjects and the opportunity to become more closely tied to the professors and peers in the class. Some of the noted benefits of taking courses in learning communities, according to "The Case for Learning Communities"[1] written by Maria Hesse and Marybeth Mason, are:

- Learning is a social endeavor and that quality learning is enhanced by quality relationships.
- Assignments are structured to promote team work.
- Students see connections between various disciplines and thus are provided with a more realistic view of problem-solving.
- An opportunity for learning critical reading, analytical writing, persuasive speaking, and computer literacy in the context of a discipline.
- Increased student persistence, as well as increased student learning and achievement.

Obviously, this is a learning environment that you will want to consider for the next semester's course work.

Fast-track (or Express) courses are delivered in a fewer number of weeks than ordinary classroom classes but with the same number of contact hours. In one semester a student can complete two mathematics courses, an economics and a political science course or any combination the college offers. Each course lasts half of the semester for double the time in class. Obviously, this choice is designed for students who can work at a faster pace.

Flipped classrooms are a relatively new method of teaching classes. Similar to the hybrid format, students spend time both in the classroom and on the internet, generally with textbook software. The

[1]Hesse, Maria and Marybeth Mason. "The Case for Learning Communities" *Community College Journal*, August/September. 76.1, 2005.

concept behind this is for students to complete online what would normally be covered in the classroom leaving the classroom open to review concepts that were difficult but also to elevate the learning of the material. In mathematics, for example, students would complete solving equations in one variable through their homework online and then work on a real-world problem when they came back to class. This method allows instructors to cover higher-level concepts that would not be possible in a traditional classroom setting.

Hopefully, you are not dizzy from reading the plethora of course options that you will want to consider in your college courses. Like most things that offer choices, it is essential that you determine which format will be the most advantageous for your academic goals. The other options mentioned will not be covered here, but be sure to check out your course catalog and semester schedules for any of these additional formats. Remember, not all colleges will offer all formats in all academic areas. Some formats work better for some subjects than others.

EXERCISE 12.10: Course Formats

Review your course selections for next semester. Locate two or three that are offered in the previously mentioned alternative formats. Then, create a two column sheet with one column dedicated to advantages and the other to the disadvantages.

Take a few minutes to record these points to determine if there is an alternative formatted class that you will want to take next semester.

Course Name:

Course Format:

Advantages	**Disadvantages**

Although these formats are great options, it is sometimes hard to work them into the schedule you need. Write a summary of what you discovered and explain why you are, or are not, enrolling in one or more of these alternative course delivery formats next semester.

___

___

___

___

___

Finally, you will want to understand the variations of lecture classes. Traditionally, lecture classes consist of a professor delivering a lecture to the class. While this delivery dominates college halls, you will find that some professors will make the lecture more student-centered and interactive. Professors who believe that knowledge is constructed through social engagement will find ways to encourage students to interact on a topic or concept. Perhaps you will be asked to debate a topic, work in groups to determine solutions to problems, or have groups that present the findings of their research. These types of assignments are going to be listed on the course syllabus, so be sure to review the professor's syllabus prior to enrolling.

© Tsibii Lesia/Shutterstock.com

Unfortunately, the course catalog will not have any symbol noting that the professor will make the course more interactive or engaging. This means you will need to ask your peers how their professor teaches and what types of assignments are offered. Additionally, as previously mentioned, locate the course syllabi for your professors. Finding the syllabus prior to enrolling in a class should not be too hard because most institutions of higher learning have a syllabus depot or something similar. Many states have laws that require the syllabi be posted on the school's homepage on the Internet. At any rate, research the way in which a professor "lectures" prior to enrolling in a course, so you will have a better understanding of the course format and delivery.

OBJECTIVE 6: Understand the Advantages and Disadvantages of the Online Format

As was briefly mentioned, online classes may include some "surprises" that create challenges for learning, so be sure to make an informed decision prior to enrolling. Understanding the structure, skills, and time needed to perform well in an online class are critical to your success.

Most online classes are structured in such a way as to allow the learner to complete assignments each week. For example, you may be required to complete a learning module or file folder each week. Most of the time the learning modules will include some combination of the following assignments:

- Class discussions
- Lab credits
- Journals
- Tests and quizzes
- Research on the Internet
- Connect to a companion website from the textbook for homework (especially mathematics classes)

The courses are designed to deliver the same information that you would receive in a face-to-face class on campus. Each professor will complete this task in the way he or she deems best to maximize learning opportunities.

Before considering taking a mathematics course online, consider the following:

- You will most likely be teaching yourself.
- You will learn primarily by reading rather than by instructor explained examples.
- You will not be able to ask questions "as they come up."
- Your instructor will probably not be available when you are working on an assignment.
- Assignments may take twice as long to finish.
- Many professors expect tests to be taken on-campus, not online (blended).

Challenges of online classes are, unfortunately, often discovered after you are enrolled. For this reason, it is good for you to consider all of the facts regarding your learning preferences and practices prior to enrolling. A few to reflect upon are personal literacy, personal motivation and persistence, and time management.

One challenge that is hidden from most first time online students is the amount of time required to succeed in the class. As was stated in Chapter 3, there is a predictable ratio that may be applied for doing well in online courses. Say you enroll in English 1301, which is a three hour credit class. For every credit hour you are earning, you will need to study three hours. An example of this is if you are taking a three-hour credit class, you will need to anticipate investing another nine hours (three-credit hours times three-preparation and participation hours). In the end you will be adding nine hours to the three-credit hours, which means you will need to allow 12-hours per week to perform optimally in the online class. Remember, this is the minimum number of hours you should allocate for this class. If you are taking a class in which you know very little, you will need to invest more time. Often students think that taking an online class is equal to less time, but an online class actually requires MORE time to master.

Most of the time, students in online class are required to be very literate in reading and writing because the directions are written, not spoken. This places the bulk of the responsibility for learning on the student. You will need to be able to read, understand, and follow directions independently. Yes, you will have a professor to assist you, but he or she may not be readily available when you are working on the course assignments. For example, many students are working on their assignments when most professors are sleeping. How will you find answers to questions in this situation? Occasionally, you may find fellow learners working at the time you are, but most often you will be alone. Thus, students who are skilled in reading and writing and can work well independently will do well in an online class.

Personal motivation and persistence are critical characteristics for online student learning. Because you are independent and alone, your motivation to learn must be high. At times you will encounter obstacles to learning online, so you must be persistent as well. The obstacles to learning online may be related to your computer's compatibility with the course delivery platform, broken Internet connections, software challenges, or your ability to trouble shoot technical issues. Remember, your professor is not a technician. The professor will not be the primary point of contact when you encounter technical concerns, so you need to know in advance who you need to contact. Often these contacts are not available when you are working, so time is once again a concern. If you are motivated to make the online learning experience successful and have the persistence to work through inevitable obstacles in your pathway, success will be the end result.

Online classes, as you have seen, require more time than taking a class on campus. Some students say that they are saving time by not commuting, which may be true. Just be sure you have planned to invest a minimum of 12-hours per week for an online three-hour credit course. This is a minimum because it does not include the time spent trouble shooting technical issues, seeking assistance with your work, or interacting in peer discussions. Obviously, planning ahead means you begin your work *no later than* prior to the day it is due. When you plan ahead, you are not operating in panic mode on the night assignments are due. Additionally, because you are not in crisis mode, the work submitted will be of a higher quality. Unfortunately, far too many online students lack this fine art of managing time for success in an online class.

Now that the ugly truth of the negative effects found in online classes has been exposed, take a look at the benefits of online courses. A few that are worthy of your consideration are flexibility, working independently, and saving time and money no longer spent commuting to campus. The first benefit to be considered in taking online classes is flexibility. Online classes allow flexibility as to when you choose to complete assignments each week. If you have demands during the day, but ample time in the evening to complete work, you are free to do the work at that time. Perhaps you have more time for course work during the weekend. If so, online classes allow you to work during the weekend. Because the class is delivered online, you can complete it anywhere the Internet is connected. If you travel for work, you can still complete your online assignments.

You can work independently, for the most part, in an online class. As a result, you can take the time you need to learn the materials. In a face-to-face class, this may not be the case as there are 20+ other students in the room with you. While there are other people taking the online class, your learning is not dependent on their understanding for the most part. Most online classes do have some social component such as discussions or critical thinking assignments, but this is not the primary means of taking in information. Thus, the online learning allows you to be an independent learner.

Finally, the savings in time and money spent to commute to a campus can be a great benefit. Perhaps the campus in which the course is based is too far to commute, but you can earn college credit without the time spent traveling. Sometimes students take classes at campuses that are in another county, state or country. Two examples of this are seen in military personnel serving in another country and students who earn internships in other states. The military student can complete the online courses while serving and protecting our country. Internships, such as those in Washington DC or with Disney, are possible to complete and still earn college credit while you are away.

OBJECTIVE 7: Understand the Best Format for Learning Preferences

Another consideration prior to enrolling in alternative course formats is which is best suited to your learning preferences. Is it possible for a student who learns kinesthetically to succeed in an online class? Take a moment to review your learning preferences as identified in Chapter 3. Then, include this vital piece of information in your consideration of course formats to take.

EXERCISE 12.11: Learning Preferences

Complete the information concerning course formats and learning preferences in the chart below. Write a brief description for each format. Then, list the ways in which this format addresses the three learning preferences.

Describe the format:	Kinesthetic Preference	Visual Preference	Auditory Preference
Online			
Hybrid			
Blended			
Service Learning			
Learning Communities (choose one of the descriptions)			
Fast-track (Express)			

Review your learning preference(s) and explain which of the course formats best suits your needs.

____

____

____

____

12.3 SELECTING A MAJOR

Did you know that the average undergraduate student changes majors three to five times before settling into the one they complete? A large number of students come to college with an ideal career (thus, major) in mind only to be shocked by the number of courses required in areas they do not like. You may be fortunate and find, early in your college career, that you simply are not interested in the field. Or, perhaps, you begin a major, spend a few years working on it, and are informed that one or two courses you need, required in sequence, will not be offered for another year. Another reason you might change majors is due to transferring to a different school. Perhaps the new college's requirements for your desired major will add another semester or more to your college career and another major will allow you to graduate as planned. Therefore, if you are not sure about what you want to study, you are not alone!

OBJECTIVE 8: Understand the Process and Options for Determining a Major

There are many different procedures you can use to understand which major is best for you. If your brother, sister, friend, or parent told you what you should do, it is time to question them and discover if they are correct . . . or not! One way to do this is to reflect on the aptitudes and interests you have. In Chapter 5 you listed your strengths, challenges, and interests. Reviewing your answers now may shed some light on what major of study you might choose.

In addition to considering your aptitudes and interests in determining your major, you will benefit from understanding your values. **Values** are the things you deem as a priority in life. Go back to Chapter 2 and review Maslow's steps of self-actualization. This may help you understand your personal values more clearly.

After reading about aptitudes, interests, and values, take time to review each and personalize it, so you can use this information to determine your major. Complete the following assessments.

Aptitude Assessment: http://www.yourfreecareertest.com/career-aptitude-test.html
Interests Inventory Assessment: http://www.vocationary.com/test/career-surveyor?a=2606
Values Assessment: https://www.mindtools.com/pages/article/newTED_85.htm

OBJECTIVE 9: Understand Resources to Support the Selection of a Major

College campuses have career services to help you more accurately determine your aptitudes, interests, and values to determine your major. Write the information for your career services here:

Building: ______________________________ Room # ________ Phone # ____________________

Once you visit this valuable resource, you will want to schedule an appointment with a career services counselor. This person is highly qualified to assist and eager to work with you in determining your major. Obviously, selecting a major is directly linked to your career choices. In addition, once you have selected a major, most counselors will help you write a resume, prepare for job interviews, and aid in recruiting firms to your campus to interview graduating students. Establishing a positive working relationship early in your academic career will be advantageous.

Additionally, you may want to find a professor working in an area that you think you have an interest to discuss his or her professional journey. Often, professors do not begin working in higher education, so many may have several perspectives to share with you on how to begin a career. This professorial advice may lead to a letter of recommendation for your future employer upon graduation.

© Potrait Images Asia by Nonwarit/Shutterstock.com

Course Connections:
Prerequisites for Hard and Soft Sciences

Generally, you will find that there are more restrictions to the order of courses you can take in the hard sciences. Because you need to know basic chemistry and Chemistry II in order to take Organic Chemistry, this will take you three semesters because you cannot move on without completing these three basic courses. As an analogy, this would resemble a formal dinner in which each course is served in a specific order.	In the soft sciences, you generally have a little more flexibility regarding when you take your courses. At many colleges English I is composition and grammar and English II is introduction to research. The order may not matter (although your composition and grammar skills really should be reviewed before trying to take a research course.) An analogy for this might be exiting a freeway, where, if you miss your exit, you can take the next one and still arrive at your destination.
 © meinikof/Shutterstock.com	 © c12/Shutterstock.com

12.4 CHOOSING A CAREER

Some students are very lucky in that they already know what their career path is prior to entering college. Therefore, they have, by default, selected their major. Some want to be teachers, so their major will be Education. Others strive to design clothing, so their choice for a major will be Fashion Design. But what if your career goal is to be a meteorologist and the closest school that offers this degree is financially out of reach? In this case, choosing a new career may be a challenge.

OBJECTIVE 10: Understand How the Choice of Major Influences Career Choice

As was seen in the previous paragraph, having a career choice pre-determined usually makes selecting a major easy. Suppose you really enjoy political science and you decide that it will be your major. What types of careers are available to people with a political science degree? If you know you do not want to teach, what are your options? Do the jobs in these careers pay well? How competitive are they? What if, on the other hand you enjoy working with computers? What are your options for majors now? Computer science, computer technology, cybercrimes, computer programming, and more would be choices for majors, and these areas generally translate directly into careers. Do the jobs in these pay well? How competitive are they?

Unfortunately, not everyone who enjoys a particular subject will want to major in it because the options for jobs may be minimal. Here lies the conundrum: do you major in what you are interested in and hope you can make a career out of it, or do you find a major that is not particularly appealing to you but whose career opportunities are wide open? Here is where you must make some tough decisions.

Additionally, consider the value you place on time with your family and extend that consideration to the future. Some careers do not lend themselves to prioritizing time with families. Perhaps money is what you value and therefore, your choice of majors will probably be in an area of current high demand.

If you place a high value on family, there are careers that lend themselves to stable marriages, "Three types of engineers—agricultural, sales and nuclear engineers—were represented among the ten occupations with the lowest divorce rates. Also reporting low marital breakup rates were optometrists (4%), clergy (5.6%) and podiatrists (6.8%)" (McCarthy[2]). Perhaps you are not interested in marriage, and/or children, in which case, any career you select will provide satisfaction.

EXERCISE 12.12: Stable Careers

Conduct research on the careers with the greatest divorce rate and list the top three. Explain why you think these are careers with such great divorce rates.

____

____

____

____

____

OBJECTIVE 11: Understand Reasons for Career Changes

The average person will change jobs an average of eleven times and careers five to seven times in their working lifetime. Do not confuse jobs with careers. In many cases, a job is merely a position with a company in which you are building your career. In other cases, a job is merely a means to make a living—there is no career involved. People change jobs for a multitude of reasons, some of which are moving to a company that pays more, earning a promotion, or being relocated. Careers, on the other hand usually have more significant reasons for change. Suppose you majored in biology and took a job performing research, which does sound exciting. However, after a few years of this, you become

[2]McCarthy, Ellen. "On Love: Study breaks down divorce rates by occupation." NY Times. 19 Sept. 2010. Web. 12 March 2014.

tired of it and want to do something else. Sometimes the economy plays a role in career changes when companies downsize or outsource their work. Suddenly there are hundreds of people with the same credentials looking for the same job. Finding a new career could mean the difference in financial security and having to accept a low-paying job just to obtain a paycheck. It is definitely in your best interest to major in a field in which multiple job opportunities exist

PERSON to PERSON

In this exercise, you will be introduced to academic planning issues. Let's discuss the possible resource options!

© Andresr/Shutterstock.com

Juan is in his last year of college, hoping to graduate this semester. He waited until the last semester to take the required College Algebra course.

He is struggling to pass the College Algebra class. It has been four years since his last mathematics course. His avoidance of the subject is due, in large part, to his perception that he has never been able to do well in the subject.

Based on this description, rank the resources as to which will provide his best opportunity to pass this class this semester and meet his graduation requirements. Where should he go for help?

Instructor ____ Classmates ____ Tutoring Lab ____ Online Tutoring ____ Family Member ____

Here is some additional information.

- He tried to take College Algebra last semester but could not due to a schedule conflict.
- He attends every class but sits quietly in the back of the classroom. He feels everyone else understands it.

Based on all the information you now know, rank them again as to what you believe is the best resources for help. Has your ranking changed?

Instructor ____ Classmates ____ Tutoring Lab ____ Online Tutoring ____ Family Member ____

continued

1. What pieces of new information do you consider to be a positive influence on his ability to graduate this semester?

____

____

____

2. What pieces of new information do you consider to be a negative influence on his ability to graduate this semester?

____

____

____

Here are your last pieces of information.

- He has used *online* tutoring services but does not have the time to attend the tutoring center due to the conflict in his work schedule and their tutoring schedule.
- His instructor has offered outside of class review sessions that only 10% of the class attend. Juan has only been able to attend one of the sessions.
- His friend took College Algebra last semester and passed the class! He has offered to help.

Based on all the information you have about this situation, rank these resources one last time as to what you believe is most the most effective option for his success.

Instructor ____ Classmates ____ Tutoring Lab ____ Online Tutoring ____
Friend/Family Member ____

1. What pieces of new information would you still like to know about the situation?

____

____

____

2. Are there any pieces of information that could be seen as both positive and negative influences on passing this class and graduating?

____

____

____

Career Connection:

© Pressmaster/Shutterstock.com

Now that you have nearly completed this course, you have acquired all the tools you need to succeed in the rest of your college career: evaluating and managing your time, thinking deeply and critically, taking good notes while reading and in class, giving presentations, resolving conflicts, planning/studying for/managing/taking tests, and finally, making informed decisions. Using these skills, you will be able to research and apply your interests and talents to find that major or certificate program that will meet your academic and personal goals.

CHAPTER SUMMARY

Your first semester is almost complete and looking forward to next semester should be an exciting prospect. Whereas your original schedule may be have prepared by an advisor or someone else, next semester, you have the opportunity to select your own courses. In this chapter, you covered what variables you should take into consideration in selecting courses for next semester, including course load, or credit hours, that you can successfully manage academically and personally.

You covered the difference between degrees and majors. Selecting a major is one of the most important decisions you will make while in college because your major will determine what kind of jobs and careers are available once you graduate. Degree plans are necessary to file with the college to provide a "roadmap" to completing your degree. If you have not decided on a major, be sure to contact career services on your campus to help you decide what your strengths and interests are in order to pair them with a major.

Some careers are better suited for family life while others tend to be more solitary. If your job requires extensive travel, especially internationally, a family might not fit with your career. However, if you are more the family type with close ties, you might want a career which will allow you close to a job with typical daytime hours.

Careers will be changed probably five to seven times during your work life for multiple reasons. You may learn that you do not like the career you have chosen and decide to move on to something else. Or, perhaps, a new opportunity comes along that you cannot pass up. And, the more flexible your degree areas are, the more likely you will be able to weather a storm of downsizing or outsourcing should one occur.

CHAPTER 12: Self-Check

Vocabulary: Define the following:

1. electives
2. minor
3. community service
4. networking
5. degree or major
6. academic or degree plan
7. prerequisites
8. core curriculum
9. internship
10. values
11. volunteerism

Concepts:

12. Identify the number of hours or lab hours included in courses.
13. Explain how to use a calendar to plan toward the number of hours to take.
14. Evaluate courses and current responsibility to create a balance in life.
15. Discuss the balance of life with regard to course selection and planning for a semester.
16. Discuss the criteria for withdrawing from a class.
17. Explain how to use a course schedule to locate courses and their availability.
18. Identify courses that are included in a student's field of study/major.
19. Evaluate prerequisites and how one meets them.
20. Define electives and discuss their importance.
21. Explain the repeat policy at your college.
22. Clarify what a minor in college is and determine if your university offers/requires them.
23. Identify the requirements for a major.
24. Compare and contrast the core courses to a major.
25. Discuss the type of courses needed for a specific field of study/major.
26. Discuss the reasons for transferring schools.
27. Explain variability of degree requirements.
28. Describe the advantages and disadvantages of transferring schools.
29. List available delivery formats: online, hybrid, blended, service-learning, learning community, and accelerated learning.
30. Explain the learning environment of each of the previous course delivery options.
31. Describe the advantages and disadvantages of each format.
32. Discuss the variations in the term "lecture."
33. Explain the structure of a week in an online class.
34. Discuss the challenges of an online class.
35. Discuss the benefits of an online class.
36. Identify the skills necessary for a student to succeed in an online class.
37. Compare and contrast each format for each learning preference.
38. Identify the best learning environment for each of the learning preferences.

39. Explain aptitude and interest.
40. Compare and contrast aptitude and interest.
41. Explain the role personal values play in determining a career choice.
42. Discuss the aptitudes, interests, and values that contribute to three different fields of study.
43. Evaluate personal aptitudes, interests, and values and two careers that match them.
44. Identify the student support services on a college campus to aid in career selection.
45. Explain how a professor can be of assistance with your career selection.
46. Determine when one should contact the career support services on your campus.
47. Identify the core curriculum at your college.
48. Explain the value of the core curriculum.
49. Identify the course catalog and various majors at your college.
50. Evaluate the course requirements for two different fields of study.
51. Compare the course requirements for two different fields of study with career options for each.
52. Explain the process of determining a major and filing it with your college.
53. Explain the difference between a job and a career.
54. Discuss how choosing major affects the courses taken in college.
55. Explain how participating in each of the previous activities can affect marketability.
56. Identify resources for locating the various opportunities of service for learning.
57. Recognize the difference between a job change and a career change.
58. Identify circumstances which might be a catalyst for a career change.
59. Describe the disadvantages associated with changing careers.
60. Describe the advantages of a career change.
61. Discuss how a career change might affect the following: feelings of self-worth, lifetime happiness, and lifetime goals.
62. Create three note cards for this chapter, the first with a true-false test question, the second with a multiple choice test question, and the third with an essay question.